The Law
in its Relations
to Physicians

The Law
in its Relations
to Physicians

By

ARTHUR N. TAYLOR, LL.B.

BeardBooks

Washington, D.C.

PREFACE.

UPON casually looking over the pages of a current legal journal the author's attention was caught by the report of a recent case in which a physician, not understanding his rights in a certain matter, had violated well-established legal principles and was held by the jury to respond in substantial damages.

The ideas suggested to the mind of the author by this case were, first, the necessity that the physician be informed regarding his legal rights and liabilities, and, second, the inaccessibility to him of such information—which ideas in turn suggested the plan worked out in the following pages.

That portion of the field occupied in common by the legal and medical professions known as medical jurisprudence has received the attention of many able writers of both professions, with the result that nearly every question of law requiring elucidation as to its medical aspect has been worked out and is accessible to the lawyer. But, upon the other hand, that portion of the field occupied by the two professions which relates to the needs of the physician in his own practice has been singularly neglected, so that the physician is left without reliable information regarding his legal rights and liabilities, and, what is equally serious, without the opportunity of having recourse to such information except as stress of circumstances may drive him to seek legal advice in some particular case.

The object of this work is to place within the reach of every physician a systematic treatment of those questions of law which present themselves most frequently in his ordinary professional work, and which he may at any moment be required to know; and to show the relation between the different questions of law, together with the reasons upon which they are based, in such a way that the physician may not only understand his rights in a given case which has been adjudicated, but will, by understanding the general principles upon which those rights are based, be able to apply those principles to new facts and conditions, and determine the rights and accountabilities of the several parties interested as unexpected or uncontemplated emergencies arise.

A. N. T.

32 NASSAU STREET, NEW YORK.

CONTENTS.

CHAPTER							PAGE
INTRODUCTION	.	.	.	.	.	.	1
I.—THE RIGHT TO PRACTISE MEDICINE AND SURGERY						.	8
II.—CONTRACT OF PHYSICIAN WITH PATIENT			.	.		.	59
III.—CONTRACT OF PATIENT WITH PHYSICIAN			.	.		.	75
IV.—RIGHTS AND LIABILITIES OF THIRD PARTIES				.		.	80
V.—RIGHT TO COMPENSATION		.	.	.	.	.	140
VI.—RECOVERY OF COMPENSATION			.	.	.	.	171
VII.—CIVIL MALPRACTICE, INCLUDING GENERAL LIABILITY OF PHYSICIAN TO PATIENT			.	.	.	.	239
VIII.—CRIMINAL LIABILITY	.	.	.	.	.	.	385
IX.—PRIVILEGED COMMUNICATIONS		.	.	.	.	.	480

v

THE LAW
IN ITS RELATIONS TO PHYSICIANS.

INTRODUCTION.

Origin and Development of Our Laws.—Our system
of laws, like our language, was brought with us from the
mother country, where it had slowly developed during
the centuries that saw the crude, barbaric Briton become
the civilized and enlightened Englishman.

Like the Englishman of modern times, our law represents not alone development but also the reception and
assimilation of foreign material from widely separated
sources. When the Britons gave way to the more powerful Saxons the laws of the Druids commingled with and
became a part of the Saxon laws and customs; the subsequent arrival of the Danes brought additional elements; afterward the invasion of the Romans, and finally the conquest of the Normans, brought much of the
civil law of continental Europe and many customs for-

eign to those of our northern ancestors; among these was the feudal system upon which is based our present law of real estate. Not only was the law greatly changed in substance by this latest arrival, but in outward form as well, Norman-French being the language in which all public proceedings were recorded and in which the records of the courts were kept from the time of William I to that of Henry III. The Latin language was substituted by Henry III, and from that time the Law Latin was used until the fourth year of George II, except during the time of Cromwell, that sturdy character evidently deeming good, terse English a better medium for expressing the law of a great nation. It is undoubtedly by reason of this slow development and liberal admixture of elements from such widely separated sources that both our language and our system of laws have acquired their wonderful degree of flexibility that is shown in the readiness with which they meet the requirements of our constantly changing and developing conditions.

General Divisions of the Law.—Our laws are divided into two kinds—the common law, or *lex non scripta*, and the statute law, or *lex scripta*.

Common Law Described.—The Latin names of these two general divisions of the law are in a measure historically descriptive. The *lex non scripta*, or common law, being those general and particular customs which have existed time out of mind, or, according to the ancient legal expression, "time whereof the memory of man runneth not to the contrary," undoubtedly had their origin at a time when writing was unknown in western Europe, some of them being said to descend from the Gallic Druids. Blackstone, who wrote at about the middle of the eighteenth century, describing the common law, said: "This is that law by which proceedings and determinations in the king's ordinary courts of justice are guided and directed. This, for the most part, settles the course in which lands descend by inheritance; the manner and form of acquiring and transferring property; the solemnities and obligations of contracts; the rules of expounding wills, deeds, and acts of parliament; the respective remedies of civil injuries; the several species of temporal offenses; and the manner and degree of punishment; and an infinite number of minute particulars which diffuse themselves as extensively as the ordinary distribution of common justice requires." * It was to this branch of the law that Lord Coke referred when he said: "Reason is the soul of the law; and when the reason of any particular law ceases, so does the law itself." † Such a system of law, it will be observed, can not be reduced to writing in the form of a code without having its entire nature changed. The

---

* Cooley's Blackstone, 67. † Coke Litt., 70 b.

universal application of the principles and customs of which it consists would be destroyed, and the system would become crystallized into a set of fixed rules incapable of organic growth and development. There is, however, some method of recording necessary to secure stability and certainty to this branch of the law, and this is accomplished by preserving the records of the courts of highest jurisdiction, which show the history of each case determined and illustrate the application of the principles of law governing it. These records are kept as precedents to guide the courts in the future application of law to similar facts coming before them for adjudication.

Common Law of the United States.—The common law of England was not found to be entirely suited to the altered conditions on this side of the Atlantic, and was therefore only adopted so far as it was applicable to our situation. The term common law as used in the United States may be generally said to include all of the law of England existing at the time of the settlement of the colonies which was found applicable to our conditions.

In contemplating the great age of our common law and the identity of its development with that of our parent nation, one can not help regarding it with a feeling of veneration and sympathizing with the Mississippi lawyer who, upon seeing the common-law rights of

dower * and courtesy † wiped out by the legislature of
his State, exclaimed: " Venerable relics of antiquity,
you have come down to us from a former generation.
You have survived the wreck of empires and change of
dynasties. Born way back in the womb of Time, whereof
the memory of man runneth not to the contrary, you
have outlived the War of the Roses,passed safely through
the Protectorate, crossed the ocean, survived the great
American Revolution, and rode out the storm of the
late great war. Whatever attendants were absent from
the bridal altar, you two at least were always there;
and when the bride and groom mutually murmured,
' With all my worldly goods I thee endow,' you as priest
and priestess sealed the covenant. Like shades you've
followed the twain blended into one, and whenever
either fell one of you administered the balm of conso-
lation to the survivor. If pure religion and undefiled
be to visit the fatherless and the widow in their affliction, thy mission has been akin to it. Venerable priest
and priestess of the common law, farewell! You have
been pleasant in your lives, and in your death have not
been divided." ‡

* Dower is the estate which the wife takes upon the husband's
death in one third of all the real property of which he was seized
during the marriage relations.

† Courtesy is the life estate which the husband takes upon the wife's
death in all of her real property, provided she had given birth to a living
child. This last condition is usually eliminated by American statutes.

‡ Soliloquy of an old lawyer, November, 1880, from Annotated Code
of Mississippi, 1892.

Statute Law.—The statute law, or *lex scripta,* consists in England of all of the enactments of parliament, or, as an English writer of the eighteenth century, in the more courtly language of the times, said, it consists of those "statutes, acts, and edicts made by the king's majesty, by and with the advice and consent of the lords spiritual and temporal, and commons in parliament assembled." In the United States the statute law includes all positive enactments of the various legislative bodies.

Whenever a question arises as to the application of a statute to a given condition not coming clearly within the purport of its meaning, the aid of the common law is invoked by the courts in interpreting and construing the act; it therefore will be seen that the common law forms the fundamental groundwork of our entire system.

Reason the Foundation of Law.—Reason being the soul of our law, as very aptly stated by Lord Coke, it necessarily follows that a clear comprehension of the law is based upon a knowledge of the reason underlying the law, and that one can not really know the law without first knowing the reason therefor.

In writing the following pages the author has endeavored to keep this fundamental truth in mind, and has, whenever possible, first developed the general principle, giving the reason supporting the same, and then illustrated its application by particular cases. Whenever that course seemed impracticable, he has endeavored to show the principle governing in the particular case and the reason for its application.

CHAPTER I.

THE RIGHT TO PRACTISE MEDICINE AND SURGERY.

No Restrictions except by Statute.—The common law * òf England did not recognize the inability of the public to discriminate for themselves between the qualified and the unqualified practitioners of medicine and surgery, and therefore imposed no restrictions upon the free exercise of the art of healing; the necessity of such a restriction was, however, recognized at an early date, and in the third year of the reign of Henry VIII a law was enacted prohibiting any person from practising medicine or surgery in London, or within seven miles thereof, without first being examined, approved, and admitted by the Bishop of London or the Dean of Paul's, who should call to their aid four doctors of physic and, for surgery, other expert persons in that faculty. The statute further provided that no person should practise outside of London and a seven-mile radius thereof without being first examined and approved by the bishop of his diocese, or his vicar-general, similarly assisted,

---

* For the distinction between common law and statute law, see Introduction, p. 2.

8

saving those practising under privileges conferred by the Universities of Cambridge or Oxford. Seven years later a charter was granted to the College of Physicians in London vesting in it the right of examining and admitting to practice formerly granted to the Bishop of London and Dean of Paul's.

Other laws relating to the subject were enacted from time to time, but, owing to their character, they were not applicable to the condition existing in the United States, and consequently never became law here.

Statutory Restrictions in the United States.—In the United States the legislature of each State has authority to prescribe qualifications which must be possessed by those practising medicine and surgery within its borders, and it may be said without exception that the legislature of each State has exercised this right to a greater or less degree. An elaborate treatment at this point of the statutes of the several States would be inconsistent with the size and scope of this work, yet a brief *résumé* will, it is thought, be of sufficient value to the practitioner to justify devoting to that purpose the necessary space.

General Classification of Requirements.—The qualifications prescribed by the several States to entitle one to begin the practice of medicine and surgery within their respective jurisdictions may be generally classed under the four heads following:

I. The candidate must have a diploma from a medical college in good standing, the length of the course being specified in many States, and ordinarily being three or four years. In addition, he must pass a satisfactory examination before a board of examiners, the subjects to be covered by this examination being frequently specified.

This is the rule in Arizona, Connecticut, Delaware, District of Columbia, Florida, Georgia, Idaho, Illinois,* Iowa, Louisiana, Maryland, Minnesota, Montana, New Hampshire, New Jersey, New York, North Carolina,† Pennsylvania, South Carolina, and Utah.

II. The candidate must pass a satisfactory examination as in the first class, but he is not required to have a diploma from a medical college. In some States of this class the time he shall have spent in the study of medicine is designated.

The following are the States within this class: Alabama, Arkansas, Maine, Massachusetts, Mississippi, North Dakota, Oregon, Tennessee, Texas, Virginia, Washington, and West Virginia.

---

* In Illinois graduates of legally chartered medical colleges of the State, in good standing, as may be determined by the State Board of Health, may be granted certificates without examination. Laws 1899.

† In North Carolina, a license or other satisfactory evidence of standing as a legally qualified practitioner of another State shall be accepted in lieu of a diploma as entitling the applicant to be examined. Laws 1899.

III. The candidate may either present an acceptable diploma or, if he has no diploma, he may be examined as to his qualifications to practise medicine and surgery.

This is the method of admitting candidates in Colorado, Missouri, New Mexico, Rhode Island, Vermont, and Wisconsin.

IV. The applicant must hold a diploma issued by a proper medical college, which must be satisfactorily shown to belong to him.

This qualification is prescribed in California, Indiana,* Kansas, Kentucky, Michigan, Nebraska, Nevada, Ohio, Oklahoma Territory,† South Dakota, and Wyoming.

Indian Territory has a peculiar arrangement which in effect allows the Indians to follow their own customs in regard to doctors or medicine men of their own race, but in the Cherokee and Choctaw Nations provides for the examination of those not citizens of the nation who desire to settle therein to practise medicine. The law also requires the candidate to secure the indorsement of four or more citizens of the nation residing

---

* In Indiana, if the college issuing the diploma presented is not rec. ognized as maintaining a sufficiently high standard of medical education, the applicant shall have the privilege of being examined as to his qualifications to practise medicine and surgery.

† In Oklahoma Territory, the candidate may be admitted upon examination if he has been actually engaged in the practice of medicine not less than five years.

in the vicinity in which he desires to practise medicine.

There is no law protecting the residents of the Creek Nation from incompetent practitioners.

Additional Requirements.—In addition to the requirements classified under these four heads there are certain other requirements which are almost universally imposed—viz., that the candidate shall be twenty-one years of age, of good moral character, and have a good general education. In some States it is provided that he shall never have been convicted of a felony.*

Removal to Another State.—There seems to be very little disposition manifested in the statute laws of the various States to facilitate the moving of a regularly licensed physician from one State to another. Several of the States make special arrangements for licensing regularly qualified physicians of sister States who change their residence and practice to those States, but in each case satisfactory evidence is required of the same or a similar degree of proficiency as that established to entitle other candidates to practise within the particular State.

Proving Diploma.—Whenever a candidate is admitted to practise medicine and surgery by virtue of a diploma, it is usually necessary for him to submit the diploma to some board appointed for the purpose of

---

* A felony may be generally defined as an offense that is punishable by capital punishment or by being imprisoned in the State prison.

passing upon the qualifications of candidates, together with an affidavit that he is the lawful possessor of such diploma, that he has attended the full course of study required for the degree, and that he is the person named in the diploma.

Issuing and Filing Certificate or License.—If upon examination of the papers submitted the board finds that the candidate has fulfilled the requirements of the law, they issue a certificate showing him to be entitled to practise medicine and surgery within that particular county or State. If the candidate is admitted upon examination, a like certificate is issued. In either case the law usually provides that this certificate shall be filed with some county officer in the county in which the physician resides and practises. The filing of this certificate with the county officer designated is an essential part of the requirements, and a physician is not entitled to practise and receive the benefits thereof until his certificate is so filed. The law generally provides that in case a physician removes to some county other than that in which he first filed his certificate he shall file a properly authenticated copy of the certificate in the county to which he removes; this copy will ordinarily be furnished by the officer with whom the certificate is originally filed upon the payment of a small fee.*

---

* As to the physician's right to attend patients in other counties without first filing his certificate in such other counties, see p. 32.

Enforcement of the Law.—In a very few States no penalty is prescribed for a violation of the law, but in nearly all States the law is enforced by fines, usually with an alternative penalty of imprisonment, and some-times by fine and imprisonment conjunctively. The amount of the fine and the duration of the imprison-ment is largely discretionary with the court, certain lim-its being prescribed for his direction, fixing the mini-mum and maximum amount of fine to be imposed and designating the longest and shortest periods of impris-onment to which the offender shall be committed.* The smallest amount of fine fixed by any State is ten dollars, and the largest amount allowed to be imposed in any is five hundred dollars; the extreme periods of imprison-ment vary from ten days to one year. In a few States, however, the payment of the fine is enforced by impris-onment until paid.

Recovery of Fee prohibited by Statute.—The stat-utes of several States expressly provide that any physi-cian practising medicine unlawfully shall not be per-mitted to recover any fee or compensation for his serv-ices.† The right of the physician to recover for such

---

* In North Carolina the discretion of the court as to the period of time for which the offender shall be committed is unlimited.

† Such provision exists in Alabama, Georgia, Kansas, Kentucky, Louisiana, Maryland, Michigan, Nebraska, North Carolina, Rhode Island, Virginia, and Vermont.

services in States where there is no express prohibition of recovery has been the subject of judicial determination, and is fully treated in Chapter VI of this work.

Privileges to Non-resident Physicians.—While every physician is, or at least ought to be, familiar with the statutes regulating the practice of medicine and surgery in his own State, it is also greatly to his interest to be informed upon the laws of the neighboring States, at least so far as they extend privileges to him as a legally qualified practitioner of a sister State.

Privilege of Attending Cases.—The States of Connecticut, District of Columbia, Indiana, Kentucky, Maine, Massachusetts, Mississippi, New Hampshire, New Jersey, New York, North Carolina,* Ohio, Pennsylvania, Rhode Island, and Wyoming accord to nonresident physicians and surgeons the privilege of practising within their border, but they are not permitted in any case to maintain an office or have a place for meeting patients generally within such States. In several of these States † the non-resident physicians' visits are restricted to " a particular case." The exact mean-

---

* In North Carolina the privilege is expressly limited so as not to permit physicians resident in a neighboring State to "regularly practise " in that State.

† In Kentucky, Maine, Massachusetts, and Rhode Island, the visit is restricted to a "particular case"; in Kentucky, to a " particular case or family "; in the District of Columbia, such physicians are permitted to attend "specified cases."

ing of this restriction does not seem to have been judicially determined.

Before exercising the privilege in Mississippi the practitioner must procure a license from the State board of health, which license is granted to him without examination, and as a matter of right, upon his showing himself to be a legally qualified practitioner of another State. The privilege given by Indiana, New Hampshire, New York, Ohio, Pennsylvania, and Wyoming is restricted to physicians living " on the border of a neighboring State." The law of New Hampshire, however, permits non-resident physicians, irrespective of their place of residence, to attend their regular patients while sojourning in the State; it also allows landlords of summer hotels to employ physicians unlicensed in the State as hotel physicians to care for their guests or employees. New Jersey allows a physician of another State to take temporary charge of the practice of a physician of that State, a written request being first made to the State board of medical examiners.

Privilege of Consultation.—It is expressly provided that legally qualified physicians and surgeons from other States may meet in consultation with resident physicians in twenty-four States, to wit: Connecticut, Delaware, District of Columbia, Georgia, Idaho, Indiana, Louisiana, Maryland, Minnesota, Montana, Nebraska, New Hampshire, New Jersey, New York, North Carolina,

North Dakota, Ohio, Pennsylvania, South Carolina, Tennessee, Utah, Virginia, West Virginia, Wisconsin, and Wyoming. The law of Georgia restricts such consultation to "a special case," and expressly provides that a non-resident physician shall not be permitted to engage in a continuous practice or consultation in connection with a resident physician or surgeon.

It will be observed that not all of the States which allow non-residents to attend patients within their borders expressly give them the right to meet resident physicians in consultation; but applying the general maxim of law, *Major continet in se minorem*, it may be stated generally that any non-resident physician having the right to enter a State to practise medicine has also the right to meet a resident physician there in consultation.

Judicial Construction of Statutes.—The statutory enactments of the various States have from time to time been construed by the courts of the respective States or of the United States; but these decisions, being usually based upon the particular wording or meaning of the statute in question, are ordinarily of little interest outside of the State in which they are rendered. Some of these decisions, however, either involve a principle of extended application or construe statutes which exist so generally as to render them of sufficient value to justify an examination.

Constitutional Validity of Medical Acts.—The con-

stitutional validity of the laws prescribing requirements
for those practising medicine and surgery has been attacked in nearly every State in the Union upon the general grounds that:

They invade natural rights.

They interfere with vested rights.

They discriminate against persons engaged in the
same business or profession, and deny them the equal
protection of the law.

Or, they are *ex post facto*.

Our courts, both State and Federal, have, however,
almost universally upheld the constitutionality of these
acts, conceding them to be invalid only where they contained some specially objectionable feature.

The authority of the legislature to enact a law of the
character of those under consideration is included in the
police power of the State. The police power is very
broad; it has been judicially defined to be that inherent
and plenary power in the State which enables it to prohibit all things hurtful to the comfort and welfare of
society. It extends to the protection of the lives, limbs,
health, comfort, and convenience as well as the property
of all persons within the State, and to accomplish this
end persons and property are subjected to all kinds of
restraints and burdens.*

* Lakeview *vs.* Rose Hill Cemetery, 70 Ill., 191. State *vs.* Noyes, 47
Me., 189.

That the practice of medicine and surgery is a vocation that very nearly concerns the comfort, health, and even life of nearly every person can not be questioned, and therefore a wholesome restraint upon those unprepared to exercise these important functions is clearly the right of the State and its duty as well.

Nearly every State makes special provisions for licensing those who had been engaged in the practice of medicine and surgery in that State for a certain length of time prior to the enactment of the law. The validity of such provisions is attacked on the ground that they create special privileges and allow those who have exercised the right for the prescribed time to continue its exercise without submitting to examination or presenting a diploma; while all who have not practised for such period are obliged to be specially examined as to their qualifications or present diplomas, or both. The answer to this attack is, that if in the wisdom of the legislature the experience gained in practising five or ten years, or any other period fixed upon, within the State is equivalent by way of preparation to the course prescribed for those about to undertake the practice of medicine and surgery, it shall be lawful and will be considered no discrimination to fix these two standards.

It has been observed heretofore that many States extend to non-resident physicians and surgeons the right of being called into the State in consultation, and sometimes the right to extend their practice into the State without being examined or licensed. This has also been attacked as being an unjust discrimination and contrary to the fourteenth amendment of the Federal Constitution. It will be found that such laws do not permit such non-resident physicians to have an office or place for meeting patients within the State, and that they usually impose further restrictions. It therefore can not be said that such non-resident physicians enjoy the same privileges and immunities as a duly licensed resident practitioner, and the law is therefore not subject to the objection urged. An Ohio court has upheld the constitutionality of the act, but based its reason for so doing on other grounds. In considering the question, the court said: " We discover nothing unreasonable in the regulations adopted by the statute in question for the admission of persons to the practice of medicine, nor any valid objection to the provision excepting therefrom physicians residents of other States. Physicians called in consultation are usually the most eminent and skillful that can be procured; and those residing on the border of an adjoining State, with a practice extending into this State, can include only those who have a legal standing and established practice in their own State, and which the law regards a sufficient evidence of their capacity and character to admit them to continue their practice here." *

* France vs. State, 57 O. St., 1; 47 N. E. Rep, 1041.

Constitutional Objections to Particular Acts.—Certain features of those acts have at times been found to be objectionable; as, for instance, a law which allowed certain privileges to a particular school of medicine, or which imposed certain burdens upon another school, would be unconstitutional.* A law punishing a duly qualified physician for what is styled "unprofessional conduct" in advertising himself as a specialist in certain diseases would be unconstitutional; for, while such conduct might be contrary to professional ethics, it would in no way be injurious to the public morals or a menace to the general welfare.† And so a law requiring all who had not practised four years in one place to procure and pay for a license, but exempted those who had practised for this period from such expense, would be unconstitutional because of the burden imposed upon one class and not upon all.‡

But against the main body of the statute law upon the subject, as it stands in the several States, there seems to be no valid constitutional objection which can be urged.

Doctor, Physician, and Surgeon Defined.—The meaning of the term doctor, or physician and surgeon, as used in the law, is not confined to any particular school or

---

* Gee Woo *vs.* State, 36 Neb., 241 ; 54 N. W. Rep., 513.

† *Ex parte* McNulty, 77 Cal., 164.

‡ State *vs.* Pennoyer, 65 N. H., 113 ; 18 Atl. Rep., 878.

schools, but is considered in the broad sense of one who professes the art of healing. Justice Daly, in a well-considered case, said: " The legal signification of the term doctor is simply a practitioner of physic. The system pursued by the practitioner is immaterial. The law has nothing to do with the merits of particular systems. Their relative merits must become the subject of inquiry when the skill or ability of a practitioner in any given case is to be passed upon as a matter of fact." *

The supreme court of Wisconsin, thirty years later, following the reasoning of this decision, held that a statute providing for the organization of a county medical society included as well the organization of homœopathists as of any other school.†

The question of whether one who " practises bonesetting and reducing sprains, swellings, and contractions of the sinews, by friction and fomentation," is a practitioner of medicine and surgery, was considered in the supreme court of Massachusetts in 1835.‡ The court was of the opinion that while such a practice does not amount to a general exercise of the functions of the science of either medicine or surgery, it forms an important part of the practice of surgery, and renders the practitioner amenable to the laws affecting the physi-

---

* Corsi *vs.* Maretzek, 4 E. D. Smith, 1.

† Raynor *vs.* State, 62 Wis., 289.

‡ Hewitt *vs.* Charier, 16 Pick, 353.

cian and surgeon; also one who gave electric treatment was held to be engaged in the practice of medicine and surgery. The court said: " It is quite unnecessary, we think, that, in order to practise medicine within the meaning of the statute, the practitioner should give internal remedies." * The services of a clairvoyant are within the meaning of the term " medical or surgical services." †

The law of Illinois, in force in 1887, provided that " no person shall practise medicine in any of its departments in this State without the qualifications required by this act." The question arose whether or not this included midwifery. The court was of the opinion that obstetrics was an important department of medicine, and that it was included within the terms of the statute.‡

Moreover, the supreme court of Nebraska, in a well-considered opinion rendered in 1894, held that a Christian Scientist, in the exercise of his practice, came within the statute which provides that any person shall be considered as practising medicine " who shall operate on, profess to heal, or prescribe for, or otherwise treat any physical or mental ailment of another." #

---

* Davidson *vs*. Bohlman, 37 Mo. App., 576.

† Bibber *vs*. Simpson, 59 Me., 181.

‡ People *vs*. Arendt, 60 Ill. App., 89.

State *vs*. Buswell, 40 Neb., 158; 58 N. W. Rep., 728.

In a more recent case, however, arising in Rhode Island, the court held that the term " practice of medicine," as used in their statutes, must be understood in the ordinary or popular sense of determining the physical condition of the patient and treating his disease or injury by the ordinary or material remedies, and that it could not be so construed as to include in its meaning the treatment of the Christian Scientist, which takes account neither of physical symptoms and conditions of the patient nor of the application of remedial substances.*

While several of these decisions were based upon the wording of particular statutes, it may be laid down as a general rule that the term doctor, physician, and surgeon, or practitioner of medicine and surgery, as legally used, is broad enough to include all those who profess and practise the art of healing in its several branches.†

Decision of Examining Board, when Conclusive.— The authority conferred upon the examining board is usually both ministerial and judicial in its character; by the law of most States the decisions of the board in refusing or in revoking licenses to practise are made subject to review on appeal to the circuit or district court. The law usually provides the manner of taking this ap-

---

* State vs. Mylod (R. I.), 40 Atl. Rep., 753.
† See post, p. 39, et seq.

peal, but is sometimes silent upon the subject; this failure, however, to provide for the manner of appealing does
not affect the right to appeal. Whenever the law provides that the proceedings of the board may be reviewed
upon appeal, it will be necessary for the party who is
not satisfied with their decision to bring the matter before the court in the manner provided by the statute; *
but when the statute makes no provision whatever for
an appeal from the decision of the board, his remedy is by
mandamus. A writ of mandamus is a command issuing from a court of law in the name of the State directed
to some inferior court, officer, or person, requiring him or
them to do some particular thing therein specified.   In
theory, a writ of mandamus will issue only to compel the
performance of a ministerial act, but will not review any
judicial proceeding or interfere with the performance of
a function requiring the exercise of judgment and discretion.   Should, however, a board refuse to give a candidate a fair examination because of his views regarding
any particular school of medicine, or should, when examined, refuse to pass him for a like reason, or refuse to
accept his diploma for a similar reason, then mandamus
would lie; but if, after giving him a fair examination,
they determine that his knowledge of medicine is not
sufficient to entitle him to practise, or if, after hearing

---

* State, Norcross *vs.* Board of Medical Examiners, 25 Pac. Rep., 440;
10 Mont., 162.

evidence against a legally qualified practitioner in the manner provided by law, they decide he has been guilty of an offense justifying the revocation of his certificate or license, such decisions are not subject to review under a writ of mandamus. In New Jersey the board has refused to register the applicant on the ground that his diploma was not issued by a reputable school or college of medicine and surgery. Under a writ of mandamus the court refused to consider the evidence as to whether the judgment of the board was correct, because the board had acted in a judicial capacity in arriving at this conclusion.*

In Missouri the supreme court, in considering practically the same facts, rendered the same decision; the judge, however, in delivering the opinion, said: " It is thought best to say this in conclusion, that, notwithstanding what has been said relative to the discretionary powers of the board of health, that [sic] according to the express terms of the provision in section 2, such discretionary power does not extend to discriminating against any particular school or system of medicine, and that, should such discrimination ever occur, the limits of discretionary power will have been passed." †

Summing up, it may be stated generally that the

---

* State ex rel. Kirchgessner vs. Board of Health, etc., 22 Atl. Rep., 226.

† State ex rel. Granville vs. Gregory, 83 Mo., 123.

action of the examining board is not final. If the statute gives the right of appeal, the court having jurisdiction will review the proceedings of the board, and by its judgment rectify errors, should any be found. And the right to review the grounds of refusal on appeal is not confined to cases of refusal for unprofessional and dishonorable conduct, but, where the statute provides for appeal in " all cases of the refusal of a certificate," the court may examine, or direct the examination, of a candidate as to his competency.* Where no right of appeal is given by statute, a writ of mandamus will lie to compel the board to do those things which the law makes it their duty to do, and even to rectify a manifest injustice resulting from an abuse of their discretionary powers.†

Illustrations.—It will be observed from the foregoing that it is the purpose of the law to guard against arbitrary and unjust or unfair conduct on the part of the examining board. A case arose in New Hampshire some years ago very aptly illustrating this. A candidate applied to the board for a license to practise medicine, surgery, and midwifery; he produced a diploma which fulfilled the requirements of the law, but the board refused to grant the license on the ground that he was

---

* State vs. District Court of First Judicial District, 48 Pac. R., 1104 (Mont.).

† Illinois State Board of Dental Examiners vs. People, 123 Ill., 227; 13 N. E. Rep., 201.

3

not worthy of public confidence. The board has the power under the law of New Hampshire, "upon due notice and hearing, to revoke any license granted by it, when improperly obtained, or when the holder has, by conviction of crime or for other cause, ceased to be worthy of public confidence." The court held that the board had no right to refuse the applicant a license solely upon the ground that he was "not worthy of public confidence," without first giving him due notice and a fair hearing. If then facts were fairly proved by evidence adduced showing him to be unworthy of public confidence, the license would be properly refused.*

And so, when the board established a rule that every medical college should by a certain date furnish the board with a list of its matriculates and the basis of their matriculation, and in the event that any college failed to comply with this request it should not be considered "in good standing," the court held that this rule could not be enforced against an applicant who had graduated from a college in good standing which had not complied with the rule, if it was shown that the college had no notice of the rule until after the date fixed.†

A Medical College can not Arbitrarily Refuse Examination.—While the following illustration is not strictly pertinent to the subject in consideration, it shows how

---

* Gage vs. Censors, 63 N. H., 92.

† State ex rel. Johnson vs. Lutz, 136 Mo., 633; 38 S. W. Rep., 323.

the courts apply the policy above illustrated to protect
students from the arbitrary action of medical colleges as
well as applicants from the unjust discrimination of
examining boards. A medical student who had paid his
fees and fulfilled all of the other conditions entitling
him to present himself for final examination, was informed by the secretary of the faculty that he would not
be allowed to present himself for final examination, nor
would he be granted a degree of doctor of medicine.
Upon a writ of mandamus the matter was brought before the court and an order issued requiring the examination of the student. The opinion of the court is both
interesting and instructive, and is therefore quoted from
at length. " In answer to this application the respondent (the medical college) presents no ground whatever
for its action, but insists that it has the right arbitrarily,
without any cause, to refuse the relator (the student)
his examination and degree. It seems to us clear that
such a position can not for a moment be entertained.
The circulars of the respondent indicate the terms upon
which students will be received, and the rights which
they were to acquire by reason of their compliance with
the rules and regulations of the college in respect to
qualifications, conduct, etc. When a student matriculates under such circumstances, it is a contract between
the college and himself that, if he complies with the
terms therein prescribed, he shall have the degree, which

is the end to be obtained. This corporation can not take the money of the student, allow him to remain and waste his time (because it would be a waste of time if he can not get a degree) and then arbitrarily refuse, when he has completed his term of study, to confer upon him that which they have promised—namely, the degree of doctor of medicine, which authorizes him to practise that so-called science. It may be true that this court will not review the discretion of the corporation in the refusal for any reason or cause to permit a student to be examined and receive a degree; but where there is an absolute and arbitrary refusal there is no exercise of discretion. It is nothing but a willful violation of the duties which they have assumed. Such a proposition could never receive the sanction of a court in which even the semblance of justice was attempted to be administered." *

Qualification of Previous Practice.—The particular period of practice of medicine which shall be accepted by the examining board or other body having authority to grant licenses, as tantamount to a proper diploma or satisfactory examination, is fixed and described by the statute of each State recognizing such mode of qualification, and in order to determine whether in any given State a candidate is qualified by his former practice to

---

* People, Cecil *vs.* Bellevue Hospital Medical College, 88 N. Y. S. R., 418; 14 N. Y. Supp., 490.

receive a license to continue in his practice recourse must be had to the statute of that State. If by a fair interpretation of the meaning of the statute the candidate has fulfilled the requirements, nothing remains but to grant the license or certificate; if, on the other hand, it does not appear that the candidate has fulfilled the requirements of the statute, such license or certificate should be refused. A recent case of some interest arose in Rhode Island, where the law provides that a physician should have " reputably and honorably " engaged in the practice of medicine prior to January 1, 1892. The applicant, who was in the shoe business, took up the study of medicine by himself during the year 1889. In the latter part of that year he began to practise, after which time he gave his whole attention to the practice of medicine, leaving his shoe business to the management of clerks, and continued his practice up to January 1, 1892, some of his patients being satisfied with his services and some not. The court said: " There is no evidence that on January 1, 1892, he had come to be regarded by the community in which he practised as a skillful and successful practitioner, and therefore had acquired the honorable reputation as a physician necessary to qualify him to practise contemplated by statute. The decision of the health board in denying a certificate is confirmed." *

---

* Paquin *vs.* State Board of Health, 38 Atl. R., 870.

In Ohio the question arose some years after the passage of an act providing that ten years of continuous practice of medicine should qualify a physician for a continued practice, whether time spent in the practice of medicine since the act should be included as part of the ten years. The majority of the court were of the opinion it should be, and it was accordingly so held.*

Registration of Certificate.—It will be remembered that the law generally provides that the physician must register his certificate or license with some designated county officer in the county in which he resides, or, if he is a non-resident, in the county in which he intends to practise; but with the exception of one or two States the statute is silent as to the right of a physician to attend patients in counties other than the one in which his certificate is recorded. Whether or not this right does exist, and if so to what extent, is a very important question, but as the matter is regulated by statutes which differ in the several States no general rule can be laid down for all States; an examination, however, of decisions which have been rendered on the subject in several States will, it is hoped, lead to a clear understanding of the governing principle.

A case was decided in the supreme court in New York in 1890 upon the following facts: A physician,

---

* Wirt *vs.* Cutler, 37 Ohio St., 347.

duly licensed by the State board and registered in Kings County, made numerous visits to a patient living in Westchester County. The court said: " No new registry is needed to visit a patient out of the county. The fact that a physician gives two days in a week out of his county to see patients does not make a new practice in a new county, unless intended as a cover for a real change of place. It is simply practising medicine in Kings County with patients in another county." * The court intimated that the opening of an office or establishing a place of meeting patients in another county would not be a violation of the law, but no court in the State seems to have expressly committed itself to this extent.

In Texas the law requires the physician to register his certificate with the clerk of the district court in the county in which he may " reside or sojourn." Under this statute the practitioner must, upon changing his residence to another county, register his certificate again with the proper officer in the county to which he has removed.†

And so in Pennsylvania, under a similar statute, a practitioner who is properly registered in one county and opens and maintains an office in another county

---

* Martiner *vs.* Kirk, 55 Hun., 474.

† Hilliard *vs.* State, 7 Tex. App., 69.

must register his certificate in such other county as a " sojourner." *

It seems fair to conclude from these cases that in all States having statutes similar to those construed, providing that a license or certificate shall be granted by a State board which shall be good in any part of the State, and which must be filed with the proper county officer in the county in which the practitioner resides, the practitioner may safely have and attend patients outside of the county in which his certificate or license is filed; but it can not be safely advised that he would have the right to open an office outside of his county, or have a regular place of meeting patients without the county, or even associate himself in partnership with a physician where the partnership office was located without the county, until he had filed or registered his certificate or license in such other county.†

In Indiana the license to practise was formerly not granted by a State board and recorded in the particular county in which the physician intended to practise, but the license itself was granted by the clerk of the district court of the county in which the physician intended to

---

* Ege *vs.* Commonwealth, 9 Atl. R., 471.

† In Illinois, the general character of the law of which conforms to the above rule, it is expressly provided that "any person practising in another county shall record the certificate in like manner" in such other county.   Laws 1899.

practise. The law of that State was therefore construed much more strictly, necessitating that a license be taken out in every county into which the physician's practice extended.*

Chief-Justice Elliott, of the supreme court of Indiana, in an opinion in which he held the law to be as above stated, expressed his opinion regarding a qualification of this construction in the following words: " It may be that there are cases where the law would hold that the statute does not apply in its full rigor, as where there is an emergency demanding prompt action, or where there is a professional visit for consultation, or the call is made because of some special skill or ability of the physician in a particular branch of his profession." †

---

* The following is the substance of the Indiana law as it was enacted in 1897 and amended March 3, 1899: " The applicant must be a *bona fide* resident of the county and State. Two freeholders must make affidavit as to the moral character of the applicant, and to the identity of the applicant and the person mentioned in the diploma. The State board of medical registration and examination will examine the same, and, if satisfactory, issue its certificate; then the county clerk is authorized to issue a license to practise medicine, surgery, and obstetrics within the State of Indiana. In case of change of residence this license may be filed with the clerk of another county and a new license obtained. A license will permit its owner to practise in any county in the State, but it must be from the clerk of the county in which the applicant resides. If there be a change of residence, however, a new license must be obtained. In case a diploma is not considered worthy of recognition, the applicant is given an opportunity to pass an examination."
—From *Medical and Surgical Monitor*, March 15, 1899, p. 98.

† Orr *vs.* Meeks, 111 Ind., 40.

Eight years later, in 1894, a case was decided by the appellate court of Indiana approving of Justice Elliott's remarks so far as they relate to emergency cases, but refusing to hold that the law would permit a physician to enter the county and practise " because of some special skill or ability of the physician in a particular branch of his profession." In this case the physician was called from an adjoining county to perform an amputation immediately necessary to save the patient's life, he being the nearest physician with the requisite skill. After performing the operation he attended the patient and dressed the wound several times. The court held that, the county seat being sixteen miles away, to which place it would have been necessary to go for a license, it would have been impracticable to have obtained the license before performing the operation, and therefore the physician was legally justified in amputating the leg, but that his subsequent visits were unlawful.*

In States in which the license to practise is issued by a county officer entitling the physician to practise in that county, as it formerly was in Indiana, instead of by a State officer or board, it will be necessary to procure a license in each county into which the physician's practice extends.

---

* Board of Commissioners of Adams Co. vs. Cole, 9 Ind. App., 474; 36 N. E. Rep., 912.

Excusable Failure to Register Certificate.—There are certain circumstances under which the physician is legally excusable for failing to properly file his certificate before practising. Such circumstances may result through ignorance of law or inadvertence on the part of the physician, as, where he honestly endeavored to comply with the law, but through error filed the certificate with the wrong officer.*

Or through ignorance of fact, as, where the physician delivered his certificate with the proper fee for recording the same to a third party, who promised to record it at once, but through sickness or other cause failed to keep his promise.†

Or such circumstances may result from the neglect or carelessness of the officer whose duty it is to register the certificate, as, where the physician applied to the proper officer to be registered, but was informed by the officer that he could not register him for he had no book in which to enter the record.‡

Under any of these circumstances the physician must have acted in good faith in his original endeavor to comply with the law, and if he desires the protection of the law to continue he must, as soon as he learns of the fail-

---

* Mayor, etc., of City of New York *vs.* Bigelow, 34 N. Y. Supp., 92; 86 N. Y. S. R., 163; 13 Misc., 42.

† Pettit *vs.* State, 28 Tex. App., 240; 14 S. W. Rep., 127.

‡ Parish *vs.* Foss, 75 Ga., 439.

ure of his effort to comply, use all due means to secure the prompt filing or recording of his certificate.

Itinerant and Traveling Doctors, Who are.—The statutes of several States contain provisions relating to itinerant or traveling doctors, which either impose burdens upon them or exclude them entirely from the right to practise. While the question of who comes within the meaning of these statutes must be determined in the light of the particular statute, the law generally is very well illustrated by the two cases following:

A statute in Texas is as follows: " From every physician, surgeon, oculist, or medical or other specialist of any kind, traveling from place to place in the practice of his profession, an annual tax of fifty dollars in each county where he may practise his profession " shall be collected. A medical specialist having two offices, one at his home and one in an adjoining county, where he meets patients twice each month, is not within the meaning of this law. The court said: " Here the physician or specialist had two places of business; part of his time he spent at one and the other part of his time at the other place. This does not carry with it the idea of itinerancy, or traveling from place to place, as we understand the meaning of this term, within the provisions of the law." *

* Hairston *vs.* State, 36 Tex. Crim. Rep., 470; 37 S. W. Rep., 858.

Rhode Island, among other restrictions upon the medical profession, provides that nothing shall " authorize any itinerant doctor to register or to practise medicine in any part of the State." A physician who resided in Boston, and made a specialty of the treatment of catarrh, made regular visits to Providence in the practice of his specialty. The evidence showed that he had also been accustomed to visiting Worcester, New Bedford, Springfield, and Lowell, Massachusetts. The State board of health decided that he was to be regarded as an itinerant doctor, within the meaning of the statute. Upon review of the decision by the supreme court the conclusion of the board was approved of and affirmed.*

These two cases show facts not very greatly differing, yet it is evidently between the two that the line of demarcation must be drawn.

What Constitutes practising Medicine.—It has been observed that the law does not exclusively recognize any particular system of medicine or class of practitioners, the legal signification of the term doctor being simply a practitioner of physic. The statutes of several States have defined what shall constitute practising medicine, with a tendency to extend rather than restrict the judicial definition of the term.

It has been held that one exercising the functions

---

* Evans vs. State Board of Health, 33 Atl. R., 878 (R. I.).

of a clairvoyant in the treatment of disease is rendering "medical services." * Also one practising Christian Science comes within the meaning of the statute making it unlawful for one not duly qualified to "operate on, profess to heal, or prescribe for or otherwise treat any mental or physical ailment of another." † Midwifery has been held to form an important department of surgery, and to come within the meaning of an act prohibiting the practice, by persons not qualified, of medicine and surgery in any of its branches.‡ And so one giving electric treatment comes within the law regulating the "practice of medicine and surgery." # And also one who professes and practises bonesetting and reducing sprains, swellings, and contractions of the sinews, by friction and fomentation, comes within the operation of the statute regulating the "practice of physic and surgery." ||

While the definitions given seem plain and explicit, it is often a very nice question whether one, not having the legal qualification to practise medicine and surgery, has performed acts which will render him amenable to the

---

* Bibber vs. Simpson, 59 Me., 181.

† State vs. Buswell, 40 Neb., 158; 58 N. W. Rep., 728.   See State vs. Mylod, ante, p. 24.

‡ People vs. Arendt, 60 Ill. App., 89.

Davidson vs. Bohlman, 37 Mo. App., 576.

|| Hewitt vs. Charier, 16 Pick, 353.

law. Whether or not a particular case comes within
the law is usually a question of fact for the jury to determine. Upon what evidence a jury will find that one
has or has not practised medicine it is impossible to say
with any degree of certainty, there being so many things,
aside from the testimony given, that the jury may take
into consideration. The best manner of illustrating this
is by examining the facts upon which juries have passed
and considering their verdicts.

Illustrations.—In the case of Richardson *vs.* State,
decided in Arkansas in 1886, the State introduced the
following evidence to show that the defendant practised
medicine:

Miss Alice Stewart said: " I am acquainted with J.
K. Richardson. I was acquainted with Mrs. Hattie
Goff. I was present on two occasions when J. K. Richardson was at Mrs. Goff's when Mrs. Goff requested me
to get some money of hers and give it to J. K. Richardson. Mrs. Goff was afflicted with dropsy and cancer.
Dr. Brandon treated her for dropsy. I saw J. K. Richardson there with Dr. Brandon at Mrs. Goff's several
times, with H. Brandon. J. K. Richardson came several times by himself and applied medicine and plasters
to Mrs. Goff's cancer. I understood that J. K. Richardson had charge of the money that I handed him at the
request of Mrs. Goff." Upon cross-examination witness
said: " I might have sworn on the trial before of this

cause, that I did not know anything about a contract with J. K. Richardson and Mrs. Goff."

The defendant offered in his behalf a deposition by H. Brandon, who said: " That during the fall and summer of last year (1885) I was practising medicine in the city of Eureka Springs, Arkansas. That while there, perhaps in the latter part of September or October, 1885, I met Dr. J. K. Richardson, who was not eligible to the practice of medicine. At the time he spoke to me he claimed to be a student of medicine, and said he wished to continue his studies under me; that if I would furnish him the books, and give him all the instructions I could, he would compensate me as much as he could; said he had but little money, but was in possession of a very excellent remedy for curing cancer. I told him if he would give me his treatment for cancer that I would get the books and take him as a student and give him instructions as much as possible, to which we agreed. He then went into my office as a student of medicine. While he was with me I treated several cases of cancer, among whom was a Mrs. Goff. I agreed to doctor her for five dollars a week, which she paid. At different times I told Dr. Richardson to go and see the case and report to me the condition of the same. I told him on several occasions that if any one wanted to.pay him any money he might receive it and report the same to me, which he did on one or two occasions. Mrs. Goff paid him some money, which he turned over to me.   Dr. Richardson never collected any money that he did not turn over to me while he was in my office to my knowledge."

In this case the jury apparently disregarded the deposition of Dr. Brandon and, looking alone to the evidence given on behalf of the State, found that the defendant treated Mrs. Goff for a certain disease and received money for the same.*

In the case of Nelson *vs.* State, decided in Alabama in 1893, the evidence showed that the defendant, being called to attend a child who was sick, responded to the call and administered medicines; that he called once or twice, but did not make any charge and did not receive any pay; that he was called doctor by his neighbors. Defendant in his own behalf testified that he called upon the child and administered certain herbs that he found in the woods; that he did not claim to be a physician or represent himself to be one, and that he made no charge for his visits, and received nothing therefor.   The jury found the defendant guilty of practising medicine; but the supreme court, in reviewing the case on appeal, reversed the judgment and sent the case back to the circuit court for a new trial.

Justice Coleman, in delivering the opinion, said: " It was the duty of the court to instruct the jury, as a matter

---

* Richardson *vs.* State, 47 Ark., 562.

4

of law, what acts amounted to a violation of the statute, and it was for the jury to ascertain whether the facts existed. We are of the opinion that it is not a violation of the statute for a person who does not solicit patronage, who does not hold himself out as a physician, and does not pretend to be a physician, but simply advises or gives medicine to sick persons, merely as a neighbor or friend, and makes no charge, and does not expect any compensation for his services." *

In the case of State *vs.* Hale, tried in Missouri in 1852, the evidence did not show that the defendant received any compensation for the services in question. The court refused to instruct the jury " that unless they believed from the evidence that the defendant received compensation for his services as a physician, that they must find him not guilty," but instructed " that unless the jury believes from the evidence that the defendant practised medicine for compensation and reward, then he is not guilty, but the State is not required to prove the actual receipt of such compensation," upon which instruction the jury found the defendant guilty. The statute upon which this prosecution was based was as follows: " No person or copartnership of persons shall follow the practice of law or medicine, in whole or in part, as a business in this State without first obtaining a li-

---

* Nelson *vs.* State, 97 Ala., 79; 12 So. Rep., 421.

cense to follow such profession according to the provisions of this act." The supreme court, in reviewing the case on appeal, held that the instruction given to the jury by the trial court correctly stated the law applicable to the case.*

It will be observed from these illustrations that in all three cases the juries found the defendants guilty. In the Richardson case the supreme court, upon appeal, criticised the verdict, and intimated that it was an injustice, but, finding no error of law in the trial, it declined to interfere with the verdict. In the Nelson case the supreme court found that the trial judge had erred in giving or refusing to give certain instructions to the jury, and therefore sent the case back for a new trial with statements of law relative to the evidence adduced, which probably resulted in a different verdict on the new trial. While in the Hale case the supreme court expressed its approval of the instruction given, and affirmed the judgment without any comments upon the verdict.

A case apparently in conflict with the Hale case comes from Rhode Island; the Rhode Island case is, however, based upon a statute providing that the unqualified practitioner shall not practise medicine or surgery "for reward or compensation." Under such a stat-

---

* State *vs.* Hale, 15 Mo., 607.

ute the instruction that "if the jury find that the defendant received no reward or compensation for his services, they must find for the defendant," is proper, and the court would commit an error if he refused to give such an instruction.*

In view, however, of the statute existing in Rhode Island there is nothing in this case really in conflict with the law as expressed in State *vs.* Hale.

In the case of Benham *vs.* State, arising in Indiana, the evidence showed that the defendant issued circulars signed Dr. ——, in which he claimed that his "treatment" of his "patients" would effect a "complete cure" of the opium habit. He also issued a number of letters from former patients addressed to him as "Doctor," testifying to the efficacy and success of his "treatment" of the opium habit. The heading of the bills and receipts given by him to his patients was: "Office of Dr. ——, No. —— —— Street, ——, Indiana." The counsel for defendant contended that the opium habit was not a disease; the jury, however, rendered a verdict of guilty, and the supreme court, upon reviewing the case, was of the opinion that the verdict was fairly sustained by the evidence.†

In a Michigan case, a party who exhibited upon a sign "Dr. ——, Magnetic Healer," and who was called

* State *vs.* Pirlot, 38 Atl. R., 656 (R. I.).
† Benham *vs.* State, 116 Ind., 112; 18 N. E. Rep., 454.

to visit and treat sick persons, and who made a certificate of death and a report of infectious diseases, was found to be holding himself forth as a medical practitioner.[*]

The selling of patent or proprietary medicines by one who does not pretend to diagnosticate a disease is in no way a violation of an act prohibiting the practice of medicine and surgery; yet if one examines patients, diagnosticates their diseases, and then prescribes or sells his own proprietary remedies, he is practising medicine, notwithstanding the ostensible and apparent motive of the defendent may be the sale of his medicines.[†]

And a man who travels from place to place with a band of music or other means of collecting people together for the purpose of selling them medicines, and in his speeches, advertisements, and pamphlets sets forth the symptoms of disease and prescribes ten different remedies as capable of curing all of such diseases, is practising medicine.[‡]

In 1831 the supreme court of Ohio held that prescribing and administering medicine to two people for a fee sufficiently shows the party to have acted in the capacity of a physician.[#]   And in 1879 the court of

---

* People vs. Phippin, 70 Mich., 6; 37 N. W. Rep., 888.
† State vs. Van Doran, 109 N. C., 864; 14 S. E. Rep., 32.
‡ People vs. Blue Mountain Joe, 129 Ill., 370.
# Jordan vs. Overseers of Dayton, 4 Ohio, 294.

appeals of Texas held that the proof of attending and prescribing for a single case by one not legally qualified to practise medicine was sufficient to support a conviction for unlawfully practising medicine.*

In accordance with the spirit manifested in the above decision, the supreme court of Nova Scotia held that one who applied plasters to tumors and cancers and gave directions for poulticing them was practising medicine.†

It will be clearly seen from the preceding illustrations that it is the policy of the law to protect the people from the ignorance and unskillfulness of the pretender or quack in all branches of medicine. The law does not, however, go to the extent of including within its restrictions one who professes to cure by manipulation of the hands, by rubbing, kneading, and pressure, such treatment being considered by the courts to be harmless, if not beneficial, and to not come within the scope of the practice of either medicine or surgery. ‡

In the trial of a case in the United States circuit court, of the sort above considered, the question arose whether or not the patient, who was called as a witness, could be compelled to produce the medicine he had received from the defendant charged with practising medicine unlawfully. The court held that he could not.

---

* Antle vs. State, 6 Tex. App., 202.
† Provincial Medical Board vs. Bond, 22 N. S., 153.
‡ Smith vs. Lane, 24 Hun, 632.

Had, however, the case been one of malpractice, it is altogether probable that he would have been required to produce the medicine.*

Emergency Cases.—The statutes of many States except from their operation services rendered in case of emergency. The question of what is an emergency was considered by the supreme court of California, in 1886, in the case of People *vs.* Lee Wah.

In this case two women who had been unable to obtain relief from their physicians called upon defendant and stated their ailments. He prepared herbs of his own selection and delivered them to the women, who took them as directed. The instructions given by the trial judge to the jury, which were approved by the supreme court, state the law fully as to what is an emergency. The following is an extract from these instructions: " Two ladies have testified before you and stated that their condition was deplorable; that they consulted in vain other physicians; and that they regarded themselves, and were regarded by their friends and physicians, as incurable, and that they repaired to this defendant as a last resort. The ladies stated upon their part it was an emergency—an exigency in which death on the one hand, and submitting themselves to that treatment on the other, were the only alternatives. I instruct

* United States *vs.* Williams, 5 Cranch. C. C., 62.

you that the emergency contemplated by the statute is not such as this case suggests. It means a case in which the ordinary medical practitioners of the schools provided for by the statutes, who are provided with the proper diplomas, and have submitted themselves to the proper examination, are not readily obtainable. This is an emergency—as where the exigency is of so pressing a character that some kind of action must be taken before such parties can be found. . . . If, however, a party is satisfied that another school of physicians or another individual can render him more efficient aid—more beneficial services than others—and he therefore seeks his aid, that is not such an emergency as the statute contemplates." *

License from Irregularly appointed Board.—A physician can not be prosecuted for practising medicine and surgery unlawfully because his license is granted by a board of medical examiners which is improperly constituted, the appointment of the members being irregular, or even unconstitutional. Such a body would be a *de facto* board, and the certificates or licenses issued by it would be sufficient to protect the parties to whom they were issued from prosecution under the statute.†

Improper Refusal of Certificate no Defense.—In a prosecution for practising medicine and surgery without

---

* People *vs.* Lee Wah, 71 Cal., 80; 11 Pac. Rep., 851.

† Brown *vs.* People, 11 Colo., 109; 17 Pac. Rep., 104; Harding *vs.* People, 10 Colo., 387; 15 Pac. Rep., 727.

a certificate the defendant can not show as a defense that the board of examiners acted improperly or unlawfully in refusing to grant him a certificate.*

Revocation of License.—The power to revoke as well as to grant licenses is generally conferred upon the examining board. The law conferring this power upon the board has been attacked upon the ground that it is unconstitutional, being a judicial function, and therefore only to be vested in the courts; but such objections have been universally held to be ill founded. The grounds usually designated by the statute upon which the board is empowered to revoke a certificate or license are "unprofessional, dishonorable, and immoral conduct." The careful examination of a few cases of this character will best show what conduct the courts consider as being unprofessional, dishonorable, and immoral.

Advertising.—The word "unprofessional," as used in those statutes, has been judicially defined as being synonymous with dishonorable and not referring to matters of professional ethics,† as it is considered unprofessional from an ethical point of view for a physician to advertise himself or his business; yet, if the advertisements contained no objectionable matter, such

---

* Krowenstat *vs.* State, 15 Ohio Cir. C. R., 73.

† State *vs.* State Medical Examining Board, 32 Minn., 324; 20 N. W. Rep., 238.

advertising would not be ground for revoking his certificate.

If, however, such advertisement contained matter which the physician knew to be false, and it was made for the purpose of deceiving and imposing upon the public, such conduct would be " unprofessional and dishonorable " in the sense contemplated by the statute. For instance, an advertisement which asserted the physician's ability to speedily cure *all* chronic nervous, blood, and skin diseases of both sexes, also *all* diseases of the eye and ear, without injurious drug or hindrance from business; *all* old, lingering constitutional diseases, where the blood is impure, causing ulcers, blotches, sore throat and mouth, pains in the head and bones, *cured for life,* etc., was held to be "unprofessional conduct of the grossest kind." *

Misrepresenting the Character of Disease.—The statutes of Ontario provide that a license may be revoked for "infamous or disgraceful conduct in a professional respect." A physician represented to patients in the last stages of consumption that they were suffering from catarrhal bronchitis and that he could cure them, by strength of which representation he obtained money from them. The court said: " It was certainly conduct disgraceful in the common judgment of mankind, and

* State *vs.* State Board of Medical Examiners, 34 Minn., 391; 26 N. W. Rep., 125.

much more in a professional respect." Moreover, it is a very serious question whether such conduct does not amount to the crime of obtaining money under a false pretense.* This question is examined under the head of Criminal Liability.

Concealing a Fœtus.—A case of considerable interest once arose in Montana, and because of its interest it is discussed at length.

A complaint was filed with the State board of medical examiners for the purpose of revoking the defendant's license for unprofessional, dishonorable, and immoral conduct. The complaint stated in substance that the defendant placed in the furnace a package containing a headless fœtus, about seven months old, with intent to destroy the same and conceal its birth; that at the coroner's inquest over the fœtus the defendant testified that he had been called to attend a woman who suffered a miscarriage; that while being delivered the head of the infant became detached; that the patient from whom the fœtus was taken asked not to have her name made public; he therefore refused to disclose the name, but stated that on the following day he would state the name to the coroner, who would use his discretion in the matter. That on the following day defendant refused to disclose the name of the patient, because she had left the State, and, without her presence to explain her con-

* *Re* Washington, Q. B., 23 Ont. Rep., 299.

dition at the time the fœtus was taken from her, his answer would incriminate him. The defendant was tried
by the board of medical examiners and found guilty
and his license revoked. He appealed to the district
court, and was there tried and found guilty. From that
court an appeal was taken to the supreme court, which,
Justice Harwood dissenting, reversed the decision of
the district court, basing the reversal upon the following reasoning:

Examining the complaint carefully, it will be found
that it states that defendant placed in the furnace a
headless fœtus, with intent to destroy the same and conceal its birth. Conceding that the evidence fully sustains
this allegation, there is no unprofessional, dishonorable,
or immoral conduct shown. It is well known that premature deliveries are liable to occur through accident or
physical weakness of the mother, and at such times the
attendance of a physician is necessary. In this case
neither the complaint alleges nor the evidence shows that
the miscarriage was procured by the defendant, and the
law will not presume him to have been guilty of a criminal act. It is quite natural that the defendant should
have become possessed of the fœtus, and when so possessed of it due regard to sanitary laws required that he
should destroy it. There can consequently be nothing
unprofessional, dishonorable, or immoral in putting the
fœtus into the furnace. As to his desire to conceal its

birth, such a desire, instead of being reprehensible, is quite laudable and wholly professional, for it is a doctor's duty to preserve secret all knowledge which comes to him in a professional capacity.

As to the second specification in the complaint, which charges that the defendant refused to disclose the name of the patient because she desired that it should not be made public, the question is not whether the defendant was legally justified in withholding the name, but whether he acted unprofessionally, immorally, and dishonorably in so doing. In view of the fact that he believed it to be his duty to withhold this information, until legally compelled to give it, there is much difficulty in seeing how his conduct was unprofessional, dishonorable, or immoral.

The third charge in the complaint, which alleges that the defendant refused to disclose the name of the mother on the ground that she had left the State, and without her presence to explain her condition at the time of the miscarriage his answer would incriminate him, presents a very nice question for consideration. Were this a criminal trial such a statement could not be taken as evidence against the defendant, but, as pointed out by Justice Harwood, in his dissenting opinion, there is a broad field of human action between moral rectitude and honorable conduct and that of crime, and, while such a refusal to testify could not be used as evidence of crime, it indicates that he seeks to avoid the light of investigation, and thereby casts dishonor upon himself.

There was, however, no specific charge in the complaint of acts amounting to unprofessional, dishonorable, or immoral conduct, nor was any evidence introduced tending to show such conduct. The court was therefore of the opinion that the conduct of the defendant in refusing to give the mother's name was consistent with that of an innocent man made overcautious by fear, knowing that his actions were liable to be the subject of judicial investigation, and that in the absence of the mother he would be unable to show his innocence.*

Effect of Former Adjudication.—It is a well-settled principle of law that a trial and judgment by a tribunal having jurisdiction is a bar to further proceedings upon the facts considered in the former trial; a court would accordingly hold that the trial and acquittal of a physician by the State board of health upon the charge of " making statements and promises calculated to deceive and defraud the public " would be a bar to an investigation by the same body for making " claims and promises which are false and fraudulent," where the evidence in the two cases is identical.†

A trial and acquittal by a medical society is, however, no bar to an investigation under the statute by the State

---

* State *vs.* Kellogg, 14 Mont., 426 ; 36 Pac. Rep., 957.

† People *vs.* McCoy, 30 Ill. App., 272.

board of health for the purpose of revoking the physician's license. Nor would an acquittal upon an indictment for procuring an abortion act as a bar to a similar investigation by the board of health, the proceedings of the court and those of the medical board being entirely distinct and independent and having different objects and results in view: the one having regard to the general welfare and criminal justice of the State, and the other simply and exclusively to the respectability and character of the medical profession, and the consequences connected with or necessarily flowing from it.*

Practice in revoking License.—The policy of the law to protect the physician from arbitrary or unjust treatment by the examining board has been considered in connection with their refusal to grant licenses; the same policy to guard against injustice is manifested in cases of revocation of license. Where the examining board revokes the license of a physician without first giving him reasonable notice of the charge against him, and the time and place of the trial thereof, the revocation will, upon appeal, be declared null and void, and the physician will be protected in continuing his practice while the appeal is pending.†

Where a physician is tried by an examining board and

---

* *Re* Smith, 10 Wend., 449.

† State *vs.* Schultz, 11 Mont., 429; 28 Pac. Rep., 643; State *vs.* Weyerhorst, 11 Mont., 434; 28 Pac. Rep., 644.

his license revoked, and he takes an appeal from the judgment of the board, but continues to practise while the appeal is pending, and is during that time convicted of practising without a license, such conviction should be reversed if his appeal results in a reversal of the order revoking his license.*

Repeal of Statutes restricting Practice.—All statutes restricting the practice of medicine are enforced by penalties prescribed for their violation, and sometimes by provisions disabling the unqualified physician from recovering for his services. It now remains to consider the effect of a repeal of such statutes. As to the criminal feature of such acts, it is a well-settled point of law that the repeal of a law creating a criminal offense renders the law inoperative as to offenses committed before its repeal; if, therefore, a prosecution is pending for the unlawful practice of medicine, and the act making such practice unlawful is repealed, the prosecution must immediately abate. And this rule holds good even if the offender has been convicted but not yet sentenced.

The removal of the inability clause imposed to prevent the collection of fees does not as a general thing enable one to collect for services rendered while such law was in force.†

---

* State *vs.* Kellogg, 14 Mont., 451, 36 Pac. Rep., 1077.

† For a full treatment of the effect of such repeal upon the right to collect fees, see p. 181, *et seq.*

CHAPTER II.

Contract Defined and Classified.—A contract has been defined by an eminent law writer of the eighteenth century as " an agreement upon sufficient consideration to do or not to do a particular thing."* This agreement may be express or implied. Where the particulars of the agreement are averred and mutually agreed upon, the contract is said to be an express contract; but where no particular terms are set forth, the law will take into consideration the relations of the parties, and will, by implication, create for them such an agreement as reason and justice would dictate. The contract is then said to be an implied contract. Such contracts may exist without our knowledge or volition, and, as a matter of fact, do arise from nearly every transaction into which we enter, thus constituting much the greater number of contracts by which we are bound.

Express contracts are either written or verbal. Written contracts are, as the name implies, reduced to writ-

* Blackstone.

ing and signed by the parties to be bound; while oral contracts are formulated only by word of mouth, and may be made either in the presence of witnesses or when the contracting parties only are present. In the absence of statutes which provide that certain contracts must be in writing, an oral contract is in all respects as binding as a written contract, the only advantage of the latter being the much greater ease and certainty with which the exact agreement is proved.

It will be readily understood from the preceding that whenever a physician or surgeon undertakes the treatment of a patient certain contracts are created by the law founded upon the relation of the parties. These contracts will be taken up and considered in the order in which they naturally follow.

Contract implied from Exercise of Professional Duties.—By merely undertaking the treatment of a patient the physician impliedly contracts with that patient that he has such skill, science, and information as will enable him properly and judiciously to perform the duties of his profession.* This is a contract which the law creates irrespective of any statutes prescribing qualifications for the practice of medicine, and one which was implied at common law before statutes existed upon the subject. The exact degree of this skill and knowledge

---

* Wood *vs.* Clapp, 4 Sneed (Tenn.), 65.

which the physician is required to possess has many times been the subject of judicial consideration. It would be manifestly unjust to the physician or surgeon to require him to possess the highest degree of knowledge or skill, while, on the other hand, the public welfare requires that the standard be kept well above that of the tyro or quack. The courts have accordingly held in all cases submitted to them that he is by this implied contract required to be possessed of " proper," " reasonable," " ordinary " knowledge and skill.* But whether or not the proper degree of knowledge and skill is brought to the particular case must be determined from the circumstances.

Advanced State of Medical Science to be considered. —It is a well-settled proposition of law that in judging of the degree of knowledge and skill in any given case due regard must be had to the advanced state of the profession at the time.† If, for instance, an operation were to be performed upon the eye of a person whose physical condition was such as to render it unsafe to put him under the influence of general anæsthetics, it would be evidence of culpable ignorance and lack of

---

* Reber *vs.* Herring, 115 Pa. St., 599; Barnes *vs.* Means, 82 Ill., 379; Gramm *vs.* Boener, 56 Ind., 497; O'Hara *vs.* Wells, 14 Neb., 403; Vanhooser *vs.* Berghoff, 90 Mo. 487, 8 West., 205; Quinn *vs.* Donovan, 85 Ill., 194; Peck *vs.* Martin, 17 Ind., 115.

† McCandles *vs.* McWha, 22 Pa. St., 261.

skill for the operator to proceed by using other than local anæsthetics; whereas about twenty years ago recognized authorities on the subject laid down the rule that chloroform should always be administered.*

Opportunities of Location to be considered.—It will also be manifest that the opportunities and location of the physician, and more particularly the surgeon, are a very important factor in determining the degree of skill and proficiency which he should be reasonably expected to attain. In the larger cities the physician and surgeon has the opportunity of attending the hospitals and clinics, of witnessing and taking part in the most difficult and complicated operations, and of attending lectures and consultations whereby he is kept in constant touch with the ablest and most advanced of his profession; whereas in the small towns and country districts the physician and surgeon has fewer opportunities of observation and practice, especially in the line of surgical work, and can not reasonably be held to possess so high qualifications as his more favored professional brother.

The law takes this condition into consideration in determining the degree of skill and knowledge which a physician impliedly contracts to possess, and accordingly requires that he have the average skill and ability ordi-

---

* Wells, Treatise on the Eye, ed. of 1880.

narily possessed by men of his profession in *similar localities.**

Test applied to all acting as Physicians.—This test of professional knowledge and skill is not applied to the regular qualified practitioner alone, but to any person who holds himself out as a healer of diseases, and who accepts employment as such.† Should, for example, one represent himself as qualified to treat and operate upon patients, who was ignorant of the most rudimentary principles of medicine and surgery, the law would extend to him no indulgence because of his unfortunate lack of scientific training, but in case deleterious results attended his treatment the same test would be applied in his case as in the case of the regularly qualified physician and surgeon practising in the same locality and at the same time—that is, he would be required to exercise at least the ordinary skill and ability possessed by physicians and surgeons in similar localities. Failing in this, he would be held to respond in damages to the extent of the injury suffered by reason of his incompetency.

Contracts to Use Care and Diligence.—The physician and surgeon also impliedly contracts that he will use reasonable and ordinary care and diligence in the

---

* Whitsell *vs.* Hill, 101 Ia., 629, 70 N. W. Rep., 750, 37 L. R. A., 830; Pelky *vs.* Palmer (Mich.), 3 Det. L. N., 198; Small *vs.* Howard, 128 Mass., 131.

† Nelson *vs.* Harrington, 72 Wis., 591.

exercise of his skill and the application of his knowledge to accomplish the purpose for which he is employed.* It is patent that a physician and surgeon may
be possessed of a very superior degree of knowledge and
skill and yet fail in the successful treatment of a case
by not using the proper care in applying his knowledge
or exercising his skill. For example, a physician of
superior learning and skill might in the hasty or indifferent examination of a patient fail to observe symptoms
characteristic of the disease from which the patient is
suffering, and treat him for a different ailment with
disastrous results, while a physician with less skill and
learning could by a more careful examination of the
patient detect the true condition, and by applying the
generally recognized remedies effect a cure.

To determine what is ordinary care and diligence
no absolute rule can be prescribed. Justice Story, in
referring to the impossibility of a fixed standard or test,
said: " Different things may require very different care.
The care required to build a common doorway is quite
different from that required to raise a marble pillar,
but both come under the description, ordinary care." †
And so in the treatment of patients, that which in one
case might be ordinary care would perhaps in another

---

* Carpenter *vs*. Blake, 50 N. Y., 696.
† Story on Bailments, § 429.

be gross negligence. The question is peculiarly one of fact, and can only be determined by taking into consideration the condition of the patient in the particular case, together with all of the attendant circumstances. If, after such an examination, it is found that the care and diligence exercised are those which an ordinarily careful physician, practising in a similar locality, would have exercised in a like case, then it is fair to conclude that the legal requirement of ordinary care and diligence has been fulfilled.

Degree of Care not Necessarily Proportionate to Character of Injury treated.—It must not be inferred from the foregoing description of ordinary care and diligence that the degree of care and diligence or care and skill necessary to be exercised in a particular case must be proportionate to the severity of that case. Such a doctrine has been urged but has been very wisely rejected by the courts.* If such a rule were adopted the conclusion would naturally and logically follow that a physician and surgeon is legally required to exercise care and skill adequate to the severity of all cases which he undertakes. Such a test is manifestly absurd and beyond the possibility of human acquirements.

Refusal of Proffered Assistance does not Alter implied Contract.—The fact that a physician or surgeon

---

* Utley *vs.* Barnes, 70 Ill., 162.

refuses to accept the proffered assistance of other medical men does not increase his liability or responsibility, but simply amounts to an implied declaration that he possesses the ability which the law requires of him.*

Physician's Contract unaltered where Services are Gratuitous.—Nor does the fact that a physician makes no charge and receives no compensation for treating a particular case alter in any degree the amount of knowledge, care, and skill which it is incumbent upon him to have and exercise.† In instructing a jury upon this question, Justice Pryor stated the law, together with the reason upon which it is based, so fully and clearly that we can do no better than to use his words : " It appears that the plaintiff was a charity patient; that the defendant was treating her gratuitously. But I charge you that this fact in no way qualifies the liability of the defendant. Whether the patient be a pauper or a millionaire, whether he be treated gratuitously or for reward, the physician owes him precisely the same measure of duty and the same degree of skill and care. He may decline to respond to the call of a patient unable to compensate him; but if he undertake the treatment of such a patient he can not defeat a suit for malpractice nor mitigate a recovery against him upon the prin-

---

* Potter *vs.* Warner, 91 Pa. St., 362.
† Du Bois *vs.* Decker, 130 N. Y , 325.

ciple that the skill and care required of a physician are proportioned to his expectation of pecuniary recompense. Such a rule would be of the most mischievous consequence, would make the health and life of the indigent the sport of reckless experiment and cruel indifference." *

This rule must, however, be understood with the qualification that a party who undertakes the gratuitous treatment of another incurs no liability unless he professes to be a physician and undertakes the treatment as such. For if he merely gives his advice or assistance as a friend or neighbor he incurs no professional responsibility.† Where, for example, one not a physician, employed in the capacity of a midwife, attempted to treat the infant's eyes, and by reason of the inefficient remedies used the child became blind, the law would not hold the midwife as contracting to possess the same skill and learning as it would a regular physician who had gratuitously undertaken the same case.‡

Dentist's Contract implies Knowledge, Skill, and Care.—It may be observed in passing that a dentist implies by the exercise of the duties of his profession that he is possessed of the same amount of knowledge and skill in his profession, and will exercise the same

---

* Becker *vs.* Janinski, 27 Abb. N. C., 45.

† McNevins *vs.* Lowe, 40 Ill., 209.

‡ Higgins *vs.* McCabe, 126 Mass., 13.

degree of care and diligence in their application, as that impliedly contracted for by the physician in the medical profession.*

Contracts to Use Best Judgment.—In addition to the contract of the physician implying that he is possessed of learning and skill and will exercise reasonable care and diligence in the treatment of his patients, it also implies that in all cases of doubt he will use his best judgment. The contract is not that his judgment will be infallible, but simply that it shall be a reasonably good judgment, and that in all cases of doubt he will fully exercise it.

In the abstract this rule appears to mean very little, but when it comes to the particular case; when the physician finds his patient suffering, perhaps, with conditions symptomatic of several diseases; when by the exercise of his best knowledge and skill, or, for that matter, the best knowledge and skill of the most enlightened of his profession, he can not determine the patient's exact condition; then the rule has a real meaning to him. In such an emergency it can not fail to be a great comfort and relief to know that an intelligent and careful exercise of his best judgment is all that is required.

If, by way of showing a further application of the

---

* Simonds *vs.* Henry, 39 Me., 155.

rule, a surgeon is requested by a patient to perform a certain operation which, in the opinion of the surgeon, is unwise, unnecessary, or will result injuriously to the patient, it becomes his duty to give the patient the benefit of his judgment, whether it is asked for or not, and if the surgeon fails to advise against such operation, but acts as requested, he becomes liable to the patient in damages for whatever injuries result to him by reason of such unnecessary or unwise operation. But, if the patient is of mature years and of sound mind, and upon being advised of the impropriety of such operation still insists upon its performance, the surgeon may accept the judgment of the patient, and, if the operation is skillfully and properly performed, he can not be held responsible to the patient because its result is injurious.*

Contracts to Follow Established Modes of Practice. —The physician and surgeon also impliedly contracts with his patients that in his treatment of them he will comply with the established modes of practice.

Such a method or system of treatment must, however, be upheld by a consensus of opinion among members of the profession before the practitioner is bound to accept and follow it in his practice.†

There are probably many cases in which the physi-

---

* Gramm *vs.* Boener, 56 Ind., 497.
† Jackson *vs.* Burnham, 20 Col., 533.

cian and surgeon possessing the skill and ability required by law can not by the exercise of due care and diligence determine the particular disease or condition from which the patient is suffering. In such case, if he uses ordinary care and skill, and by the exercise of his best judgment determines upon a particular disease, and then applies the recognized remedy or mode of treatment for that disease, he is fulfilling his contract with the patient and doing all the law requires of him in the particulars considered. But if he experiments with some other mode of treatment he does so at his peril. Justice Goddard, in the case of Jackson *vs.* Burnham, said: " In other words, he must be able in case of deleterious results to satisfy the jury that he had reason for the faith that was in him, and justify his experiment by some reasonable theory." *

Duty to Instruct Patient and Nurse.—It is also incumbent upon the physician and surgeon to give all reasonable and necessary instructions for the proper treatment and care of the particular disease or injury for which he is treating the patient; and should injury result from his failure to exercise this precaution he will be held to respond in damages.† This obligation extends not only to giving instructions for the period

---

* Jackson *vs.* Burnham, 20 Col., 533.
† Carpenter *vs.* Blake, 60 Barb., 488.

during which the physician is attending the patient, but also for the period of convalescence immediately following. Therefore a physician should, upon dismissing his patients, carefully tell them what to avoid, and advise them to exercise that care which in his judgment is best calculated to restore their natural health and strength.*

The physician should not, however, be held to anticipate and advise against improbable conduct on the part of the patient. Where, for instance, a patient who is under the care of a physician at a hospital leaves the hospital without informing the physician of his intent so to do, it will be unjust to hold the physician to the duty of anticipating the patient's departure and advising him to remain.†

Does not Contract to Cure.—Without a special contract to that effect the physician and surgeon is never considered as guaranteeing that he will effect a cure, or even benefit his patients.‡ A physician may, however, enter into such a contract by express agreement providing that he shall be paid only in case he effects a cure, and such a contract, when entered into, will be binding though no definite sum is named as the compensation

---

* Beck vs. German Klinik, 78 Ia., 696, 7 L. R. A., 566.

† Richards vs. Willard, 176 Pa. St., 181, 35 Atl. Rep., 114.

‡ Styles vs. Tyler, 64 Conn., 432, 30 Atl. Rep., 166; Leighton vs. Sargent, 27 N. H., 460; Haire vs. Reese, 7 Phil. (Pa.), 138.

for performing the cure.* When no specified sum is agreed upon, the physician will, upon performing the cure, be entitled to a reasonable amount for such services, to be determined in the ordinary manner.

Continuation of Attendance.—A physician may by special contract, when undertaking the treatment of a case, limit his attendance to a longer or shorter period, or may at any time during the treatment of the case discontinue his attendance by first giving reasonable notice of his intention so to do; but if he does not limit his attendance by express contract or give such reasonable notice of his intention to discontinue his visits, he is bound to continue his visits as long and as frequently as the requirements of the case may demand, and he is held to the use of ordinary care and skill in determining when his visits may be safely discontinued.†

Contagious Disease.—It is the duty of the physician, and he impliedly contracts, to protect his patients in all reasonable ways from contagious and infectious diseases. If he himself has such a disease, and with knowledge of his condition visits his patients without apprising them of the fact, and thus communicates the disease

---

* Mack *vs.* Kelly, 3 Ala., 387.

† Ballou *vs.* Prescott, 64 Me., 305; Boom *vs.* Reed, 69 Hun, 426; Barbour *vs.* Martin, 62 Me., 536; Williams *vs.* Gilman, 71 Me., 21; Dashiell *vs.* Griffith, 84 Md., 363; Becker *vs.* Janinski, 27 Abb. N. C., 45.

to them, he is clearly guilty of a breach of duty. Moreover, it is his duty, in passing from patients who are afflicted with an infectious and dangerous disease to others who are not so affected, to take such precautions as experience may have shown to be necessary to prevent the communication of infection, and he will be held responsible for his failure so to do.*   When the physician has effected a cure of a patient afflicted with a contagious or infectious disease, it becomes his duty to employ all proper and necessary means to disinfect the premises, and the law will protect him in fulfilling such duty, even though it may involve destruction of property.†

Contract for Medical Treatment Includes Surgical Cases.—A physician who enters into a contract with a patient or with a third party, agreeing to give " medical " treatment or to " perform the duties of a physician " for a certain period of time, there being no express understanding regarding surgical cases, or nothing to show that it was clearly the intent that surgical cases should be excluded, will be required under the contract to perform surgical operations as well as to give general medical treatment during the period.‡

Privileged Communications.—Last, but by no means

---

* Piper vs. Menifee, 54 Am. Dec., 547, 12 B. Monroe, 465.

† Seavey vs. Preble, 64 Me., 120.

‡ Wetherell vs. Marion Co., 28 Iowa, 22 ; Clinton Co. vs. Ramsey, 20 Ill. App., 577.

least in importance, the physician contracts with his patients that he will preserve sacred and inviolable all
knowledge which comes to him in a professional way.
So sacred is this knowledge held that in many States the
physician is not required to disclose the same in a court
of justice without the patient's consent. Knowledge of
this sort is technically known in the law as privileged
communications. The questions arising under this
privilege being many and varied, they are made the subject of a separate chapter.*

Importance of the Foregoing Principles.—By way of
general observation it may be said that the foregoing
contracts and obligations implied on behalf of the physician form nearly the whole groundwork of the law regulating the subject of civil malpractice, and if the physician carefully remembers and applies these rules he may
hope to escape being required to face an injured patient
in a court of justice, and certainly to avoid being
mulcted in damages.

---

* See chap. ix, Privileged Communications.

CHAPTER III.

Contract Implied on the Part of the Patient.—A contract on the part of the patient, as well as on the part of the physician, is created by law. Such contract, like the one of the physician, is based upon and grows out of the relations of the parties, and is in its nature complementary to the contract of the physician.

Contract to Pay Physician's Fees.—The right of the physician to charge and recover compensation for his services is very seldom the subject of an express agreement between the physician and patient; yet the physician is quite as secure in this right as though it were fixed by formal agreement, it having been long settled that where a person avails himself of the benefit of services done for him, even though without his positive authority or request, the law supplies the formal words of contract and presumes him to have promised an adequate compensation. It may therefore be laid down as a general rule that whenever a patient employs or receives the services of a physician he is bound to pay a reasonable compensation for such services.*

---

* Crane *vs.* Baudoine, 65 Barb., 260; Peck *vs.* Martin, 17 Ind., 115.

A notable exception to this rule formerly existed under the law of England, which treated the services of the physician as honorary and gratuitous, and did not permit him to recover compensation therefor unless the patient was bound by a special agreement to pay. The services of the surgeon were not considered of the same honorary character, and he was therefore able to recover his fees without a special agreement. Under the medical act passed in the twenty-first and twenty-second years of the reign of Victoria, physicians, if duly registered, are entitled to recover reasonable compensation for their services without any express contract providing for such compensation, thus being placed on the same footing in this regard as physicians in the United States.

Liable for Subsequent Visits.—It will be remembered that a physician undertaking the treatment of a case is bound to continue his visits as long as the condition of the patient requires his attention. The counterpart of this obligation may be found in the implied contract which the law creates requiring the patient to pay the physician not only for the first visit, which he has expressly requested, but for all further visits or services which the physician and surgeon makes or renders by reason of the necessities of the case.*

---

* Dale *vs.* Donaldson Lumber Co., 48 Ark., 188.

Liable for Fee of Consultant.—The patient is bound not only to pay the attending physician, but also the physician who is called to a consultation, and this has been held to be the law notwithstanding there is an agreement between the attending physician and patient that the attending physician shall pay the expenses of such consultation.*

The reason for this rule may be readily seen. It has been observed that where a party knowingly and without objection permits another to perform services for him, the law implies a promise to pay what the services are reasonably worth. Consequently, when a physician is called to a consultation, even though it be by the attending physician, it is fair for him to presume that the consultation is for the benefit of the patient, and to rely upon the promise of payment which the law makes for the patient. The agreement of the attending physician to pay the consultant is unusual and exceptional, and being contrary to the ordinary presumption of law the consultant will not be bound unless he has notice of such arrangement before or at the time of rendering the services.

It is doubted, however, whether a patient is bound by an implied contract to pay for medical services of a physician called in by her attending physician for the mere purpose of convincing her that he is doing all that

---

* Shelton *vs.* Johnson, 40 Iowa, 84 ; Garrey *vs.* Stadler, 67 Wis., 512.

can be accomplished for her, where such physician, in fact, rendered no services for her and was not called in at her request.*

It is pertinent to state at this point that should the patient be required to pay the consulting physician after the attending physician has agreed to defray this expense, the patient may recover the amount so paid by him from the attending physician, or he may treat it as a counterclaim and deduct the amount from fees earned by the attending physician.

Contract of Obedience.—It is a well-settled proposition of law that it is the duty of the patient upon placing himself in the hands of a physician to follow strictly all instructions and conform to the necessary prescriptions and treatment, if they are such as a physician or surgeon of ordinary skill and care would adopt or sanction. As a disregard of this obligation results to the injury of the patient only, it does not give the physician a cause of action against the patient; yet if the patient endeavors to recover damages from the physician for injuries which he claims result from unskilled treatment, the physician and surgeon may, by showing that the patient is guilty of such negligence or disobedience, prevent his recovery.†

---

* Schrader *vs.* Hoover, 87 Ia., 654, 54 N. W., 463.

† Haire *vs.* Reese, 7 Phila. (Pa.), 138; Davis *vs.* Spicer, 27 Mo. App., 279; Jones *vs.* Angell, 95 Ind., 376.

Sunday Contracts.—In the absence of statutes to the contrary, any contract executed on Sunday is as valid and binding as though executed on a week day. Each State has, however, passed laws requiring the observance of Sunday. In all States labor is prohibited, and in most States the transaction of business is made unlawful upon the Sabbath. In those States which go so far as to prohibit labor only, one is free to enter into contracts and to execute promissory notes and other instruments which are perfectly valid; but in those States which prohibit the transaction of business, any instrument or contract made or entered into on Sunday is invalid and can not be enforced even though one of the parties may have performed his part of such contract. If, for instance, in a State prohibiting the transaction of business on the Sabbath goods are sold and delivered on Sunday, or services are rendered on that day, the party receiving the goods or enjoying the benefit of the services is under no obligation to pay for them.

These statutes, however, unanimously except from their operation contracts made to carry out works of necessity or charity, and the courts have held, whenever the question has been raised, that the contract of the physician falls within this exception, and that it is binding in all respects both upon him and upon the patient.[*]

* Smith *vs.* Watson, 14 Vt., 332; Aldrich *vs.* Blackstone, 128 Mass., 148.

CHAPTER IV.

Who are Third Parties.—The term third party, as used in this article, means any interested person other than the patient. While the physician may consider that he is dealing with the patient individually, it happens more frequently than otherwise that third parties are interested, either having rights of which the physician should be informed and prepared to respect, or incurring liabilities which if understood and taken advantage of may conduce to the physician's financial welfare.

Liability of Third Parties for Fees.—In treating this subject, attention will be first given to the question of when third parties become liable to the physician for the payment of his fees.

Liability of Parent.—That the parent is bound to provide for the maintenance of his minor children is a rule of natural law. But the question to what extent the parent becomes liable for necessaries furnished to his minor child is one that is sometimes perplexing. When necessaries are furnished, either in the shape of goods delivered or services rendered, with the knowledge and consent of the parent, there can be no question about his liability to pay. But it is laid down as a general rule that no action can be maintained against the parent for goods purchased on credit by his minor child, even though they may be necessary, unless the father has expressly or impliedly authorized the credit.

The authority of an infant to bind his parent for necessaries, such as food, clothing, and medical attendance, will be inferred from very slight evidence. The following cases will illustrate the principle:

Illustrations.—If a child who is away from home attending school is taken sick, the parent will be liable to the physician for the amount of his bill, authority to bind the father being inferred from the nature of the case.[*] A girl of fourteen, with the consent of her father, went to live at a place thirty miles distant, where for three years she contracted for, earned, and controlled her own wages, her father neither furnishing nor agreeing to furnish her with necessaries; while these circumstances showed that she was emancipated from the duty of service to the father for the time she was so employed, there was no such complete emancipation as to release him from liability to a physician who attended her in sickness, though the father had no knowledge of such attention.[†]

---

[*] Parker *vs.* Tillinghast, 19 Abb. N. C., 190.

[†] Porter *vs.* Powell, 79 Iowa, 151.

And so, where a child leaves home through fear of violence, he carries implied authority to bind his father for necessaries.* But if the child, having no reason to fear violence or mistreatment, leaves his father's home without the father's consent, for the purpose of seeking his fortune in the world, or to avoid the discipline and restraint so necessary for due regulation of families, he carries no credit, and the father is under no obligation to pay his necessary bills.†

It will be observed that the case above cited, of the girl who left her father's house and had been employed for three years, is not in conflict with this proposition, for in that case the father had given his consent to the employment. If, however, the child, after leaving home against his father's will, being taken sick, returns home and is received by the father, he becomes liable to the physician for medical services rendered to the child at his house and with his knowledge and assent.‡

It seems quite well settled by a number of recent decisions that the parent is bound to pay for necessaries

---

* Stanton vs. Willson, 3 Day (Conn.), 37; Pidgin vs. Cram, 8 N. H., 350; Kimball vs. Keyes, 11 Wend. (N. Y.), 34; Walker vs. Laighton, 31 N. H., 111; Van Valkinburgh vs. Watson, 13 Johns (N. Y.), 480.

† Weeks vs. Merrow, 40 Me., 151; Owen vs. White, 5 Port. (Ala.), 435; Hunt vs. Thompson, 4 Ill., 179; Raymond vs. Loyl, 10 Barb., 483; Walker vs. Laighton, 31 N. H., 111; Reynolds vs. Sweetser, 15 Gray (Mass.), 78.

‡ Deane vs. Annis, 14 Me., 26.

furnished to his minor child who is living apart from him with his consent when the parent refuses to furnish them.*

Upon the death of the father, the mother becomes the head of the family, but it seems she is not bound by the same obligations of maintenance and support as those which formerly bound the father. Under the rule most commonly in force the child, if he has a separate estate, will be required to pay for his own medical attendance from his estate; and only in the absence of such an estate will the mother be subjected to that burden.

In case of separation or divorce it is of practical value to determine whether the father or mother is liable for necessaries for the child. While there are general principles of law governing the liability, it will be impossible to state generally where it rests, an examination into the circumstances of the particular case being always necessary. In case of voluntary separation of the parents the father is *prima facie* liable for the support of the children, though they may be in the custody of the mother; but if the mother, without just cause, leaves the father and takes the children with her, no authority is implied to bind him for their support or

* Dewane *vs.* Hansow, 56 Ill. App., 575; McMillen *vs.* Lee, 78 Ill., 443; Porter *vs.* Powell, 79 Iowa, 151.

necessary expenses, her possession of the children being unlawful.* But should the court, by a decree or order, give her the custody of the children, then her possession of them becomes rightful and the father becomes liable for their support.†

In Rhode Island it has been held that where the mother wrongfully left the father's home, taking a child, the father, by suffering the child to live separate from him with the mother, constituted her his agent to contract for the child's necessities.‡ When a divorce is granted, the custody of the children is usually regulated by decree. If the divorce is obtained by the wife and the husband is shown to be an improper person to care for and educate the child, the court will decree the custody of the child to the mother. Whether or not the father is liable for the support of the child under such circumstances can not be stated generally, for different rules are applied in different States, and in some States the circumstances of the particular case will govern the matter. In such a case the only safe rule for the physician to be guided by is to have an express contract for payment with some responsible party before the services are rendered.

When the child becomes of full age a different rule

---

* Hyde vs. Leisenring, 107 Mich., 490.
† Shields vs O'Reilly, 68 Conn., 256.
‡ Gill vs. Read, 5 R. I., 343.

of liability attaches; the parent then ceases to be under obligation to furnish him with necessities, even though he remains at his father's home. It is true the father may become liable for medical attendance upon his adult child by an implied agreement to pay, but it seems the law places the father of an adult child in the same category as a stranger, and will not find him liable on any less or weaker evidence than that required to fix such liability upon a mere friend or acquaintance. So a request by a father to a physician to attend his son, of full age, and at his house, raises no implied promise on the part of the father to pay for such services.* A married daughter of more than twenty-one years of age came with her husband and child to her father's home; she being sick, her husband requested a physician, to whom he was unknown, to call at the house of the father, saying the father wished him to attend his daughter; the physician called, usually met the father, who expressed great interest in his daughter's welfare, expressed a wish to be present at a consultation which was held, and never in any way disclaimed his liability. The court said: " It is true that a person may not avail himself of the benefit of services done for him without coming into an obligation to reward them with a reasonable recompense. But he can not be said, in the mean-

---

* Boyd *vs.* Sappington, 4 Watts, 247.

ing of the law, to avail himself of services as so done when they are not for his individual benefit, nor for that of any one for whom he is bound to furnish them. The acquiescence of one in the rendering of service or benefit to another, not entitled to call upon him therefor, is not equivalent to an acknowledgment that it is rendered at his request. So far as the legal responsibility was concerned, the defendant, though the father of the patient, was a stranger to her and her necessities. He could neither require of her, nor be required upon by her." *

Liability of Husband.—The liability of the husband for necessities furnished to the wife is much more certain than that of the parent for necessities furnished to the child; in the latter case there is a question of authority on the part of the child to bind the parent, but in the former case, if the husband and wife are not separated by reason of the improper conduct of the wife, or by reason of her leaving him against his will, almost the only question that can be raised is whether the goods furnished or services rendered were necessary. If the husband and wife are living apart by mutual consent, and the husband has entered into a contract with the wife to furnish her with a certain amount each month for her support and maintenance and all family ex-

* Crane *vs.* Baudouine, 55 N. Y., 256.

penses, and pays such amount, he will still be liable to a physician who renders services to her at her request, the physician not knowing they are living apart and that the husband makes her a fixed monthly payment in lieu of supporting her.*

It has been heretofore observed that the patient is bound to pay the physician not only for the first visit which is made at his request, but for all subsequent visits which the nature of the case requires; and so the husband who employs a physician to attend his sick wife is liable for services rendered throughout the illness. Should the wife be removed to her father's home during her illness, without the husband's knowledge or consent, he will still be bound to pay the physician whom he employed before such removal for services rendered to the wife at her father's home.† If, however, the husband notifies the physician at the time of the removal that he will not pay for services subsequently rendered to her, the physician can not collect from him without showing by clear and satisfactory evidence that the husband was guilty of gross abuse, neglect, and misconduct justifying such removal.

A physician who attends a woman, supposing her to be a wife, can collect for such services from the man

---

* Lawrence vs. Brown, 91 Ia., 342, 59 N. W., 256.
† Downing vs. O'Brien, 67 Barb., 583.

holding himself forth as her husband, even though they are not in fact married.*   But, it seems, if the physician is cognizant of the fact that they are not married, he can not collect from the supposititious husband, unless such husband employed him to render the services, thus becoming liable upon a direct undertaking to pay.

The liability of the husband for necessary food, clothing, and medical attendance furnished the wife in his absence does not include the services of a clairvoyant who does not profess to be a physician or to have any medical skill or knowledge of diseases or their remedies. The court in passing upon this question said: " It does not appear that the plaintiff (*clairvoyant*) professed to be a physician or to have any medical skill or knowledge of diseases or their medical remedies, and of course it does not appear that he has furnished the wife with any necessaries within the rule of law for which the husband can be rightfully charged.   The law does not recognize the dreams, visions, or revelations of one in a mesmeric sleep as necessary for a wife, for which the husband, without his consent, can be held to pay.   These are fancy articles, which those who have money of their own to dispose of may purchase, if they think proper, but they are not necessaries, known to the law, for which the wife can pledge the credit of her absent husband." †

---

* Gerlach *vs*. Turner, 89 Cal., 447, 26 Pac. Rep., 870.

† Furlong *vs*. Leary, 62 Mass., 406.

Liability of Master for Attendance on Servant.—It is a well-settled doctrine that the master is not by reason of his relation to the servant liable for medical attendance upon such servant.* If, however, a physician is called by a master to attend a servant in his employ, such engagement has been held to amount to a direct undertaking by the master to pay; but if he is called by the master's wife, even with an express agreement that her husband will pay, the husband is not bound unless it can be shown that the agreement is made with his knowledge and consent, or that he subsequently ratified the hiring. The reason for this rule may be readily perceived; the husband is never bound by the contracts of his wife except for necessaries furnished to her or to her children; therefore a contract imposing a liability upon him for medical attendance upon a servant, which he is not primarily liable to pay, is beyond the scope of her authority.†

Liability of Vessels for Attendance upon Seamen.— For the information of those physicians living in cities and towns located on the oceans, great lakes, or other navigable waters of the United States, the general rule of liability of vessels for the care and medical attendance upon their sick and disabled seamen is given.

It is a well-established rule of law that shipowners

---

* 4 Waite's Actions and Defenses, 400.

† Baker *vs.* Witten, 1 Okl., 160, 30 Pac. Rep., 491.

and masters are bound to provide suitable care and
medical treatment for seamen who become disabled by
sickness or injuries received in the discharge of their
duties, and a physician attending such seamen may hold
the vessel, the master, or the owners to pay for his
services.*

The extent of the period covered by this liability is
the subject of much conflict; some cases hold that the
seaman is entitled to care and medical treatment until
he recovers, while others restrict the right to the period
covered by the voyage for which the seaman is engaged.
It seems that where the injury or sickness is the result
of culpable negligence or mistreatment by the master
or officers of the vessel the courts have held the liability
to extend over the entire period of sickness or disability;
whereas, when the sickness or injury could not be im-
puted to such cause, they have considered the liability
as terminating when the voyage for which the seaman
was engaged was completed and he was discharged.†

This is a question upon which the law books present
a great amount of material—some of it conflicting—
but, owing to the comparatively small number of the
profession who are interested in its discussion, it is not
thought advisable to use the space necessary for an ex-

---

* Holt *vs.* Cummings, 102 Pa. St., 212, 48 Am. Rep., 199.

† The Ben Flint, 1 Abb. U. S., 126 ; The J F. Card, 43 Fed. Rep.,
92 ; *contra* The Lizzie Frank, 31 Fed. Rep., 477.

amination of particular instances of the application of the general principles laid down.

Statute of Frauds.—The question of when a third party not in the relation of husband, parent, or master is liable for the services of the physician is often a very nice one. Section four of the English Statute of Frauds provides, among other things, that "no action shall be brought whereby . . . to charge the defendant upon any special promise to answer for the debt, default, or miscarriage of another person . . . unless the agreement upon which such action shall be brought, or some memorandum or note thereof, shall be in writing and signed by the party to be charged therewith."

This section of the statute has been re-enacted, with certain unimportant modifications, throughout the United States.*

At first glance it would seem that in order to enforce the liability of a third person of the class we are now considering, his contract of obligation must in all cases be reduced to writing and signed. This statute is, however, not so broad in its application as it at first appears. As a matter of fact, the contract or agreement fixing the liability of the third party is more frequently without than within the operation of this statute.

---

* In Pennsylvania it does not apply to any contract the consideration of which is less than twenty dollars.

In order to bring a case within the statute, a third person who is in no way liable for the debt or default in question must promise to pay it if not paid by the debtor. If the promise is of such a nature as to act as an assignment or sale of the security for the debt, or of the debt itself to the third party, it does not come within the statute, nor if the third party assumes to be the paymaster, making himself directly and unconditionally responsible for the debt, is it necessary to reduce such agreement to writing.

It will be observed that the promise to pay must, to come within the statute, be conditional: thus, if a third party says to a physician, " If the patient does not pay you I will," the promise comes within the statute, and to be binding must be reduced to writing. But if the third party says, " Attend such a patient and I will pay you," the promise does not come within the statute, and the oral promise is binding,* for in such a case the third party does not agree to answer for the debt of another, but by his contract makes the debt his own.

It is a well-established rule of law that all valid contracts must be based upon some good or valuable consideration. If, therefore, a third party says to a physician, after the services are rendered and the indebted-

---

* Buchanan *vs.* Sterling, 63 Ga., 227; Boston *vs.* Farr, 148 Pa. St., 220, 23 Atl. Rep., 901 ; Thomas *vs.* Leavy, 62 Ill. App., 34.

ness is incurred, " I will pay the bill of ——," such a promise is not binding, whether written or verbal, because there is no consideration upon which to found the contract. A sufficient consideration need not be one of money. When, for example, the promise is made before services are rendered, the consideration for assuming the obligation is that the physician will render such services; or, if the services have been rendered, and a third party agrees to assume the indebtedness, provided the physician will forbear from bringing a suit upon the account, or will dismiss a suit already brought, such condition will be a sufficient consideration upon which to found the contract of liability. A physician who was attending a patient was approached by the patient's son with the following statement: " You do what you can for father, and you charge this bill to me, and what you do afterward, and I will leave you some money before I leave town." This was a direct undertaking, and therefore not required to be in writing; but, so far as it related to the fee for services already rendered, was without consideration and void, although good and binding for services rendered after the date of the promise.*

But if a physician who is attending a patient refuses to continue his services unless guaranteed that he will

---

* Chappell *vs.* Barkley, 90 Mich., 35, 51 N. W., 351.

be paid for both past and future services, and a third party undertakes to make such payment upon condition that the physician's services shall be continued, the continuation of the services will be a sufficient consideration upon which to base the obligation.

It is hoped that the foregoing explanation has clearly shown the difference between an original undertaking, which is valid and binding whether in writing or not, and a collateral obligation for the payment of another's debt, which must be in writing to comply with the statute. An examination will therefore be made of a few cases which tend to show what circumstances will amount to a direct and original undertaking by a third party.

Liability of Party asking Physician to attend Another.—Whether or not the mere request by a third party for a physician to call upon a particular patient, without stating that he acts as agent for such patient, will render the third party liable to the physician for services rendered the particular patient is a question upon which there is some conflict, the courts in the State of New York holding the third party liable in such cases, while those of other States in which the question has arisen renounce the doctrine of liability under such circumstances.

An extreme case of the sort arose in New York city in 1873. A person called at the office of a physician.

The physician being absent, he wrote upon his business card, " Call on Mrs. ——, at No. — Broadway," and left it with the clerk, with the request to hand it to the physician and tell him to come as soon as possible.

The jury rendered a verdict for the physician, and the court to which the case was appealed refused to disturb the verdict. The court, in the opinion, said: " There was nothing on the card to indicate to the plaintiff, before he rendered the services, that the defendant had called at his office at Mrs. ——'s request, and that he was therefore only acting as her messenger.

" The defendant might very readily have secured himself from all liability by simply writing the memorandum on a blank card, or by adding to what he wrote on his own card something that would have apprised the plaintiff of the fact that he acted in the transaction for Mrs. —— as her agent.... Having neglected to do this, the plaintiff was, under the circumstances, justified in believing that he was employed and would be paid by the defendant." *

Later, in 1896, the supreme court refused to disturb the verdict of the jury fixing the liability upon a son who summoned a doctor to attend his father by the following words: " Doctor, I want you to come and attend my father. He had a doctor who was not satisfac-

* Bradley *vs.* Dodge, 45 How. Pr., 57.

tory." In the opinion the court cited the case of Bradley *vs.* Dodge with evident approval.* These cases repre-sent an extreme view, and, as the question has never been passed upon by the court of last resort in the State of New York, it is impossible to say what that tribunal will determine the law to be.

The better rule of law, it is thought, and probably the one which would be followed in any State except New York, is that the mere calling for a physician, or requesting him to call upon a certain patient, will not make one liable to such physician for his fees in the par-ticular service. This is shown by these cases:

The superintendent of a cooperage company sent a messenger to a physician summoning him to the works of the company to attend an injured employee. The court of appeals for Missouri, in considering the matter, said: "We take it that the law will not imply, upon this evi-dence, a contract either on the part of the corporation or on the part of Mr. —— (the superintendent) to pay for these services. The general rule, no doubt, is that, where a person requests the performance of a service, and the request is complied with and the service per-formed, the law raises an implied promise to pay the reasonable value of the services. But this implication does not obtain where one person requests a physician

---

* Foster *vs.* Meeks, 18 Misc., 461, 41 N. Y. Supp., 950.

to perform services for a patient, unless the relation of
the person making the request to the patient is such as
to raise a legal obligation on his part to call in the
physician and pay for the services. Where a husband
calls in a physician to attend upon his wife, or where a
father calls in a physician to attend upon his minor
child, the law implies a promise on his part to pay the
reasonable value of the services, because there is a legal
obligation on his part, in either case, to furnish necessaries for the patient's benefit. But no such implication
arises where one calls in a physician to attend upon a
stranger, or upon one to whom he is under no legal obligations." Quoting further in the same case, the court
said: " The reason and policy of this rule are obvious,
especially in cases like the present. When a person is
dangerously wounded, and perhaps unable to speak for
himself, or suffering so much that he does not know how
to do it, any person will run to the nearest surgeon in
the performance of an ordinary office of humanity. If
it were the law that the person so going for the surgeon thereby undertakes to become personally responsible for the surgeon's bill, and especially for the surgeon's bill through the long subsequent course of treatment, many would hesitate to perform this office, and
in the meantime the sufferer might die for the want of
necessary immediate attention." *

* Meisenbach *vs.* The Southern Cooperage Co., 45 Mo. App., 232.

A case stronger than the one above given is reported in Vermont. A brother who had been acquainted with a physician took him to see his insane brother and earnestly requested him to undertake the treatment of the insane patient. There was no express agreement as to the payment for the services. The court, in considering this case, said: " It appears that all of the services were performed for the brother of the defendant, who, though insane, was liable therefor. The services were not beneficial to the present defendant, and he was under no legal obligation to pay for them unless as an express undertaking, or unless it may fairly be inferred from the evidence that it was the intention of both parties that the plaintiff should perform the services and the defendant should pay therefor." *

In the case of Rankin *vs.* Beale, a father sent for a physician to attend his adult son at the father's house, and after the services were rendered agreed with the physician to pay for them. The court held that the father was not bound by merely sending for the physician to pay his fee, and the promise of payment being made after the services were rendered was without consideration and void.†

A third party, acting as messenger, was sent for a certain physician to assist in the performance of an

* Smith *vs.* Watson, 14 Vt., 332.
† Rankin *vs.* Beale, 68 Mo. App , 325.

operation. Not finding him in, he went to the office of another physician and said: "I have come after you to go and see a sick man." The third party went part way with the physician to the patient's house, when, meeting with another person going to see the patient, he separated from the physician. Upon arriving at the patient's house, the doctor who was in attendance on the sick man explained to him what had occurred, and said that the physician who had just arrived would assist in the operation, which was assented to, and the operation was performed. The court said: "The evidence tended to show that the plaintiff (the physician) was aware of the fact that the defendant acted merely as a messenger, and did not intend, or expect, to make himself personally liable for the services which were to be rendered to the sick man. If, upon the explanation made by the doctor in attendance, the plaintiff was not willing to assist at the instance and on the credit of the sick man, it was his duty then to make known his objections.

"To hold the defendant liable under these circumstances would deter every one from doing the charitable office of going after a doctor for a sick neighbor." *

A physician attending a patient who was injured and lying at his son-in-law's house proposed on several

---

* Smith *vs.* Riddick, 5 Jones Law (N. C.), 342.

occasions to discontinue his services, when he was requested not to do so by the son-in-law. After the patient's death the physician presented his bill, amounting to five hundred dollars, to the son-in-law, as a claim
against him personally, and asked its payment. He did
not deny his responsibility, but objected to the amount;
and after a dispute and some angry words he wrote an
order upon an attorney for two hundred dollars to be
paid out of a certain claim when collected, and handed
it to the physician, saying he would give him that, and
would not pay him another cent, and if he did not take
that he would not get anything. The account was
charged upon the physician's books to the patient, and
when the bill was presented to the son-in-law he was
the patient's administrator; but that was unknown to
the physician. The court said: " Though the physician
in the beginning, may have rendered services solely upon
the patient's responsibility, in the absence of a special
contract he was not bound to continue to do so, and had
the right to discontinue, and enter into a contract with
the son-in-law to become responsible for his subsequent
services; but, in such case, the burden is on him to show,
not only a discontinuance, or a proposal to discontinue,
but also an agreement on the part of the son-in-law to
be responsible. There is no pretense of an express agreement; in the absence of such, it was necessary for the
physician, in order to entitle him to the affirmative

charge, to prove facts undisputed, from which the law would conclude an actual, though implied, agreement. The cause of the physician's proposal to discontinue his attendance does not appear. . . . Every person who may go for the regular attending physician when needed by his patient, or who, from considerations of friendship or humanity, may request him not to discontinue his attendance, does not render himself responsible for the services of the physician. Whether he does or not, depends upon the attendant circumstances." *

In the following cases circumstances have been shown which were considered equivalent to a direct contract or undertaking to pay the indebtedness.

In the case of Clark and Meigs *vs.* Waterman, a physician was called by the defendant to attend a girl who had lived with him from the time she was eight until she was eighteen years of age, and who had spent nearly seven eighths of her time subsequent thereto, up to the time of her sickness and death, in his household. The defendant manifested much interest in the case, was dissatisfied with the services of the first physician employed, discharged him, and employed another physician to attend the patient; he called for the bills of the physicians to lay before the town, " to see if they would not assist him." These facts were considered sufficient to show that the defendant intended and gave the plaintiffs

---

* Curry *vs.* Shelby, 90 Ala., 277, 7 So. Rep., 922.

to understand that he was himself the employer, and he was accordingly held liable.*

The employee of a lumber company was injured, not while in the course of his employment, but in a private brawl. The secretary, treasurer, and general business manager of the company sent a telegram to a physician as follows:

" To Dr. ——: Come here immediately by quickest means; man shot in breast.

[Signed.]   " ———— Lumber Company."

The doctor responded, and continued his visits for six weeks. The bill was presented to the company, but they denied liability and refused to pay. The secretary-treasurer and manager denied his liability, but offered, by way of compromise, to pay ten dollars, the price of the first visit. The offer was refused, and suit brought against the company and the officer who sent the telegram. It will be observed that the telegram by which the physician was summoned was not a request for him to attend any particular person, but an order for him to report to the company direct. So far as the reported case shows, the sufficiency of this order to bind them, had it been properly authorized, does not seem to have been questioned; but the company contested the claim on the ground that the officer sending the telegram had no authority, express or implied, to bind it to pay for

---

* Clark and Meigs *vs.* Waterman, 7 Vt., 76.

such services. The officer's excuse for using the company's name was that he was personally unknown to the physician, and was afraid the physician would not come unless summoned in the company's name. The trial court found that the company was not liable, but the secretary was personally liable. The principle upon which the secretary was held liable is that if the agent exceeds his authority, so that his principal is not bound, he will himself be liable for the damages thus occasioned to the other contracting party, although he may have been innocent of any intention to defraud.*

A landlord sent orders to a physician requesting him to call upon his tenants. The physician understood from the orders that the landlord intended to pay, and accordingly charged the services to him and made no efforts to collect from the tenants. The landlord testified that he did not consider that the orders made him personally responsible; afterward, however, he offered the physician some fodder to apply on the account, and also promised to make a payment of money at a stated time. The trial justice gave judgment against the landlord for the full amount of the claim, and the appellate court refused to disturb the judgment, as there seemed to be evidence to support such a judgment.†

The question whether or not an implied promise by

* Dale and Banks *vs.* Donaldson Lumber Co., 48 Ark., 188.
† Speer *vs.* Meschine, 46 S. C., 505, 24 S. E. Rep., 329.

a third person to pay exists in a particular case is nearly always one of fact, to be determined by the jury, whose duty it is to consider all of the attendant circumstances and carefully weigh the evidence of the parties, plaintiff and defendant, and, when such evidence is conflicting, to consider the character and reputation for truth and veracity of the witnesses, their intelligence and opportunity for knowing the real truth, and all other matters which bear upon the question at issue.

Liability of Corporation for Employment by Agent. •—A prolific source of litigation is the question of whether or not the employment of a physician by an agent or officer to attend an injured employee binds the corporation or company whom he represents to pay the physician's fee.

This question arises more frequently in connection with railroad companies than with all other concerns, the character of the employees' duties being such that they are liable to become seriously injured at almost any time and at any point on the line of the employer. When such accidents occur the services of a physician are needed at once, and it is usual for an employee having the highest authority in the immediate locality, usually the station agent or conductor, to summon and employ for the company the nearest competent physician and surgeon. The railroad companies, instead of meeting such obligations promptly, have manifested a preference to avoid paying for the services rendered in such cases when the circumstances of hiring are not such as legally to bind them to pay. A careful examination, therefore, of what will and what will not amount to a binding obligation on the part of the company will be of material value.

General Rule of Liability.—It may be stated as a general rule that a company or corporation is under no legal obligation to provide medical attendance for persons injured in its service; and if a physician or surgeon seeks to recover from a company for attendance upon an employee so injured, he must show that he was employed to render such services by a servant or officer of the company having authority to employ him; or, if the person employing him did not have authority so to do, he must show a subsequent ratification by those having authority to act for the company in such capacity.*

Who has Authority.—It is a general rule of law that one who deals with an agent is bound to know at his peril the extent of the agent's authority. This rule should be kept in mind while considering who has and who has not authority to bind his principal.

---

* Toledo, Wabash, and Western Ry. Co. *vs.* Prince, 50 Ill., 26. This rule is probably changed in South Carolina by a statute which imposes upon the railroad company the duty of giving notice to the most accessible physician of all accidents which occur on its road. Rev. Statutes of South Carolina, § 1690.

The president of a railroad company has authority to employ a physician and surgeon to attend its injured employees, and by so doing binds the company to pay for such services.

It is pretty well settled that a general superintendent has the same authority.* In the case of Cincinnati, Indianapolis, St. Louis, and Chicago Railroad Company *vs.* Davis, the company endeavored to escape liability on the ground that it employed a chief physician and surgeon whose duty it was to employ surgeons to give professional attention to persons injured by its trains. Justice Elliott said: " It would be unreasonable to require a surgeon to give professional assistance to a person injured by the company's trains, and then deny him compensation upon the ground that the superintendent had no authority to employ him because that authority was lodged in a chief surgeon. Nor are we willing to sanction a rule imposing upon the surgeons whose services are requested by the superintendent the duty of making specific inquiry as to the scope of the superintendent's authority. Such a rule would operate harshly in many cases, for, if the surgeon must stop to make inquiries before leaving his home or office, the injured man might perish. Better railroad companies should be held responsible for the acts of such a high

* Atchison and N. R. Co. *vs.* Reecher, 24 Kan., 228 ; McCarthy *vs.* Missouri R. Co., 15 Mo. App., 385.

officer as a general superintendent, although as between him and his principal that officer may usurp authority that is vested in a subordinate agent, than that a surgeon who obeys the summons of a superintendent should be compelled to go unpaid." *

This is undoubtedly the correct rule, notwithstanding the superior court of the city of New York held in 1853 that the superintendent of the New York and Harlem River Railroad Company would not be presumed to have authority to bind his company to pay for medical services engaged by him as officer of such company. The evidence showed that the superintendent had a general supervisory control over the whole line of the road, everything connected with the running of the road being under his supervision and control, and that he paid money to drivers, conductors, and other persons employed by him as superintendent, but had no direction over the treasury. The court argued from this evidence that it did not appear that the superintendent had authority to arrange and liquidate claims made against the company for damages resulting from the negligence of its agents and servants, and that the power exercised in employing a surgeon to attend one employed by the road was analogous thereto,

---

* Cincinnati, Indianapolis, St. Louis, and Chicago R. Co. *vs.* Davis 126 Ind., 99, 9 L. R. A., 503, 25 N. E. Rep., 878.

and was consequently not within the scope of his authority.*

As this case was not decided by a court of highest authority in the State, and is in direct conflict with reason and justice, and as well with the courts of all other States which have passed upon the question, it is doubted whether the decision would be regarded as a proper precedent to follow even in New York State.

The division superintendent also has authority to employ physicians and surgeons on behalf of the company.† The supreme court of Kansas recognizes, however, a distinction between professional services rendered to employees and those rendered to injured passengers upon the request of the division superintendent; while in the former case they uphold the presumption of his authority to bind the company, in the latter they repudiate the doctrine.‡

A general agent or general manager of a railroad company, which are judicially defined as being the same, is likewise presumed to have power to procure medical attendance for an employee injured in the service of their company.#

---

* Stephenson vs. New York and Harlem River R. Co., 2 Duer, 341.
† U. P. R. Co. vs. Winterbotham, 52 Kan., 433.
‡ U. P. R. Co. vs. Beatty, 35 Kan., 265.
# Atlantic and P. R. Co. vs. Reisner, 18 Kan., 458.

Any agent, employee, or servant of the company, if properly authorized, and acting in accordance with his instructions, may bind the company for services of a physician or surgeon rendered at his request. Where an inspector of a street-railway company who was instructed by the company " to see that those injured were taken somewhere where medical aid could be given," employed a physician to attend a passenger who was injured in getting off the car, the company was held to pay the physician's fee.* And so, when a physician was employed by an agent or employee of a brewing company to attend an employee who had been injured, and the physician inquired of the agent employing him who would be responsible for his medical attention to the injured employee, the agent replied that he had no authority to bind the company, but he would write to them and let the physician know. On the following day the agent showed the physician a telegram from the company as follows: " Have the negro treated." The physician relied upon the telegram, and the court held that he was justified in his conclusion that the agent was authorized to procure medical services on behalf of the company to " have the negro treated." †

For an agreement by a company to pay a physi-

* Hanscom *vs.* Minneapolis St. Ry. Co., 53 Minn., 119, 20 L. R. A., 695, 54 N. W. Rep., 944.

† Montgomery Brewing Co. *vs.* Caffee, 93 Ala., 132, 9 So. Rep., 573.

cian's fees to be of such a character as to enable the physician rendering services to avail himself of it, such agreement or contract must be made with him direct, either by an officer or agent of the company properly authorized to make such contract.*

If, for example, a physician is called by one injured in a railroad accident to attend him, the physician's contract is with the patient; and the relation does not change even though the president of the railroad calls upon the patient and tells him to employ any physician or surgeon he chooses and the company will pay the expense.† This promise to the patient does not create a privity between the company and the physician. If, however, the promise were made to the physician direct and acted upon by him, the company would be bound to him in the full amount of his fee.

Where a company contracts with a physician to attend an employee who has been injured, and reserves the right to determine what is a reasonable compensation, the court has held that the physician was bound by such reservation, and would not be permitted to recover a greater amount than that fixed upon as a reasonable compensation and tendered by the company.

---

* Thomas Mfg. Co. *vs.* Prather, 65 Ark., 27, 44 S. W. Rep., 218.

† Canney *vs.* S. P. C. R. Co., 63 Cal., 501.

The reason upon which the court holds the physician to this arbitrary determination of the amount of his fee is that the company is under no legal obligation to supply such medical attendance, and therefore if it does assume such obligation it has the right to impose such conditions as it sees fit.* It is doubtful, however, whether the courts will extend the application of this doctrine, or will apply it to this extent where the employee is injured by reason of the negligence of the company.

It is pertinent to state in passing that a contract by a physician with a railroad company to render professional services to employees of the company, or to those to whom the company is liable for personal injuries, does not bind the physician to render services to persons injured while trespassing on the property of the company.†

Who has not Authority.—It seems well settled that the authority to employ a physician on behalf of the company is not included in the general power and authority vested in the conductor, roadmaster, or station agent by virtue of his office or position.‡ And it makes no difference however positively such employee

---

* Fraser *vs.* San Francisco Bridge Co., 103 Cal., 79.

† Directors of Poor *vs.* Donnelly *et al.*, 5 Cent. Rep. (Pa.), 269.

‡ The Peninsular Railroad Co. *vs.* Gary, 22 Fla., 356 ; Tucker *vs.* St. Louis, K. C., and N. R. Co., 54 Mo., 177 ; Sevier *vs.* Birmingham S. and T. R. R. Co., 92 Ala., 258.

promises that the company will pay, such engagement and promise are wholly outside of the scope of their general authority.* Nor is there any such authority lodged in an engineer.† Nor is the attorney or solicitor of the road presumed to have such authority.‡

The courts have also held that the employment of a physician or surgeon for the treatment of injured employees does not come ordinarily within the scope of the duties of a general manager of an ordinary manufacturing business,# nor of the manager of a plantation.||

In this regard, it will be observed, a distinction is drawn between a railroad company, which is bound by such contracts made by its general manager or general agent, and an ordinary manufacturing business.

Whether or not a physician regularly employed by a railroad company to treat its injured employees has power to bind the company for board and care of such injured employees has several times been considered, and the courts have held that he has no such authority.△ In the case of St. Louis, Arkansas, and Texas Railway

---

* St. Louis and K. C. R. Co. vs. Olive, 40 Ill. App., 82.

† Cooper vs. N. Y. C. and H. R. R. Co., 6 Hun, 276.

‡ St. Louis, Ark., and Tex. R. Co. vs. Hoover, 53 Ark., 377.

Chaplin vs. Freeland, 7 Ind. App., 676, 34 N. E. Rep., 1007.

|| Malone vs. Robinson, 12 So. Rep., 709 (Miss.).

△ Chicago and E. R. Co. vs. Behrens, 9 Ind. App., 575, 37 N. E., 26; Bushnell vs. C. and N. W. R. Co., 69 Ia., 620.

Company *vs.* Hoover, it was held that the railroad company was under no obligation to refund money advanced by the physician for such board and care rendered to an injured employee.[*]

An exception to the rule that a conductor or employee of the class just considered is unauthorized to employ a physician is found in the humane doctrine of emergency, which is recognized as law by the courts of Indiana, but which has not been followed by the courts of any other States.

This doctrine is based upon the theory that the conductor or employee of highest authority in the immediate locality represents the company, and that in case of a sudden and pressing emergency extraordinary authority and powers arise in him, adequate to the urgent and immediate demands of the occasion.[†]

This extraordinary power in the conductor or other representative is only coextensive with the duration of the emergency which gives rise to it.[‡] If, therefore, an employee is seriously injured, or injured in such a way that immediate attention should be given him, the conductor or employee of highest authority is empowered to engage the services of a physician and

---

[*] St. Louis, Ark., and Tex. R. Co. *vs.* Hoover, 53 Ark., 377.

[†] Terre Haute and Indianapolis R. Co. *vs.* McMurray, 98 Ind., 358.

[‡] Ohio and M. R. Co. *vs.* Early, 141 Ind., 73, 28 L. R. A., 546, 40 N. E. Rep., 257.

bind the company in so doing. This contract, how-ever, can only be binding upon the company for such services as are immediately and urgently necessary.

In a case where a large number of employees are in-jured, and there being present only one of the com-pany's surgeons, who is unable to attend all of the wounded, the conductor is authorized to employ another surgeon to amputate the leg of one of the persons in-jured, and the company is bound to pay for such opera-tion, but not for attention given to such employee after the operation was performed.* This doctrine empower-ing minor agents to bind the company for medical services rendered in case of emergency, it will be re-membered, has been recognized as law only by the courts of Indiana. Whether or not this doctrine will gain recognition in other States can not be predicted with certainty, but, as it is founded upon good reason-ing and justice, a more extended adoption of the rule may be hoped for.

Ratification.—While the railroad company is ordi-narily under no obligation to pay for the services of a physician employed by an employee or inferior officer, it frequently happens that the company becomes liable for the payment of a physician's fee when he is pri-

---

* Evansville and R. R. Co. *vs.* Freeland, 4 Ind. App., 207, 30 N. E. Rep., 803.

marily so employed, through the ratification of such employment by the conduct of the higher officers of the company.

It is a well-established rule of law that such a hiring can not be ratified excepting by an officer whose power and authority are sufficient to enable him to make the contract primarily which he assumes to ratify by subsequent words or conduct.*

The question of whether or not the facts in a given case amount to a ratification of an unauthorized hiring is usually one for the jury to determine. The doctrine can therefore be better illustrated by examining a few cases than in any other way.

In the case of Pacific Railroad Company *vs.* Thomas, a physician was employed by the assistant master mechanic and the section boss to attend an employee who was injured. This hiring did not have the effect of obligating the company to pay the physician for his services, notwithstanding both the section boss and assistant master mechanic said that they would see that the railroad company paid him; but the physician, before he had finally completed the services, sent a letter to the superintendent of the railroad, explaining the circumstances of his employment and inclosing a bill for his services. The superintendent paid no attention to this

---

* T., W., and W. R. R. Co. *vs.* Rodrigues, 47 Ill., 189.

letter and bill. The jury found upon this evidence that the superintendent had by his acquiescence ratified the original contract of hiring.*

The station agent requested one Rodrigues to nurse and take care of a brakeman who had been injured, and told him that the railroad company would pay him for the services. Soon after he wrote to the general superintendent, informing him what had been done, but received no reply. Rodrigues, after performing the services, presented his bill to the station agent for payment. Soon afterward the superintendent conferred with the station agent in reference to the various items, and as to whether the charges were reasonable. The superintendent made no objection at the time, but said if the charges were reasonable he would pay the account. This was held a ratification.†

In the case of the Terre Haute and Indiana Railroad Company vs. Stockwell, the conductor of a train which ran into and injured a man employed a physician to dress the wound and take care of the injured man. He then sent a telegram reporting the affair to the general superintendent and general agent, and that evening, upon arriving in St. Louis, he reported to the general superintendent in person that he had struck a man and

---

* Pac. R. Co. vs. Thomas, 19 Kan., 256.
† T., W., and W. R. R. Co. vs. Rodrigues, 47 Ill., 189.

had employed a physician to dress his wounds. The physician, after rendering the services, addressed a letter to the president of the company, stating the circumstances of the employment, the services he had rendered in a general way, and demanding pay therefor. The railroad company never questioned or repudiated the employment as made by the conductor, not even after receiving the physician's letter. From this evidence the court found that the employment of the physician by the conductor was ratified and confirmed.*

Where the station agent employed a physician to treat an injured employee with the understanding that the company would pay, and the general superintendent on the following day came to the town where the injured employee was and inquired of the station agent regarding him, and seemed to be informed regarding the character of the injury and the treatment of the surgeon, but made no objection or complaint in reference to the action of the station agent in employing a surgeon, of which he was apprised, and a few weeks later the general superintendent in conversation with the physician informed him that the pay would be all right, the contract of the station agent was considered ratified.†

---

* Terre Haute and I. R. Co. *vs.* Stockwell, 20 N. E. Rep., 650, 118 Ind., 98.

† Cairo and St. Louis R. Co. *vs.* Mahoney, 82 Ill., 73.

In the case of Toledo, Wabash, and Western Railroad Company *vs.* Prince, a surgeon was employed by the station agent to take charge of a wounded man. The station agent reported the case to the general superintendent a few days afterward, and heard nothing further until he presented the bill. The superintendent then refused payment. The jury found a verdict for the plaintiff on the ground of ratification. The supreme court of Illinois sustained the judgment of the trial court, and in commenting on the case said: "If the superintendent desired to save the company from being held responsible, he should, on receiving the report of the case, have dissented from the action of the station agent, and directed him to apprise the surgeon of such dissent, instead of allowing the latter to continue his services under the belief that he was in the employ of the company." *

In apparent conflict with this and some of the preceding cases is a recent case decided by the supreme court of California, upon a statement of facts very similar to the case above given. The trial judge instructed the jury that if the defendant knew that the plaintiff was treating the injured man on its account, and relied for compensation on the defendant, and the defendant made no objection thereto, then the defendant

---

* Toledo, Wabash, and Western R. Co. *vs.* Prince, 50 Ill., 27.

was liable. Upon this instruction the jury rendered a verdict for the plaintiff, but the supreme court reversed the judgment, stating its reason as follows: " We conclude that knowledge upon the part of defendant that the plaintiff was rendering services to the injured man, and also knowledge of defendant that plaintiff was relying on it for compensation for the performance of such services, taken in connection with the fact that defendant, possessing such knowledge, made no objections thereto, are circumstances wholly inadequate to create a legal liability against defendant." *

While those physicians living in the States in which the cases above cited were determined know how the courts of their respective State will hold, those living in States where the particular question has not been adjudicated can not predict with certainty which precedent their courts will follow; it therefore behooves them to be well within the requirements of the rule recognized by the California courts. To do this, a physician should immediately upon being employed by an inferior officer or agent of a company to render services for such company, write to some officer who has power to make such a contract, informing him of the hiring, stating that he has undertaken the treatment

* Deane *vs.* Gray Bros. Artificial Stone Paving Co., 109 Cal., 433, 42 Pac. Rep., 443.

of the patient on behalf of the company and expects them to pay his fee; and if the agent originally hiring him is without authority so to do, he desires to be notified at once and to be instructed whether or not to proceed with the treatment of the patient.

In the case of Burke *vs.* Chicago and West Michigan Railroad Company, a physician who was attending an injured employee, not having been employed in the first instance by any one assuming to act for the railroad company, attempted to fix the liability upon the company by virtue of a letter which he received from the chief surgeon of the company, which was as follows: "I am informed that you are now attending ——, an employee of the Chicago and West Michigan Railroad Company, who was injured a few weeks ago. Will you be kind enough to inform me as to his present condition? Has he completely recovered? I would like a history of the case since you took charge of it. Please send your bill for services, itemized to me, if you are through with the case." It was shown by the company that the chief surgeon had no authority to employ a physician or surgeon to act generally in a case, but only to act temporarily in case of emergency; moreover, the court held, there being no original employment by a representative of the railroad company, the chief surgeon's letter could not be construed a ratification of such employment, even though ratification were authorized by him, nor could the letter be construed as a contract of employment.*

Liability of Counties and Towns for Services to Paupers.—Another prolific source of litigation is the question of the liability of counties and towns for medical services rendered to their paupers. This right is based upon statutes which differ in the several States; therefore a satisfactory treatment of the subject will necessarily be by States, and will require a greater amount of space than should be devoted to the subject in this chapter.

The various States have enacted laws calculated to afford relief to the distressed poor who through age, disease, or other infirmity are unable to provide necessary food, clothing, shelter, and medical attendance for themselves; but the extent of the class included in such charitable enactments, as well as the extent of the aid afforded them, varies considerably. In some States only those poor people are entitled to medical attention at public expense who have been formally declared paupers by the proper tribunal; while in others all persons unable to pay for necessary medical attention, whether declared paupers or not, and in some States whether residents or non-residents, are entitled to have their physicians' bills paid from the town or county treasury.

---

* Burke *vs.* Chicago and W. M. Ry. Co , 72 N. W. Rep., (Mich.) 997.

In some States, if the officer whose duty it is to authorize the medical treatment of a poor person wrongfully
withholds such authorization, the physician must secure
authority by appeal to the proper tribunal, treat the
patient at his own cost, or leave him to suffer without
attention. In others he may treat the patient and sue
for and recover the value of his services, notwithstanding
the wrongful withholding of authority for such treatment. In case of an accident, where persons without
property or ability to pay for their own medical treatment are severely injured, the physician may in some
States give them immediate attention and recover from
the town or county the value of such services; while in
others he must leave the patient to suffer and perhaps die until he secures instructions from the over-
seers of the poor to render medical services, if he
wishes to be secure in the collection of his fee for such
services.

The liability of the town or county for medical
attendance upon prisoners confined in the county jails
is also subject very largely to the regulation of local
statutes.

Post-mortems at Coroner's Inquest.—The right of
the physician to recover from the county for services
in making a post-mortem examination when summoned for that purpose by the coroner is in many States
regulated by statutes which vary not only in their form

of expression but in the substance of their provisions as well, and which are the subject of such frequent change as to render an extended examination of them of no lasting value. The common-law liability of the county and also the meaning of many of these statutes have been the subject of judicial examination on numerous occasions and, as these cases serve to illustrate the policy of the law with regard to the compensation of physicians for this class of services, they are examined to some extent.

Upon the common-law liability of the county for the physician's fee for services at a coroner's inquest the supreme court of Arkansas, in a recent case, expressed itself as follows: " The statute makes it his (the coroner's) duty to *use all proper means* to ascertain the truth concerning the death of the person over whose body he is required to hold an inquest. It sometimes occurs that the cause of death can only be ascertained by skillful physicians, and by them only by making an autopsy. How can the coroner discharge the duty imposed on him in such cases? He may summon the physician to testify and compel him to swear to his opinion on a superficial view of the body, but can not compel him to touch it, or do the more nauseous and dangerous work of opening it, because such an act is not within the office of a witness. The coroner is not expected or required to make the autopsy with his own hands.

9

It is not within the line of his official duties, and no
fee is allowed for such work, for the reason stated.
Yet he is authorized to ascertain the truth concerning
the death. The conclusion is unavoidable: he must in
such cases employ a physician to make the autopsy and
ascertain the cause of death, as in that case it would
be the only proper means by which the truth could be
ascertained." Commenting further upon the liability
for the payment of the physician's fees for such operation, the court says: " Is he (the coroner) or the county
responsible for the services of the physician? . . . Such
services, though ancillary to the purpose of some inquests, are not official, and consequently were not considered by the legislature when it fixed the fees of
coroners. But there is not only no fee fixed, but no
fund set apart to the coroner for such expenses. To
hold, then, that he is responsible, under such circumstances, would be to require him to contribute so much
gratuitously to the administration of justice and to
the enforcement of the laws. . . . Such a requirement
would be unjust and oppressive, and contrary to the
spirit of our laws. As a rule, the counties are responsible for the expense of the administration of criminal
laws. Both justice and policy demand an adherence to
the rule in this case, and that the county should pay
a reasonable compensation for such services when needed
and performed—that is to say, what they are reasonably

worth." * This case is cited with approval and followed in a later Arkansas case decided in 1895.†

In 1865 the supreme court of New York held that where a physician was employed by a coroner to perform a post-mortem examination at the inquest, with no special agreement that he should receive his compensation from other source than the coroner, his only recourse was to compel that official to pay his fee; but that the coroner had the right to recover from the county the amount paid to a physician in such a case.‡ The legislature, however, passed an act in 1874 making the physician's fee in such a case a direct charge against the county. Since the passage of this act the physician must look to the county for his pay, as the coroner is released from this liability.#

In California the liability of the county for the payment of the physician's services in making post-mortems is recognized, but the legislature has enacted a law providing that "the board of supervisors must not hear or consider any claim in favor of an individual against the county unless an account, properly made out, giving all the items," is presented to the board. A

---

* St. Francis Co. vs. Cummings, 55 Ark.. 419.

+ Clark Co. vs. Kerstan, 60 Ark., 508, 30 S. W. Rep., 1046.

‡ Van Hoevenbergh vs. Hasbrouck, 45 Barb., 197.

People vs. Board of Supervisors, 38 N. Y. S. R., 964, 15 N. Y. Supp., 680.

claim of a physician which was properly verified by the coroner was presented to the board for allowance. The account was for "making a trip from Petaluma to Timber Cove, and making a post-mortem examination of the body of ——, and taking the stomach of said deceased to San Francisco for analysis." This account was held not to fulfill the requirements, as it did not give "all the items." It should have given the number of miles traveled in going from Petaluma to Timber Cove, and the length of time consumed in making the post-mortem examination; also the number of miles traveled, the time consumed, and the expense incurred in taking the stomach to San Francisco for analysis.*

In Colorado the right to collect from the county is fixed by statute, which provides that where the "jury shall deem it requisite," the coroner may summon one or more physicians, and may allow a reasonable compensation subject to the confirmation of the board of county commissioners. The wording of this statute does not, however, render it incumbent upon the physician, when summoned, to inquire whether or not the jury deemed it requisite to make such an examination. It is his duty when so summoned to obey the summons, and he has a right to assume that the coroner acted

---

* Christie *vs.* Board of Supervisors of Sonoma Co., 60 Cal., 164.

correctly in summoning him, and to rely upon such official act.*

In Indiana the liability of the county has been recognized for many years. The supreme court said in 1852: " We have no doubt that in a case where a post-mortem examination is really necessary the coroner may, by his employment, bind the county to the payment for a sufficiency of professional skill to make the examination. To that extent, at least, he must be the agent of the county." † The matter is now regulated in the State by statute, which provides that when a surgeon or physician is required to attend an inquest held by a coroner, and make a post-mortem examination, the coroner shall certify such service to the board of county commissioners, who shall order the same paid out of the county treasury. The fact that an inquest is conducted by a justice of the peace, who is there authorized to perform all the duties of a coroner, and the physician employed and the certificate of services made out by the justice, does not in any way affect the liability of the county to pay the physician for such services.‡ Nor does it release the county from their liability in the premises because the physician is

---

* Co. Commrs. Pueblo Co. *vs.* Marshall *et al.*, 11 Col , 84, 16 P. Rep., 837.

† Gaston *vs.* Board Commrs. Marion Co., 3 Ind., 497.

‡ Stevens *vs.* Board of Commrs. Harrison Co , 46 Ind., 541.

in the employ of the county to treat the poor of the
asylum, nor even where the subject operated upon was
during his life a pauper whom it was the physician's
duty to treat when sick.* Incident to the coroner's
duty to hold inquests is his right not only to employ
a physician to perform a post-mortem examination, but
also his right to determine who that physician shall be.
In the case of the Board of Commissioners of Dearborn
County *vs.* Bond, the county commissioners employed a
physician to render such services, and when the coroner
refused to recognize their selection, but employed another physician and certified to his claim, the board of
county commissioners refused to allow the same. The
matter was appealed, and finally reached the supreme
court, where the claim was allowed. Justice Best said:
" This duty is imposed upon the coroner, and for the
purpose of enabling him to discharge it he is empowered
to employ such means and to select such physician or
surgeon as in his judgment will enable him to ascertain the cause of death. The duty thus imposed necessarily confers the authority to make his own selection
in the faithful discharge of his duties, and, in this
respect, he can not be superseded by the board of commissioners, upon whom no such duty rests." †

There is in Indiana, by virtue of a statute, a limited

---

* Lang *vs.* Board of Commrs. Perry Co., 121 Ind., 133.
† Board of Commrs. of Dearborn Co. *vs.* Bond, 88 Ind., 102.

exception to the general rule of liability of the county—thus: where money and other valuables are found upon the body of the deceased this property is first subjected to the payment of the expenses of the inquest.*

The statute law of Iowa relative to the subject provides that " when he (the coroner) or the jury deem it requisite, he may summon one or more physicians or surgeons to make a scientific examination, who, instead of witness fees, shall receive such reasonable compensation as may be allowed by the county board of supervisors." † Under this law the amount allowed by the county board is conclusive and can not be increased upon appeal unless fraud can be shown in fixing such amount.‡

In Pennsylvania the courts hold that the coroner has the power at common law to employ a physician to perform an autopsy and to bind the county for the physician's pay. The physician when summoned is under no obligation to investigate and determine whether the inquest should be held; this is a matter left to the discretion of the coroner, and the physician may safely rely upon the mere fact that he is summoned.#
Nor have the county commissioners the right to appoint

---

* Thornton's Ind. St. 1897, § 8341.

† Code of Iowa, § 529, McClain's Code, § 503.

‡ Moser vs. Boone Co., 91 Ia., 359, 55 N. W. Rep., 327.

County of Northampton vs. Innes, 26 Pa. St., 156.

a regular physician to perform such services, thereby precluding the coroner from making his own selection.*

Upon the question of the liability of counties for the payment of the fees of physicians for performing post-mortem examinations at coroners' inquests, the courts of the State of Texas seem to stand alone. The supreme court in 1888 held that there was no such liability at common law, and that there was no statute in the State fixing such liability upon the counties.† Again, in 1891, the same court refused to permit a physician to recover the amount of his reasonable fee with the laconic statement: "The law permits no recovery for the services rendered." ‡ This construction of the law being for the second time brought to the attention of the profession by the highest court of the State, they evidently realized its injustice, and, taking the advice of the court in the case of Fears *vs.* Nacogdoches County, sought relief through legislative enactment. At the next session of the legislature, which convened on January 10, 1893, a law was enacted authorizing coroners to call in the county physician; or, if impracticable to secure his services, to summon any regularly practising physician to perform a post-mortem, and providing that the county in which such in-

* County of Allegheny *vs.* Shaw, 34 Pa. St., 301.

† Fears *vs.* Nacogdoches County, 71 **Tex.**, 337, 9 S. W. Rep., 265.

‡ Frio Co. *vs.* Earnest, 16 S. W. Rep. (Texas), 1036.

quest is held shall pay the physician a fee of not less than ten dollars or more than fifty dollars, the excess over ten dollars to be determined by the county commissioners' court after ascertaining the amount and nature of work performed in making such autopsy.*

Liability of Employer for Neglect, etc., of Physician. —The liability of third parties, as contemplated heretofore in this chapter, is only that which arises in favor of the physician. Questions frequently arise as to the liability of third parties to the patient, based upon the transactions between the physician and patient. While such questions are not of direct interest to the physician, it is thought best to give them brief attention.

Employers, such as railroad companies, steamboat companies, mining companies, and the like, very frequently employ physicians to treat their wounded or sick employees; in case of negligence or malpractice of the physician, it has been a very common occurrence for the injured employee to sue his company to recover damages for the injury or loss suffered by him by reason of such negligent or improper treatment by the employer's physician or surgeon; but it is now a well-settled proposition of law that the employer is not liable for the improper treatment by a surgeon in such a case. The relation between the employer and physician or surgeon is not that of master and servant, which in

---

* Laws of Tex., 1893, 155.

the law implies that the servant acts under and according to the instructions of the master. In the case of employer and physician the very nature of the physician's duties precludes the possibility of this relation, as the physician is bound to exercise knowledge, skill, and judgment, and it is because he is capable of this that he is selected. It therefore follows that the employer is not responsible to his employees for the manner in which they are treated by the physician or surgeon whom he procures for them.* The law does, however, require that the employer use reasonable care in selecting a physician and surgeon of ordinary skill, otherwise he might be liable to his employee for his own negligence in making a careless selection.†

Nor is a county or other municipal corporation liable to a patient for unskillful or improper treatment by a physician while in the county hospital or similar institution.‡

---

* A., T., and S. F. R. Co. *vs.* Zeiler, 54 Kan., 340, 38 P. Rep., 282; O'Brien *vs.* Steamship Co., 154 Mass., 272; South Fla. R. Co. *vs.* Price, 32 Fla., 46, 13 So., 638; Richardson *vs.* Carbon Hill Coal Co., 10 Wash., 648, 39 Pac. Rep., 95; Quinn *vs.* Kansas City, M., and B. R. Co., 94 Tenn., 713, 28 L. R. A., 552, 30 S. W. Rep., 1036; Union P. R. Co. *vs.* Artist, 60 Fed. R., 365, 23 L. R. A., 581; York *vs.* Chicago, M., and St. P. Ry. Co., 98 Ia., 544, 67 N. W. Rep., 574; Clark *vs.* Missouri P. R. Co., 48 Kan., 654, 29 Pac. Rep., 1138; Pittsburgh, C. C., and St. L R. Co. *vs.* Sullivan, 41 Ind., 83, 40 N. E. Rep., 138.

† Laubheim *vs.* DeK. N. S. Co., 107 N. Y., 228.

‡ Sherbourne *vs.* Yuba Co., 21 Cal., 113; Brown *vs.* Vinalhaven, 65 Me., 402; Summers *vs.* Daviess Co., 103 Ind., 262, 1 West Rep., 217.

While the liability of the physician to the patient can not properly be discussed under the present chapter, it is thought pertinent to state that the immunity of the third parties in the cases just referred to does not in any way relieve the physician from his liability to the patient.*

Rights of Third Parties.—Having examined those cases in which third parties are liable to both the physician and patient, we will now pass to a consideration of the rights of third parties.

Rights of Husband.—It has been observed that the husband is subject to certain liabilities arising from the treatment of his wife; it is therefore natural to suppose that he has certain rights in the premises which should be respected.

In case it becomes necessary to operate upon a patient, is it necessary to first obtain consent from her husband? In the case of M'Clallen *vs.* Adams a husband placed his wife under the care of a physician whom he knew, at a distance from his own residence, for treatment for a scrofulous tumor of the breast; while the wife was under the doctor's care a cancerous condition developed, and the physician without the husband's knowledge amputated the breast, from which operation the patient never recovered. The court was of the opin-

---

* DuBois *vs.* Decker, 130 N. Y., 325, 14 L. R. A., 429. See Ch. VII.

ion that the husband, in placing his wife in the care of the physician under the circumstances stated, "impliedly requested him to do all such acts, and adopt such course of treatment and operations, as in his judgment would be most likely to effect her ultimate cure and recovery, with the assent of the wife, and therefore that the operation in question was within the scope of the authority given him." The court, commenting upon the case, further said: "Although it might have been an act of prudence in the [physician] to give the [husband] notice of the situation of the wife, and of his intention to perform a dangerous operation, yet we think he might safely trust to the judgment of the wife, to give her husband notice from time to time of her situation and intentions, and that it was not necessary, in point of law, for the [physician] to give such notice, or to have any new request or authority." *

The court, in the case of State, etc., *vs.* Housekeeper *et al.*, decided in 1888, in considering a similar state of facts, said: "The consent of the wife, not that of the husband, was necessary. The professional men whom she had called in and consulted were the proper persons to determine what ought to be done. They could not, of course, compel her to submit to an operation, but if

---

* M'Clallen *vs.* Adams, 19 Pick, 333.

she voluntarily submitted to its performance, her consent will be presumed, unless she was the victim of a false and fraudulent misrepresentation, which is a material fact to be established by proof." In this case the evidence showed that the wife had been afflicted with a lump in her right breast, supposed to be an innocent tumor, but afterward ascertained to be a cancer. The physicians operated for cancer, removing the entire breast. The husband testified that he supposed the operation was for the purpose of removing a tumor, and that he would never have consented to the operation which was performed. The evidence did not show whether the wife was informed of the character of the operation to be performed, but the court stated the law relative to this question as follows: " The party who allows a surgical operation to be performed is presumed to have employed the surgeon for that particular purpose." *

It is a rule as old as the common law itself that the husband is entitled to the society and services of his wife; if, therefore, the physician, through improper care or inattention, prolongs the sickness of the wife, he can be held to respond in damages to the husband for the value of his wife's society and services during such peri-

---

* State, etc., *vs.* Housekeeper *et al.*, 70 Md., 162, 16 Atl. Rep., 382. As to necessity of securing consent before operating, see *post*, p. 313.

od of prolonged sickness, also for the expense of caring for her during this period.*

And, finally, when the wife dies, the husband is entitled to have her body in the condition in which the breath leaves it for the purpose of interment. Should the physician violate this right and perform an autopsy upon the body without the consent of the husband, it seems well settled that he can be held to respond in damages to the husband; the amount of damages would be assessed by the jury, and the principal element upon which it would be based would be the injury to the husband's feelings.†

This right to the body of the deceased is primarily in the surviving husband or wife; if there is no surviving husband or wife it is in the next of kin.‡

Thus a father who places his child in the care of a physician has the right to immediate possession of the body upon the child's death, and can maintain an action against the physician for any violation of this right.#

This proposition is, of course, to be understood with the qualification that, where the circumstances of the death are such as to render a coroner's inquest necessary,

---

* Nixon vs. Ludlam, 50 Ill. App., 273; Stone vs. Evans, 32 Minn., 243, 20 N. W., 149.

† Foley vs. Phelps, 37 N. Y. Supp., 471, 1 App. Div., 551.

‡ Larson vs. Chase, 47 Minn., 307. For law respecting the right to perform an autopsy, see *post*, p. 315.

Burney vs. Children's Hospital, 169 Mass., 57, 47 N. E. Rep., 401.

the physician who performs the autopsy under the coroner's orders is protected in so doing if he treats the body with ordinary decency and does not wantonly or unnecessarily disfigure it.*

Right of Third Parties Generally.—It has been observed that the doctor's duty requires him to sometimes destroy property which is infected with any contagious disease; but when such property belongs to third parties, have they any recourse against the physician who ordered its destruction?

A case occurred in Maine in 1874 † in which the owner of a house in which small-pox patients had been, sued the physician for ordering the paper removed from the wall, the plaintiff claiming that its removal was not necessary to properly disinfect. The trial court gave the plaintiff a judgment of thirty-five dollars against the physician, but the supreme court sent the case back with an opinion of law which relieved the physician from all liability in the premises. In this case the court, speaking through Justice Walton, said: "When the small-pox or any other contagious disease exists in any town or city the law demands the utmost vigilance to prevent its spread. . . .

"To accomplish this object, persons may be seized and restrained of their liberty or ordered to leave the State; private houses may be converted into hospitals

---

* Young *vs.* College of P. and S., 81 Md., 358, 32 Atl. Rep., 177.

† Seavey *vs.* Preble, 64 Me., 120.

and made subject to hospital regulations; buildings may be broken open and infected articles seized and destroyed, and many other things done which, under ordinary circumstances, would be considered a gross outrage upon the rights of persons and property. This is allowed upon the same principle that houses are allowed to be torn down to stop a conflagration. *Salus populi est suprema lex*—the safety of the people is the supreme law —is the governing principle in this case.

"Where the public health and human life are concerned the law requires the highest degree of care. It will not allow of experiments to see if a less degree of care will not answer. The keeper of a furious dog or mad bull is not allowed to let them go at large to see whether they will bite or gore his neighbor's children . . . nor is one using a steam engine to see how much steam he can possibly put on without bursting the boiler. No more are those in charge of small-pox patients allowed to experiment to see how little cleansing will answer; how much paper spit upon and bedaubed with small-pox virus it will do to leave upon the walls of the rooms where the patients have been confined. The law will not tolerate such experiments. It demands the exercise of all possible care. In all cases of doubt the safest course should be pursued, remembering that it is infinitely better to do too much than to run the risk of doing too little."

It will seem conclusive after reading this forcible opinion that third parties have no right whatever to interfere with the physician in taking such reasonable steps as he deems necessary for perfect disinfection, and that he can only be held responsible for or restrained from wholly unnecessary or willful destruction.

A peculiar case touching the liability of a physician to a third party recently arose in Massachusetts. A physician was employed by a father to examine a young man, who was engaged to be married to his daughter, to determine whether or not he was affected with a venereal disease. The young man had accidentally injured himself, and the physician, after making the examination, reported that he was suffering from gonorrhœa, by virtue of which statement the engagement was broken off.

The injured man sued the physician, and the supreme court held that if he did not possess ordinary skill and learning, and use ordinary diligence and care in their exercise, he was liable to the plaintiff, and that the breaking of the plaintiff's marriage engagement in consequence of the wrong diagnosis was not too remote a damage to sustain the action.* Whether or not he did possess ordinary skill and learning and exercise proper care and skill in conducting the examination, was a question for the jury to determine from the evidence adduced at the trial.

---

* Harriott vs. Plimpton, 166 Mass., 585, 44 N. E. Rep., 992.

CHAPTER V.

Right Usually Founded upon Implied Contract of Patient.—It has been observed that a patient impliedly contracts with a physician, when he engages his services or when he receives the physician's professional attention, that he will make a reasonable and proper compensation therefor. The right of the physician to his fee is probably governed in nineteen out of twenty cases by this implied contract. Occasionally, however, there is a special contract superseding the one implied by law, and, probably with still greater frequency, there are peculiar circumstances attending the case which materially affect the contract as ordinarily implied. The implied promise of payment may arise from either one of two circumstances: First, from the employment of the physician to attend the patient, or second, from the mere attendance of the physician and the acceptance of his services, even though he is not expressly employed.

From the fact that the mere employment of the physician creates a liability for the payment of his fee,

140

it follows that if a physician is sent for to attend a certain patient, and upon promptly responding to the call the physician is informed that another physician is in attendance, or that the trouble is passed, or that for any other reason his services are not required, he will, nevertheless, be entitled to the ordinary and reasonable compensation for making the call.*

The mere acceptance of the services of a physician being sufficient to bind the patient to pay therefor is another sufficient reason for the rule of law heretofore observed, that the physician is entitled to compensation not only for the first visit made at the patient's express request, but also for all subsequent visits which the patient's condition requires.

Right to Compensation for Services of Student.— The physician is entitled to a fee for services rendered by students who attend upon his patients under his directions, and the fact that such students are not legally qualified to practise medicine and surgery in their own names and collect fees for such services does not affect this right.† And so, where a physician employs another physician to assist him, he is entitled to recover for the services of such assistant.‡

---

* See Bartlett *vs.* Sparkman, 95 Mo., 136 ; Wheatley *vs.* City of Covington, 11 Bush, 18.

† People *vs.* Monroe, 4 Wendell, 200.

‡ Jay County Commiss. *vs.* Brewington, 74 Ind , 7.

Right of Irregular Practitioners to Recover Fees.— One practising an irregular branch of medicine, such as Christian Science, spiritualism, or the like, if not prohibited so to do by the law of his State, is entitled to fees for such services. In the case of Wheeler *vs.* Sawyer, the defense interposed was " that the so-called ' Christian Science' is a delusion; that its principles and methods are absurd; that its professors are charlatans; that no patient can possibly be benefited by their treatment." The court said, " We think this all immaterial. We are not required here to investigate ' Christian Science.' The patient chose that treatment, and received it, and promised to pay for it. There is nothing unlawful or immoral in such a contract. Its wisdom or folly is for the parties, not the court, to determine." *

The question whether or not a physician who has not fully complied with the requirements of the law can recover his fees is treated at length in the following chapter.

Sunday Contracts Valid.— The contract of the physician being construed to be one of necessity and charity, comes within the exception provided for by the statutes, which declare all work done and contracts entered into

---

* Wheeler *vs.* Sawyer (Me.), 15 A. Rep., 67, 6 N. Eng. Rep., 826. See, however, p. 88.

on Sunday to be unlawful, and therefore the physician is entitled to his regular fees for medical services rendered on that day.*

Amount or Rate of Fee Collectible.—The amount of fee to which a physician is entitled is not a question of law, but is rather one of fact, and is determined by the customs of the locality and by the circumstances of the particular case. In many localities one dollar is the regular fee for making an ordinary day call, and in such localities the physician would not be entitled to collect a larger fee for an ordinary day visit without a special understanding, for customs of this sort may assume the force and effect of unwritten laws; in other localities custom allows a larger fee. It is presumed, however, that the rate of fees is based upon the condition existing in the particular locality, and that a careful examination and comparison of the rates of fees and of the conditions of their respective localities will show a wise and equitable adjustment of the question throughout the country. What constitutes a visit may also be regulated by custom. If a visit is required to be prolonged beyond a certain period, custom may establish the practice of charging extra for all time expended beyond the limit fixed, or a physician may establish such a custom for himself

---

* Smith *vs.* Watson, 14 Vt., 332; Aldrich *vs.* Blackstone, 128 Mass., 148. See p. 79.

by generally announcing it among his patients. His right to the added compensation would at first, however, be dependent upon the announcement of his special terms to the particular patient, and this announcement would, if acted upon, be equivalent to a special contract for such increased fee. But after the custom became generally known and recognized no special notice would be required to fix the liability upon the patient.

The fees for performing operations are also subject, to a certain extent, to customs; there are, however, many operations of an unusual character which from the nature of the case can not be provided for by customs. Many operations being of a difficult character, it becomes advisable often to acquire the services of a surgeon specially skilled in that line of work, or specially qualified to perform the particular class or kind of operation. The services of such men are not, and can not be, subject to the customs prescribing the rate of fee in the particular locality in which the services happen to be rendered. Also, a physician who is called from a distance because of his special fitness, or for other reasons, may collect for such services, basing the amount of his fee upon the rate customarily charged by him and not upon the rates charged at the place where he visits the patient.

Where, however, a physician is called from a distance to see a person either on business or social matters, and while there attends him professionally, he is not entitled to the same compensation as though he were summoned to attend him professionally; in the latter case he would be entitled to a greater compensation based upon the loss or abandonment of home practice, while in the former case he would merely be entitled to a compensation for the time spent in attending the sick person professionally, and perhaps for the expenses of the trip. The allowance or disallowance of the last item would depend very much upon the circumstances of the case.*

Upon the same principle it has been held that where a physician lives at his brother's house as a member of the family, he is not entitled to compensation for uninterrupted medical attendance and services during the entire time of the brother's sickness. In this case Justice Hanna said: " The testimony shows that the claimant, while he attended his brother, the decedent, did not devote all his time and attention to his patient, but that he acted as a member of the family, sleeping and taking his meals in the house, going out and returning at his pleasure; and though, no doubt, he rendered many kind, thoughtful, and affectionate attentions to his suffering brother, yet they formed no part of his duties as a physician, and can not after the death of that

---

* Succession of Dickey, 41 La. Ann., 1010, 6 So. Rep., 798.

brother be made the basis of pecuniary compensation. The most the claimant is entitled to is to be paid for the professional visits made, and the number of operations performed by him, at the usual rate of practising physicians." *

The supreme court of Louisiana has held that a physician's charges against an estate for services rendered to the deceased are not to be based entirely upon the physician's skill and the character of the services, but that the ability of the estate to pay for such services should be considered in determining the amount of the fee. In this case the deceased had stricture of the œsophagus, probably cancerous in its nature. He could not be fed through the mouth and artificial means had to be resorted to. The purpose was for a time accomplished by inserting a flexible tube through which liquid nourishment was given him, but this means soon failed, the stricture becoming complete and rigid. The physician then resorted to the operation of gastrotomy, after which the patient survived twenty-one days, having been under the care of the physician for a period of sixty days. The physician rendered a bill of $2,500. The supreme court, in considering the amount of the fee, said: " The physician should be paid, but the charge is disproportionate to the man's estate and condition

---

* *In re* Moffett Est. (Pa.), 32 Leg Int, 218.

in life. His estate is inventoried at $8,705. The lower court allowed $500. We increase it to $1,000.*

A case is reported in the *Pacific Record of Medicine and Surgery* † in which not only the character of the operation performed, but the ruling of the court upon the effect of the value of the patient's estate upon the amount of fees recoverable therefor, are strikingly similar to those in the above case. Here an operation of gastrotomy was performed upon a patient who was seventy-two years of age, and who was afflicted with cancer of the œsophagus. The physician charged $1,500 for the operation, $100 each for night detentions, and $100 each for visits, his bill amounting in all to $9,200. Upon trial, the physician's lawyer, against the strenuous objection of the defendants, introduced in evidence the inventory of the decedent's estate, showing it to be appraised at $250,000. The only question involved in the trial was the one of the amount to which the plaintiff was entitled, the executors having previous to the trial offered to pay $2,750 in full of the claim, and the plaintiff having offered to accept $4,000. The trial judge, after instructing the jury at some length upon the conditions they were to regard and the effect they were to give the evidence of the experts in fixing

---

* Czarnowski *vs*. Succession of Zeyer, 35 La. Ann., 796.
† *Pacific Record of Medicine and Surgery*, April 15, 1899, p. 298.

the amount of the fees, referred to the importance
which should be attached to the value of the patient's
estate in the following words:

" While you may take into consideration, in estimating the value of the plaintiff's services, all the circumstances surrounding such services, the time consumed
in the operation and in attendance upon Mr. Goldberg,
the responsibility involved in the operation, and in this
connection you may consider the financial situation of
the patient and the value of his estate, the reputation
and skill of the plaintiff, as well as the income which
he derives from his practice, the number of visits and
duration as well as the loss of time incurred by the
plaintiff in traveling back and forth, the nature and
extent of the services, and the benefit to the deceased,
yet this does not mean that you may arbitrarily fix any
sum you may see fit as the amount to be recovered by
the plaintiff in this case. He is entitled to recover only
such a sum as will be a reasonable compensation for his
services rendered the decedent considering all the circumstances. The doctrine known to maritime law as
salvage does not apply to cases like the one at bar.
That is to say, while you may take into consideration
the value of the estate as one of the elements to determine the value of plaintiff's services, yet that element
is not controlling. In other words, the plaintiff is only
entitled to recover the reasonable value of his services

rendered to the decedent prior to his death, and for the purpose of fixing and determining such value you have the right to take into consideration the other elements mentioned."

With these instructions the jury retired and returned with a verdict for the plaintiff of $6,500, which itemized, amounted to $1,500 for the operation and $60 each for the visits.

Courts have, however, repeatedly held that the rate of fees chargeable by physicians is in no way affected or altered by the financial circumstances of the patient. This is probably the law as applied in suits between physician and patient, but when the claim is being enforced against the estate of a deceased patient, as in the above cases, then the court may be more disposed to follow them as precedents.

A recent case which may well illustrate the impossibility of laying down a fixed rule for the regulation of professional fees in surgical cases, or cases requiring unusual or peculiar skill and ability, is that of Heintz vs. Cooper.* In this case, the patient had sustained a compound fracture of the leg and dislocation of the ankle joint. Both bones were broken and protruded through the flesh, and six or seven pieces of the bone were removed. The physician's services commenced

* Heintz vs. Cooper, 47 Pac. Rep., 360 (Cal.).

July 12th and continued through until October 13th following, during which time plaintiff testified he made about two hundred visits and about seventy of these were for the purpose of dressing the wound; that five dollars to ten dollars a visit when the wound was dressed, and two dollars and fifty cents a visit for all other visits, was a reasonable charge; and that for reducing a compound fracture of the leg, two hundred and fifty dollars to five hundred dollars was a reasonable compensation. On the other hand, the professional evidence introduced by the defendant was that five hundred dollars was a reasonable compensation for all services rendered in the case. The jury returned a verdict for seven hundred and fifty dollars. Upon the appeal of this case, Justice Haynes said: " It appeared, however, that in no case in Monterey County within the knowledge of the medical witnesses had so large fees, in the aggregate, been paid in case of compound fracture, though in none of the instances mentioned was the character of the fracture or the number of visits stated; and it is now contended on behalf of appellant (the patient) that the prices so paid in those other cases in that county determine what is a reasonable compensation for plaintiff's services in this case, or, as counsel stated it, ' the usual price at the time and place of performance is the rule.' The cases cited in support of this proposition relate to ordinary services, as to which there is a reason-

ably uniform established rate of compensation, and
not to professional services, where the skill and learning
of the person, as well as the almost infirite variety
in the character and circumstances of the subject
upon which he devotes his services, precludes the
establishment of any fixed rate of compensation
which could be applied to more than a very restricted class of cases and the more common class of
services."

In short, the amount of the fee which a physician
and surgeon is entitled to charge is governed, in the
case of ordinary and usual services, by the generally
recognized customs prevailing at the time and place
where the services are rendered, or, if he is called from a
distance to perform such services, then by the custom prevailing in his locality.   But in case of unusual
or peculiar services no such general custom will rule;
all of the attendant circumstances must be taken into
consideration and a fair and equitable amount thereby
determined upon.   A more definite and certain rule
than the above can not be well given.

Consultant's Fee.—In case of consultation, the custom seems so well established, that the patient will pay
the fee of the consultant, that an agreement between the
patient and attending physician that the physician will
pay the consultant's fees does not release the patient
from paying such fees unless the consultant is in-

formed of such arrangement before the services are rendered.*

Where, however, an attending physician takes another physician to a patient's house to convince the patient that he is doing all that can be done, and the physician so called in does nothing whatever for the patient, and is not, in fact, called in at the patient's instance or request, the patient is under no obligation to pay him anything.† Nor does it necessarily follow where a patient employs two physicians, who, in fact, meet at his bedside at each call, that each meeting will rank as a consultation. In the matter of Succession of Duclos, the court said: "As to the pretension that, from the moment more than one physician is called in, and attends regularly upon a case, every visit made by every physician employed takes rank as a consultation, it can not be listened to, even supposing that the visits are made at the same hour, so that the physicians actually meet at the patient's bedside. The difference of the charge for what is technically styled a consultation, and for a simple visit, would make it ruinous to most patients and unreasonably onerous to all, to avail themselves of the lights of more than one of the faculty in time of need." ‡

---

* Shelton *vs.* Johnson, 40 Ia., 84; Garrey *vs.* Stadler, 67 Wis., 512. See p. 77.

† Schrader *vs.* Hoover, 87 Ia. 654, 54 N. W. Rep., 463.

‡ Succession of Duclos, 11 La. Ann., 406.

Failure to Benefit Patient no Bar to Recovery of Compensation.—A consideration of those things which may be urged as defeating the right of the physician to compensation brings us first to the effect of the failure by the physician to benefit his patient. The contract of the physician that he is possessed of ordinary skill and knowledge, and will use due care and diligence in exercising them, does not guarantee his ability to effect a cure in all cases, nor indeed is it an assurance that his services will even be beneficial. If, therefore, the test of a successful treatment is to be considered a prerequisite to the physician's right to recover for such services, it is patent that a new requirement is interposed by the law. This, however, is not the case; it has been laid down as law that if the physician possesses ordinary knowledge and skill and uses reasonable and due care in their exercise, he does all the law requires of him; this proposition is correct, and is therefore applied as a test of the physician's right to recover regardless of the benefit or injury following his treatment. The court well stated the law in a Pennsylvania case in the following words: " The fact that a professional man does not succeed in accomplishing that for which he is employed, can not affect his right to recover for services rendered, unless actual want of skill be specifically shown." *

* Teedman *vs.* Loewengrund (Pa.), 2 W. N. C., 272.

Illustrations.—Whether or not a physician has complied with the requirements of the law in a given case is a question of fact to be determined by the jury by the aid of expert evidence. In a recent Illinois case the evidence showed that the patient was thrown from his buggy and his left shoulder joint dislocated by the fall. On the following day he called upon the doctor, who, the evidence tends to show, properly reduced the dislocation. In three or four days he called again, according to the physician's instructions, and the shoulder appeared to be doing well. The patient was not again seen by the physician for about forty-five days, when the shoulder was found to be in an ankylosed condition, and unable to be moved. On the following day the patient returned to the doctor's office by appointment; the doctor administered anæsthetics to him and proceeded to break up the adhesions, but in doing so ruptured the axillary artery. The next day the physician and patient went to Chicago, where an eminent surgeon performed a surgical operation on him. He cut down upon the blood-vessel, cleaned out the cavity, which was filled with blood clot, sought out the bleeding vessel, tied it, sewed up the wound, and dressed it. He testified that the head of the humerus was in the socket where it belonged. The patient never fully recovered from the injury, and, as the evidence tends to show, his arm is stiff and the humerus out of place.

The physician brought suit to recover his fee, and the patient contested it on the ground that the dislocation was never in the first instance reduced, and that caused the ankylosis and the necessity of breaking up the adhesions from which the subsequent trouble resulted. The patient also contended that if the shoulder had been properly reduced in the first instance, and ankylosis had set in, it was not proper practice to break up the adhesions; that he would have got proper motion in the lapse of time without it. The doctor introduced the evidence of several of the most eminent physicians of Chicago, who gave their opinion that the treatment of the patient's wound was good practice at every step. Upon the advisability of breaking up the adhesions, one physician testified as an expert witness as follows: "Patients don't always get the benefits that we hope they will get in cases where the shoulder has been dislocated, but that advice was such as a surgeon in good practice would give under the circumstances."

The evidence also tended to show that the surgical operation necessitated by the rupture of the axillary artery was the probable cause of the shoulder becoming again dislocated.

The jury concluded from the evidence that the physician had treated the patient's shoulder in a reasonably skillful manner according to the practice of surgeons, and accordingly gave him a verdict. The appellate
11

court sustained the verdict, and, in commenting on the case, said: "A physician is not an insurer of the success of his treatment, and is entitled to pay for his services whether he succeeds in curing his patient or not, provided he uses the skill of an ordinarily skillful physician." *

In a Tennessee case of some years ago an amputation was performed, a large butcher knife and a carpenter's sash saw being the surgical instruments used. The operation, however, appeared to have been well performed, and the patient, under a proper treatment, soon recovered. The representative of the patient contested the collection of the physician's fee upon several grounds. The court held that the operation seemed to have been performed with a reasonable degree of skill, and accordingly sustained the verdict of the jury giving the physician his fee. The supreme court, in commenting on the case, said: "It certainly requires some degree of skill in anatomy and surgery to perform an operation of the kind, and the success that attended it, though not conclusive, is a circumstance from which the skill may be inferred. The instruments employed, drawn from other vocations, not the most congenial for the special occasion, were certainly unusual and extraordinary for such a purpose. But we are not to infer from this circum-

---

* Yunker *vs.* Marshall, 65 Ill. App., 667.

stance alone that the surgeons had not sufficient art and skill in the use of them. Besides, it is possible that the delay necessary to procure proper instruments might have been fatal to the patient." *

It does not necessarily follow that a physician has failed in performing his legal duty to his patient, and is therefore not entitled to compensation, because he has mistaken the nature of his disease and treated him for an ailment from which he is not suffering. In a recent case brought in New Jersey by a physician to recover a fee, the defendant interposed the defense that the physician had prescribed and administered remedies for a disease which he had not. The trial justice instructed the jury that this insistment of the defendant, even if true, would not prevent a recovery; that the question was whether the physician exercised proper care and skill as a physician; that if the jury should conclude that the doctor was mistaken in the nature of the defendant's disease, they must then go still further, and say that a want of care and skill was exhibited. If no want of care or skill appeared, he was entitled to a fair compensation, although he fell into a mistake. This is undoubtedly a correct statement of the law, and in applying it to a given case it remains for the jury to determine whether or not, as a matter of fact, the physi-

---

* Alder *vs.* Buckley, 1 Swan (Tenn.), 69.

cian has failed in bringing the proper amount of knowledge to the case or in exercising a reasonable and ordinary degree of skill and care.*

**Effect of Incompetency or Neglect upon Right to
Recover.**—Whether a physician's failure to possess the
proper degree of learning and skill, or neglect to use
proper care in their exercise, does *ipso facto* preclude
him from all right to compensation is a question upon
which there is a direct conflict of authority.

The courts of New York hold that such failure on
the part of the physician does defeat all right to compensation; and as a corollary to this proposition they
hold that a judgment obtained in a suit for the value
of services in a given case conclusively establishes the
propriety of the physician's treatment in that case, and
that an action for malpractice can not afterward be
based upon the same case.† The supreme court of
Maine expresses itself in harmony with the New York
courts and this proposition when it says: " The same
facts which would authorize a recovery for malpractice
would constitute a defense in a suit for professional
services." ‡

In a later case, in Wisconsin, the court repudiated

---

* Eli *vs.* Wilbur, 49 N. J. L., 685.

† Bellinger *vs.* Craigue, 31 Barb., 534; Gates *vs.* Preston, 41 N. Y.,
113.

‡ Patten *vs.* Wiggin, 51 Me., 594.

this doctrine, and held that the physician's claim for fees and the patient's claim for damages resulting from malpractice were two separate and distinct claims.* The doctrine laid down by the supreme court of Wisconsin has been approved and followed by a recent case in Iowa. The court in that case says: " It does not necessarily follow that because a physician or surgeon may be guilty of negligence, which causes some inconsequential or inconsiderable injury, he is to be deprived of all compensation for his services on account thereof. Whether he shall lose the value of his services depends upon the amount of damages suffered by reason of his neglect to perform his duty. No penalty beyond the amount of the actual damages sustained is to be visited upon him because of his negligence or want of skill." †

The latter doctrine is thought to be the better law, and the Iowa and Wisconsin cases will probably be followed as precedents by the courts of those States which are not already committed to the contrary doctrine.

Rights under Contract " No Cure, No Pay."—The contract of " no cure, no pay " is probably one which is not very frequently entered into by the most reputable class of the medical profession, although there is, at least, no legal reason why it should reflect any suspi-

---

* Ressequie *vs.* Byers, 52 Wis., 651.

† Whitesell *vs.* Hill, 101 Ia. 629, 66 N. W. Rep., 894.

cion of discredit upon the physician who is a party to it. When a physician agrees to such an arrangement, and there is no specific price fixed as the compensation for performing a cure, the physician will be entitled to the reasonable and usual sum for performing such services. But before he is entitled to any compensation whatever he is bound to show that he has fulfilled his agreement and effected a cure. A physician undertook the treatment of a patient upon the plan under consideration, and soon afterward, fearing that the patient was financially irresponsible, persuaded the patient's son of the propriety of securing the payment by his own written obligation, whereupon the son gave the doctor a memorandum reading as follows: " I hereby agree that I will be holden to Dr. J. S. for the payment of his bill for medicine and attendance upon my father and his wife "—this agreement of the son, while positive in form, was subsequent in time to the original agreement of the physician, the basis of which was " no cure, no pay," and was therefore held by the court to be collateral to it, and the physician was accordingly not permitted to collect upon the written agreement without first showing that he had effected a cure.*

When a patient enters into an agreement with a physician to be treated upon the basis of " no cure,

---

* Smith *vs.* Hyde, 19 Vermont, 54.

no pay," he is bound by such agreement to submit to all reasonable treatment prescribed for such a time as may be reasonably calculated necessary to effect the cure. Should the patient refuse to do this, thus rendering it impossible for the physician to complete the cure and reap the benefit of his skill and labor, he is entitled, upon showing such facts, to receive compensation without performing any further services. The amount of compensation to which he would be entitled would depend upon the terms of the contract. If the contract fixed a specific amount as the price of successful treatment, he would be entitled to receive that amount at once; but if the contract was silent as to the amount of compensation, he would be entitled to a reasonable and usual fee for the services already rendered. The patient might, however, in the latter case, for the purpose of proving the services to be without value, introduce evidence to show that the treatment prescribed was not calculated to produce beneficial results, and that the medicine used was worthless and possessed no efficacy in producing the results desired; and for the purpose of proving this the physician may be required to testify as to the ingredients of the medicine used, even though it be a secret preparation of his own.*

A Tennessee case of some years ago, based upon a

---

* Jonas *vs.* King, 81 Ala., 285.

contract of the character in consideration, was tried, which somewhat amusingly illustrates the predilection of a certain class of laymen to avoid the payment of a professional bill whenever possible.

In this case a physician contracted with an habitual drunkard to cure him of his unfortunate affliction in consideration of the payment of five hundred dollars.

The treatment seems to have been successful to such an extent that the patient, after using the medicine prescribed, quit his habits of intoxication, and told his friends that he had lost his appetite for ardent spirits, but that he thought he could again acquire his appetite for spirits by beginning with cider or wine. He continued sober for about nine months and then returned to his habits of intoxication. How he acquired the appetite again is not shown.

The question of whether or not drunkenness is a disease that can be cured by medical skill was interposed; the jury was instructed that if the physician was entitled to recover they must find it so to be, and that the physician had not only suppressed or suspended the appetite for a season during the operation of the medicine, but had so far removed it that it would not return unless the patient indulged in such a manner as to a temperate man brings on the propensity. Upon this instruction the jury rendered a verdict for the patient, and the physician promptly appealed.

The supreme court theorized to some extent upon the nature of drunkenness, and concluded that it was a disease produced by the indulgence of a habit, and that if the disease or disposition to drink were destroyed, its return by renewed indulgence proved a disregard of that sense of moral principle which a rational being would be expected to exercise. Applying these theories, the court said: " To admit that after being so placed (the disposition to drink being destroyed) he might return, is to admit that by his own voluntary act he could defeat the physician of his promised reward; and it would hence follow that, by taking advantage of his own wrong, the physician would have the twofold mortification of losing his fee and seeing his skill mocked at. Therefore it should have been left to the jury to say whether, if the propensity had been destroyed, the patient returned to his habits of drunkenness with the dishonest purpose of evading the contract." The judgment of the trial court was reversed and the case sent back for a new trial upon the lines indicated in the opinion.*

Relevant to the question in consideration is a case which was decided in South Carolina in 1829 and which was never officially reported, but is preserved in the manuscript of the court. In that case a physician

---

* Fisk *vs.* Townsend, 7 Yerg. (Tenn.), 146.

undertook to cure a child of a chronic disease with the understanding that he would not charge more than five dollars if not successful. The parent, believing that the child was cured, promised to pay him one hundred dollars, but it afterward appeared that the disease was not cured, but only suspended. The court refused to hold the parent to his agreement to pay one hundred dollars made under his mistaken belief, but remitted the physician to his original agreement.*

Intent that Services shall be Gratuitous; Effect.— Whether or not the intent of the physician at the time he renders services to a patient that such services shall be gratuitous will defeat his right to compensation is a question upon which there is some conflict. The supreme court of North Carolina lays down the rule that if such services " were intended to be, and were accepted as a gift or act of benevolence," then the physician is not entitled to compensation; but if the patient did not understand that such services were intended as gratuitous, and accept them as such, the physician is entitled to compensation, even though he originally intended to make no charge.† On the other hand, the court of appeals of Missouri holds that if the physician rendered his services intending them to be gratuitous,

* Harris *vs.* Oberly, So. Car., MS., Dec., 1829.
† Prince *vs.* McRae, 84 N. C., 674.

he could not subsequently change his mind and collect for them, even though the patient did not know when the services were rendered that they were intended to be gratuitous.*

A careful and critical examination of the reasoning upon which these two decisions are based leads to the opinion that the North Carolina decision is not well founded, and that the Missouri court expresses the true doctrine.

The North Carolina court subjects the transaction to the same test as that required to demonstrate the validity of an ordinary contract—viz.: that there shall be a meeting or concurrence of minds of the parties, and that there shall be a mutual understanding which is agreed to by both. These undoubtedly are necessary elements to the validity of a contract, but, as a matter of fact, the transaction in consideration is not a contract, but a gift, and is accordingly to be governed by the law relating to gifts.

The essential elements of a gift are that the donor or giver shall actually or symbolically deliver the property which is the subject of gift to the donee with the intention that it becomes the donee's without the payment of any consideration. In this case the physician represents the donor, the patient the donee, and the services ren-

---

* Lippman *vs.* Tittman, 31 Mo. App., 69.

dered constitute the subject of gift. The services are rendered by the physician with the intent that they shall be gratuitous; the services being received, the gift is completed and perfect, whether the patient knew them to be gratuitous or thought them to be otherwise and expected to pay; for, to quote the words of Chief-Justice Sterrett, of the supreme court of Pennsylvania: "lt is now too well settled to admit of question that, upon the ground of implied benefit, the assent of a donee will be presumed; and the title will vest *eo instanti* the gift is made, even though he be ignorant of the transaction, and will continue in him until he rejects it." * More-over, if the services were intended as a gift when ren-dered, the physician can not subsequently change his mind and collect fees for such services even though it may have been through a misapprehension or mistake of facts that he was induced to originally intend the services as gratuitous.†

Whether or not it was the physician's intention that his services should be gratuitous is a question of fact which in the court of trial must be determined by the jury from the evidence submitted to them. All of the attending circumstances of the treatment, the re-lation of the physician and patient, the statements of

---

* Tarr *et al. vs.* Robinson *et al.*, 158 Pa. St., 60.

† Pickslay *vs.* Starr, 149 N. Y., 432.

the physician relative to compensation for such treatment, and the fact of whether or not the physician made a charge for such services at the time they were rendered, as shown by his books of original entry, are all circumstances to be taken into consideration in determining the intent.

Intoxication of Physician, Effect of, upon Right of Recovery.—A physician who attempts to render medical services when in such an intoxicated condition as to be unable to exercise proper skill and judgment is not entitled to any compensation for such services; but a patient who continues to employ a physician after he has rendered services in an intoxicated condition is not in a position to refuse paying his fee because of such past drunkenness.*

Services among Physicians; Right to Compensation.—There is among physicians a custom to render services for each other without compensation. Whether or not this custom is sufficiently established and so generally understood as to defeat the right of a physician to compensation for services rendered to another physician has been considered by the supreme court of Georgia to be a matter of fact, which must be proved by evidence. If the evidence shows that it merely exists as a courtesy, and is not of universal observance, then the

---

* McKleroy *vs.* Sewell, 73 Ga., 657.

physician is entitled to compensation, unless, of course, there was an understanding or intention that the services were to be gratuitous. If, on the other hand, the evidence shows that the practice is so universal as to justify a physician treated in the belief that the custom becomes a part of the contract, then the right of compensation does not exist.*

Carelessness in Regard to Contagious Diseases, Effect of.—It has been observed that a physician is bound to take such precautions as may be necessary to prevent the transmitting of a contagious disease from one patient to another. It naturally follows that if a physician disregards this duty, and a patient thereby becomes afflicted with such contagious disease, the physician's right to compensation for services rendered to him is defeated, to the extent of the damages suffered from the contagious disease,† if, indeed, not *in toto*.‡

Promissory Note for Future Services Conditional.— Physicians sometimes undertake the treatment of a patient for a certain fixed fee or sum, and at the beginning of the treatment require the patient to execute a note for all or a part of the fee agreed upon. The consideration upon which such a note is based is the future rendering of professional services, and this class of serv-

---

* Madden *vs.* Blain, 66 Ga , 49.
† Piper *vs.* Menifee, 12 B. Monroe (Ky.), 465.
‡ See p. 158 *et seq.*

ices necessarily means personal services, and not the services of some assistant or other doctor; it therefore follows that if the physician entering into such a contract is from sickness or other cause rendered incapable of performing such services when due, under the contract the patient is relieved from his obligation to pay, and the note may be repudiated for failure of consideration.*

Partial Allowance by Municipality Extinguishes Claim against Patient.—A physician who attends a poor person under such circumstances as to bind the town or county for the payment is entitled to look for his compensation either to the municipality or to the patient; but if he presents his bill for such services to the municipality, and it is audited and allowed either at its face value or for a less amount, and the physician accepts the amount allowed, the indebtedness is completely extinguished both against the patient and the municipality. A case recently arose in New York involving this question. A physician rendered services to the value of eighty dollars. The patient being a poor person, he submitted the bill to the town " as health officer," and received twenty-five dollars. The patient subsequently performed services for the physician to the amount of twenty dollars, against which the physician proposed to offset his " balance " of fifty-five dollars.

---

* Powell *vs.* Newell, 59 Minn., 406, 61 N. W. Rep., 335.

The supreme court was of the opinion that the trial court was authorized in finding from the facts that the physician's bill, interposed as a counterclaim, was for services performed for the town, and for which the town was liable. The court said: " The sum audited he accepted, and the effect of said transaction was necessarily to extinguish the claim against the town. If there was any liability on the part of the plaintiff (patient), as well as the town, for the defendant's (physician's) attendance upon his family, which defendant might have properly claimed, his presentation of the bill to the town, and acceptance of the amount at which it was audited, we think must have the effect of also extinguishing the claim against the plaintiff." *

The judgment of twenty dollars in favor of the patient for services rendered to the physician was therefore approved and sustained by the supreme court.

* Wood *vs.* Munson, 70 Hun, 468, 53 N. Y. S. R., 621, 24 N. Y. Supp., 287.

CHAPTER VI.

Demand.—The first step to be taken by the physician to recover compensation for services performed is to make a demand on the patient for the amount which is due. This is usually and most properly done by presenting the patient with a bill. Should this means prove ineffectual and other amicable efforts likewise fail in producing the desired result, more drastic measures would then become necessary; but before departing from peaceful methods of collection and attempting to enforce the payment of the money by legal measures, it is well to first consider whether the legal status of the creditor is such as to enable him to invoke the aid of the court.

Is Physician Legally Qualified to Practise?—In passing upon the physician's standing in court, the first questions that naturally occur are, has he fully complied with the requirements of the law so as to be entitled to practise medicine, and, if not, what legal rights has he in the premises?

The first question is one of fact, to be determined

12   171

by carefully examining the statutes of the State in which the physician practises, and learning whether or not all of the requirements are fulfilled. If a license from the State board is prescribed, has this license been obtained? And if this license must be filed with a certain county officer, has it been so filed? Should such an examination show a defect in the physician's legal right to practise, a careful examination of the law then becomes necessary to determine what rights he really has.

Rights of Unqualified Practitioners.—It has been observed that the statutes of several States expressly provide that any physician practising medicine unlawfully shall not be permitted to recover for his professional services.* In the majority of the States, however, there is no express provision upon the subject, and in such States the right of the unqualified physician to collect is the subject of judicial construction.

It is a familiar rule of law that no compensation can be recovered in a court of justice for performing an act which is unlawful, or which is prohibited by statute.† Upon this principle the courts of nearly all of the States have based their decisions, and have accordingly declined to aid the physician who has failed to comply with the

---

* Such provisions exist in Georgia, Indiana, Kansas, Kentucky, Louisiana, Maryland, Michigan, Nebraska, North Carolina, Rhode Island, Vermont, Virginia, and Wisconsin.

† Dickerson *vs.* Gordy, 5 Robinson's Rep., 489.

requirements of the law in recovering fees.* The supreme court of Tennessee refused to permit a physician to recover where he had not procured and filed his license before the services for which he sought to obtain payment were rendered, but had secured and filed such license before suit was brought. The court said: " Where a statute has for its manifest purpose the promotion of some object of public policy, and prohibits the carrying on of a profession, occupation, trade or business, except in compliance with the statute, a contract made in violation of such statute can not be enforced." †

In Texas the court of civil appeals held that a physician who had graduated from a medical college recognized by the American Medical Association, but who had failed to procure a certificate from the board of medical examiners and have the same recorded, should not be entitled to a judgment for fees, notwithstanding no board of medical examiners had been appointed.‡

And so it has been held by an early decision in Massachusetts (1822) that a physician duly qualified by the law of another State to practise in such State shall

---

* Gardner *vs.* Tatum, 81 Cal., 370; Roberts *vs.* Levy (Cal.), 31 P. Rep., 570; Dickerson *vs.* Gordy, 5 Robinson's Rep., 489; Fox *vs.* Dixon, 34 N. Y. S. R., 710.

† Haworth *vs.* Montgomery, 91 Tenn., 16, 18 S. W. Rep., 399.

‡ Kenedy *vs.* Schultz, 6 Tex. Civ. App., 461.

not thereby be entitled to come within the borders of Massachusetts and recover for services rendered. The court said: " The object of the act was to guard against the evil effects to be apprehended from the practices of ignorant and unskillful practitioners. This purpose can not be completely obtained, if those of this description, if any such there be, on the borders of the commonwealth, may be permitted to practise within its limits." *

This rule must, of course, be understood as subject to the privilege since extended to regularly licensed practitioners of neighboring States to attend patients within its borders.†

The court of appeals of the State of Missouri stands alone in holding that an unqualified practitioner of medicine is entitled to recover a fee in the absence of an express statutory provision to the contrary. The court says: " Whatever may be the rule in some States, we must consider it as well settled in this State for the present that, where a contract is not prohibited by law, and has been fully executed by the person rendering the services, he may recover their value from the person who received their benefit, though in rendering the services the person was guilty of a misdemeanor, because he rendered them without a proper certificate or license for

---

* Spalding *vs.* Alford, 1 Pick. (Mass.), 33.
† See p. 15, *et seq.*

doing so." * From a critical examination of this statement it will appear that the court discriminates between those contracts which are *malum in se* and those which are in themselves lawful, but whose execution is restricted to persons possessing prescribed qualifications; refusing to aid in collecting in the former case, but enforcing a payment in the latter, even though the party proves himself to have committed a misdemeanor in establishing his right to recover.

This is undoubtedly the law in Missouri at the present time, but the fine-haired distinction upon which it is based dwindles in importance when compared with the forceful reasoning by which the courts of other States have arrived at the contrary conclusion.

Chief-Justice Ruffin, of the supreme court of North Carolina, commenting upon this distinction, said: " The distinction between an act *malum in se* and one merely *malum prohibitum* † was never sound, and is entirely disregarded; for the law would be false to itself if it allowed a party through its tribunals to derive advantage from a contract made against the intent and express provisions of the law." ‡

---

* Smythe *vs.* Hanson, 61 Mo. App., 286.

† *Mala in se* are those acts which are wrong in themselves, such as murder; as opposed to *mala prohibita*, or those acts which are only wrong because they are prohibited by law. Rapalje *vs.* Lawrence, Law Dictionary.

‡ Sharp *vs.* Farmer, 4 Devereux and Battle's Law, 122.

The Missouri court is not content with discriminating between things *mala in se* and those *mala prohibita,*
but it goes a step further and says that the practice of
medicine is a thing not even *malum prohibitum* except
as to those unqualified to exercise its functions; and that
because it is not in itself prohibited the court ought
not to refuse its aid to one who has unlawfully practised medicine, an office not in itself wrongful, and
which might lawfully be exercised by another.

Notwithstanding these distinctions, the question remains clear and distinct, May one unqualified to practise medicine exercise the functions contrary to the
law and recover compensation by the aid of our courts?
Justice Learned, of the New York supreme court, said:
" It is a settled principle that one can not recover compensation for doing an act to do which is forbidden by
law and is a misdemeanor. The contrary rule would
make an absurdity. It would permit one to hire another to commit a misdemeanor and would compel the
payment of the contract price for doing what the law
forbids." *

Justice Clopton, of the supreme court of Alabama,
said: " It is too well settled in this State to require further argument, that a penalty, imposed by statute, implies a prohibition; and a contract founded on its vio-

---

* Fox *vs.* Dixon, 34 N. Y. S. R., 710.

lation is void, though not so expressly declared by statute." *

It may be safely understood from the foregoing that
the law is well settled that one practising medicine or
surgery without first complying with the requirements
of the statutes can not enforce the payment of his fees,
whether the statutes expressly so declare or are silent
upon the subject—the State of Missouri being an exception to this rule.

No Recovery for Medicines furnished.—The physician being disqualified to practise can not recover for
services rendered, but what effect does this disqualification have upon his right to recover for medicines which
he has actually furnished to the patient?

An instructive case upon this question was decided
in the supreme court of New York about seventy years
ago. A medical practitioner who was not licensed was
called to attend a patient after other physicians were
unable to benefit her. Quoting from the opinion of
Chief-Justice Savage: " He (the physician) came and
prescribed for the patient, and cured her by the use of
two phials of medicine and a box of ointment. What
the medicines were the witness knew not. She was asked
the value not of the medicines simply, for her answers
show that she estimated the value of the services of the

---

* Harrison *vs.* Jones, 80 Ala., 412.

(physician) as worth sixteen or eighteen dollars, because the patient was cured. The medicines at the apothecary's shop would probably have been worth only a few shillings. . . . Where the same person officiates as physician and apothecary he comes within the decision of this court that an unlicensed practitioner is incapable of suing for services rendered or medicines furnished as a physician. As the patient was cured, it is to be regretted that (the physician) was not paid; but if unlicensed pretenders to skill in diseases can recover, as in this case, the statute may become a dead letter; the country will be filled with mere quacks, peddling their nostrums, and deceiving and destroying the ignorant and credulous, the very mischief which the statute is intended to prevent. I do not say that the (physician in this case) is a mere pretender, for he cured his patient, and in honor and honesty should have been paid; but it is our duty to administer the law." * In a later case an unlicensed physician attempted to recover for medicines to which he had a patent, and which he had prescribed and furnished to a patient, but the court refused to give him judgment because he was in effect " peddling his nostrums in the character of a physician, and inducing people to buy and use them in consequence of their reliance on his pretended skill." " Such

---

* Allcott *vs.* Barber, 1 Wend. (N. Y.), 526.

practices," says the court, "the law of the State has declared to be dangerous to the public health." *

In harmony with the cases above quoted from, the supreme court of Alabama holds that the question whether the unlicensed practitioner may recover for drugs and medicines furnished depends upon whether such drugs and medicines were administered and furnished by him acting in the capacity of a physician; or whether he sold them to the patient acting in the capacity of a druggist or apothecary. If in the former capacity, he can not recover for the value of such drugs, but in the latter he should be allowed to recover.†

In full accord with the cases considered upon this point is a recent Kansas case in which the supreme court by a process of cogent reasoning concludes that a physician who furnishes drugs to a patient does so in the capacity of a physician and not as an apothecary, and that, if he is unlicensed to practise medicine, he can not recover the value of the drugs so furnished.‡

In this case Justice Green said: "Can the plaintiff recover for the medicine alone, having furnished it as an attending physician? The statute in question forbids any one from practising medicine for reward or com-

---

* Smith *vs.* Tracy, 2 Hall (N. Y.), 465.

† Holland *vs.* Adams, 21 Ala., 680.

‡ Underwood *vs.* Scott, 43 Kan., 714, 23 Pac. Rep., 942.

pensation, without having the qualification prescribed therein. The object of this law, doubtless, was to prevent unauthorized and unqualified persons from practising medicine in any of its branches. The right to practise the calling of the physician is, by this statute, taken from certain unqualified persons, and the statute should not be so construed as to give a person the privilege of exercising a right which is in violation of any of its provisions. To hold that a person who furnished medicine, as a physician, could recover compensation for the medicine so furnished or prescribed, would, in our judgment, render the statute nugatory, and any unauthorized person might prescribe for a patient and simply charge for his medicine and thus defeat the very object of the law. The practice of medicine may be said to consist in three things: First, in judging the nature, character, and symptoms of the disease; second, in determining the proper remedy for the disease; third, in giving or prescribing the application of the remedy to the disease. If the person who makes a diagnosis of a case also gives the medicine to the patient, he is, in our judgment, practising medicine within the provisions of the statute in question; and if unauthorized to practise, or is acting in violation of the provisions of the statute, he is not entitled to compensation for the medicine, which he furnishes at the time, as a physician; and the instruction of the court, which said to the jury that the plaintiff below (the physician) could recover for the medicine furnished, though he might not have been entitled to practise medicine, was erroneous." *

It therefore is safe to conclude that outside of Missouri the unlicensed physician is unable to recover through the courts either compensation for professional services rendered or the cost of medicines furnished to patients by him in the capacity of a physician; and that it will accordingly be unwise for one not legally qualified to practise medicine and surgery at the time and place of rendering professional services to resort to suit for the recovery of his fees.

Repeal of Disqualifying Act, Effect on Services Previously Rendered.—But what effect, if any, does the repeal of a disqualifying act have upon the physician's right to recover for services which were unlawfully rendered before such repeal? Here again we find some conflict of authority, the supreme court of Massachusetts being of the opinion that the disqualifying act was not designed to prevent the debt from accruing, but was intended to deprive the physician unlawfully practising from the means of enforcing the payment of such debt, and therefore when the disqualifying act was repealed the obligation stood complete, and the means of enforcing it by legal proceedings were immediately available.†

---

* Underwood *vs.* Scott, 43 Kan., 714, 23 Pac. Rep., 942.

† Hewitt *vs.* Wilcox, 1 Met., 154.

The courts of all of the other States which have passed upon the question have, however, repudiated this doctrine, they holding, with better reason, it seems, that such contracts are void in their inception, and that the repeal of the disqualifying act can therefore raise no obligation on the part of the patient and create no right to recover on behalf of the physician.* It has been heretofore observed that the repeal of an act making it a penal or criminal offense to practise medicine without legal qualifications takes from the court the power of enforcing the penalties incurred under such repealed law; the distinction made between the criminal and civil rights in such a case may be regarded as another evidence of the policy of our law to throw about the accused every reasonable protection.

Steps for Consideration in Enforcing a Claim.—If, on the other hand, the physician has perfected his legal status, as nearly all practising physicians and surgeons have done, it then becomes pertinent to consider the various steps in the process of enforcing payment by legal measures.

Action will lie in this Country for Physicians' Fees. —It has been observed that in England, until the medical acts passed during the present reign, the physician

---

* Puckett vs. Alexander, 102, N. C., 95, 3 L. R. A., 43, 8 S. E. Rep., 767; Bailey vs. Mogg, 4 Denio, 60 (N. Y.); Nichols vs. Poulson, 6 Ohio, 305; Warren vs. Saxby, 12 Vt., 146; Quarles vs. Evans, 7 La. Ann., 544.

was not entitled as a matter of legal right to recover compensation for his services, the law considering them of so exalted and honorable a character that it would not encourage the suspicion that they had been rendered from so unworthy a motive as that of a mercenary. Moreover, Lord Kenyon, in a case in which he refused to enforce the payment of a fee, expressed his doubt whether the physicians would not disclaim a right which would place them in society on a footing with common men.* However justified the opinion of Lord Kenyon may have been at the time and place of its expression, it was not approved by the wisdom of the succeeding century in his own country, nor has it ever been considered suitable to the conditions in this country. Justice Stevens, of the supreme court of Indiana, in considering the application of the English doctrine by our courts, said with perspicuity and unanswerable logic: " It is true that we have adopted the common law of England, but it is a qualified adoption. We have only adopted so much of it as is of a general nature and not local to that kingdom, and not inconsistent with our own laws. We have not adopted any part of it that is peculiar to that country, or that is contrary to, or inconsistent with, the spirit and practice of our own institutions. It is at least doubtful whether the prin-

---

* Chorley *vs.* Bolcot, 4 T. R., 317.

ciple here contended for was any part of the common law at the time the States of this Union dissolved their allegiance to that kingdom; but if it were, it is clearly a principle which is local to that country, and is inconsistent with the spirit and genius of all our institutions and the practice of our courts. Our institutions and laws are all based on the great and broad principles of liberty and equality, and know nothing about nobles and ignobles, honorables and common men. There is but one class known: all stand upon the same footing, and bow with equal submission to our common master—that is, the law of the land. We have no privileged orders known to the law, either as to suing or being sued." *

The physician entering court upon the common plane of all litigants must come prepared with proper and sufficient evidence to show those facts upon which he bases his right to recover.

Limitations of Actions.—Perhaps the first question to consider at this stage is the age of the claim: is the account barred by the statute of limitations? If so, would the patient be willing to plead such a defense to defeat recovery?

The statutory period of limitation upon the different classes of debts and obligations varies so greatly in

* Judah *vs.* McNamee, 3 Blackf. (Ind.), 269.

the several States that no general statement of the law can be made; but recourse must be had in each case to the statutes of the particular State to determine whether or not the claim is within the period of limitation.

If the account consists of a single item, it is a simple matter to determine whether it is within or beyond the prescribed period; but perhaps the account consists of a series of items extending over a period of several years, the earlier of which items are beyond the limit. Is the right to recover such items barred? Nearly every State recognizes the doctrine of mutual accounts, which is founded upon the presumption of a mutual understanding that the parties to the account will continue each to credit the other until either desires to terminate the dealing, when the balance will be ascertained and will be considered as accruing at the date of the last item of the account. Neither Louisiana * nor Texas, however, accept this doctrine, but in case of a continuous account consider the statute of limitations as running against each item from the date of its entry. New Hampshire also denies the rule, excepting as between merchant and merchant.†

Whether the ordinary account of a physician—that is, an account consisting of charges for professional

---

* Arbonneaux *vs.* Letorey, 6 Rob., 456.

† Blair *vs.* Drew, 6 N. H., 235.

services on the one hand, and of credit for the payment of fees by the particular patient on the other hand— will constitute a mutual account is a question upon which the courts of the different States are divided.

The doctrine more commonly accepted is that an account to be mutual must be the result of a mutual exchange of commodities or services, the mere payment of money on one side not being considered sufficient to make the account mutual so as to prevent the bar of recovery. This is the law in California, Georgia, Indiana, Maine, Maryland, New York, and Pennsylvania.

On the other hand, the supreme court of Michigan holds that a payment made upon an account will render the whole account open and mutual, so as to take the earlier charges out of the operation of the statute of limitations.*

This question seems, unfortunately, to be one upon which there is considerable conflict and uncertainty, the court of the same State even contradicting itself in the course of a few years; † therefore the only safe method one can adopt in carrying long accounts of the sort is to have an occasional settlement or accounting in which the balance is either liquidated by cash or note, or is carried forward as a new account, or for the new

---

* Hollywood vs. Reed, 55 Mich., 308.

† See Madden vs. Blair, 66 Ga., 49 ; and Lark vs. Cheatam, 80 Ga., 1.

period of time; in such a case the statute of limitations will run anew from the date of such settlement or accounting.* If the settlement is effected by carrying the balance forward, it is essential that the debtor should have the account before him, and should agree either expressly or impliedly to the correctness of the new balance.

In case the account is found to be barred, it then becomes necessary to determine whether the patient would avail himself of a defense of this character, for suit may be commenced upon a claim against which the statutory period has run, either in whole or in part, and unless the defendant specially pleads the statute as a defense, judgment may nevertheless be entered in the plaintiff's favor for the full amount of the claim.

Is Proof of License Necessary?—Perhaps the first question to decide upon commencing suit is whether it is incumbent upon the physician, or plaintiff, to prove that he has fully complied with the law of his State and was duly qualified to practise medicine at the time the services in question were rendered; or whether this will be presumed until contradicted or disproved by the defendant. Upon this question there is again a difference of opinion in the courts of the different States.

Probably the rule best founded on reason and jus-

---

* Schall *vs.* Eisner, 58 Ga., 190.

13

tice is that in civil suits between physician and patient the physician's right to practise medicine will be presumed until disproved, or at least disputed; while in cases of a criminal prosecution against one for practising medicine unlawfully, he must prove himself to have complied with the law. This rule is very clearly laid down by Justice McAllester, of the Illinois appellate court, who says: " After a thorough examination of the authorities, and a full consideration, we are of the opinion that the rule with its proper distinctions may be thus stated: Where the question of license or qualification of a physician arises collaterally in a civil action between party and party, or between the doctor and the one who employed him, then the license or due qualification under the statute to practise will be presumed; but in case of a prosecution on behalf of the public the rule is otherwise, and in such cases license or due qualification under the statute is not presumed, and it rests with the defendant to prove it." *

A sound reason for this rule is that when an act is required by positive law to be done, the omission of which would be a misdemeanor, the law presumes that it has been done, and therefore the party relying on the omission must make some proof of it.†

---

* Williams *vs.* People, 20 Ill. App., 93.
† City of Chicago *vs.* Wood,24 Ill. App., 40.

There is considerable doubt cast upon the full application of this rule in Illinois by a more recent opinion
of the supreme court of that State. The court, after
referring to the decision sustaining the above rule, expresses a desire not to commit itself in the case they
were then considering, which was one between third parties in which the physician's qualifications arose only
collaterally, but they said: " If he (the physician) were
himself suing to recover for his professional services, he
would doubtless be required to show affirmatively his
compliance with the law, but between third parties the
fact that he is and has for a long time been practising
as a physician and surgeon is sufficient to show, *prima
facie*, that he is lawfully authorized so to do." *

At an early date the supreme court of New York
decided squarely upon the point, holding that in a suit
by the physician for his fees a license would be presumed until the contrary was shown.†

The supreme court of Louisiana, also at an early
date, held that where one acknowledged a physician as
such by employing him to render professional services
such acknowledgment was *prima facie* evidence that
he was duly qualified,‡ but that when the defendant

---

* North Chicago Street Ry. Co. *vs.* Cotton, 140 Ill., 486.

† McPherson *vs.* Chesdell, 24 Wend., 15; Thompson *vs.* Sayre, 1
Denio, 175.

‡ Prevosty *vs.* Nichols, 11 Martins, 21.

in the suit propounded interrogatories to the physician regarding his license, and he failed to answer them, such failure would be taken as confessing that he had no license to practise.*

On the other hand, the rule that a physician must, upon suing, prove that he has secured a license in conformity with the law, was acknowledged as the law in Delaware in 1849.†

The supreme court of Georgia declared such rule to be the law in that State as early as 1850.‡ In 1855 the supreme court of Alabama said: " The effect of these statutes, taken together, was to prohibit all persons from practising as physicians, unless they were licensed by a medical board in their State, or their names were enrolled according to the provisions of the statute, or unless they practised on the botanic system alone; and the necessary result of this prohibition would be to prevent a recovery in all actions founded on contracts for medical services, unless it was proved that the persons rendering such services were not within the prohibition." #

The same rule is held to be the law in New Jersey ‖ and Massachusetts.△ The supreme court of Indiana, in

---

* Dickerson vs. Gurdy, 5 Robinson, 489.
† Adams vs. Stewart. 5 Harr., 144.
‡ Bower vs. Smith, 8 Ga., 74.
# Mays, Adams, etc., vs. Williams, 27 Ala., 267.
‖ Dow vs. Haley, 30 N. J. L., 354.
△ Spaulding vs. Alford, 1 Pick., 33.

a recent decision, after reviewing all of the principal cases on both sides of the question, expresses itself as believing that good reason exists in civil suits for the rule of presuming the physician qualified until the qualification is disputed or disproved, but the court adds: " The statutes under which these several rulings have been made, while similar to our own, none of them, so far as we know, provide, as does ours, that no cause of action shall lie in favor of any person for services as physician who has not, prior to the rendition of such services,procured a license to practise." The court then argues that this clause in the statute has the effect of compelling the physician to prove that he has complied with the requirements of the law before recovering in a suit brought to collect the value of professional services.*

The statutes of some States contain the reasonable provision that no evidence of authority to practise medicine will be required as a prerequisite to a recovery for professional services unless notice is given by the defendant that he shall require proof upon that point. The court of appeals of South Carolina held in an early case that the physician's right to practise would be presumed unless the defendant gave him reasonable notice that proof upon that point would be required.†

---

* Cooper vs. Griffin, 13 Ind. App., 212, 40 N. E. Rep., 710.

† Crane vs. McLaw, 12 Richardson, 129.

Regarding those States in which the question has not been decided, it is pertinent to say that no better advice can be given than: Assume that no presumption of law will be indulged in favor of the physician's right to practise, and have your case prepared accordingly.

In case of suit brought in one State for services rendered in another, no proof is necessary of the right of the physician to practise in the State in which the services were rendered, for the courts of the State in which suit is brought will not presume that the practice of medicine was restricted in that State.*

Proof of Authority to Practise.—The character of proof required to show that one is qualified to practise medicine and surgery depends almost entirely upon the statutes of the particular State, and the preparation of this proof can be intrusted only to those skilled in the law; therefore it will be idle to give more than a very cursory review of the law upon this point. Probably the fundamental rule of evidence in making this proof is the simple one that *the best evidence of which the case, in its nature, is susceptible will be required.* This rule means that if a right is to be proved which has its origin or foundation in a diploma or license, then the right can be proved only by producing and proving the original diploma or license. Should, for instance, one

---

* Downs *vs.* Minchew, 30 Ala., 86.

living in a State requiring as a qualification to practise medicine that he shall have graduated from a regularly incorporated medical college, desire to prove that he has complied with this law, he must not only produce his original diploma, but he must show the incorporation of the college. And if the college does not owe its corporate existence to a special act of the legislature of that particular State, he must produce the act of incorporation; he must also show the college to have existed at the time the diploma purports to have been issued.*

Should the law not, however, provide that the degree shall have been issued by an incorporated body, then a production of the corporate records is not necessary.†

The courts at an early date required strict proof of all of these facts, never admitting a diploma as proof *per se* of its genuineness, but requiring that the genuineness of the parchment should be proved *aliunde*.‡   The rigor of the law has, however, been somewhat ameliorated by statutes which frequently provide that when the physician has presented his diploma to the State board of health or State board of medical examiners, and verified its genuineness, the board shall issue a certificate to that effect, and that such certificate and diploma shall be proof of the holder's right to practise

---

* People *vs.* Nyce, 34 Hun, 298; Hunter *vs.* Blount, 27 Ga., 76.

† Holmes *vs.* Hale, 74 Me., 28.

‡ Hill *vs.* Boddie, 6 Ala. (O. S.), 56.

medicine. In case of provisions of this sort the certificate serves to prove and identify the diploma. The statutes sometimes make the license issued by the designated board competent evidence without proof of the signature. Under such a statute it is incumbent upon the physician to simply offer the license in evidence as full proof of his rights.*

Proof of Employment.—The physician having shown himself authorized to practise medicine, the next step in establishing his right to recover is to show his employment. If the suit is instituted for the purpose of recovering for services rendered to the defendant himself or any immediate member of his family for whose medical services he is primarily responsible, then the mere fact of the services having been rendered by the physician and accepted by the patient is sufficient to establish employment. If, however, the services have been rendered to some third party, for whose medical attendance the defendant is not primarily liable, this step in proving the case may require great care and skill. The law governing the liability in such cases is fully examined in a preceding chapter.†

Proving Services Rendered.—Having passed very briefly over the method of proving the physician's right to practise medicine, and his proof of employment, we

---

* White *vs.* Mastin, 38 Ala., 147.   † See p. 91, *et seq.*

will pass to the next and, to him, more important step of proving the services rendered.

The question of how far a physician may go in giving testimony upon this point is often a very nice one, for the statutes of many States place a seal of secrecy upon the lips of the physician with regard to knowledge obtained in a professional way. The Civil Code of New York provides that a physician " shall not be allowed to disclose any information which he acquired in attending a patient in a professional capacity and which was necessary to enable him to act in that capacity." In New York a physician brought a suit to recover for services, and the patient filed a general denial to the physician's complaint or preliminary statement of facts upon which he relied for recovery. The question then arose as to what facts the physician would be permitted to testify to under the law from which this quotation is taken. He attempted to, and, in fact, did, in the trial court testify to the defendant's physical condition and the disease for which he treated him; but upon appeal the judgment was reversed because the physician had no right, under the law above quoted, to disclose such information, the patient not having waived his privilege. It was urged by the physician's counsel that the patient, by his general denial, waived the privilege. The court, however, held this ground to be untenable, notwithstanding the general denial did make it incumbent upon the physician to prove all of the facts upon which he based his case; had, however, the patient set up, as a defense, incompetency, unskillfulness, or misconduct, he would then have put in direct issue the manner of treating the disease, and would doubtless have been held to waive the privilege, thereby permitting the physician to testify to the condition he found existing in the patient and to the treatment which he prescribed. It was also urged in this case that if the physician were not permitted to describe the disease with which the patient was afflicted he could not show the value of the services, but the court was of the opinion that such a result did not necessarily follow. Justice Haight, who wrote the opinion, said: " The physician can still testify to his employment, to the number of visits made, to the examinations, prescriptions, and operations, and if the defendant objects to his describing them the physician may testify as to their value." *

This rule would preclude the physician from corroborating his testimony as to the value of the services because he could not communicate the character of the services rendered to another physician to enable him to form an opinion as to their value; but it is obvious that the defendant could not produce a witness to dispute the value of such services without making

---

* Van Allen *vs.* Gordon, 83 Hun, 379, 31 N. Y. Supp., 907.

public the facts which the plaintiff was forbidden to disclose, thereby enabling the plaintiff to produce expert evidence in corroboration of his own testimony as to the value of the services rendered.

In those States in which the physician is not precluded by express statutes from disclosing information obtained by him in a professional capacity, he will be permitted, at the proper stage in proving his case, to testify fully and particularly as to the extent, character, and value of the services rendered.*

Books of Account in Proving Claims.—Unless the services upon which the suit is brought have been very recently rendered it will be extremely difficult, if not impossible, for the physician to testify to the time of making each visit and the value of the same without having recourse to his books of account.

At such a time the physician's books of account may generally, if properly kept, be made use of for a double purpose: first, they may be used to refresh the mind of the physician in testifying to the facts referred to therein, and, second, they may be introduced as evidence to prove the account upon which suit is brought. As a means of refreshing his memory, it is proper for a physician upon testifying to have recourse to his books

---

* For a list of States containing statutes which disqualify the physician to give such evidence, see p. 481, n.

either where he recollects the facts and can testify from memory, or where he does not recollect the facts, but made or saw the writing when the facts were fresh in his mind and remembers that it then stated the facts correctly.*

No general rule can be given as to when, where, and under what circumstances the books of account are admissible as evidence of the facts stated in them, as the subject is one upon which the decisions from the courts of the several States are irreconcilable; moreover, many States have statutes regulating the subject which are peculiar to the particular jurisdiction. In New York the physician's books of account are admissible as evidence upon his showing them to be his regular books of account, and proving that he kept no clerk who was familiar with his business and competent to testify regarding the facts stated in the books; that some of the work or services charged was performed, and that he kept correct accounts.† The proof that the physician keeps correct books of account should be made by patients who have settled bills by his books.‡ The physician's wife, who transcribes or enters items into the physician's books, is not a clerk within the meaning of

---

* Chase's Stephen's Dig. of Evidence, Art. 137, N.

† Vosburg *vs.* Thayer, 12 Johns., 461; Atwood *vs.* Barney, 80 Hun, 1.

‡ Beatty *vs.* Clark, 44 Hun, 126.

the above qualification.* In Pennsylvania the physician's books of original entry are admissible in evidence upon being properly proved to be such.† In Indiana it is very doubtful whether books of account are competent evidence.‡ The rule as it exists most generally is that the books of original entry are admissible when properly proved. If the entries are in the handwriting of the party himself, then he may prove the same; if in the handwriting of a clerk, then such clerk must identify or prove the account; but if the person who made the entries is dead, mentally incapacitated, or beyond the jurisdiction, the books may be received in evidence upon proof of the handwriting of such person.# This rule must, however, be understood as subject to many qualifications and exceptions.||

It is generally required that the books be those of original entry. Such is the requirement in many of the States.△ In Pennsylvania it is held that a book containing entries transferred from time to time, as the parties had leisure, from a blotter, which is preserved

---

* Smith vs. Smith, 13 N. Y. App. Div., 207.

† In re Fulton Est., 178 Pa. St., 78.

‡ 9 A. and E. Encycl. of L., 2d ed., 905.

McBride vs. Watts, 1 McCord (S. C.), 384.

|| See 9 A. and E. Encycl. of L., 2d ed., 903 et seq.

△ The courts of Kentucky, Maine, Massachusetts, Minnesota, Missouri, New Jersey, Pennsylvania, South Carolina, Texas, and Vermont require that the book shall be one of original entry.

and in the possession of the party offering the book, is
not admissible as a book of original entries, the blotter
being the permanent record of the transaction.* If,
however, such entries are first made upon slips of paper
or cards and then copied into a book, such book becomes
one of original entries.† If these temporary memo-
randa are made by one person and transcribed into the
book by another, it will probably be necessary to call not
only the person transcribing them to prove the entries
made in the book, but persons making the original mem-
oranda as well, to prove that at or about the time the
charges were made services were performed similar to
those charged in the book.‡

Particularity of Items of Account.—As to the particularity with which the account must set forth the
items of the bill upon which suit is begun, it may be
stated generally that this depends upon the nature of
the account. If the account is one upon which there
has been no settlement or liquidation of the character
referred to in a preceding paragraph,# each item should
be charged separately and under the date upon which
the particular service was rendered, with a specific sum

---

* Breinig *vs.* Meitzler, 23 Pa. St., 156.

† Davison *vs.* Powell, 16 How. Pr., 467; Patton *vs.* Ryan, 4 Rawle
(Pa.), 408.

‡ Chicago Lumber Co. *vs.* Hewitt, 64 Fed. Rep., 314; Miller *vs.* Shay,
145 Mass., 162; Paine *vs.* Sherwood, 21 Minn., 225.

See Limitations of Actions, p. 184.

charged for each visit or item entered upon the account. There are cases holding that such particularity is not necessary,* but there is not sufficient authority to justify one in ever keeping or preparing an account with less particularity.

In an early South Carolina case the bill sued upon contained an item of " thirteen dollars for medicine and attendance on one of the general's daughters, in curing the whooping-cough." A new trial was asked for on the ground that the physician ought to have given a specific bill of the medicine and attendance. The court, speaking through Justice Smith, said: " I did think otherwise on hearing this case; but on mature consideration I think the charges were too general, and am, therefore, for granting a new trial." † The question of whether or not the account is sufficiently specific must be decided by the court according to the prevailing usage in similar cases.‡

Regarding the character of the visits or services performed, and the kind and amount of the medicines charged, it does not seem necessary that the bill should be descriptive. In an early New Hampshire case in which the items were specified as " to visit " and " to medicine," the court said: " Had this been shown to be

---

* Van Bibber *vs.* Merritt's Exr., 12 Weekly, N. C., 272.

† Hughes *vs.* Hampton, 2 Tread. Const. (S. C.), 745.

‡ Schmidt *vs.* Quin, 1 Mill Const., 418 (S. C.).

different from the usage of medical men, it might be proper to inquire into the character of the disease and the circumstances under which the services were performed; but the charge stands well enough until something is shown to the contrary. There is nothing upon the face of the charges to create any suspicion of their correctness; and we can not, without evidence, make any presumption against them. Or, if there had been a general charge for visits and medicines throughout the year, and a gross sum affixed thereto, for compensation to the physician and for medicines furnished, there might be some reason for inquiring into it. But here is a specific sum charged for each visit; and it was competent for the defendant to show that the services were not rendered and that the charges were unreasonable, if such had been the facts." *

From the preceding quotation the reader will realize the necessity in case of an unusual charge of specifying the character of the services rendered. If, for instance, a minor operation were performed, or if unusual services of any character were rendered while making a visit, and yet the item appeared upon the bill as a " visit," with the proper amount charged for the real services performed, the difference between the sum charged and the amount ordinarily charged for a mere visit would

---

* Bassett *vs.* Spofford, 11 N. H., 167.

be so great as to create a suspicion as to the correctness of the bill.

Books of Account, How to be Kept.—It is advisable to refer more particularly at this point to the manner and method of keeping the physician's books of original entry. It has just been observed that a physician may be required to state specifically the nature of each service rendered and charged upon the account, especially if the amount charged for the same is of an unusual character; it therefore is necessary that some explanation be entered with each item which will enable the physician to refresh his memory and testify to the particular services rendered.

Upon the other hand, if the books are desired to be used in evidence in those States extending to professional communications between physician and patient the privilege of secrecy, they must not divulge matters coming within the protection of the statute, otherwise they will be objectionable and will be excluded upon motion of the patient or his personal representatives. Generally speaking, any information obtained by the physician in his professional intercourse with his patients which was necessary to enable him to treat them, and also the character of treatment advised or prescribed by him, are within the protection of the statute.* Here is clearly

---

* See chap. ix, Privileged Communications. For a list of States in which the privilege is recognized, see p. 481, n.

14

a case where the requirements of the law on the one
hand, and the prohibition of the law upon the other,
conflict in such a way as to subject the physician to a
severe hardship. This hardship it is thought may be
overcome if the physician living in a State which enjoins
silence as to all knowledge professionally obtained will
invent a code of arbitrary signs and characters, and by
the use of these characters describe the ailments for
which he treats his patients, together with the services
rendered by him. Such characters when used must,
however, be completely unintelligible to others, and it
can not be safely advised that he would be permitted to
disclose his system to another and still claim the privilege of having his books containing such characters admitted in evidence.

Illustrations.—Should the physician have been so
indiscreet as not to keep a book of accounts, and is unable to recall and testify specifically to the items of the
account upon which he brings suit, or is prohibited from
so doing by reason of the death or mental unsoundness
of the patient, his ability to recover is a matter of very
grave doubt. In the case of Administrator, etc., of Galtney *vs.* Leggett, Dr. Leggett brought suit to recover
among other sums one upon an open account for medical services rendered Galtney and his wife, children,
and servants during the years from 1836 to 1842, and
which amounted in the aggregate to one hundred and

forty dollars. Leggett's only witness was John W. Mo-
nett, Galtney's regular family physician, by whom it was
proved that Leggett attended Galtney's family in his
absence. He testified that he had seen Leggett at Galtney's house two or three times, but did not say at what
time. He did not know anything about any of the
charges made, nor of Leggett's making any visits at the
time charged; he knew nothing of the items; that he had
heard Galtney frequently say that he had employed Leggett as his physician when he was absent; that Galtney's family, white and black, numbered nearly one
hundred persons, and they were often sick; that he had
called two or three times in consultation with Leggett at
Galtney's house; that the prices charged for the services were according to the usual rates; that Galtney and
Leggett were very intimate, and that it was not unusual
for men situated as they were to suffer accounts to run
on uncollected for a long time. Justice Thatcher, in
commenting upon the case, said: " The evidence, however, upon which the jury found for the plaintiff some
portion of the account for medical and surgical services
seems extremely vague and uncertain. The only witness called by the plaintiff to establish this account
could speak neither as to the time or the character of the
services charged, and, in point of law, gave no testimony as to the account filed. It is true that it is
difficult for accounts of this character to be strictly

proved, nor indeed is it necessary; but it would seem to be always in the power of a physician or surgeon to show that he was in the habit of keeping correct books of accounts, and that the account sued upon had been correctly copied from his books. It is also true that the court will not lightly disturb the findings of a jury in cases of this kind where they are particularly the proper judges of the weight of the evidence; but in the present instance the evidence does not seem at all to warrant the verdict upon the account."

And, again, in the case of Simmons *vs.* Means, in which suit was brought to recover a hundred and fifty dollars for medical services generally and medicines furnished to defendant and his family, and in which the jury found a verdict for the plaintiff for a hundred and thirty dollars, the evidence showed that during the period charged in the account the plaintiff was the family physician of the defendant, and was seen several times going to and from the defendant's residence, and was frequently at the house of the defendant; and that the charges contained in the account filed were in accordance with the customary rates in that locality.

Justice Thatcher, passing upon this case also, said: " The evidence introduced to prove the account was to the effect that the plaintiff below was the practising physician in the family of the defendant, and that he was seen passing to and from the defendant's house, during the time included in the account; and that ' he did practise in his family' during the period, together with proof that the amounts charged in the account were according to the customary rates. The items of the account do not appear in the record. The bill of exceptions does not show of what character the professional services or medicines supplied were, or that any, in fact, were supplied. The evidence that the physician practised in the family, and was seen going and returning from his house, is not sufficient to create a legal presumption of indebtedness by the defendant. This court has gone so far as to authorize a physician to recover in an action against his patient by establishing upon a trial the facts of his habit of keeping correct books of accounts, and that the account sued upon had been correctly copied from his books. But with this exception, physicians must be held, like others, to the customary rules of evidence. In this view the finding (of the jury in favor of the physician) in this case was plainly unwarranted by the evidence." *

Nor has the jury any right to assume, because most of the items of such an account have been positively proved to be correct, that all of the items are correct. The court, in a case involving this point, speaking through Justice Fisher, said : " The plaintiff must either

---

* Simmons *vs.* Means, 16 Miss., 397.

prove his account by direct and positive proof, or show that he keeps correct books, and that his accounts have been correctly transcribed." *

And, again, in the case of Déjol *vs.* Johnson, admr., in which a physician's bill had been allowed and paid to the amount of $612.55, Justice Spofford said: " The large medical bill is not justified by the evidence. There is no detailed account of items. Two or three visits to the parish of Calcasieu, about forty miles from Dr. Thornton's residence in Flat Town, and constant attention to the deceased for a fortnight in his own house, whither Déjol was removed before his death, together with the furnishing of medicines, are all the services specifically proved. It is true a witness states that the doctor attended the deceased for six or eight months before his death. The disease was also a loathsome one. But the opinion of this witness that the bill was a just and correct one can not supply the lack of data to support such an opinion. Upon a survey of the evidence we are satisfied that three hundred dollars would be a liberal allowance for the services as proved, and the item charged as paid to Dr. Thornton must be reduced to that sum." †

In proving that professional services have been ren-

---

* Moore *vs.* Joyce, 23 Miss., 584.

† Déjol *vs.* Johnson, admr., 12 La. Ann., 853.

dered, it is competent for the physician to produce a witness to testify that the physician left his office, taking medicine with him, and said he was going to visit the particular patient, and started in the direction of the place where he lived.* It will be understood from the preceding cases that this evidence is simply corroborative in effect and is valuable only for the purpose of strengthening the evidence of the principal witness who testifies as to the particular services rendered.

Proof of Amount of Claim.—There is no presumption of law concerning the value of a physician's or surgeon's services, and there is no presumption that a jury can ascertain it without testimony of some kind from persons knowing something about such value.† It has been shown that the plaintiff is a competent witness to testify to the value of the services which he has sued to recover, the patient being alive and of sound mind. Should any other physician be cognizant of the character and extent of the services upon which suit is brought, it will also be competent for him to testify to their value; or, if the case is such that the plaintiff is not precluded from disclosing the character of the defendant's disease and the nature and extent of his services, then he may call upon any regular physician

---

* Autauga Co. *vs*. Davis, 32 Ala., 703.

† Wood *vs*. Barker, 49 Mich., 296.

to testify as to their value. When such testimony is given regarding the value of the services rendered and none is given to contradict it, the jury is not permitted to disregard the evidence and form an independent conclusion, but must find in accordance with the evidence.* Should conflicting evidence upon this point be adduced by the parties, it then becomes the duty of the jury to scrutinize it and deliberate upon the matter with care, so as to arrive as nearly as possible at the true value of the services performed.

The supreme court of Louisiana lays down the rule that where the witnesses differ as to the proper charges to be made by physicians, the correct rule is to allow the lowest estimate.†

Should the case be one of a difficult operation, and the ability and professional standing of the physician specially high, these facts are proper for the consideration of the jury and will justify a greater compensation.‡ A witness who is produced to show the value of the services in question must testify regarding the value of the particular services upon which suit is pending or those of the same character.# It is not necessary that the physician should prove the value of the services to

---

* Wood *vs.* Barker, 49 Mich., 296.

† Succession of Duclos, 11 La. Ann., 406.

‡ Lange *vs.* Kearney, 4 N. Y. Supp., 14, affirmed, 127 N. Y., 676.

Trenor *vs.* Central P. R. R. Co., 50 Cal., 222.

the patient, the value to be proved by him is the ordinary and reasonable price for services of that nature.* The reasonableness of the charges can not be established by a witness proving what the same physician had charged him in a similar case,† nor is one not a physician competent to testify as to the value of such services.‡ While in epidemics custom may sanction an increased rate of charge, such conditions will not justify exorbitant fees, and in estimating the correct amount the court is inclined to the lowest estimate given by witnesses.#

The case of Board of Commissioners of Marion County vs. Chambers is instructive as to the character of proof requisite and permissible to determine the amount of fee to which the physician is entitled. While this case was one in which a physician brought suit against a county to collect fees due him from the county, yet the rules of law which were held applicable to that case would govern equally in a like action where the plaintiff and defendant were both natural persons. In this case Dr. C. was employed by the coroner to conduct a post-mortem examination, for which he filed a claim of $180. The commissioners allowed him $105, and from that order he appealed to the

---

* Styles vs. Tyler, 64 Conn., 432.

† Collins vs. Fowler, 4 Ala., 647.

‡ Mock vs. Kelly, 3 Ala., 387.

Collins vs. Graves, 13 La. Ann., 95.

superior court, where a verdict was given him for the full amount of his claim. The case was then appealed to the supreme court, which reviewed the trial of the case in the superior court and affirmed the judgment of that court. There being much evidence fully sustaining the value of the doctor's services as charged and allowed, the court confined itself to an examination of alleged errors of the superior court in admitting and rejecting certain evidence.

The counsel for the board of commissioners asked the doctor, "What has been the average daily income from your profession for the two years past?" The doctor's counsel objected to the question, and the court sustained the objection. The supreme court, in passing upon this ruling, said: "Whether the income of the appellee (the physician) was much or little was entirely immaterial. If a surgeon properly performs a surgical operation he is entitled to recover the reasonable value of his services, neither more nor less, whether his professional income be ten or ten thousand dollars a year. The value of the services can not be measured by the professional income of any series of years. If the physician or surgeon possesses the requisite skill and knowledge, and exercises such knowledge and skill properly, he is entitled to be paid the reasonable value of services rendered by him, irrespective of the question of his yearly professional income." The plaintiff produced two physicians and surgeons to testify in his behalf as to the value of the services performed; these witnesses testified upon their examination in chief that they were physicians and surgeons, and that they were competent to testify to the value of services rendered in making post-mortem examination; but, on cross-examination, one of them said: "I don't know what physicians have charged for making post-mortems for the county; I know nothing of the prices at which services can be procured; I judge from what I think it would be worth." The other witness said upon cross-examination: "I have never made examinations for the county; my testimony is based upon all the circumstances. I base my opinion on what I think is the value of such services, irrespective of the price charged or paid." The counsel for the board of commissioners then asked to have the testimony of these witnesses stricken out, which the trial court refused to do. The supreme court said: "No error was committed in overruling appellant's motion. The testimony was competent, for the witnesses were shown to be experts, and to possess such knowledge, skill, and acquaintance with the subject under investigation as entitled them to express their opinions to the jury. They may have had some knowledge of the value of such services, without knowing anything at all about what others were charging for like services. . . . It is clear, from the statements of the witnesses, that they were skilled in their professions, and that they did have sufficient acquaintance with the nature and value of services rendered in post-mortem examinations to entitle their opinion to go in evidence." The board of commissioners' counsel put the question to one of the members of the board: " At what price could you have procured competent physicians to make post-mortem examinations during the years 1877 and 1878?" The physician's counsel objected to the question, and his objection was sustained. Upon the correctness of this ruling the supreme court said: " The question in issue was, not what others would have done the work for, but what was the reasonable value of the services of appellee (the physician). It was no more competent for the appellant (the board) to introduce the offered evidence than it would have been for the appellee to prove that any other surgeon would have charged twice as much as the sum claimed by the appellee. It was competent for appellant to call competent witnesses to give their opinions of the value of the services, but not to prove particular bargains or offers." *

In case of medical services rendered to counties or towns, the statutes of some States authorize the board having charge of such matters to limit the amount of relief to be furnished. With such a statute the board

* The Board of Commissioners of Marion County *vs.* Chambers, 75 Ind., 409.

may, before the relief is furnished or services rendered
establish a limit, but where no such limit has been es
tablished, the board must allow the reasonable value o
the services rendered.*

Defense.—The physician having shown his employ
ment, established the fact that the services were ren
dered, and proved the value of those services, it then be
comes incumbent upon the patient to show some jus
reason why he should not pay, and, if he fails in this
judgment will be rendered against him. Experience ha
shown that the human mind is very fruitful in devising
excuses and discovering reasons for avoiding obliga
tions; it therefore usually happens that the defendan
has a defense. Perhaps the most common defense, when
the suit is between the physician and patient, is that o
general denial, which simply necessitates the strict proo
that the services were rendered as alleged, and that the
are of the value claimed. Frequently the defendant pro
duces witnesses, who, it has been heretofore shown, mus
be physicians, to prove that the services are of a les
value than that claimed. In such a case the plaintif
should be careful to secure as his witnesses men of goo
professional standing whose judgment is esteemed and
integrity undoubted. The defense has been interposed
that, excepting for those visits specially requested, the

patient is not liable unless the physician shows some reasonable necessity for the additional visits. This defense has no legal weight; a physician, being employed to attend a patient, is the proper and the best judge of the number and frequency of visits necessary, and, in the absence of proof to the contrary, the court will presume that all professional visits made were deemed necessary and were properly made. Justice Temple, of the supreme court of California, said: " It would be a dangerous doctrine for the sick to require a physician to be able to prove the necessity of each visit before he can recover for his services. This is necessarily a matter of judgment, and one concerning which no one, save the attendant physician, can decide. It depends not only upon the condition of the patient, but, in some degree, upon the course of treatment adopted." *

In the case of Jeffries *vs.* Harris the defendant attempted to show the character of the physician, but was not permitted to do so. The court said: " Character was not put in issue by the nature of this action, and the defendant is equally liable on his assumpsit, whether the plaintiff's character were good or bad; for, if he chose to employ him as a physician, it is not competent to him, afterward, to say that he is not a good one, and, therefore, that he will not pay him. If, indeed, the

---

* Todd *vs.* Myres, 40 Cal., 355.

plaintiff had imposed on the defendant by false pretensions to skill, he would have been responsible for any injury done him; but, in this case, the plaintiff is entitled to compensation for skill and labor, whatever they
may be." *

A very common sort of defense is that in which the
defendant admits the rendering of the services but
claims that they were so unskillfully rendered as to be
injurious; and frequently he files a counter-claim for
damages resulting from such unskillful or negligent
treatment. The constant recurrence of cases in which
this sort of defense is interposed will justify a careful
examination of the law governing the proof. Many of
the trial courts seem to have been of the opinion that
when a patient pleaded as a defense to a physician's suit
to recover compensation for professional services that
such services were not rendered with skill, this plea
immediately cast the burden upon the physician of showing by a fair preponderance of evidence that the services
rendered by him were performed with all necessary or
required skill. The courts of last resort have, however,
universally declared this to be a mistaken view, they
holding the law to be that where the physician has made
a *prima-facie* case by proving his professional character,
his employment by the defendants, the rendition of the

---

* Jeffries *vs.* Harris, 3 Hawks. (N. C.), 105.

services and their value, he is entitled to judgment unless the defendant can show by competent evidence that
he has been guilty of negligence or want of proper skill
in treating the particular patient.* Nor will the fact
that a patient grew worse under the plaintiff's treatment
and grew better after he was discharged show that the
physician was guilty of negligence or unskillfulness in
treating him. To illustrate more fully and show the
character of evidence required, a quotation is taken from
a case in point: The patient in this case had sustained
a serious injury by the explosion of a dynamite cartridge
and the plaintiff had been called as a specialist to treat
his eyes and ears. The defense interposed was that of
improper treatment. In commenting upon the evidence
offered to establish this defense the court said: " It is
claimed that the plaintiff improperly applied and used
a tube of hot water over the nose to cure the ailment or
injury to his eyes; that the heat was so great as to be injurious. Other physicians were in attendance on the
patient, but their evidence was not produced. No surgical or medical witness was called by the defendant to
say that the treatment was improper or negligent in the
least degree, whatever uneducated persons or non-ex-
perts might conjecture on the subject. The plaintiff

---

* Robinson *vs.* Campbell, 47 Ia., 625; Styles *vs.* Tyler, 64 Conn.,
432; Baird *vs.* Morford, 29 Ia., 531; Wooster *vs.* Paige, 1 Pac. Coast
L. J., 324.

could not be convicted of malpractice on such evidence. He could not be held responsible simply because he failed to cure the defendant's son, nor for mere mis-judgment in treating him, if the treatment was such as a physician and surgeon of ordinary knowledge and skill would apply." *

Nor is it a valid defense to a suit by a physician to recover the value of his services to show that the nurses in the hospital to which the patient went upon the phy-sician's advice were negligent or careless, it not being shown that the physician was proprietor or manager of the hospital.†

Drunkenness is also sometimes pleaded as a defense to such an action. If a physician who is called to attend a patient is in such an intoxicated condition as to be unable to fulfill the duties of his profession, this is not only a complete defense to an action commenced to re-cover compensation for those particular services, but there is, under the law of some States, a criminal liabil-ity involved. If, however, a patient, after the doctor has treated him in an intoxicated condition, continues to send for or employ him, he will be held to have waived all objection to his habits of intoxication and will not be permitted to plead such a defense.‡

* Wurdeman vs. Barnes, 92 Wis., 206, 66 N. W. Rep., 111.
† Baker vs. Wentworth, 155 Mass., 338, 29 N. E. Rep., 589.
‡ McKleroy vs. Sewell, 73 Ga., 657.
15

Effect of Judgment for Recovery of Fee.—A judgment being entered in favor of the physician in a suit commenced by him to recover the value of his professional services, it is interesting and valuable as well to inquire what effect such a judgment will have upon a possible right of action against him and in favor of the patient growing out of unskillfulness in the performance of the same services for which he has just recovered. It is a general principle of law that a judgment of a court of concurrent jurisdiction directly upon a point is a bar to an action upon the same point and between the same parties in another suit.

The court of appeals of New York has applied this doctrine to its full extent. In this instance suit had been commenced by a patient to recover damages, laying the amount at five thousand dollars, from his physician for unskillful and negligent treatment of a dislocated elbow and fractured arm. The physician then commenced an action before a justice of the peace to recover the value of his services in the treatment complained of from the patient, who was plaintiff in the malpractice suit. The patient appeared in the suit instituted before the justice of the peace for the recovery of fees, but interposed no defense, and judgment was entered against him to the amount of six dollars and fifty-eight cents. The physician, then, as a defense to the patient's action for damages from malpractice, set up the judgment rendered by the justice of the peace. Upon the principle above given the supreme court, and afterward the court of appeals, held that the judgment of the justice was a complete bar to the action for damages.* The courts of West Virginia have declared themselves in harmony with this decision;† so also have those of New Jersey ‡ and Arkansas.# The contrary view has, however, been taken by the courts of Indiana,|| Ohio,△ and Wisconsin.◊

Collections from Estates of Decedents.—There now remains to be considered before closing this chapter the manner of presenting and proving claims for physicians' fees against estates of deceased persons, together with a general survey of the law regulating the subject.

The administration of estates is governed in each State by statutes which are more or less peculiar to the particular jurisdiction. It will therefore be impossible in a limited space to give more than a very general view of the manner of administration, but the proving of claims, when contested, in which the doctor is most deep-

---

* Gates *vs.* Preston, 41 N. Y., 113.

† Lawson *vs.* Conway, 37 W. Va., 159, 16 S. E. Rep., 564.

‡ Ely *vs.* Wilbur, 49 N. J. L., 685.

Dale *vs.* Donaldson Lumber Co., 48 Ark., 188.

|| Goble *vs.* Dillon, 86 Ind., 327.

△ Sykes *vs.* Bonner, 1 Cinn. R., 464.

◊ Ressequie *vs.* Byers, 52 Wis., 650.

ly interested, is governed by pretty much the same law in all jurisdictions, and will therefore be examined more particularly.

The first step in the administration of the estate of a deceased patient or debtor in which the doctor is interested is that at which the time arrives for presenting his claim for payment. Of the arrival of this time he is usually given notice, either actual or constructive. In the presenting of such claims the doctor should always be prompt, remembering that unless the claim is presented within the period fixed by the law of his State it is totally barred—at least, such is the law of many States—and that, should the law of his State, being more indulgent, allow him to present his claim after the first period fixed has expired, he will be entitled to his proportion of only those assets which remain after the payment of the claims filed and allowed at the proper time. The time fixed for the presentation of claims refers as well to those not due as to those which have already accrued. In some jurisdictions future debts of the estate are paid at their present value at the same time as the other debts; in others, arrangements are made for paying them at maturity.

Claim, by whom Presented.—The claim against a decedent's estate must be filed or presented by the person who owns it or has an interest in it, with the right of enforcing its collection,* or by his lawfully authorized agent.†

Claim, to whom Presented.—The presentation, to be beyond question, must be made to a legally qualified administrator or executor, although a presentation to an executor before his qualification has been held valid.‡ A presentation to an administrator after his discharge is, however, of no effect.# When there are two or more executors or administrators of an estate, a presentation to one of them is sufficient.||

Presentation of Claim.—The sufficiency of the presentation of a particular claim is a question that can be decided in the light of the statutes existing in that jurisdiction, and the preparation of a claim for presentation should never be undertaken without first consulting the statutes of the State in which it is to be filed. In some States the claim is not required to be presented in writing, although this is probably the exception. No harm can result from doing more than the law requires in matters of this kind, and the claim should therefore always be carefully prepared in writing, describing the general

---

* McDowell *vs.* Jones, 58 Ala., 25.
† Marshall *vs.* Perkins, 72 Me., 343.
‡ Branch Bank *vs.* Hallett, 12 Ala., 671.
# Gibson *vs.* Mitchell, 16 Fla., 519.

nature,* amount, and value of the services with as much particularity as possible. If a note or other instrument has been given, and the claim is filed upon such instrument, then a copy of it should be attached to the claim.

Claims for medical services should always be verified by affidavit of the claimant or doctor, sworn to before some officer having authority to administer oaths.

The affiant should in his affidavit of verification set up the facts that he is a physician and surgeon, and has been duly licensed or is duty qualified under the law of the particular State to practise medicine and surgery; that the annexed account against the estate of decedent, amounting to the sum of —— dollars, is just, after allowing all just credits, deductions, and set-offs, and is now due and unpaid. An affidavit setting up these facts in proper form will comply with the law of nearly every State, but before making an affidavit the local statutes should be examined and their requirements carefully followed.

After a claim has been duly presented the executor or administrator will in most States examine the same, and, if he is satisfied that it is a just and proper claim against the estate, either in full or in part, he will allow

---

* The description of the nature of the services rendered should not be so specific, when filed in those States holding professional communications privileged, as to violate the law.

the same, either at its face or *pro tanto,* accordingly as he is convinced of its merits.

Should the claim be rejected, either in full or in part, the claimant is required, within a short period of time, usually ranging from three months to one year, to bring an action against the executor or administrator to recover the claim or the part of the same which is disallowed; otherwise his rights in the premises will be barred.

Advisability of Prosecuting Claim.—At this point it becomes advisable to consider the condition of the decedent's estate and determine whether or not there are sufficient assets to pay the claim when proved, or whether the reward will be so small as not to justify the fight. Should the estate be solvent, it then is necessary to carefully scrutinize the claim and determine whether or not it is legally valid, and if valid, whether it can be proved.

Solvency of Estate.—In considering the solvency of the estate it is necessary to examine the order of the payment of debts, for the estate may be solvent as to a certain class of debts and pay them in full, while those of a subsequent class would receive but a small percentage of their face value, or perhaps nothing at all. At common law the debts of the decedent were paid in the following order: 1. The necessary funeral expenses. 2. The necessary expenses of administration. 3. Debts of record due to the crown. 4. Debts of record due to the subjects, which included judgments, decrees, statutes, and recognizance. 5. Debts by specialty * founded upon a valuable consideration. 6. Simple contract debts † based upon valuable consideration. 7. Voluntary bonds or covenants. 8. Other voluntary debts.

Under this scheme the physician's bill would rank in the sixth class, unless he had been so fortunate as to secure a bond in liquidation of it, when it would be advanced to the fifth class, or had reduced it to judgment during decedent's lifetime, in which case he would enjoy the advantage of belonging to the fourth class. In paying these debts, if the estate is solvent, all the creditors are paid in full; but if there is a deficiency in the estate, all the creditors of each class are paid in full in the order of their class until the estate is exhausted, those coming in the subsequent class or classes getting nothing, or perhaps only a *pro rata* share of their indebtedness. To illustrate, under the above scheme, an estate having only enough money to pay the first five classes of creditors would pay them in full. Should there, however, be a sum left after paying the first five classes, but not equal to the total sum of the debts owing under the sixth class, this amount would then be divided among the

---

* Debts by specialty are those arising out of a contract or other instrument under seal.

† Simple contracts include all not under seal, whether oral or written.

creditors of the sixth class in proportion to the amount of their claims.

The common law order of creditors has been altered in every State, the preference of debts growing out of specialty contracts over those arising from simple contracts being nearly always withdrawn; in some States, however, judgments obtained in the lifetime of deceased are given preference over simple contract debts.

The most common order now existing in the United States is the following: 1. Funeral expenses. 2. Expenses of administration. 3. Expenses of last illness. 4. Judgments (abolished in a number of States). 5. Public debts. This order in many States ranks after the funeral expenses and expenses of administration. 6. Simple contract liabilities.

Probably the most striking change, as shown by comparison of the order existing at common law and the one last above given, is the addition of the class " expenses of last illness." This class is quite generally recognized in the United States, but it is not universally accepted.

What is Included in Expenses of Last Illness.—Generally speaking, this includes the necessary medical attendance and nurse hire incurred during the last sickness. What the term " last illness " means is a question that is not entirely free from doubt. We have an early case from the supreme court of Louisiana in which, by reason of the peculiar statute defining the term "last sickness," a hardship is worked upon the physician. In that case the patient was afflicted with a fatal disease, of which the physician would have been unable to cure him, but the immediate cause of the patient's death was a pistol wound. The physician would have been entitled to a privileged claim for attending the patient during that which, in fact, was his last sickness; but the code specified that "the last sickness is considered to be that of which the debtor died," * thus defeating the claimant's preference.

An early case comes to us from South Carolina in which a preference was asked for nursing during the decedent's "last sickness." The period of such services extended through the last year of the decedent's life, during which time he was lingering under the disease which finally terminated his existence. The refined and humane sentiment expressed by the court of appeals in giving their interpretation of this act demands a quotation of the opinion: " The issue made up presented the question, and the jury have decided that the services were rendered during the last sickness.

" The court can lay down no rule or limitation for the duration of the last sickness of a man, nor for the degree of attention to be paid him. A wounded man

---

* Succession of Whittaker, 7 Rob. (La.), 91.

may linger a long time in a helpless state, and chronic diseases and some cancers run through more time than a year. The act concurs with the principles of Christian civilization, and is remedial of a common want and necessity—attention and services during last sickness. We must therefore construe it liberally, and let it inure to its proper end, the full relief of the sick and the infirm. The court and the jury were the proper judges in the particular instance; and they appear to have assessed the amount of the plaintiff's account with justice and discretion." *

In the matter of Reese's estate the evidence showed that Mr. Reese received an injury from a fall; he was attended by the claimant for some time, and so far recovered as to be able to attend to his ordinary business, and the claimant's services were dispensed with. Afterward he had a relapse and called in another physician. Soon after that he died, probably from the effect of the fall, from which he never entirely recovered. The question arose whether claimant's bill was entitled to precedence as " medical attention given during the last illness." The court thought that the clause refers to proximate and not remote causes of death, and that the attendance must be during the last sickness, but could not be rendered at intermittent periods.

---

* Percival admr. ads. McVoy. Dudley (S. C.), 337.

In the case of Huse *vs.* Brown, exr., the services were rendered by the claimant between January 19th and June 28th. The decedent was suffering from a cancer in his nose, from which he died in December following. The trial court instructed the jury that if they should decide the testator died of the cancer under which he was laboring when the plaintiff attended upon him, and that it was a continuing complaint or disorder until his death, they might consider it his last sickness. The supreme court, in referring to this instruction, said: " And why not, whether any such instruction had been given to them or not? It would seem to a plain understanding to be an indisputable fact that the sickness which is terminated by the death of a patient is his last sickness. . . . Sickness assumes so many forms, and death approaches in so many different ways, that we know not how to lay down any legal principle in such cases that can be applied by way of construction of the words ' last sickness.' What is to be considered a man's last sickness seems to be a question properly determinable by the jury upon the facts in each case, and which can seldom, if ever, be the same in two instances. There may probably be in a multitude of cases a strong resemblance. On a trial for homicide it is always a question for the jury whether the deceased died a natural death or in consequence of the act of the person accused. So it may be a question whether the sickness of which a person dies is the same under which he labored when confined and receiving medical aid one or two months before. In the case before us, the questions as to the cause of the testator's death and the continuance of his sickness have been settled by the jury whose business it was to settle it." *

In addition to the above opinion no comment is necessary. Should the estate be insolvent, and the services of such a character as to be urged as a preferred claim, or should the estate be solvent, then the next question to be considered is the validity of the rejected claim.

Validity of Claim against Estate.—Generally speaking, the same questions may arise to defeat the collection of a claim against the estate of a deceased person as those which are invoked by a living defendant for the same purpose, and which have been considered in the preceding pages.

There are, however, a few questions which, from the nature of the case, can only arise in the class of cases now under consideration. For instance, it has been observed that the husband is liable for the medical treatment of his wife; for that reason a claim for services rendered to a deceased wife should be presented to the

---

* Huse *vs.* Brown, exr., 8 Me., 167.

husband for payment, and not filed against her estate unless the husband has no property with which to pay the claim.*

Where services are rendered a decedent under the expectation and mutual understanding that compensation will be made for the same by way of legacy, or otherwise, but with no special agreement to that effect, the person rendering such services may, upon the failure of decedent to provide for such legacy, collect the reasonable value of his services from the estate.† But where the services are performed in the mere expectation or hope of a legacy, without the intention of making any charge therefor, no claim can be maintained against the estate, even though the claimant's hope of a legacy is not realized.‡

In case of claims of the sort rendered for members of the claimant's family there is a presumption that the services were intended to be gratuitous; this presumption, however, may be rebutted by proof of an express contract to pay therefor, or by evidence of facts or circumstances showing that when the services were rendered the parties contemplated a pecuniary compensation. The strength of this presumption is dependent

---

* *In re* Weringer's estate, 100 Cal., 345, 34 Pac., 825.

† Starkey's Appeal, 61 Conn., 199; Harrison *vs.* Lindley, 104 Ill., 245; Martin *vs.* Wright, 13 Wend (N. Y.), 460.

‡ Clark *vs.* Todd, 16 N. Y. Supp., 491.

upon the degree of relationship becoming weaker as the relationship is more distant.

Without dwelling further upon the character of the claim, which is regulated by the same law as that regulating claims between ordinary litigants, we will pass to the mode of proving these claims against estates of decedents, which presents new difficulties.

Proving Contested Claims against Estates of Decedents.—The manner of proving ordinary contested claims has been carefully examined in the preceding pages, together with the amount and character of proof necessary to satisfactorily show the indebtedness. These same rules and precedents may all be considered as regulating the proof of a claim against the estate of a deceased debtor, with the single and important exception that in ordinary claims the physician himself is a competent witness to testify regarding the transactions out of which the indebtedness arose; while in a claim of this sort his lips are sealed and he can only prove his case by submitting his books of account and by producing such other competent witnesses as may have knowledge calculated to corroborate the account.

The reason for this condition is the following: At common law no interested party to a suit was a competent witness to testify in his own behalf. While the older law works laud the good sense and sound policy of this rule, it does not seem to have proved satisfactory in this country, for it has been abrogated by the legislature of every State, so as to permit the parties to a suit to freely tell all they know of the transactions or conditions out of which the litigation grows, the policy now being to consider the party's interest as affecting the credibility of his statements rather than disqualifying him from making such statements. It is obvious, however, that whenever a suit grows out of a transaction one of the parties to which is dead or insane, the grossest injustice might be done by permitting the other party to testify regarding the nature of such transaction, or to relate any conversation or communication which took place between them relative thereto. For this reason the modern lawmakers, in sweeping away the ancient rule disqualifying the parties as witnesses, have gone only so far as to permit them to testify where they are both living and mentally capable; but where the lips of one party are sealed by death or insanity they allow the law to stand as before, closing the mouth of the other.

This disability, together with the one imposed upon the physician by the law relating to privileged communications, is peculiarly serious to him. If the books of account disclose the nature of the patient's affliction or the character of the treatment prescribed, then they are objectionable in those States having statutes protecting privileged communications; if, on the other hand, the books contain no such information, or if such information is recorded in characters unintelligible to others than the physician, then they are subject to the criticism of being too indefinite to prove the account, and must be supported by strong corroborating evidence. Moreover, it is a matter of very grave doubt whether or not the physician may even prove his books of account and have them accepted in evidence in a suit against the estate of a deceased or insane person. In New York there are two distinct lines of conflicting decisions, one holding that the physician's books are admissible in evidence in a case of this sort,* and the other holding that the books can not be received in evidence.† There is probably no subject in the law upon which the decisions are more conflicting and the rights of the respective parties more uncertain and vague, nor in which the opportunities offer themselves for the lawyer to more fully exercise his knowledge, skill, and judgment in behalf of the interests of his client.

Is Physician's Wife Competent to Prove such Claims?—The person who is most commonly possessed

---

* Young *vs.* Luce, 21 N. Y. Supp., 225; Clark *vs.* Smith, 46 Barb., 30; West *vs.* Van Tuyl *et al.*, 119 N. Y., 620; Wetmore *vs.* Peck, 19 Alb. L. J., 400.

† Ross *vs.* Ross, 6 Hun, 182; Davis *vs.* Seaman, 64 Hun, 572.

16

of information necessary to corroborate such claims is the physician's wife, but whether or not she is a competent witness to prove the facts within her knowledge is a very nice question. At common law the wife could not testify for or against her husband in a suit to which he was a party. This rule has been altered in many States, but not in all. In those States in which the rule has not been altered the wife unquestionably has no right to testify. In those States in which the disability has been removed, and the wife permitted to testify with her husband, the question arises, in cases of this sort, whether her interest in her husband's suit against the estate of the decedent is such as to render her with her husband an interested party, and therefore an incompetent witness, or whether she shall be considered as having no interest, and accordingly permitted to testify.

The reasons given by the courts at common law for denying to the wife the privilege of testifying in a suit to which the husband was a party were, first, that it was against public policy, such an act being thought a menace to the harmony of the domestic circle and a violation of the confidence subsisting between husband and wife; second, because of the identity of their legal rights and interests. If this second reason is considered applicable to-day, there can be no alternative but to deny the wife the privilege of giving evidence in behalf of her

husband's claim; but as the marked tendency of legislation during the past half century has been toward establishing a severalty of legal rights and interest, it is
not surprising that some of our courts should consider
the second reason so greatly weakened as to regard the
wife no party to such a suit, and not legally interested
in the result, and therefore accept her evidence in support of the claim. This is a question, however, upon
which the courts are unfortunately divided, and in those
States where a decision has not been rendered by the
court of last resort the question must be considered as
still open.

In cases of this sort the testimony of the wife has
been held competent in the following States: Maryland,[*] Mississippi,[†] New Hampshire,[‡] and New York.[#]
It is probable that the rule would be held the same in
Nebraska.[||]

On the other hand, such testimony has been
held incompetent, and rejected by the courts of
last resort in the following States: Illinois,[Δ] Indi-

---

[*] Trahern *vs*. Colburn, exr., 63 Md., 99.

[†] Rushing *vs*. Rushing, admr., 52 Miss., 330.

[‡] Clements *vs*. Marston, 52 N. H., 31.

[#] Whitman *vs*. Foley, 125 N. Y., 651; Porter *vs*. Dunn, 131 N. Y.,
314.

[||] Wylie *vs*. Charlton, 43 Neb., 840, 62 N. W. Rep., 220.

[Δ] Bevelot *vs*. Lestrade, 153 Ill., 625.

ana,* Iowa,† Maine,‡ Pennsylvania,# and West Virginia.||

The claimant, upon producing satisfactory proof of the legality and justness of his claim, is entitled to a judgment for the amount he has shown to be due to him, which judgment the executor or administrator must pay in due time, either in full or in part, as the assets of the estate may justify.

---

* Scherer *vs.* Ingerman, 110 Ind., 428. This case simply declares the wife incompetent because the statute provides that she shall be in such cases.

† Muir *vs.* Miller, 82 Iowa, 700. Code excludes such evidence.

‡ Berry *vs.* Stevens, 69 Me., 290.

Sutherland *vs.* Rose, 140 Pa., 379.

|| Kilgore *vs.* Hanley, 27 W. Va., 451.

CHAPTER VII.

CIVIL MALPRACTICE, INCLUDING GENERAL LIABILITY OF PHYSICIAN TO PATIENT.

Purpose of the Chapter.—The purpose of this chapter is to make a careful examination of the law governing the civil liability of physicians and surgeons, illustrating its application by particular instances and cases as fully as the limit of the work will permit. The examination will extend through the subject of civil malpractice, and will also include those instances of civil liability arising from acts either of omission or of commission which do not amount to malpractice.

No Liability for Refusal to take a Case.—In some localities there is a popular belief that a physician, by reason of the rights and privileges which he enjoys as such, is bound to undertake the treatment of any patient who requests from him professional services. There is in the law no foundation whatever for this belief. A well-known law writer, in referring to the subject, says: " No question can exist as to the legal right of a physician, unless he be an officer of the government charged with specific duties, which he thereby violates, to decline ·

to take charge of a particular case." *   But having once
assumed charge of a case, we have observed in a preceding chapter,† he immediately sets in operation numerous implied contracts and presumptions of law regarding
his qualifications to properly treat that case, and, should
he fail to fulfill these implied contracts, or comply with
the presumptions of law, a civil liability immediately
arises in favor of the patient to the amount of damages
thereby sustained.

General Professional Requirements.—Perhaps the
most fundamental of the professional requirements that
we have heretofore observed are that one who undertakes to render medical services, holding himself out as
a physician or surgeon, will be held by the law, first,
to possess a reasonable degree of knowledge, skill, and
experience; second, to exercise ordinary care and diligence; and third, to use his best judgment in all cases
of doubt as to the best course of treatment.‡

Application of Rule.—Whether or not the amount
of knowledge displayed or the degree of skill, care, and
judgment exercised is sufficient in any case to fulfill the

* Wharton on Negligence, § 731.

† See p. 60, *et seq.*

‡ Leighton *vs.* Sargent, 27 N. H., 460; McNevins *vs.* Lowe, 40 Ill.,
209; Long *vs.* Morrison, 14 Ind., 595; Branner *vs.* Stormont *et al.*, 9
Kan., 51; Patten *vs.* Wiggins, 51 Me., 594; Wood *vs.* Clapp, 4 Sneed,
65; Ritchey *vs.* West, 23 Ill., 385.

requirements of the law is a question of fact for the
jury to determine from the evidence produced at the
trial. To illustrate the application of the rule we will,
as in previous chapters, examine the records of a few
prominent trials. In the case of Boldt *vs.* Murray *
the patient was suffering with a fracture of the inner
condyle of the humerus. The evidence does not tend
to show that the bone was not properly set. The evidence of the plaintiff was to the effect that the bandage
was not put on the arm in the approved manner, but
was rolled from the upper to the lower part of the arm,
and so tightly as to prevent circulation, and that, although the hand and arm became swollen and the latter
discolored, the bandage was left on; and that, by reason
of the improper bandaging and the permitting of the
bandage and splints to remain on in such condition, the
circulation of blood was cut off, and, as a consequence,
the flesh of the arm, being deprived of sustenance,
sloughed off. The physician, on the other hand, gave
evidence to the effect that the arm was properly bandaged, and that the unfortunate result of the injury was
caused by the failure of the patient and his parents to
obey the physician's directions, etc. Here was a case
of direct conflict of evidence from which it was the province of the jury to determine the real facts. The court

* Boldt *vs.* Murray, 2 N. Y. S. R., 232.

instructed the jury upon the law applicable to the case, as set forth in the above rule, whereupon they retired and found a verdict for the plaintiff, evidently believing the evidence given by the plaintiff and disregarding that given by the defendant. The judgment based upon this verdict the general term of the supreme court refused to reverse, stating in effect that the evidence of the plaintiff, if true, was sufficient to show that the defendant did not come within the legal requirements as to knowledge, care, and judgment, and that as to the truth of such evidence the jury was the proper judge.

In the case of Link *vs.* Sheldon * *et al.,* the plaintiff, a lad of thirteen years of age, had fallen, striking with such force upon his hand and forearm as to produce a Colles's fracture and a dislocation of the ulna. The defendants were called and dressed the arm, placing a certain metallic splint, which should have been adjusted to the palmar surface of the hand, upon its back. The plaintiff's evidence was to the effect that the bandaging of the hand and arm had been so tight as to cause an inflammation and resultant suppuration, which in healing drew in the thumb and permanently deformed the hand.

The accident took place on Friday. It appears that the patient's parents became dissatisfied with the defendants' treatment of the case, and, hearing of the suc-

---

* Link *vs.* Sheldon, 136 N. Y., 1.

cess of another doctor, employed him and dismissed the defendants on the following Tuesday morning, and that the defendants had nothing further to do with the case.

The evidence adduced by the defendants was to the effect that the injury was not an ordinary Colles's fracture, but that the position of the bones was so reversed that the splint had to be used as applied by them; that the physical condition of the patient, in addition, was bad from feverishness; that the bandages were rightly adjusted; that the great inflammation discovered when the doctor who succeeded to the case was called in was due to their having been prevented by the parents from redressing the arm on Monday evening, as they desired to do; and, finally, that had the succeeding physician properly treated the hand in its inflamed and swollen condition by lancing instead of poulticing, no distorted condition of the hand would have resulted.

The jury returned a verdict for the plaintiff to the amount of four thousand dollars. The court of appeals, in refusing to reverse the judgment, said: " The evidence upon the material points was conflicting. There was more or less disagreement among the doctors; but it is impossible to say that there was not evidence tending to establish a lack of skill, or some neglect, on the part of the defendants. It was not necessary, in order to sustain the action, that there should have been proof of gross culpability upon the part of the defendants.

It was sufficient to warrant a verdict against them that there was evidence of any failure on their part to exercise proper care, or of any neglect in the discharge of the duty they had assumed toward the plaintiff."

While the legal effect upon the liability of the defendants, from dismissing them at an early stage in the treatment of the case and employing another physician, is not pertinent to the question now in consideration, it is perhaps of sufficient interest to justify digressing. In considering this question in the above case the court laid down the rule that the liability of the defendants in such a case extends not only to injuries directly resulting from the ignorant, unskillful, or negligent treatment to which they have subjected the patient previous to the time of their discharge, but they are liable as well for all injuries directly resulting from such improper treatment, even though they are not manifest until after the case has passed to the care of another physician. If, however, such injuries are the result of any other cause than that of the improper treatment of the defendants', they are not liable therefor. Upon this point the trial judge charged that " if the jury find, from the evidence, that it is just as probable that the injury complained of was caused either by the original severe injury, or by the interference of the plaintiff's parents (in refusing to allow the defendants to redress the arm), or by the subsequent manipulations and treatment of Dr. —— (who succeeded defendants in the treatment of the case) and others, as from the pretended tight bandaging, it is the duty of the jury to find a verdict for the defendants." This instruction was held by the court of appeals to properly state the law.

After laying down the general rule requiring a reasonable degree of competency, care, and judgment, the court, in commenting upon the evidence in the case of Ritchey *vs.* West,* said: " The concurring evidence of all of the physicians shows that the splints and bandages were not properly applied. Had they extended below the wrist, the evidence seems to show that they would have confined the wrist to its proper place. It is probable that such a practice would have tended, notwithstanding the fracture, to have held the broken bone more nearly to its place until a union was formed, and thus have prevented to some extent, if not altogether, the deformity and disability to use the hand. The physicians also agree that the splints employed were not of sufficient width, as well as too short, for the treatment of the fracture, even if they had been midway between the wrist and elbow, as he supposed. And from this evidence it would seem that there must have been a want of ordinary skill, or great negligence, in the treatment

---

* Ritchey *vs.* West, 23 Ill., 385.

of the case, in not detecting the dislocation of the wrist joint. The physicians all agree that this portion of the injury could have been easily detected by ordinary care and skill, and the fact that it had been and was still dislocated was afterward detected by a person who did not profess surgery or skill in such matters, and had previously had only slight experience in cases of fractured limbs. Then, if the evidence of the medical men who were examined as witnesses is to be credited, and it is supported by the fact that the dislocation of the joint was detected by a person professing to have no skill, there was a want of ordinary care or skill, or both, manifested in the treatment of the case."

Failure to Discover Extent of Injury.—It must not, however, be inferred from the preceding case that the failure of the surgeon to discover a serious injury is a fact from which incompetency or negligence will necessarily be inferred. This is well illustrated by the case of Gedney *vs.* Kingsley.* In this case the patient was thrown from her carriage and sustained a fracture of her right arm. The defendant, a physician, was called and made an examination, but did not discover the nature of the injury, and supposed it to be no more than a bad bruise. Upon the second visit he informed the patient that her arm needed further atten-

* Gedney *vs.* Kingsley, 41 N. Y. S. R., 794, 16 N. Y. Supp., 792.

tion, but she thought she was getting on toward recovery, and said that she would send for him if she needed him further. The arm became very greatly swollen, and it was finally discovered that one of the bones was fractured. By reason of the delay in discovering the fracture the injury became in a measure irreparable. As usual, the parties differed in their remembrance of the facts. A physician who had examined the arm before the defendant, supported the defendant in his statement that the extent of the swelling prevented an examination which was needed to discover the fracture. The medical experts also differed upon the question whether a skillful surgeon ought to have discovered the fracture, but all agreed that the swelling should have been reduced; but, as to this, the court very properly expressed the opinion that if the patient prevented that by directing the physician to make no more calls until he was notified, he could not be blamed for omission to diligently look after the case. The jury found that the arm was so swollen that a complete assurance of the extent of the injury could not be made from a careful and skillful examination, and that the swelling was suffered to continue because the physician was told to wait until he was sent for to attend further. They consequently exonerated him.

Failure to Reduce Dislocation.—While in some cases, like the one above given, the question of the physician's liability for unskillfulness and negligence grows out of his failure to discover the extent of the injury sustained, it more frequently happens that the question of liability arises where the character and extent of the injury are discovered, but the fact of whether or not the physician effected the relief attempted is disputed. Questions of this sort frequently arise in cases of dislocation in which the injury is treated with supposed success, but after weeks, or perhaps months, it is found that the bones are not in proper place. Upon the trial of this class of cases the testimony is almost always conflicting, that of the patient tending to show that the dislocation was never properly reduced, while that of the physician positively denies the failure to properly reduce the dislocation, and accounts for the bones subsequently being found to be dislocated by negligence of the patient or his failure to observe instructions, or other similar cause.

In the case of Rowe vs. Lent,* the patient suffered a dislocation of the right shoulder. The family physician, after considerable effort and some difficulty, succeeded, as he claimed and still claims, in reducing the dislocation. The injury occurred in January, and the physician continued to attend the patient until July 24th following, when he claimed a cure had been effected. He frequently saw the patient, however, and examined

---

* Rowe vs. Lent, 42 N. Y. S. R., 483.

the shoulder between this date and August 13th, when the patient left his home, going to the seashore to take sea baths. On about the 14th of August the patient was examined at a New York city hospital, and it was found that his shoulder was dislocated. The surgeon in charge made an attempt to reduce the dislocation, but was unsuccessful. The injury still continues and is conceded to be permanent. Upon the question of whether or not the dislocation had ever been properly reduced, there was some non-professional testimony introduced at the trial that the right shoulder did not look like the left; but some of the expert testimony tended to show that the difference in appearance might exist even if the dislocation had been properly reduced.

The case was submitted to the jury, who found for the plaintiff. The general term of the supreme court refused to disturb the verdict of the jury, and, after laying down the general rule that a physician must possess a reasonable degree of learning and skill, said: " The test, however, seems to be, whether in the case on trial the requisite skill, care, and diligence were employed, and not whether the practitioner is reputed to possess such skill. But the surgeon is not necessarily chargeable with want of the requisite skill, or negligence and want of care, simply because he does not succeed in accomplishing the desired result. Human skill can not · relieve all infirmities, ills, or injuries to which mankind is subject, and the only test, therefore, that can be applied is whether in a given case the surgeon has exercised reasonable skill and attention in his treatment of the patient who has placed himself under his care, and whom the latter has undertaken to treat. As we have seen in this case, that the question was before the jury upon evidence somewhat conflicting, and the whole case was fully and fairly left to them by the charge of the trial judge given in an able and impartial manner, to which no exception was taken by the counsel for the defendant, and the jury upon this conflicting evidence found in favor of the plaintiff. While perhaps they might, upon this evidence, have found either for the plaintiff or defendant, there is sufficient evidence in support of their conclusion to uphold a verdict, and the court upon appeal can not say their verdict was either against the evidence or unsupported thereby." The foregoing quotation is made at this considerable length for the reason that it so clearly marks the policy of the courts and of the law in suits of this character.

An interesting suit, based upon the alleged failure of the physician to reduce a dislocation, is that of Carpenter *vs.* Blake, decided by the supreme court of New York in 1871. The patient was thrown from a horse and her elbow joint dislocated. The defendant was called to attend the injury and claims that he properly reduced the dislocation; the patient, on the other hand, claims that he did not succeed in restoring the bones to their places, or, if he did succeed in the original operation, that he failed to employ proper measures to keep them there, and upon this theory brought suit.

The evidence produced at the trial was voluminous and conflicting. The injury occurred on June 28th, and the defendant was called at once to attend the injury. The plaintiff testified that the physician simply drew the arm around his knee and placed it on a pillow at her side, bent at nearly a right angle; that she did not hear the characteristic " snap " caused by the bones falling into place, and that there was no relief from the pain.

The defendant testified that upon setting the joint he extended and rotated the arm and applied his hand to the joint, satisfying himself that the bones were in place; the plaintiff denied that he applied either of these tests. It is conceded that the defendant did not measure the arm to determine beyond peradventure that the bones were in proper position. The plaintiff and other witnesses testified that they observed a protuberance at the elbow joint the night of the injury, and compared it with the other elbow and inquired what it was. It appeared that the arm retained, when not controlled by splints, about the same position it was in after the first attempt to reduce the dislocation, and at no time could the plaintiff move it without pro-

17

ducing severe pain. The defendant insisted that she must move it. When she attempted it, the pain was so great she had to call for help, and even then had to cease the attempt because of the suffering it caused. This was known to the defendant, and yet it did not seem to put him on inquiry whether he had not failed to properly set or treat the arm. The plaintiff was satisfied that the joint was never properly set, and so told the defendant; and, to ascertain whether or not her suspicions were correct, called other doctors. This was in the latter part of August, about two months after the injury was received. The defendant deserted the case at about this time. Other physicians were then called, and, after rendering the patient unconscious by the use of anæsthetics, reduced the dislocation. The bones, however, soon returned to their former position, and have remained there ever since. The jury upon this evidence found for the plaintiff, assessing the damages sustained at two thousand dollars.

Failure to Apply Extension.—In the case of Barnes *vs.* Means * the improper treatment complained of was the failure of the physician to properly extend the broken limb from which the patient was suffering, whereby the wound healed improperly. The evidence showed that the fracture of the larger bone was oblique, and

---

* Barnes *vs.* Means, 82 Ill., 379.

near the upper part of the lower third of the limb; the fracture of the smaller bone was transverse, and was from two to three inches above the ankle joint. The defendants were called at once and dressed the injury within twenty or thirty minutes after the bones were broken, but did not use extension or counter-extension. The excuse made by the defendants for not extending the limb and using counter-extension to hold it in place was that the extreme tenderness and swelling would not permit of their so doing, and they introduced evidence to show that some days after the fracture was adjusted they did attempt extension and counter-extension, but that the patient could not endure it. Upon the question of the condition of the limb at the time the injury was first adjusted there were several witnesses who were then present and who testified that no swelling had then occurred.

An expert testified before the jury that the shortening was caused by the lapping of the bones; that the first duty of the surgeon was to bring the bones to their proper position by extension and counter-extension. If necessary he placed the patient under the influence of chloroform, and that if the patient would not allow a proper adjustment of the fracture he would abandon the case.

The trial judge, in instructing the jury upon the law applicable to the case, said: " That if you believe, from the evidence that, in the treatment of fractures of bones, regard should be had to the direction in which the break occurred; and if the jury believe, from the evidence, that the fracture of the bones of the plaintiff, which the defendants treated, required extension in order to secure the proper adjustment of the parts to each other, and that the defendants did not use any means to secure extension, but, by want of skill, or by negligence, suffered the broken fragments to be or become displaced, and that thereby the plaintiff has suffered and become permanently lame and disabled, as charged in the declaration, you should find the defendants guilty." Upon this instruction, which was held to be a correct statement of the law applicable to the case, the jury found for the plaintiff and assessed the damages at one thousand dollars.

The foregoing cases being thought sufficient to illustrate the application of the general rule of liability, a more critical examination will now be made as to the particular requirements of the rule.

Degree of Knowledge, Skill, and Care Required.— The part of the general rule upon which the courts seem to have found the greatest difficulty in agreeing is that relating to the amount or degree of knowledge, skill, and care that the physician is obliged to possess and exercise to escape from liability for injurious results that may follow his treatment. To place the test as that degree exercised by the *thoroughly educated* members of the profession would be manifestly unjust to the great majority of the physicians and surgeons, while a test requiring only that skill exercised by the *moderately educated* members would be equally unjust to the public. Upon this reasoning the supreme court of Iowa placed the test as the average of the skill and diligence ordinarily exercised by the profession as a whole.* While this rule is probably a just one and about right in theory, it is doubted whether any practising physician knows what is the " average of the skill and diligence ordinarily exercised by the profession as a whole," and, as he is the proper judge of whether a given act will stand this test, the utility of the rule is doubted.

While the degree of care necessary to be bestowed in a particular case is governed in a great degree by the requirements of that case, a rule of law demanding that the degree of care and skill required shall be proportionate to the severity of the injury or disease treated would manifestly work a great hardship upon the profession. Such a rule was very wisely and justly rejected by the supreme court of Illinois.†

The location of the particular practitioner should

---

* Smothers *vs*. Hanks, 34 Ia., 286; Almond *vs*. Nugent, 34 Ia., 300.
† Utley *vs*. Burns, 70 Ill., 162.

also be taken into consideration in determining the amount of knowledge and science he shall possess and the degree of care and skill he shall exercise, because, for reasons heretofore referred to, the physician and surgeon practising in our large cities may be reasonably required to possess higher qualifications than those in small towns or rural districts. This indulgence should not, however, be allowed to the country practitioners to the extent of permitting them in each particular neighborhood or community to establish by their own professional standing the standard of requirement for that community; for, in the words of Justice Worden, " there might be but few practising in the given locality, all of whom might be quacks, ignorant pretenders to knowledge not possessed by them, and it would not do to say that because one possessed and exercised as much skill as the other he could not be chargeable with the want of reasonable skill." After due regard for all of these conditions, a number of our courts in well-considered decisions have determined the proper test to be that there shall be required of the physician and surgeon that amount of knowledge, skill, and experience, and the exercise of that degree of care and skill which physicians practising in *similar localities* ordinarily possess and . exercise.*

* Whitesell *vs.* Hill, 101 Ia., 629, 37 L. R. A., 830, 70 N. W. Rep., 750.

Illustrations.—A case illustrating the application of the law very nicely is that of Small *vs.* Howard.* In this case the plaintiff, the whole inside of whose wrist had been cut through to the bone in such a manner as to sever all the arteries and tendons, called upon the defendant for treatment. The defendant was a physician and surgeon residing in a country town of about twenty-five hundred inhabitants, and had no experience in surgery beyond that usually had by country surgeons. The result of the treatment not being satisfactory, suit was commenced for malpractice in dressing and caring for the wrist. Upon the trial one expert called by the plaintiff testified that he did not think the average country surgeon would be likely to possess the requisite skill to care for this wound. The evidence of the experts regarding the propriety of the treatment given the injury was conflicting, some testifying that it was properly treated, others the contrary. The court, upon the principle in consideration, instructed the jury that " the defendant, undertaking to practise as a physician and surgeon in a town of comparatively small population, was bound to possess that skill only which physicians and surgeons of ordinary ability and skill, practising in similar localities, with opportunities for no larger experience, ordi-

* Small *vs.* Howard, 128 Mass., 131.

narily possess; and he was not bound to possess that high degree of art and skill possessed by eminent surgeons practising in large cities, and making a specialty of the practice of surgery. He is not responsible for want of success, unless it is proved to result from want of ordinary care and attention, and then only to the extent of the injury caused by his want of skill and neglect, nor for the whole consequence of the particular original injury or disease. He is not presumed to engage for extraordinary skill or extraordinary care and diligence."

The jury, applying this instruction to the evidence before them, found a verdict for the defendant. The plaintiff, being dissatisfied, appealed, but the trial of the case, including the instruction of the trial judge, from which the above quotation was taken, was approved by the supreme court.

The case of Hathorn *vs.* Richmond* is somewhat peculiar, and one in which there is considerable law. The plaintiff, whose leg was fractured, sent for his regular physician. The regular physician declined to take the responsibility of reducing the fracture and laid the leg on a double inclined splint, to make the patient as comfortable as possible. On the following day the defendant was sent for and reduced the fracture. The regular physician continued to attend the case nearly every

---

* Hathorn *vs.* Richmond, 48 Vt., 557.

day for about twenty-two days, when another physician was called to take his place. The defendant, who had reduced the fracture, did not call again until five days after the operation, and then only by reason of a letter written him by the regular physician at the request of the patient's friends, especially requesting him so to do. At the time of making this call the patient did not seem to be dissatisfied with the services rendered by the defendant and made no claim of improper treatment. For what purpose he was called, or what he did, if anything, while there, the report of the case does not show. It seems that the leg was bandaged too tightly, and as a result the injury followed for which suit was brought. The defendant claimed that he was only sent for to take charge of setting the leg with the assistance of the regular attending physician, and that he did this properly, and then left plaintiff in the hands of the regular physician as his patient, without any expectation of again visiting the case unless specially sent for. All the surgeons called on the part of the defendant testified that the surgeon applying the dressing in any such case could not tell whether the bandage might prove too tight or too loose, but that this matter must necessarily be left with the attending surgeon, whose duty it was to examine carefully in reference thereto, and adjust the dressing and bandages as might be needed. No evidence was offered to contradict this.

It was conceded and treated in the trial that the course taken with the limb in the interval between the time defendant left the patient after he had finished dressing the injury and his second visit, five days later, was lacking in proper and ordinary skill and care.

In the matter of general professional requirements, the trial judge instructed the jury, in effect, that the defendant would be held to possess such knowledge and skill and exercise such care and judgment as that ordinarily possessed and exercised by doctors in the same general neighborhood and in the same general lines of practice; and that they should determine from the evidence whether the defendant did possess such knowledge and skill; and if they decided this question in the affirmative they should determine whether he used ordinary care in dressing the leg. This instruction the supreme court held to be correct.

The trial judge continued with his instruction to the jury, charging them that if they found the defendant was wanting in the proper exercise of skill in the tightness of the bandage, still, if his employment ceased when he had set and dressed the limb, and the treatment of the case fell to the attending physician, and it was the duty of the attending physician to discover that the bandage was too tight and to loosen it and redress the limb, and if by such proper loosening and redressing of the limb the injury of the tight bandage could have been prevented, then the defendant would not be liable for the injury. The supreme court denied the correctness of the instruction upon the following grounds: It will be observed that this instruction assumes that the bandage was negligently applied by the defendant. From this fact it will necessarily follow that the improper application of the bandage will begin to exert an injurious influence upon the limb from the moment it is applied, and therefore it would be manifestly unjust to assert that the defendant is not liable for the injury inflicted by this negligently and improperly applied bandage during the ten or, perhaps, twenty-four hours which must elapse before the attending physician can detect the improper bandaging and give relief. Moreover, the court declined to intimate whether it would relieve the defendant from liability for the injury resulting from his improper bandaging after the time when the attending physician should have discovered that the bandage was too tight and given relief, or whether it would hold him liable for all damages resulting from his own improper bandaging and the assistant's negligence in failing to readjust the bandage. The judgment rendered for the defendant in the original trial was accordingly reversed and the case sent back for a new trial. In view of the open question left by this decision, it can hardly be considered prudent for a surgeon to dress an injured member and leave all subsequent treatment to the regular attending physician, relying upon him to correct any inadvertency which may have attended the original operation or treatment.

Rules for Determining Skill. — In determining whether or not a physician is possessed of the requisite amount of knowledge, or exercises the proper degree of skill, due regard must be had: First, to the school of medicine which he practises; and, second, to the advanced state of the profession at the time the particular services were rendered.

Practice of the Particular School Governs.—There being different and distinct schools of medicine, recognizing different principles and different modes of treatment, it follows that the treatment of a physician of one school must be tested by the general doctrines of his own school, and not by those of other schools.*

While the justice and, in fact, the necessity of this law are almost too evident to permit of comment, it will perhaps be desirable to examine one or two cases.

A case in which the rule was extended to a degree to which it could not be at this day, because of the more adequate laws protecting the public from quacks, is that of Bowman *vs.* Woods.† In this case the defendant

---

* Patten *vs.* Wiggin, 51 Me.. 594.
† Bowman *vs.* Woods, 1 Greene, Ia., 441.

claimed to be a botanic physician. The cause of action arose from alleged unskillful treatment of a patient in a confinement case. About thirty-six hours after the delivery a Dr. C. was called in as consulting physician, and upon the trial he testified in effect that at the time he arrived the placenta was not removed; that the patient was greatly prostrated by the severity of the labor and the loss of blood; and that she was also suffering from a distention of the bladder, which had not been evacuated since parturition. He gave it as his opinion that the placenta should have been removed and the distended state of the bladder relieved at a much earlier period; and that such delay would be likely to produce puerperal fever. Several other physicians, as witnesses, concurred in Dr. C.'s views of the practice.

The defendant then offered as evidence in his own behalf the testimony that he was a botanic physician, and that, according to the botanic system of practice and medicine, it is considered improper to remove the placenta, and that it should be permitted to remain until expelled by the efforts of Nature. The proof of these facts being objected to, they were ruled out by the trial judge. The supreme court, upon reviewing the case, was of the opinion that the trial court erred in not admitting the proffered evidence of the defendant. Justice Greene, after observing that the several schools of medicine were then alike unprohibited and enjoyed equal legal rights in Iowa,* said: "A person professing to follow one system of medical treatment can not be expected by his employer to practise any other. While the regular physician is expected to follow the rules of the old school in the art of curing, the botanic must be equally expected to adhere to his adopted method. But on the part of every medical practitioner the law implies an undertaking that he will use an ordinary degree of care and skill in medical operations, and he is unquestionably liable for gross carelessness or unskillfulness in the management of his patients; and still the person who employs a botanic practitioner has no right to expect the same kind of treatment or the same kind of medicine that a regular physician would administer. The law does not require a man to do more than he undertakes, nor in a manner different from that which he professes. Therefore, if in the case the defendant below could show that he was employed as a botanic physician, and that he performed the accouchement with ordinary skill and care, in accordance with the system he professed to follow, we should regard it as a legal defense. It would show a full compliance with his profession and undertaking; and if injury resulted from it to the plaintiff, he could properly blame no one but himself.

. . . .

" The people are free to select from the various

---

* This decision was rendered in 1848.

classes of medical men, who are accountable to their employers for all injuries resulting from a want of ordinary diligence and skill in their respective systems of treating diseases. It is to be lamented that so many of our citizens are disposed to trust health and life to novices and empirics, to new nostrums and new methods of treatment. But these are evils which the courts of justice possess no adequate power to remedy. Enlightened public opinion and judicious legislation may do much to discountenance quackery and advance medical science."

Upon reading this case one can not help rejoicing in the approximate realization of the prophetic hope expressed by the court, for at the present day, excepting in a few States, a defendant would be unable to invoke the protection of an unwilling court by showing that his vicious ignorance of the laws of medicine and of health was sanctioned by the so-called school he professed to follow.

A recent application of the rule is found in the case of Force *vs.* Gregory.* There the patient was treated for ophthalmia by the defendant, who is a homœopathic physician, and who introduced evidence to show that in treating the plaintiff he adopted the remedies prescribed by the homœopathic practitioners. The

---

* Force *vs.* Gregory, 63 Conn., 167.

plaintiff showed that the old-school practitioners would have treated such a case differently, and that she should have received the latter mode of treatment. The defendant's counsel asked the court to instruct the jury that the propriety of the treatment of the patient must be tested by the doctrines of the defendant's school of medicine. The court refused to give the instruction asked, but instead instructed the jury in such a way as to leave it uncertain whether the defendant's treatment was to be judged by the rules and practice of his own school alone, the instruction given being of the sort calculated to direct the attention of the jury to the relative merits of the two systems. Under this instruction the jury found a verdict for the plaintiff. The supreme court, in reviewing the case, disapproved of the instruction and reversed the judgment. In criticising the instruction given the jury Justice Fenn said: " The jury, we think, should have been told that the relative merits of the two schools were in no sense before them for their consideration; that so far as the defendant was to be judged by either, it was by the tenets, rules, principles, and practices of his own school, not by those of another; and if the defendant adopted the treatment laid down by his own school, the fact that another school prescribed another treatment tended in no wise to show that the defendant was chargeable with lack of skill or negligence. It would seem that if it could be held negligent or unskillful in a given case to use the treatment prescribed by the school to which the practitioner belonged, such negligence or want of skill must consist either in the mode of use, the application of such remedies under improper circumstances, or because they were intrinsically wrong, inappropriate, or inadequate. If there be any valid objection to the language quoted from Patten *vs.* Wiggin—viz., 'The jury are not to judge by determining which school, in their own view, is best'—it is in the failure to incorporate with the general statement the further one that the test there given does not exclude the duty of keeping pace with the progress of professional knowledge, ideas, and discoveries, to the extent that a faithful, conscientious, and competent practitioner, of whatever school, may be reasonably expected, and is therefore lawfully required to do."

Perhaps the case of greatest interest recorded in the law reports in which this question was raised is that of Nelson *vs.* Harrington.* In this case the defendant was a spiritualist or clairvoyant physician. The evidence showed that the patient, a boy of about fifteen years of age, accompanied by his father, called upon the defendant about September 1st. The boy was suffering from a disease of the hip joint, but the defendant diagnosti-

---

* Nelson *vs.* Harrington, 72 Wis., 591, 1 L. R. A., 719, 40 N. W. Rep., 228.

18

cated the disease as rheumatism and prescribed treatment accordingly. He continued to treat the case until about the middle of the January following, and during that time encouraged the patient in persistent walking, asserting that walking was beneficial to him. In January the leg became so much worse that he was unable to walk and suffered great pain. Other physicians were then called in and the patient was benefited, but will remain a cripple for life.

The counsel for the defendant urged that he professed the clairvoyant system of medicine, and that if he treated the patient with due care and skill in accordance with the rules and practice of that school or system of medicine he complied with the requirements of the law and was not liable for unfavorable results of his treatment.

The supreme court, in determining the weight to be given to this defense, carefully reviewed the methods of the alleged school of clairvoyants, which may be described as follows: The mode of diagnosis consists in going into a sort of trance condition, and while in such state discovering the condition of the patient and prescribing for the malady so disclosed. The spiritualist professes to have no medical knowledge, but trusts implicitly to the correctness of the diagnosis made and prescription given while in such state.

To constitute a school of medicine there must be

rules and principles of practice for the guidance of all its members, as respects diagnosis and remedies which each member is supposed to observe in any given case, and each competent practitioner of a certain school would treat a given case in substantially the same way. The court says: " And so one school may believe in the potency of drugs and bloodletting, and another may believe in the principle of *similia similibus curantur;* still another may believe in the potency of water, or of roots and herbs; yet each school has its own peculiar principles and rules for the government of its practitioners in the treatment of diseases." The court then observes that clairvoyants recognize one mode of practice only to the extent of obtaining a knowledge of the condition of their patients, but that the treatment prescribed by different clairvoyants differs as greatly in similar cases as that prescribed by physicians of entirely different schools, and that by prescribing such different remedies for the same disease they can be said to violate no rule or system of clairvoyant treatment. The court therefore concludes that those practising medicine as clairvoyants form no school of medicine, and have no particular system or rules by which they can be judged.

Regard must be had to the Advanced State of Medical Science.—The idea expressed by the court in the last part of the quotation from the opinion in the case of

Force *vs.* Gregory brings us to the subject next in order of consideration, which is, that in judging of the knowledge and skill displayed in a given case due regard must be had to the advanced state of medical science at the time the particular services were rendered. In referring to the improvements in medical and surgical science, and the right of the patient to the benefit of these improvements, Justice Woodward said nearly fifty years ago: " Discoveries in the natural sciences for the last half century have exerted a sensible influence on all the learned professions, but especially on that of medicine, whose circle of truths has been relatively much enlarged; and besides, there has been a positive progress in that profession resulting from the studies, the experiments, and the diversified practice of its professors. The patient is entitled to the benefits of these increased lights. The physician or surgeon who assumes to exercise the healing art is bound to be up to the improvements of the day." *

The application of the test is very well illustrated in the case of Gates *vs.* Fleischer.† In this case the plaintiff had recently given birth to a child, from which she suffered a slight laceration of the cervix. Not regaining her strength satisfactorily, she called in the de-

---

* McCandless *vs.* McWha, 22 Pa., 261.
† Gates *vs.* Fleischer, 67 Wis., 504.

fendant, about five or six weeks after the delivery of the child, to treat her. The defendant made a local examination, and stated that she was suffering from uterine disease, and applied caustics to the cervical canal on the theory that those parts were ulcerated. This treatment was continued for several months.

The defendant, deriving no benefit from this treatment, after a lapse of about eight months consulted a specialist, who found the cervical canal entirely closed. This was opened by artificial means. The evidence also showed that during the entire time of her illness the plaintiff was suffering from septicæmia.

Upon the trial of the case evidence was given to the effect that there was no ulcerated condition of either the uterus or the cervical canal, and that the treatment with caustics was unjustifiable; that advanced medical science discards the use of caustics in cases of ulceration, as a dangerous practice; and that the treatment applied had caused cicatrix in the cervical canal, etc. The trial court, in instructing the jury upon the law applicable to the case, told them that the physician was bound to bring to the treatment of the case such skill as is ordinarily possessed and exercised by physicians and surgeons in such localities, " having regard to the advanced state of the profession at the time of the treatment." This instruction the supreme court held to be entirely proper and suited to the evidence adduced at the trial.

In the case of Almond *vs.* Nugent,* the opinion of Chief-Justice Beck reviews several important features of the ground just passed over in such a masterly way that the following extended quotation is taken therefrom. The chief justice said : " The first one [of the instructions] is clearly objectionable in holding the civil responsibility of the surgeon to be governed by the same rules of law as those that apply to mechanics and to others engaged in some of the other pursuits mentioned. As a general rule, mechanics are answerable for results, and the real test of their skill is the success of their work. Not so with the physician and surgeon. They are required to exercise due skill, but are not responsible if the desired result fails. The skillful mechanic will always be successful. The materials which he undertakes to shape and fashion are subject to known laws, and are completely under his control. The surgeon and physician apply their skill to human bodies which are subject to laws, both physical and mental, almost infinite in number—many uncertain and many unknown. The diseases which they combat are not under the full dominion of human skill and wisdom. They are not expected to resist and avert the approach of death, which ultimately destroys all.

" The third instruction above quoted is equally ob-

---

* Almond *vs.* Nugent, 34 Ia., 300.

jectionable. The thought that the physician and surgeon are required to keep up with the progress of the day in their respective professions accords with my views (expressed in a previous case). . . . But the rule announced, that the practitioner must apply himself to the 'most accredited source of knowledge,' imposes a requirement that can not be admitted. It demands that the surgeon shall be educated by instructors of the most established reputation, that he shall resort to schools of the widest fame, and study books of the first authority. The rule condemns all knowledge not acquired in this way, and fixes, as a standard of ordinary skill, attainments gained from the prescribed course of preparation for the discharge of professional duties. . . . Humble and unknown instructors of obscure schools may be sources from which the professional man may gain thorough knowledge of the principles of his profession. . . . The law requires skill and makes no inquiry as to the source whence it is obtained.

" The last sentence of the instruction under consideration is, if possible, more faulty. It holds the surgeon liable in damages if he fails to exercise his art or profession rightly and truly as he ought. Here absolute accuracy and certainty are demanded. No allowance is made for failure to administer the proper remedy in cases where the highest skill will leave the professional man in doubt at the time he is required to act. As we have before remarked, many laws of Nature, applicable to the administration of remedies for the diseases of the human body, are not fully understood; many are unknown. In obedience to an occult law an approved remedy may fail. Symptomatic indications often refuse to inform the physician or surgeon of the real disease which his skill is called upon to combat, and an autopsy reveals, too late, conditions of the organs of the patient, that could have been discovered in no other way, which demanded a different course of treatment. As it is impossible for the surgeon or physician, possessing even the highest degree of skill, always to act rightly and truly as he ought, the practitioner should not be held liable if, in the faithful and honest exercise of ordinary skill, which is only demanded, he fails to use the right remedy."

Best Judgment Required.—It will be remembered that the general standard of professional requirements is that the physician must possess a reasonable degree of knowledge, skill, and experience; second, that he must exercise ordinary care and diligence; and third, that he will use his best judgment in all cases of doubt. Having scrutinized the first two requirements of this standard, attention will now be particularly given to the third.

It may be considered an axiom, *de facto* as well as legal, that one can not use good judgment in the treatment of a case without first possessing the adequate amount of knowledge and skill and exercising the proper degree of care. Dr. McClelland,* in his collection of malpractice cases, cites the case of Courtney *vs.* Henderson, decided in the marine court of New York, in which a man, fifty-seven years of age, who had been under the care of an eye infirmary for eight weeks, was induced to withdraw from that institution and put himself under the defendant's treatment. While in the infirmary there was a gradual improvement of his eyes, but soon after placing himself under the care of the defendant the improvement ceased, the disease became more aggravated, and the eyesight gradually failed. The defendant treated the eyes about three months, and during this time performed an operation upon them and put some kind of powder into them. At the end of the three months' treatment the plaintiff returned to the eye infirmary, but his vision was gone, never to return. The only expert evidence offered was that of two physicians from the infirmary, who testified that they had no doubt the plaintiff would have recovered under proper treatment. They also testified to their mode of treatment in such cases, which differed materially from that of the defendant. It seems that no expert evidence was offered showing that the defendant's treatment was

* McClelland on *Civil Malpractice*, p. 273.

either skillful or proper, nor any evidence to show that he was a qualified physician and surgeon. The defendant's counsel urged that the failure of the defendant to properly treat the plaintiff was the result of an error in judgment, and for that he was not liable. The court held that this was a good defense when applied to one skilled in the science of medicine, but that the defendant, knowing nothing of anatomy, surgery, or physics, was incapable of having judgment in the matter. The court accordingly affirmed the judgment rendered in favor of the plaintiff and against the defendant for malpractice.

The law, it has been observed, requires only that the knowledge possessed and the care and skill exercised shall be " ordinary " or " usual," but the judgment must be the physician's *best judgment.* What is one's best judgment is, from the nature of the case, absolutely impossible to determine, the judgment of no two men being the same in all respects. Because of the uncertainty of a rule of liability based upon the judgment of the party whose actions were the subject of litigation, an English court refused to entertain the plea that an error of judgment was a defense. Justice Tindal, in that case, said: " Instead, therefore, of saying that the liability for negligence should be coextensive with the judgment of each individual, which would be as varied as the length of the foot of each individual, we ought rather to adhere to the rule which requires in all cases a regard to caution such as a man of ordinary prudence would observe." * The justice did not, at the time of uttering these words, have in mind the judgment of a professional man exercised in performing the functions of his profession, yet the principle will apply, for the exercise of judgment must be such as not only to preclude the idea of professional incompetency and of a want of reasonable care, but the judgment itself must be consistent with the use of that degree of skill that it is the duty of every surgeon to bring to the treatment of a case, according to the standard of skill and care indicated.† For this reason nothing short of one's best judgment is adequate.

A physician who possesses the requisite amount of knowledge and skill, and exercises his best judgment in determining upon such treatment as experience has shown him to be best, is not liable in damages from an injury resulting from an error of judgment.‡ Such judgment, in order to be a complete protection to the physician, must, however, have been exercised in a case where competent physicians might honestly doubt as to the nature of the disease or the proper method of treating it. In such a case all that the law requires is that a physician shall summon to his assist-

---

* Vaughan *vs.* Menlove, 3 Bing., N. C., 468.

† West *vs.* Martin, 31 Mo., 375.

‡ Vanhooser *vs.* Berghoff, 90 Mo., 488.

ance all of his knowledge and skill, and in the light of
their aid exercise his best judgment. If, however, the
case is such a one that no physician possessing ordinary
knowledge and skill would doubt or hesitate, and but
one course of treatment would be suggested by a competent professional man, then any other course of treatment might be evidence of a want of ordinary knowledge
or skill, or proper care or attention.* In determining
whether or not a physician may safely exercise his judgment in a given case he should first consider his general
qualifications as a practitioner of medicine and his competency to handle the particular case; for if he is competent to treat the case, but is in doubt as to the nature
and extent of the injury or the proper mode of treatment, he is justified, and it is his duty, to use his best
judgment in deciding upon the nature of the disease or
injury and fixing upon a course of treatment, and also
as to whether or not he will consult with some other physician and surgeon. But if, on the other hand, he is not
competent to treat the case, or feels that he is not competent, he should recommend the patient to some other
physician.†

Theoretically, it is not difficult to lay down a rule
which commends itself both to our reason and our sense
of justice, defining those errors of judgment from which

---

* Patten *vs.* Wiggin, 51 Me., 594.
† Mallen *vs.* Boynton, 132 Mass., 443.

no cause of action should arise. Such a rule is the one
laid down by Justice Richmond, which is that " Physicians are not responsible for the errors of an enlightened judgment, where good judgments may differ; and
I can come to no other conclusion than that, when there
are reasonable grounds for doubt and difference of opinion, the professional man, after the exercise of his best
judgment, admitting that he possesses the necessary
knowledge, is not responsible for errors of judgment or
mistakes, and is only chargeable with errors which could
not have arisen except for the want of or the exercise of
reasonable skill and diligence." *   But it is in the practical application of such a rule that the difficulty lies.
What things must the physician know as a matter of
knowledge and what may he assume through the exercise of his best judgment?   In the case of Du Bois *vs.*
Decker † the plaintiff had a portion of his foot crushed
beneath the wheels of a locomotive. The physician, hop-
ing to save the foot, deferred amputation for nine days;
then, seeing that the foot could not be saved, amputated
the leg just above the ankle. Shortly afterward gangrene appeared, rendering further operation necessary.
At the trial evidence was given tending to show that the
bones of the foot were so crushed that immediate amputation of the injured portion was necessary, and that

* Burnham *vs.* Jackson, 1 Colo. App., 237.
† Du Bois *vs.* Decker, 130 N. Y., 325.

the appearance of gangrene was in consequence of the delay in operating. The counsel for the defendant claimed that the defendant, in the exercise of his best judgment, believed the foot might be saved, and that he could not be held liable for an error of judgment. But the court failed to agree with the defendant's counsel; it said: " But his judgment must be founded upon his intelligence. He engages to bring to the treatment of the patient care, skill, and knowledge, and he should have known the probable consequences that would follow from the crushing of the bones and tissues of the foot." On the other hand, if the injury sustained in such a case were not so serious as to preclude the probability of the recovery of the injured member, and the defendant were to produce competent and skilled physicians at the trial to testify that a recovery might be reasonably expected, and that the course of treatment adopted by the defendant was proper or best calculated to effect a recovery, then no reason can be seen why the defendant should not have been released from all liability.

A physician in the exercise of his judgment is not bound to anticipate or foresee any unusual or improbable result of his treatment. In the case of Bogle vs. Winslow,* the plaintiff, who had a few days previously received a severe blow on the head, called upon the de-

---

* Bogle vs. Winslow, 5 Phil. (Pa.), 136.

fendant, a dentist, for the purpose of having some teeth extracted. The defendant administered chloroform and took out the teeth. A few hours afterward the plaintiff complained of numbness of one side, which in a few days was followed by a stroke of paralysis. The plaintiff brought suit against the dentist, claiming that the paralysis was the direct result of the chloroform. Considerable expert evidence was given, most of it to the effect that paralysis could not result from the use of chloroform. Some testified that it might result from the use of such an anæsthetic. There was also evidence that the severe blow on the head received by the plaintiff might have produced a latent disease only requiring some exciting cause to rouse it into activity.

The judge was of the opinion that if the administering of the chloroform or the extraction of the teeth was the cause of plaintiff's paralysis, still it would not be just to make the defendant answer in damages for consequences which he could not foresee, and which were not the ordinary or probable result of what he did. The jury was so instructed and found a verdict for the defendant.

The rule that a physician is bound to exercise his best judgment being one of universal application, it necessarily follows that when he is called upon by a patient to perform an operation which in his judgment is unwise or unnecessary, he is bound to advise against such operation whether his opinion is asked or not. In the case of Gramm *vs.* Boener * the defendant had set the plaintiff's arm. Several weeks after, the bones appeared slightly out of place, either from having become displaced or from not having been originally accurately adjusted. The plaintiff asked the defendant to rebreak and readjust the bones, but the defendant advised against the operation. He told the plaintiff that to rebreak the bones would be of no use; that it had better be left alone, and that he ought not to think of it. But upon the plaintiff's insistence, he finally performed the operation. The result was so unsatisfactory that suit was brought. In the supreme court, upon the appeal of the case, the question arose whether the defendant was justified in finally deferring to the judgment of the patient and breaking the arm, or whether he should have refused to operate altogether when such an operation was contrary to his own best judgment. The supreme court was of the opinion that the defendant had incurred no liability under the circumstances in operating. Upon this question Justice Worden said : " But if a surgeon, when thus called, advises a patient who is of mature years and of sound mind that the operation is unnecessary and improper—in short, advises against the performance—and the patient still insists upon the per-

* Gramm *vs.* Boener, 56 Ind., 497.

formance of the operation, in compliance with which the surgeon performs it, we do not see upon what principle the surgeon can be held responsible to the patient for damages, on the ground that the operation was improper and injurious. In such cases the patient relies upon his own judgment, and not upon that of the surgeon, as to the propriety of the operation; and he can not complain of an operation performed at his own instance and upon his own judgment, and not upon that of the surgeon."

If in the physician's best judgment it is advisable to withhold from a patient in a particular emergency a knowledge of the danger and extent of his disease, he will be justified in so doing. So, when a physician, in attending a patient who was suffering from a felon, told her that her hand was doing well, and that she ought to be thankful that it was so well, he was held to have incurred no liability thereby, it not appearing that the patient desired to secure counsel, or was deterred by the physician's statement from so doing.*

Nor is there any legal necessity that the physician should acquaint the patient with the character of the operation or treatment he proposes to employ.† The advisability of such a step is purely a matter of judg-

---

* Twombly vs. Leach, 65 Mass., 397.
† Boydston vs. Giltner, 3 Ore., 118.

ment, and in such matters the exercise of the physician's best judgment is all that the law requires.

Refusal by Physician of Proffered Assistance does not Increase his Obligations.—Having once assumed charge of a case, the degree of knowledge, skill, and care which the law requires a physician to possess and exercise is not altered by the fact that he refuses the proffered assistance of other medical men. His refusal in such a case is simply an implied declaration of his ability to treat the case properly, and its effect is neither to increase nor decrease the degree of knowledge, skill, and care which the law makes it his duty to have and exercise.*

Admission of Inadequate Skill.—If, on the other hand, the physician frankly informs the patient that he has not sufficient skill or experience to treat the particular case or injury, the degree of skill that can reasonably be required of him is thereby materially decreased.† Such an admission will not, however, relieve the physician from liability when he continues his services with the assistance of another physician or surgeon. In a case of this sort the liability is a question of fact to be determined by the jury, who, in arriving at their conclusion, must determine whether there was such a degree of ignorance or unskillfulness displayed

---

* Potter *vs.* Warner, 91 Pa. St., 362.

† Shearman and Redfield on Negligence, § 607.

as to justify holding the defendant liable to the plaintiff in damages, notwithstanding his admission. In the case of Lorenz *vs.* Jackson,* the plaintiff had been injured by being struck by a piece of steel from a broken hammer, which passed through two pairs of trousers and buried itself in his left leg above the knee. After receiving the injury he rode about a mile on a handcar, and then walked about five hundred feet to his home. Soon afterward the defendant arrived and examined the wound, but was unable to find the piece of steel; he announced that the wound was of a serious character and that he did not regard himself as sufficiently experienced in surgery to properly treat the case, and advised that a more skilled and experienced surgeon be called in. Another doctor was accordingly secured. Together the doctors administered ether, and the physician last summoned probed for the piece of steel, widening the wound in the limb, and thereafter applied bandages. The doctor first summoned remained with the patient all night, administering to him hypodermic injections of morphine and atropine. The treatment continued for about eight days, when it was discovered that dry gangrene had ensued. A third physician was then called to take charge of the case, who soon determined upon and performed an amputation. Much evi-

* Lorenz *vs.* Jackson, 88 Hun, 200.

dence was given upon the trial respecting the treatment of the patient by the first two physicians called, but what that evidence was the report of the case does not show. The judge, upon submitting the case to the jury, charged them in effect that " if the practitioner frankly informed the patient of his want of skill, or if the patient is in some other way fully aware of it, he can not complain of the lack of that which he knew did not exist." Notwithstanding, the jury returned a verdict in favor of the plaintiff, assessing his damages at three thousand dollars. This verdict the supreme court refused to disturb.

Liability for Negligence of Student.—It has been observed that a physician and surgeon is entitled to compensation for the services of his apprentice or student practising under his direction. As a logical result, he should be held responsible for the negligence or want of skill in such assistant. This has been held to be the law in England,* and this case will probably be considered an authoritative precedent in America.

Must follow Established Practice.—One of the rules which the law strictly enforces for the protection of the public is that when there is an established practice or mode of treatment for a particular disease or injury the physician must conform to professional custom and

* Hancke *vs.* Hooper, 7 C. and P., 81.

adopt the established treatment, but will not be permitted to experiment without incurring liability for resulting injuries.*

The reason for the rule, also an indication of the extent to which it will be enforced, is well expressed in the case of Carpenter *vs.* Blake,† where the court said: " Some standard, by which to determine the propriety of treatment, must be adopted; otherwise experiment will take the place of skill, and the reckless experimentalist the place of the educated, experienced practitioner. If the case is a new one, the patient must trust to the skill and experience of the surgeon he calls; so must he if the injury or the disease is attended with injury to other parts, or other diseases have developed themselves, for which there is no established mode of treatment. But when the case is one as to which a system of treatment has been followed for a long time, there should be no departure from it, unless the surgeon who does it is prepared to take the risk of establishing by his success the propriety and safety of his experiment.

" The rule protects the community against reckless experiments, while it admits the adoption of new remedies and modes of treatment only when their benefits have been demonstrated, or when, from the necessity of

---

* Hesse *vs.* Knippel, 1 Brown (Mich. N. P.), 109.

† Carpenter *vs.* Blake, 60 Barb., 488.

the case, the surgeon or physician must be left to the exercise of his own skill and experience."

The question of when a method of treatment is considered sufficiently settled or established as to be the only safe one for a physician to adopt has given the courts some trouble. This question is, however, one rather of fact, to be determined from the evidence with the aid of testimony of expert witnesses, than of law. In the case of Slater vs. Baker and Stapleton,* decided in England in 1767, the evidence showed that a surgeon and an apothecary were employed to treat a leg which had been broken and set. In treating this leg they rebroke it and applied a new instrument. The evidence of experts was to the effect that when the callus had formed to any degree it was bad practice to rebreak the leg; and that in the present case the callus must have formed to such a degree as to render the operation improper and contrary to recognized practice. The surgeon who performed the operation was a man of recognized ability and high professional standing. The court refused to set aside a judgment for the plaintiff and closed its opinion by saying: " For anything that appears to the court, this was the first experiment made with this new instrument, and if it was it was a rash action, and he who

---

* Slater vs. Baker and Stapleton, 2 Wilson's R., 359.

acts rashly acts ignorantly; and although the defendants in general may be as skillful in their respective professions as any two gentlemen in England, yet the court can not help saying that in this particular case they have acted ignorantly and unskillfully, contrary to the known rule and usage of surgeons."

In the case of Winner vs. Lathrop * the patient was suffering from a- fracture of the radius. The defendant reduced the fracture several hours after the injury, and, so far as the evidence shows, seems to have performed the operation skillfully and in accord with the most approved methods known to the profession. There was, however, evidence given by the defendant to the effect that the defendant directed that the injured part be bathed in a decoction of wormwood and vinegar, which the expert testimony condemned.

The injured arm was not perfectly restored to its former usefulness; the wrist remained to some extent stiff, the rotary motion of the arm was obstructed, and the usefulness of the hand was permanently impaired. For this reason suit was brought, and judgment obtained in the trial court against the defendant for fifty dollars. The supreme court, upon appeal, was of the opinion that no unskillfulness in the treatment of the arm had been shown, and that application of wormwood

---

* Winner vs. Lathrop, 67 Hun, 511.

and vinegar to the injury, even if proved, was not such a departure from approved medical treatment as to justify a recovery against the defendant.

A case rich in instruction upon the point in consideration is that of Jackson *vs.* Burnham.* The plaintiff was suffering from phimosis, and the defendant, instead of slitting up the prepuce, applied a flaxseed-meal poultice, which aggravated the malady and accelerated gangrene, and resulted in the destruction and loss of the organ. Upon the trial of the case the trial judge instructed the jury, among other things, that: " If you find from the evidence that this defendant, in the treatment of the plaintiff, omitted the ordinary or established mode of treatment, and pursued one that has proved injurious, it is of no consequence how much skill he may have; he has demonstrated a want of it in the treatment of the particular case, and is liable in damages." The supreme court, upon review of the case, criticised this instruction, saying, in effect, that as an abstract proposition of law it was not absolutely correct, because it did not give an opportunity for the exercise of enlightened judgment in cases involving doubt, or where there was reasonable ground for difference of opinion as to the nature of the disease and the proper mode of treatment. But as

* Jackson *vs.* Burnham, 20 Colo., 532.

applied to the present case, where the evidence showed by a strong preponderance that the disease from which the plaintiff was suffering was phimosis, and that the proper method of treating this condition is to slit the prepuce to the corona, relieving the tension or strangulated condition and permitting the restoration of circulation, the instruction could not have misled the jury to the prejudice of the defendant.

In cases of this sort the court held that the test by which to determine whether a physician is bound to follow a particular mode of treatment for a given condition is whether or not that mode of treatment is upheld by a consensus of opinion of the members of his profession. The court said when the method of treatment is so upheld, "it should be followed by the ordinary practitioner; and if a physician sees fit to experiment with some other mode, he should do so at his peril."

For the purpose of more fully illustrating the application of the rules and principles of law laid down in the foregoing pages of this chapter the character of the defense of the defendant in this case will be examined. The defendant admitted that the proper remedy for phimosis was that testified to by the expert witnesses and above given; but he denied that the plaintiff was suffering from phimosis. He maintained that the swollen condition of the organ was the result of an ulceration of the urinary canal and that the treatment prescribed for him was proper for such a condition. The defendant's counsel urged that, admitting the defendant had erred in diagnosticating the case and that the true condition was phimosis, then the error was one of judgment for which the defendant could not be held responsible.

Upon the trial of the case, after all of the evidence was introduced, the trial judge properly instructed the jury upon the duties of the physician: that he must possess ordinary, etc., skill and knowledge; that he must use ordinary care and diligence; and that in all cases of doubt he must use his best judgment; but that in cases where competent physicians might honestly differ as to the nature of the disease the defendant should not be held responsible for an error of judgment reached by the exercise of due skill and care, etc. While the records of the case do not show that there were any special findings of fact returned by the jury, yet the conclusion necessarily follows from their verdict, which gave the plaintiff damages to the amount of five thousand dollars, that they found, from the evidence submitted, either that the defendant was incompetent or, if competent, that he did not exercise ordinary skill and care in diagnosticating the case; and that the case was not one in which competent physicians might honestly differ in their opinion as to the nature and extent of the disease after making a careful and proper examination.

Failure to give Proper Instructions.—Nor does the physician's liability necessarily end when he has treated the patient with all due skill and care, exercising proper judgment and using the most approved methods of treatment.

If the character of the injury or disease is such that any particular method of nursing is necessary to avoid an aggravation of the injury or prevent a relapse, or if the patient's welfare requires that he shall observe certain rules or practices, or shall avoid any particular indulgence, the physician is bound to inform the nurse or patient, or both, as the case may require, of the condition he wishes to avoid, and give them proper instructions as to the care and treatment best calculated to conduce to a cure. In the case of Carpenter *vs.* Blake the court said: " If, in case of dislocation of the elbow joint, it is enough for the physician to replace the bones, and to put the arm on a pillow, with the part below the joint at a right angle with that above it, and direct the application of cold water, it would seem to be proper, if not necessary, that the attending surgeon should inform the patient, or those having charge of him or her, of the necessity of maintaining that position; and if there is a tendency in the limb to become straight, or if in consequence of the severity of the injury to the ligaments about the joint there is great pain, which renders the patient nervous and restless, thus increasing the

tendency of relaxation, or to straighten, and, as a consequence, to stiffen the joint, the danger should be disclosed, to the end that all proper precaution may be
taken to prevent it. It is insisted that these dangers
were imminent, and yet no word was given. This was,
in my judgment, culpable negligence; much of the suffering the plaintiff has undergone, and much of the
loss she has sustained, might have been prevented had
the defendant done what it was clearly his duty to do,
if he knew the consequences which might result from
redislocating the joint or straightening the arm." *

In the case of Beck vs. The German Klinik et al., †
the evidence showed that the plaintiff, who had broken
his leg, employed the defendants, viz., the German Klinik, an incorporated hospital, and certain physicians
and surgeons members of that concern, to treat him;
that the methods and appliances which were used in the
treatment of the case were such as were used and approved of by physicians who were possessed of and who
exercised at least the average skill of the medical profession as a body at that time; and that the treatment
seemed to have been proper and skillful, and the leg,
when the splints and bandages were removed, appeared
all right. The evidence also showed that after the gyp-

---

* Carpenter vs. Blake, 60 Barb., 488.
† Beck vs. German Klinik et al., 78 Ia., 696, 43 N. W. Rep., 617,
7 L. R. A., 566.

sum bandages, used to keep the bones in place, were removed, the defendants directed the plaintiff to use his limb and to walk with crutches, but that they gave him no further directions as to the manner or extent of such use. The evidence further showed, or tended to show, that the broken bone had not well united, either because of improper treatment or because of its diseased condition, and that when the bandages were removed, or soon thereafter, the limb at the wounded part was crooked, and that it became necessary to perform an amputation. An expert witness testified upon examination of the limb after amputation, that there was a diseased condition of the bone which might have been caused by " a splinter or a muscle getting between the bones; and in that case walking would irritate and produce a tendency to disease." He further said: " I would instruct my patient not to walk on a leg I found not united." " The least weight of the foot, after patient commenced walking, would tend to separate at the top " (pointing to a portion of the bone, having the amputated limb before him). " If the bone, when set, confined in its apparatus for eight weeks, came out in that crooked condition or form, then the tendency of the use of that limb in walking would impair its efficiency and would induce disease." The court, in commenting upon the legal effect of the evidence above given, said: " The jury were authorized to find that plaintiff had no correct instructions as to the proper care and use of his wounded leg; and that he had wrong instructions which directed him to use his leg; that the diseased condition was caused or aggravated by the use of the leg, which the defendants directed, and that with proper instructions, which we will presume plaintiff would have followed, his leg would have been saved, or at least the disease of the bone would have been ameliorated and he would have escaped much suffering." " Defendants may have exercised proper care and used proper skill in all things, yet, under the law of the case, if they omitted to give plaintiff proper instructions for the care and use of his wounded leg they were rightly held liable by the jury. As we have said, the jury were authorized to find for plaintiff under the evidence on the ground of defendants' negligence by omission to discharge their duty to instruct plaintiff as to the care and use of his injured leg."

In a recent Ohio case * the trial judge, in instructing the jury regarding this duty of the physician, stated the law very clearly; he said: " It is the duty of the surgeon, when he takes charge of a case, such as a broken femur bone, to give his patient all necessary and proper instruction as to what care and attention the patient should give his broken limb in the absence of the sur-

---

* Tish vs Welker et al., 4 Ohio Leg. News, 433.

geon, and the caution to be used in the use of the limb before it is entirely healed."

The case in which this instruction of law was required by the facts at issue happened to be one in which the patient had suffered from a fracture of the femur—hence the narrowness of its scope; the law applies equally well, however, whether the patient be suffering from a fractured femur or a fractured rib, or whether the affliction be typhoid fever or mumps. Proper and necessary instructions are in all cases required by the law.

Liability for Improperly Discontinuing Attendance. —In an earlier chapter of this work the implied contract of the physician that he will continue his attendance upon the patient so long as his condition shall require it has been considered. Should a physician fail to pay due regard to this obligation and cease his attendance at a time when by the exercise of an honest and properly educated judgment he might have determined that his services were still required, he will be liable to an action for damages resulting therefrom.*

Justice Pryor, in an instruction to the jury, expressed the law very clearly and forcibly. He said:"The defendant was called to treat the plaintiff for a miscar-

---

* Dale *vs.* Donaldson Lumber Co., 48 Ark., 188.

riage. He visited her the day of her misfortune and the two succeeding days; but he never came afterward. It is not denied that when he ceased his visits she was not cured of her malady. His retainer was for no definite period. Upon this state of facts the question is, Did the defendant violate his duty to the plaintiff by his abandonment of her? When a physician engages, as here, to attend a patient without limitation of time, he can not cease his visits except, first, with the consent of the patient; or, secondly, upon giving the patient timely notice, so that he may employ another doctor; or, thirdly, when the condition of the patient is such as no longer to require medical treatment, and of that condition the physician must judge at his peril. Here it is not shown that the plaintiff was no longer in need of medical attention; so that the defendant had no right to discontinue his attendance, unless either the plaintiff consented or he gave her proper notice; and if he left her without such consent or such notice he was guilty of grave professional negligence. The defendant swears that at his last visit he notified the plaintiff that he was going out of town, and indicated to her a physician who would attend her in his stead. If this statement be true, the defendant's absence is excused, and you must exonerate him from this imputation of neglect. But the defendant's story is denied by the plantiff's witnesses, and their testimony tends to prove that he abandoned her without leave and without notice." *

Upon the law governing this liability there seems to be no question or disagreement, it is upon the facts that the parties conflict, the defendant usually testifying that he notified the patient of his inability to render further services; the patient, on the other hand, testifying that no such notice was given.†

In the cases considered above the services of the physicians were rendered at the patients' homes, but the principle of law controlling is the same when the services are rendered by the physician at his office. Of course, if the patient comes to the office of a physician from whom he has received proper treatment and then fails to return for further treatment, in consequence of which he suffers injury, the physician is not liable to an action for such injury.‡ But if a physician who is receiving and treating a patient at his office fails through his own fault or neglect to meet the patient at the usual or proper time and place, whereby the patient suffers injury, then the physician is liable in damages to the amount of the injury so sustained.

Right to Leave Practice Temporarily.—The preceding question brings us to the consideration of when and

<hr>

* Becker *vs.* Janinski, 27 Abb. N. C., 45.

† Ballou *vs.* Prescott, 64 Me., 305; Barbour *vs.* Martin, 62 Me., 536.

‡ Dashiell *vs.* Griffith, 84 Md., 363.

20

under what circumstances the physician may with legal safety go away and leave his practice. The law books show very few cases throwing light upon this question, which probably argues that physicians exercise great care in determining when they may safely leave their practice, and also in selecting competent substitutes to whose care the health and lives of their patients are to be temporarily intrusted.

As a general rule it can be laid down that a physician should never go away and leave his practice without arranging for some competent physician to attend his patients,* but under what circumstances and conditions he is justified in leaving his patients in the care of such a physician is not quite so clear.

It is very easy to see upon principle that a physician, possessing adequate skill and knowledge to enable him to understand the condition of his patients, who, by the careful exercise of his good judgment, determines with a reasonable degree of certainty that they are beyond the point of danger, may safely leave them under the care of a competent substitute; but whether the law will require so high a test of care is doubted. We have but just quoted an instruction from Justice Pryor, in which he said: "The defendant swears that at his last visit he notified the plaintiff that he was

---

* Pelky *vs.* Palmer, 109 Mich., 561, 67 N. W., 561.

going out of town, and indicated to her a physician who would attend her in his stead. If this statement be true, the defendant's absence is excused, and you must exonerate him from this imputation of neglect." *
While in this case the patient was without doubt in grave need of medical attendance, yet there is no evidence shown in the report that her life was in imminent danger or that she was even in a critical condition. And, again, in the case of Dashiell *vs.* Griffith.† Justice Roberts says: " If the defendant had in his treatment of the finger, prior to the 24th of February, exercised reasonable care, skill, and diligence, and then, because of the illness of his father, had turned the plaintiff over to Dr. ——, a competent physician, for the further treatment of her finger, and the plaintiff refused to go to Dr. —— for treatment, then the liability of the defendant ceased." But here again the plaintiff was merely suffering from a felon, and when the defendant last saw the patient it was thought that the diseased member was doing as well as might be expected. In the case of Ewing *vs.* Goode,‡ decided in the United States circuit court, the defendant had operated upon the plaintiff for a cataract. The operation took place on the 25th of September; it

---

* Becker *vs.* Janinski, 27 Abb. N. C., 45.

† Dashiell *vs.* Griffith, 84 Md , 363.

‡ Ewing *vs.* Goode, 78 Fed., 442.

was characterized a smooth and successful operation, and the wound was quite healed in about ten days. About the 19th of November following the plaintiff complained of pain in the eye; the defendant carefully explored the eye with the ophthalmoscope, but could discover no cause for the pain. The pain continued, and repeated examinations were made at short intervals apart, but, as no cause for the pain could be found in the eye, it was diagnosticated as neuralgia of the fifth nerve and treated as such. On the 9th of December the defendant thought he saw a slight increase in the tension of the eye, but was doubtful about it. This was a symptom indicating glaucoma, and one for which the eye had been carefully examined at short intervals since the pain commenced; the defendant accordingly prescribed eserine. On the 10th of December the defendant examined the eye again and found no increased tension and no other evidence of a glaucomatous condition, though the pains continued. On the 11th of December he confirmed his conclusion that there was no increased tension by making another examination. After this he remained in the city until the 18th of December, and receiving no calls from the plaintiff went away, leaving his practice in the hands of a competent physician, who understood the plaintiff's case and had assisted in the operation on the eye and had examined it after the pain commenced. On January

6th the defendant returned and found an increased tension amounting to $+1$ and distinct symptoms of glaucoma. An operation was promptly performed with the hope of relieving the pain and retaining the eyeball. This operation proving unsuccessful in accomplishing the desired effect, the eyeball was finally extracted. The court gave special attention to the right of the defendant to leave his practice on the 18th of December as he did. After carefully reviewing all of the above facts, Judge Taft said: "As to the right of (the defendant) to leave the city on the 18th of December, when his patient had not called him for a week, and while she was presumably following the precautionary and alleviating prescriptions of eserine and phenacetine, I do not think there can be any doubt, if he made provisions for the attendance of a competent oculist in case of a call."

All of the cases cited above are those in which the physician's right to temporarily leave his practice is upheld, and a careful examination of the reports has failed to discover a precedent in which the right of the physician to leave his practice in the hands of another competent physician is denied; yet it seems that the right to leave one's practice should depend upon the same principles which ordinarily are applied as a test of liability—viz., if the physician, by the careful exercise of ordinary skill and knowledge, believes that he may safely leave his patients to the care of another, he will be justified in so doing; if, on the other hand, a patient's condition is such that a physician in his best judgment thinks a change of physicians would be injurious, nothing short of dire necessity should induce him to permit the substitution.

Liability of Physician for Negligence of One whom he Recommends.—Having determined that the physician has under ordinary circumstances the right to leave his practice in the hands of a competent substitute, it becomes pertinent to consider what, if any, responsibility such physician bears for the acts of his substitute. Should the physician recommended be in a legal sense the agent of the physician recommending him, —that is, if he is employed by him as an assistant—then the law applies the legal maxim *qui facit per alium facit per se*, and holds the recommending physician liable for all negligent or improper professional conduct of his agent. But if, on the other hand, the physician recommended is in independent practice, and is properly esteemed a man of ordinary professional ability and of proper discretion, the physician recommending him will not be held responsible for any error he may commit.

When a regular railroad physician, upon going away for a short time, gave instructions that if anything happened the railroad company should call upon a certain

other doctor, and an accident did occur and the designated physician was called in and improperly treated
the case, it was held that the regular physician was not
liable for such improper treatment, there being no evidence to show that the physician recommended was in
the employ of the defendant.*

In the case of Myers vs. Holborn,† a physician
promised to attend a patient during confinement. A
short time before the event took place he left the city
for a three days' vacation, but first visited the patient
and made an examination of her condition, from which
he concluded that his services would not be required for
several days. During his absence, however, the child
was born, and according to arrangements made by the
defendant, before leaving, the patient was attended by
another physician, who severed the umbilical cord so
near the child's body that it was impossible to tie it, in
consequence of which the child died. An action was
brought by the husband against the physician employed
to attend the case for this negligence of his substitute,
but the liability was denied by the court, which,
speaking through Justice Gummere, said: " Dr. ——
(the physician recommended to attend the patient) and
the defendant were each of them practising physicians
within the State, having no business connections with

---

* Hitchcock vs. Burgett, 38 Mich., 501.

† Myers vs. Holborn, 29 Vroom, 193, 33 Atl. Rep., 389.

one another, except that Dr. —— was attending the patients of the latter while he was temporarily absent. Even if it be admitted, therefore, that Dr. —— was employed by the defendant to attend upon the wife of the plaintiff, that fact did not render the defendant liable for his neglect or want of skill in the performance of his service, for an examination of the authorities will show that a party employing a person who follows a distinct and independent occupation of his own is not responsible for the negligent or improper act of the other."

It will be observed from the foregoing opinion that in New Jersey the courts go so far as to hold that a physician can not be held for the negligence of another physician whom he employs to perform certain professional services, if such other physician has a distinct and independent practice. While there is no question about the correctness of the principle of law by which the court arrived at this conclusion, it is doubted whether the courts of other States will find the principle applicable to this particular condition; therefore, a physician can not be safely advised to employ another physician to attend to his practice, even though such other physician does enjoy an independent practice, if he desires to escape liability for the professional errors of such other physician.

A question which might be suggested by those pre-

ceding is one which arose in the case of Jones *vs.*
Vroom.* In this case the defendant, a physician in
general practice, who was attending the plaintiff for
typhoid fever, was informed by her that she had a pain
in one of her eyes and that the sight was beginning to
leave it, and was asked to send her an oculist. The defendant laughed at her, and told her there was nothing
the matter with the eye, but upon further request promised to send her an oculist. He did not comply with the
request, however, and as an excuse for not doing so said
he had forgotten the matter. Finally the nurse tele-
phoned for an oculist, who said, upon examining the
eye, that he could do nothing for it, but that he might
have done something if he had been sent for sooner.
The plaintiff sued the defendant for not securing the
oculist when requested, but the defendant's liability
was denied. The court said: " The defendant was employed to treat her for fever, and his employment imposed no duty on him to provide her with a specialist
for her eye." This case was tried simply upon the
question indicated in this quotation; it therefore is possible that other questions might have been raised upon
which a different decision could be reasonably expected.
Any way, it is never safe for one to undertake to do a
thing without fulfilling the agreement, whether there is

* Jones *vs.* Vroom, 8 Colo. App., 143.

a consideration or not, and a physician can not safely ignore complaints regarding conditions which by any probability relate to the condition for which he is treating the patient.

That Services were Gratuitous is no Defense.—In examining the contract of the physician as implied from his relations to his patients it was observed that the fact that his services were rendered without compensation or reward did not alter the character of his obligations to his patient or relieve him from liability for the breach of such obligation. This was not always considered the law, nor is it now the law as applied to the ordinary relations and affairs of life. Under the common law the degrees of negligence are usually characterized as slight, ordinary, or gross, and the particular degree of negligence of which the defendant must have been shown to be guilty in order to fix liability upon him varied in inverse ratio to his compensation. If he was well paid for performing certain services he could be guilty of slight negligence only at his peril; if, on the other hand, he received no compensation, nothing short of gross negligence would be considered culpable; but where the compensation was the usual and ordinary amount liability would attach for damages suffered from ordinary negligence.

This was the rule which the courts applied at an early date in fixing the liability of physicians for pro-

fessional errors.* The courts very soon, however, detected the pernicious effects which might be reasonably
expected to follow the application of such a rule of liability to the practice of a learned profession like that
of medicine, which deals not only with the health and,
in a great measure, the happiness of the people, but
their very lives; and, accordingly, by a line of well-considered decisions they have held the physician strictly
to the prescribed requirements of professional ability
and care, whether his services are paid for or gratuitous.† The reason and the necessity for this rule are
clearly and urgently expressed in an instruction delivered by Justice Pryor, from which an extended quotation is made in Chapter II of this work.‡

The application of the rule of liability for error
or neglect in medical treatment, whether compensation
is made or not, is only applicable, it must be remembered, in cases where the defendant holds himself out
as a physician and surgeon. If one not professing to
be a qualified physician, and the patient not understanding him to be one, undertakes to render medical
services without compensation, such services, though
improperly rendered, will be considered by the court as

* Shearman and Redfield on Negligence; Richey *vs.* West, 23 Ill.,
385.
† Du Bois *vs.* Decker, 130 N. Y., 325; Becker *vs.* Janinski, 27 Abb.
N. C., 45; McNevins *vs.* Lowe, 40 Ill., 209; Baird *vs.* Gillett, 47 N.Y., 186.
‡ See page 66.

a mere kindly or neighborly office and incapable of supporting an action for damages.*

Liability of Other than Qualified Physicians for Malpractice.—From the foregoing paragraph it must not be inferred that one who, in fact, is not a qualified physician, but who holds himself out as such, may escape any of the liability which attaches to a regular physician for improper treatment. The mere fact that one solicits patients, representing himself as competent to treat them, brings with it all of the penalties to which the regular physician is liable. Justice Lyon, in the case of Nelson *vs.* Harrington,† said the rule is elementary that a physician or surgeon, or one who holds himself out as such, whether duly licensed or not, when he accepts an employment to treat a patient professionally, must exercise such reasonable care and skill in that behalf as are usually possessed and exercised by physicians or surgeons in good standing, of the same system or school of practice, in the vicinity or locality of his practice, having due regard for the advanced state of medical or surgical science at that time. In this case the defendant was a clairvoyant physician or spiritualist, who professed to have no medical education or training; yet the mere fact that he held himself out as being possessed of ability to treat patients

---

* Higgins *vs.* McCabe, 126 Mass., 13.

† Nelson *vs.* Harrington, 72 Wis., 591.

through the occult aid vouchsafed him, and accepted the duties and undertook the functions of a physician, rendered him amenable to the same law governing their liabilities.

Whether or not in such cases the defendant does hold himself out as a physician is usually a question of fact for the jury to decide from the evidence, and it is often a question requiring nice discrimination. In an early Wisconsin case the evidence adduced at the trial to show that the defendant held himself out as a physician was that he was called as a physician in the first instance; that he attended the case and consulted with a certain doctor; and that he was called doctor during his attendance. The evidence showed that he attended as surgeon seven weeks, assuming the whole direction and treatment of the injured limb, and went into consultation with other physicians and surgeons. Regarding this evidence the supreme court said: " These facts, though not perhaps direct proof of his holding himself out as a physician and surgeon, are sufficient to go to the jury as circumstantial evidence." *

In an early Ohio case the evidence showed that a farmer represented himself as a cancer doctor, having skill and experience in the treatment and cure of cancers. He claimed also to be in possession of a certain

* Reynolds *vs.* Graves, 3 Wis., 416.

recipe or prescription, procured from a certain cancer specialist, that would remove cancers without affecting sound tissue. This evidence was considered sufficient to render him subject to the same liability as a qualified physician in the treatment of a malady of the character he professed to treat.*

And in a more recent Illinois case one suffering from an injured finger went to a druggist for treatment, supposing him to be a physician. The druggist treated the finger wrongly, which resulted in an aggravation of the injury and final loss of the finger.

The court was of the opinion that the druggist, by treating the finger, the plaintiff believing him to be a doctor, held himself out as such, and was consequently chargeable in that character.†

General Scope of Physician's Liability.—Innumerable questions of liability diversified in their nature and character may, and as a matter of fact do, arise, both from inadvertent and willful violation by the physician of his duties and obligations to his patients. The cases heretofore considered are those in which the physician has failed to treat his patient with proper skill or care, or has been deficient in performing some duty nearly related thereto. An examination will soon be made of a few cases arising from acts either of omission or of com-

---

* Musser *vs.* Chase, 29 Ohio St., 577.

† Matthei *vs.* Wooley, 69 Ill. App., 654.

mission, which contravene duties of a wider scope that he owes to his patients or employers. It will be observed, however, that in many of the illustrations following the familiar principles heretofore discussed will be involved.

Necessity of Consent to Surgical Operations.—As a general proposition of law, a surgeon must have consent before operating upon a patient. As a matter of law, however, the courts are disposed to imply consent to perform the particular operation from the fact that the patient has placed himself under the surgeon's care. A recent English case, which has justly provoked considerable unfavorable comment, is that of Beatty *vs.* Cullingworth.* In this case the plaintiff, an unmarried woman, who was about to submit to the operation of ovariotomy, told the defendant, who is said to be one of the most eminent London surgeons, that if both ovaries were found to be diseased he must remove neither. He replied, "You must leave that to me." The plaintiff denied hearing this remark. Both ovaries were found diseased and were removed.

The plaintiff was engaged to be married, but upon learning that both ovaries had been removed broke her engagement, and later brought suit against the surgeon for malpractice. Justice Hawkins, upon the trial

* Beatty *vs.* Cullingworth, Q. B. Div., 44 Cent. L. J., 153.

of the case, charged the jury in effect that the plaintiff had tacitly consented to the operation, whereupon they returned a verdict for the defendant. A prominent legal journal, in commenting on the case, says: " The action of the court in this case has met with very general criticism upon the ground that the facts involving a direct prohibition would seem to exclude the possibility of implying consent. As a contemporary says, it is one thing for a surgeon to refuse to operate unless unlimited discretion is confided to him and quite another thing to deliberately disobey express instructions. Undoubtedly the defendant's wisest course would have been to refuse to operate unless the scope of his authority was agreed upon in advance." *

This case can not be safely considered the law in this country, for an American court would not, it is thought, instruct the jury, under like circumstances, that there was a tacit consent to the operation, but would leave it for the jury to determine whether the evidence before them showed a tacit consent. In short, in nearly all cases of this sort the question is one of fact, for the determination of the jury, rather than of law.

An important question of law arises, however, when an operation is performed upon a wife or upon a child,

* 44 Cent L. J., 153.

as to whether or not the surgeon must first secure the consent of the husband or parent. In a well-considered case the court of appeals of Maryland denies that a husband has the right to withhold his consent to the performance of a necessary surgical operation upon his wife. The court, speaking through Justice Yellott, said: " Surely the law does not authorize the husband to say to his wife, You shall die of the cancer; you can not be cured, and a surgical operation affording only temporary relief will result in useless expense. The husband has no right to withhold from his wife the medical assistance which her case might require." *

Following the reasoning of this decision, one can not see why a physician should be required to secure the consent of a parent before operating upon a child, provided the child was of proper age and discretion to understand the nature and effect of the operation proposed. As there seems to be no precedent upon this particular point, the question can not be authoritatively answered until a case involving the question shall arise which the parties thereto think sufficiently important to take to a court of last resort.

Right to Perform Autopsy.—Somewhat analogous to the right of the surgeon to operate upon a patient is the right of the physician to perform an autopsy, except that, from the nature of the case, the consent of

---

* Janney *vs.* Housekeeper *et al.*, 70 Md., 162.

21

the subject can not be gained in the latter class of operations.

Upon the legal status of a dead body there is an almost confusing wealth of legal lore coming down to us through the English courts from the early days of Christian England. The burial of the dead in church-yards in England is supposed to have been introduced by Cuthbert, Archbishop of Canterbury, in the year 750. Whereupon the protection and control over the repose of the dead gradually passed from the authority of the secular courts to that of the ecclesiastical tribu-nals. The secular courts, being deprived of all author-ity over the dead, looked upon the cadaver as not being the subject of a property right, but confined themselves to the protection of the monument and other external emblems of grief erected by the living. Lord Coke, chief-justice of England, expressed this condition in the learned and ponderous style of his time as follows: " It is to be observed that in every sepulchre that hath a monument two things are to be considered—viz., the monument, and the *sepulture*, or buriall of the dead. The buriall of the *cadaver*—that is, *caro data vermibus* —is *nullius in bonis*, and belongs to the ecclesiastical cognizance; but as to the monument, action is given, as hath been said, at the common law for the defacing thereof." *

* Third Inst. (Coke), 203.

That adequate protection to the dead is necessary is too obvious to permit of discussion; and as the ecclesiastical court is unknown to our government, the functions which in England vested in that court must here be exercised by our courts of law.

In exercising these functions relative to the subject under consideration, they have, perhaps with a single exception, in respect to the learned precedents of the English courts, refused to hold a dead body as strictly property, yet they recognize and protect the right of the relatives of a deceased person to the custody and control of the body.

The relatives in whom this right vests are, first, the husband or wife of the deceased; second, if no husband or wife survives, then the children; third, if there is no husband or wife and no children, then, first, the father, second, the mother; fourth, after them the brothers and sisters of the deceased; fifth, after them the next of kin, according to the course of the common law, to the remotest degree, according to the law of descent of personal property.

This right involves and carries with it a duty; more particularly, it is both a right and a duty: a right to the custody, care, and protection of the body of the deceased from the moment the breath leaves it, and the duty of according to it decent Christian burial.

In referring to this right, in the case of Foley *vs.*

Phelps,* Justice Patterson said: " The right is to the possession of the corpse in the same condition it was in when death supervened. It is the right to what remains when the breath leaves the body, and not merely to such a hacked, hewn, and mutilated corpse as some stranger . . . may choose to turn over to an afflicted relative." In this case the question arose, for the first time in New York, whether one performing a post-mortem examination without the consent of the widow of deceased was liable to her in damages. The court in a learned and elaborate opinion examined the law and the principles applicable to the case, and came to the logical conclusion that whenever the widow's " right to the possession of the corpse in the same condition it was in when death supervened " was violated, such violation furnished a ground for a civil action for damages.

Practically the same question had arisen in the case of Larson vs. Chase,† in which the court not only held there was a cause of action, but that mental suffering caused by the unlawful act was a distinct element of damages.

In the case of Burney vs. Children's Hospital,‡ a father placed his child in a hospital for treatment; the child died, and a post-mortem examination was per-

---

* Foley vs. Phelps, 1 App. Div., 551.
† Larson vs. Chase, 47 Minn., 307.
‡ Burney vs. Children's Hospital, 169 Mass., 57, 38 L. R. A., 413.

formed without his consent. The father brought suit against the hospital for damages. The court, following the reasoning of the former decision, said: " The father, as the natural guardian of the child, was entitled to the possession of its body for burial. Being entitled to the possession of the body for the purposes of burial, is not his right against one who unlawfully interferes with it, and mutilates it, as great as it would be if the body were buried in his lot, and was thence unlawfully removed? That an action may be maintained in the latter case we have already seen, and we are of the opinion that it may be in the former."

As both reason and justice commend the conclusion arrived at by these courts, there can be no doubt that the precedents will be followed whenever the question arises, and that a physician who performs an autopsy without the consent of the person having the right of custody of the deceased, does so at his peril.

There are, however, cases in which such operations may be performed without consent and yet no liability exist; these cases are where the post-mortem is performed in accordance with the directions of law. The statute law of most States provides that whenever a person is found dead, and the cause of his death is not apparent and can not be ascertained from the evidence given or from a superficial examination of the body, the coroner shall order an examination to be made. Such an examination, to be safely made, requires no consent from the relatives of the deceased, for it is sanctioned by positive law. An interesting case of the sort is that of Young *vs.* College of Physicians and Surgeons of Baltimore City.* In this case the deceased, who, in coupling cars, sustained a severe injury to his right leg, it being mashed below the knee and almost severed from the body, was taken to a hospital, where he died next day. The evidence showed that the deceased was a strong, stout man, and of good nerve. A fellow-laborer testified that he had worked with deceased five years, during which he had lost no time. After the death a post-mortem examination was ordered by a Dr. G., a coroner, and performed by a certain Dr. K., both of whom were made defendants to the suit. Evidence was offered on the part of the plaintiff for the purpose of showing that the post-mortem was without the widow's consent; that the body was wantonly cut, mutilated, and disfigured, and the feelings of the relatives of the deceased were inhumanely outraged.

On behalf of the defendants it was shown that Dr. G. was a coroner, and that Dr. K. was medical examiner, appointed by the board of health; also that the post-mortem was ordered by Dr. G. as coroner. Dr. G. tes-

* Young *vs.* College of Physicians and Surgeons of Baltimore City, 81 Md., 358, 32 Atl. Rep., 177.

tified that he ordered the autopsy because he wished to know the cause of death; that it had been reported to him that the man's leg had been cut off by the train and that he had died within thirty-six hours after he was brought to the hospital, that he did not think the loss of the leg in this way sufficiently accounted for the death, and that he could not give the death certificate without having a post-mortem. Dr. K. testified that he did not think in the majority of cases persons in ordinary health, when the leg was crushed below the knee, would die from shock. A certain expert testified that if a healthy man should have his leg crushed off, he would not think it a sufficient cause to explain the death, and in such case, if his official duty required him to give a death certificate, he would make every effort to obtain a post-mortem; and that it was so unusual for a death to occur from accident under the conditions surrounding the deceased that other explanations were more probable. Another expert testified that when a man's leg is cut off below the knee, and he dies within thirty-six hours after the injury, the accident would not be an entirely satisfactory explanation of the death, if the man was ordinarily healthy and muscular; and, if he was required to determine definitely the cause of death in such a case, he would not consider that he had done his duty without having an autopsy. Dr. K. described his proceeding in making the autopsy—the

taking out of the brain, the opening of the body, the removing and cutting into the different organs, the liver,
spleen, kidney, lungs, and heart. He testified that an examination of all the vital organs was necessary to determine the cause of death; that the cause of death was
persistent heart shock; that deceased had fatty kidneys
and fatty degeneration of the heart; that the injury
itself was not of such a nature as to have caused persistent heart shock, unless there was something else
besides the injury that helped to produce it. Expert
evidence was also given to the effect that a complete
examination could not be made without removing and
opening the brain.

In the city where the present case arose the law
provides that " when any person shall die in the said
city it shall be the duty of the physician who attended
during his or her last illness, or the coroner, when the
case comes under his notice, to furnish within forty-
eight hours after death . . . a certificate setting forth
as far as the same can be ascertained . . . the cause,
date, and place of death." In summing up the conclusion of the court in this case, Justice Roberts said : " The
evidence before us exhibits the case of a public officer,
whose duty it is to find out and certify the cause of a
death which is brought to his notice. The accident
preceding his death, and disabling him, is not, in his
opinion, sufficient to cause the death of a healthy per-

son. There must, therefore, as he thinks, be some diseased condition of the injured man which contributed to bring about this result. His opinion is shared by other reputable physicians who have testified in the case. He could not honestly and conscientiously give the certificate which the law required him to give unless he made proper inquiry into the case. In his judgment, and in the judgment of the professional witnesses, proper and sufficient inquiry could not be made without an autopsy. So far as the evidence in the case shows, or any rational inference from it, the coroner did simply his plain and positive duty in ordering the autopsy. And the medical examiner, Dr. K., was equally obliged by his duty to obey the order of the coroner."

Under the law quoted above, in compliance with which the coroner directed the post-mortem examination, no reason can be detected why the attending physician might not with equal right and justification have conducted the examination in the coroner's absence. A case involving this particular question arose in Denver not many years ago. There a law was in force similar in effect to the one above quoted, which required the physician to give a certificate of death before a burial permit could be obtained. In this case the deceased was stricken dead while riding in a carriage, and was taken to an undertaker's to be prepared for burial. While there, deceased's regular attending physician was applied to by the undertakers for a death certificate, whereupon he performed a post-mortem. Suit was commenced against the undertakers and the physician, but the court held that they were not liable. Justice Richmond, in his opinion, said: " I think that the evidence discloses circumstances which would warrant any physician in declining to issue a certificate designating the cause of death, and permitting burial, without a post-mortem examination. It is true that the physician may have had a belief as to the cause of death, but the circumstances under which death occurred warranted him in hesitating to give the certificate required by the ordinance of the city of Denver in this case. This being so, and the proofs showing conclusively that the body was not mutilated, and that the autopsy was performed in a decent and scientific manner, with due regard to the sex of the deceased and the feelings of all parties interested, I can not conceive what possible damages could be proved to a jury." *

The matter may be summed up as follows: An autopsy performed with the consent of the relative who is entitled to the custody of the dead body can never be questioned if properly performed. Such an operation, when performed under direction of law, is never subject to legal punishment, yet the existence of the two cases

---

* Cook et al. vs. Walley et al., 1 Colo. App., 163; 27 Pac. Rep., 950.

last examined should be a sufficient reason to convince the cautious practitioner of the advisability of always securing such consent when possible. Where consent is withheld, and the physician feels that a conscientious performance of the duty before him requires that a post-mortem examination be made, he should, in furtherance of his own safety, turn the case over to the coroner, or at least act under the direction of that officer.

Liability for Presence of Unprofessional Attendant. —A peculiar case of liability arose a number of years ago in Michigan from an act which, although apparently done in good faith, was reprehensible indeed.

The evidence showed that a doctor who was sick and fatigued from overwork, and who was compelled to go a considerable distance over roads so bad that a horse could not be ridden or driven over them, to attend a case of confinement, secured the reluctant consent of a young unmarried man to attend him and assist in carrying his lantern, umbrella, and other articles necessary for the occasion, the night being dark and stormy. The plaintiff's house consisted of one room, with a bed, sink, or alcove, in front of which there was a curtain, and in which the doctor expected to find the patient. Upon arriving at the house the doctor told the husband he had brought a friend to help carry " his things." The husband said "All right," and invited them in and made no objection to the young man. Upon entering they found the patient in the main room, and it was there she was delivered of the child. The young man conducted himself in a respectful manner, and excepting once, when called to hold the patient's hand, while in a paroxysm of pain, sat facing the wall. Both the patient and her husband claimed they did not know the non-professional character of the young man, but supposed he was a physician or a student practising under the attending physician, and therefore made no objection to his presence.

In the trial court judgment was rendered for plaintiff, from which defendant took an appeal. Chief-Justice Marston, of the supreme court, in reviewing the case, said: " It would be shocking to our sense of right, justice, and propriety to doubt even, but for such an act the law would afford an ample remedy. To the plaintiff the occasion was a most sacred one, and no one had a right to intrude unless invited, or because of some real and pressing necessity, which it is not pretended existed in this case. The plaintiff had a legal right to the privacy of her apartment at such a time, and the law secures to her this right by requiring others to observe it, and to abstain from its violation. The fact that at the time she consented to the presence of the young man, supposing him to be a physician, does not preclude her from maintaining an action and recovering substantial damages upon afterward ascertaining his true character. In obtaining admission at such a time and under such circumstances, without fully disclosing his true character, both parties were guilty of deceit, and the wrong thus done entitles the injured party to recover the damages afterward sustained, from shame and mortification upon discovering the true character of the defendants." *

Liability for Wrongful Certificate of Insanity.—The duty which a physician is frequently called to perform, of passing upon the mental state of a fellow man, who, by virtue of his judgment, is either permitted to remain at large or is confined in a lunatic asylum, is a most grave and responsible one. An error of judgment may, on the one hand, mean a menace to the peace and even safety of the community, or, on the other hand, an unjust and lamentable deprivation of that most important of all rights, personal liberty.

The purpose of the present examination of law is, however, to examine the physician's liability for an improper exercise of these functions, and not the physician's duties and obligations to society or to the person whose sanity is in question, except in so far as they affect the real subject of inquiry.

The method of determining the mental condition of

* De May vs. Roberts, 46 Mich., 160.

one suspected of being insane is regulated in the several States by statutes differing somewhat in the different jurisdictions. A common method, however, of obtaining summary protection from the violence or possible violence of a lunatic is to confine him upon the certificate of two reputable physicians. What civil liability the physician incurs who errs in making this certificate is the question to be considered.

The first step to be taken in passing upon the liability of a physician is to determine whether or not the certificate is in itself correct or false. If the certificate is found to be correct, this, it seems, is a complete bar to a civil action against the physician for damages, for, in the absence of a statute imposing a penalty for a failure to comply with a certain method or mode of procedure in determining the mental condition of the party examined, the physician incurs no liability for the inefficiency of the modes which he pursued in reaching and certifying a correct conclusion.* Moreover, it has been held that the burden of proof is upon the plaintiff to show that at the time the certificate of insanity was given he was in fact sane, and that until this fact is shown by a preponderance of evidence the physician signing the certificate can not be held liable.†

It appearing that the certificate of insanity is in-

---

* Pennell *vs.* Cummings, 75 Me., 163.   † *Ibid.*

correct, and that the physicians have erred in their conclusion and certified to a condition which did not exist, does it then follow that a civil action for damages in favor of the person who has been wrongly imprisoned will lie against them? The answer to this question is practically the same as that which has been made to nearly every question arising in the cases of malpractice examined in these articles—viz., if the defendants were possessed of the ordinary amount of knowledge and skill which the law requires for the proper exercise of their duties, and if they used ordinary and reasonable care in making the examination and exercised their best judgment in determining the party's mental condition, then they are not liable, whether their conclusion is correct or not. There is a prominent English case * in which this question was passed upon and the law governing the defendant's liability lucidly and elaborately expounded by Justice Crompton in his instruction to the jury. The case is rather voluminous, covering over thirty pages in the volume of reports where it is recorded, yet a brief examination of the facts and the law which was held to be applicable will probably compensate in enlightenment for the time required. The plaintiff was a shopkeeper in London, who lived very discordantly with his spouse—in fact, the want of do-

---

* Hall *vs.* Semple, 3 F. and F., 337.

mestic harmony was frequently manifested in outbursts of violent temper, in which the use of abusive and obscene epithets was common, and even physical violence to the wife's person had been complained of. The plaintiff complained, among other things, of the wife's extravagance, and the evidence did show that she had taken articles from the shop and pawned them. The wife was accustomed to go to certain physicians with her complaints regarding the husband's treatment, among whom was one of the physicians who subsequently signed the certificate of lunacy. Upon one occasion when the husband met this physician and his wife together he made a remark which the physician construed as an imputation against the wife's chastity, but which the husband apparently did not so intend. The wife also claimed that the husband slept with a drawn sword by his bed and that he repeatedly threatened her life. The defendant in the case, together with the physician above referred to, perhaps from a desire to relieve the wife from the hardship of the husband's persecutions, after a few minutes' conversation held with him at different times, signed separate certificates of his insanity in which they respectively assigned the grounds for believing him insane, as follows:

First Certificate: 1. Facts indicating insanity observed by myself: He had a wild and staring look, with restless eyes and nervous, agitated manner. He represented to me that his wife was ruining himself and business, and he intimated that she was improperly associating with other men; he is evidently laboring under delusions, and he acts upon these delusions.

2. Other facts (if any) indicating insanity communicated to me by others.

He is guilty of repeated acts of violence; he constantly threatens his wife and often assaults her; he sleeps with a drawn sword by his bedside, and declares he will murder any one who approaches him, and he has often threatened to stab his wife.

The defendant who signed this certificate had not seen the sword at the time of certifying the plaintiff insane, but he afterward learned that the " drawn sword " was a theatrical or court dress sword.

Second Certificate: 1. Facts indicating insanity observed by myself: He had a restless, irritable, and excited manner, with a glaring look, and expressed much vindictiveness toward his wife, and said, " I must be a fool to mind what that woman has said." He said she had her fellows continually running after her, and intimated that I was one of them.

2. Other facts (if any) indicating insanity communicated to me by others:

On a former occasion, when I had called to see him, he had just before broken the looking glass to pieces, also the marble mantel and bedstead; had been

22

brandishing knives over his wife's head, and using hor-
rid language, sometimes kicking her, tearing her bon-
net and clothes off, and all without provocation, as I
find from neighbors and old acquaintances that she is a
discreet, sober, prudent, and patient woman.

This certificate was based upon an interview had
more than seven days previously, and was accordingly,
under the English statute, irregular, and of no effect. The plaintiff was released when the irregularity
of the certificate was discovered, and he soon thereafter commenced suit against the defendant for
damages.

The law which was held to govern in the case can
probably be no better expressed than in the words of
Justice Crompton taken from his charge to the jury.
Therein the judge said: " Take me as saying to you in
point of law that if a medical man assumes under this
statute the duty of signing such a certificate, without
making and by reason of his not making a due and
proper examination, which a medical man under such
circumstances ought to make and is called on to make,
not in the exercise of extremest possible care, but in
the exercise of ordinary care, so that he is guilty of
culpable negligence, and damage ensues, then, that an
action will lie, although there has been no spiteful or
improper motive, and though the certificate is not false
to his knowledge.

" The true ground of plaintiff's complaint is the negligence of the defendant, and the want of due care in the discharge of the duty thrown upon him; and I think that if a person assumes the duty of a medical man, under this statute, and signs a certificate of insanity which is untrue, without making the proper examination and inquiries which the circumstances of the case would require from a medical man using proper skill in such a matter, if he states that which is untrue and damage ensues to the party thereby, he is liable to an action, and it is to that I desire to call your particular attention. It is not that a medical man is bound to form a right judgment so as to be liable to an action if he does not. There are cases of insanity which are very difficult to deal with or to understand. But what he is required to do is to make an examination, and, if it be necessary, to make such inquiries as may be required. It would be unjust if a man were to be visited, in cases of this kind, with consequences arising from mere error of judgment or mistake of fact.

" There must be, to make him liable, negligence in the discharge of those proper duties which it must be taken he has assumed in undertaking to sign the certificate of insanity, and if you are satisfied that there has been negligence with reference to these matters—culpable negligence, as I have described—then he is liable. Now, I can not help thinking in a matter of this kind, which is not like a mere preliminary inquiry before a magistrate, but a proceeding upon which a man is to be at once confined to imprisonment as a lunatic, very considerable care is necessary. One can hardly say precisely what that degree of care may be. It is said that one man may be satisfied with a quicker examination than another. We, for instance, would take a long time before we should be able to form a judgment in a matter of this kind. A person experienced in such matters might decide more quickly, while an ordinary medical practitioner might require a longer time. We take it as clear, however, that considerable care ought to be used."

The jury in this case rendered a verdict for the plaintiff, assessing his damages at one hundred and fifty pounds.

The principles which were held to govern in the English case have been accepted as the law by American courts whenever this question has arisen,* and will undoubtedly continue to be so accepted. Therefore, as long as the physician possesses proper knowledge and science and conducts the examination with reasonable and ordinary care the result of his conclusion will never despoil his estate, even though in the exercise of his best judgment he may have been in error.

---

* Williams *vs.* Le Bar, 141 Pa., 149; Ayers *vs.* Russell, 50 Hun, 282, 3 N. Y. Supp., 338; Hurlehy *vs.* Martine, 31 N. Y. S. R., 471, 10 N. Y. Supp., 92.

Other cases might be shown to illustrate, possibly more fully, the application of the principles, but it is thought that further elaboration will be superfluous.

Liability for Erroneous Conclusion in Examination. —A peculiar case of injury resulting from an erroneous conclusion of a physician is shown in a recent Massachusetts case.* In this case the plaintiff, who was engaged to be married, had accidentally injured himself in such a way as to require the attention of a physician and the application of remedies to his private parts. The father of the plaintiff's *fiancée*, hearing that the plaintiff was afflicted with a venereal disease, took him to the defendant, a physician, for the purpose of learning his real condition. The physician examined the plaintiff and reported that he had gonorrhœa, whereupon the plaintiff's *fiancée* broke the engagement, and the plaintiff brought suit against the physician for damages.

It will be observed that this case presents conditions differing from all others heretofore considered: a third party employs a physician to examine a man, the physician does so, and erroneously reports his condition. Is the physician beholden to the man examined for damages resulting from his incorrect diagnosis? Here there is no contractural relation existing between the physi-

* Harriott *vs.* Plimpton, 166 Mass., 585.

cian and the man whom he examines, for he is in the employ of the third party. We have seen, however, that a physician who undertakes the treatment of a case gratuitously is under equal obligation to the patient as though the patient paid him for the treatment. So, also, is the physician bound to possess the same qualification and exercise the same skill in the treatment of a patient where he is paid for such treatment by a third party.* Therefore in this case the fact that the physician was employed by a third party to conduct the examination can not be urged as a bar to the plaintiff's right to recover. But does the mere fact that the physician made an erroneous report of the plaintiff's condition entitle the plaintiff to recover from him for damages resulting therefrom? Here, again, we find the old familiar rule that the physician is not liable for his incorrect report if he has the ordinary skill and learning of a physician, and exercised ordinary diligence and care in their application to the case; otherwise he is liable. Nor does the fact that the purpose of the examination was information and not medical treatment have any material effect.

Examining without Consent.—An English case arising from an examination similar to the one related above, in which the party examined submitted only with reluc-

---

* Du Bois *vs.* Decker, 130 N. Y., 325.

tance, and afterward sued the physician for assault in making the examination under coercion, presents quite a different question for consideration. In this case a housemaid was accused by her mistress of being in the family way; the girl denied the accusation, but the mistress sent her to her room and sent for a physician to examine her. The physician on arriving went to the girl's room and told her he had come to examine her; the girl objected, and said she did not like to be examined; the doctor explained that he was a professional man and told her how to prepare herself for examination; she did as directed, and submitted to the examination, crying all the time. The doctor found that the mistress's belief was mistaken and so reported. The servant afterward brought suit against the doctor for assault upon the theory that his examination was only submitted to through fear and duress. Upon the trial a verdict was rendered in favor of the doctor. From this court an appeal was taken to the Manchester Assizes. The two justices who heard the question there disagreed upon the law, Justice Lopez expressing his opinion that the girl had only submitted to the examination through fear of evil consequences that would follow her refusal, and that her submission could not therefore be considered a consent to the examination. Justice Lindley, however, was of quite a different opinion, and thought there was no evidence of want of consent as distinguished from a reluctant obedience or submission, and that, in the absence of all evidence of coercion as distinguished from an order that she could have obeyed or not, she had no cause of action. The court being evenly divided, the judgment was allowed to stand. An appeal was then taken to the court of appeals, the justices of which agreed with Justice Lindley. The appeal was accordingly dismissed and the judgment permitted to stand in favor of the doctor. This case is cited particularly for the purpose of pointing out a possible danger. The mere beginning of a suit of this sort, whether or not the plaintiff succeeds in obtaining a judgment against the doctor, is greatly to his damage; therefore he should never attempt an examination of the kind unless the consent of the party to be examined is fully and freely given.

Contagious Diseases.—Questions of liability of the physician to his patients growing out of his conduct in cases of contagious disease have arisen in two separate and distinct classes.

The first and most important, which has been heretofore referred to,* is that growing out of a breach of duty on the part of the physician to protect his patients in all reasonable ways from contagious and infectious diseases. The liability of this class is very

* See page 72.

well illustrated in the case of Piper *vs.* Menifee.* Here the physician was told by the patient's wife that if he attended a certain case of small-pox he must not come to see her husband. The physician said that " he would not, unless the (small-pox patient) would be bound for his fee." The next day, when he returned, the patient's wife again told him that if he visited any small-pox patients he must not come there. He replied that he would not visit any small-pox patients. Ten days later the patient's wife again pressed him strongly about small-pox patients, again repeating the interdiction. In answer he neither admitted nor denied that he visited such patients, but said that if he visited them he would change his clothes, and there would be no danger. After the physician had been attending the patient for about three weeks for typhoid fever, and when he was getting better and began to recover from the fever, he broke out with small-pox, and some time after the patient's son broke out with the same disease. The patient also offered evidence to show that the physician was attending small-pox patients while attending him. The court held that this statement of facts constituted a good cause of action against the defendant. Justice Marshall, who rendered the opinion, said: " Suppose a physician, knowing that he has an infec-

---

* Piper *vs.* Menifee, 12 B. Mon. (Ky.), 467, 54 Am. Dec., 547.

tious disease, continues to visit his patients without apprising them of the fact, and without proper precautions on his own part, and thus communicates the disease to one of them. Clearly the physician thus acting would be guilty of a breach of duty and of his implied undertaking to the patient, which, whether it be regarded in the light of carelessness or negligence or fraud, would render him liable for consequent damages, including as well the suffering and danger and loss of time as the expense necessarily occasioned by the second disease thus produced by his own wrongful act.

. . . .

" The actual case, as presented by the evidence which was offered, is even stronger for the (patient) than that which has been hypothetically stated, inasmuch as it may be inferred that the continuance of the plaintiff's employment in the first disease was induced by his promise not to visit small-pox patients while he was visiting the (patient)."

From the very nature of the physician's professional duties it is necessary for him to pass from patients suffering from infectious or contagious diseases of the more ordinary and less virulent type to those not so affected. Modern science has, however, shown that antiseptic precautions will greatly decrease the danger of contagion, and if the physician adopts those measures best calculated to insure the safety of those with whom he comes in contact he will be considered as exercising due skill and care as judged by the advanced stage of the medical science.

The second class of cases in which the physician's conduct has been questioned consists of those in which he has incorrectly reported a patient to the board of health as being afflicted with a contagious disease. In this class of cases it seems that the question of liability depends upon the good faith of the physician in making the report rather than upon his skill and care. In passing upon a case of this sort Justice Sedgwick, of the New York supreme court, said: " Nor, as I view the case, can it be maintained that the defendants' (the physicians') omission, if there were such an omission, to use ordinary skill as physicians, in coming to their opinions, was actionable under the facts in this case. There was no improper or hurtful treatment or medication in pursuance of the opinion. These opinions led them to make an honest report to the health board. The statutes had made it their duty to report cases of contagious disease. The performance of this duty was not part of the functions of a physician in his relation to a patient, but rather to the public. My opinion is that in order to give the public the protection due to it, according to the intention of the statute, any physician that possesses in fact an opinion that a patient has a contagious disease is bound to report the case, whether he has or not used ordinary professional skill and knowledge. A physician of skill in everything but cases of small-pox, which happily are not numerous, may, unexpectedly to himself, be called to a case which presents to him the appearance of small-pox. It may be said that he can call in counsel. It can not, however, be said that private counsel should be called in rather than such as the law has appointed. Certainly, if he really thinks the case to be one of small-pox, it is his duty to communicate his opinion to the public authorities, who furnish skilled physicians peculiarly competent to pass upon the case. They are the experts that the law points out for the physician. The attendance of those experts upon a patient can cause no injury, and therefore the responsibility rests solely upon the public officers." *

It is evident that the logic of this opinion will not apply in cases where the act of the attending physician in reporting cases of contagious disease to the board of health is not a mere ministerial one, and where no regular physician is provided by law to make the examination by virtue of which the patient is quarantined. It is therefore believed that where a patient is quarantined by virtue of the examination of the attending physician he will be held to exercise ordinary skill and diligence in conducting that examination.

* Brown vs. Purdy, 8 N. Y. S. R., 143, 54 N. Y. Super. Ct., 109.

A case of liability arising from the conduct of a doctor in reference to a contagious disease, although not coming under either of the foregoing classes, or, in fact, growing out of a professional relation between the parties to the suit, is reported in the *New York Supreme Court Reports*. In this case a physician directed the plaintiff to whitewash a house in which there had been small-pox patients. The plaintiff objected to going into the house, but was informed by the doctor that the house had been thoroughly disinfected, and that no danger of contagion existed. Relying upon the doctor's statement, the plaintiff performed the services and in due time broke out with the disease. This case came before the court upon a question of law. It was decided that the facts as stated showed a cause of action, and that it was for the jury to determine from the evidence whether the doctor had acted toward the plaintiff with due care and prudence, and whether the plaintiff had acted rashly and inexcusably in entering the house under the circumstances.[*]

Negligence in Writing Prescriptions.—The physician may become civilly liable in damages as well for injury resulting from a negligently or ignorantly written prescription as from any other form of malpractice. Nor does the negligence of the druggist who compound-

---

[*] Span *vs.* Ely, 8 Hun, 255.

ed the prescription without discovering the error and directing the doctor's attention to it relieve the physician from his liability.*

Deceit and Misrepresentation.—It is a general rule of law that a statement which amounts to an expression of opinion, even though erroneous, does not furnish ground for action. Deception, to be actionable, must relate to existing or past facts, and not to representations made as to facts to transpire in the future. The reason most commonly given for this condition and the one upon which the law is probably founded is that one to whom an opinion is expressed as to a future event has no right to rely upon it.† And so a purchaser may not rely upon the representation of a vendor regarding the quantity or value of an article which is open to his inspection, but must depend upon his own judgment.‡ And also where statements were made by a real-estate agent to a widow to induce her to exchange her homestead for other property—that she was making a good trade and bettering her condition, and that she could sell enough of the other property to pay for a house—such statements are considered mere expressions of opinion and not misrepresentations; for while the person to whom such representations are made may rely upon

---

* Murdoch *vs.* Walker, 43 Ill. App., 590.
† Homer *vs.* Perkins, 124 Mass., 431.
‡ Evans *vs.* Bolling, 5 Ala., 550.

them, he is supposed to be equally able from his own opinion to come to as correct a conclusion as the other party, and therefore can not claim to be misled by such opinion.*

As the law is always, or nearly always, based upon reason, it is natural to expect to find an exception to this general law in cases where the reasons for its existence do not apply. Such an exception does exist in those cases where an opinion is expressed with intention to deceive, and where the other party has a right to rely upon the opinion; and also in cases where the facts are not equally known to both parties, but where the opinion is expressed by the one party and is founded upon special skill or knowledge by which he alone is able to form an opinion.†

The expression of an opinion by a physician and surgeon relative to the subject of his profession comes peculiarly within the exception, and we therefore shall expect to see him held responsible for any deceit or misrepresentation. The case of Hedin *vs.* Minneapolis Medical and Surgical Institute ‡ is one of some importance in which this question was adjudicated. In this case the plaintiff, an illiterate man, who had been

---

* Brady *vs.* Cole, 164 Ill., 116.

† Conlan *vs.* Roemer, 52 N. J. L., 53.

‡ Hedin *vs.* Minneapolis Medical and Surgical Institute, 62 Minn , 146, 64 N. W. Rep., 158, 35 L. R. A., 417.

badly injured in an accident, was suffering from a fracture at the base of the skull and was physically a
wreck. He consulted the defendant. After being examined, he was positively assured by the surgeon that he
could be cured by receiving treatment at that institute,
but that he must pay a fee of five hundred dollars. By
virtue of these representations the plaintiff paid the
money demanded and submitted to the treatment, but
upon failing to receive benefit therefrom, brought suit
to recover the money paid to defendant, basing his
action upon the deceitful misrepresentation of the defendant's surgeon. The jury rendered a verdict of five
hundred dollars in favor of plaintiff, from which defendant appealed, but the supreme court affirmed the
judgment. Justice Collins, who gave the opinion of the
court, expressed himself upon the law applicable to the
case as follows: "Considering the circumstances and
relations of the parties, there was something more in
the defendant's statements than the mere expression of
his opinion upon a matter of conjecture and uncertainty. It amounted to a representation that the plaintiff's physical condition was such as to insure a complete recovery. The doctor, especially trained in the
art of healing, having superior learning and knowledge,
assured plaintiff that he could be restored to health.
That the plaintiff believed him is easily imagined, for
a much stronger and more learned man would have

readily believed the same thing. The doctor with his skill and ability should be able to approximate to the truth when giving his opinion as to what can be done with injuries of one year's standing, and he should always be able to speak with certainty before he undertakes to assert positively that a cure can be effected. If he can not speak with certainty, let him express a doubt. If he speaks without any knowledge of the truth or falsity of a statement that he can cure, and does not believe the statement true, or if he has no knowledge of the truth or falsity of such a statement, but represents it as true of his own knowledge, it is to be inferred that he intends to deceive. The deception being designed in either case, and injury having followed from reliance upon the statements, an action for deceit will lie."

Contributory Negligence.—In Chapter III of this work it has been observed that it is the duty of the patient to follow all reasonable directions and instructions given him by his physician, and that while a breach of this duty, resulting as it does principally in the injury of the patient, will not give rise to an action in favor of the physician, yet it is a fact which the physician may plead as a defense to an action commenced against him by the patient for negligent or unskillful treatment in the particular case. This failure of the patient to follow the instructions of the physi-

23

cian and conduct himself in a manner suggested by ordinary caution and prudence is known in the law as contributory negligence.

The instructions of the physician, in order to be binding upon the patient, must be such reasonable and proper instructions as a physician of ordinary skill would give; if, however, they impose unnecessary burdens or suffering upon him, he will be legally justified in disregarding them. In the case of McCandless vs. McWha,* the patient was suffering from a comminuted, oblique fracture of both tibia and fibula. The defendant attempted to effect extension and counter-extension by binding splints on the fore and back part of the leg, reaching from the ankle to the knee. These splints were bound on in such a way as to impede circulation, and to irritate the parts and cause them to be considerably swollen, thereby causing much pain. The patient, unable to stand the pain, loosened the bandages. This act, the defendant claimed, contributed to the injury, and should therefore be a defense to the action, but the court thought not. Justice Lewis said: "A patient is bound to submit to such treatment as his surgeon prescribes, provided the treatment be such as a surgeon of ordinary skill would adopt or sanction. But if it be painful, injurious, and unskillful, he is not

* McCandless vs. McWha, 22 Pa. St., 261.

bound to peril his health, and perhaps his life, by submission to it. It follows that before the surgeon can
shift the responsibility from himself to the patient, on
the ground that the latter did not submit to the
course recommended, it must be shown that the
prescriptions were proper, and adapted to the end in
view."

If, however, the instructions given the patient were
proper and adapted to the end in view, although the
physician's treatment of the case may have been improper, and the patient fails to follow the instructions
and injury ensues, what effect will such failure have
upon his right to recover from the physician for the
injury sustained? A casual examination of the cases in
which this question is treated leads one to believe that
there is considerable conflict of authority, but a more
critical scrutiny shows that the conflict is only apparent, and that it results from a confusion of the two
classes into which acts of this sort as a defense are divided.

The true doctrine, in general terms, seems to be
that the physician having been guilty of negligence in
the treatment of the case, the contributory negligence
of the patient, when contemporaneous with the physician's negligence, or when uniting or cooperating with
it in such a way as to conduce to the deleterious result
of the physician's treatment, may be pleaded as a com-

plete defense to an action against such physician. But if the contributory negligence is subsequent in point of time to the negligence of the physician, or if the effect of the physician's negligence and that of the patient can be separated in such a way as to show distinctively the deleterious result of each, then the patient's negligence will be received as a defense only in the way of mitigation of damages.* The case of Du Bois *vs.* Decker † affords an excellent illustration of the application of the second rule. The patient had through the improper treatment of the physician been subjected to two amputations. The physician set up as a defense that after the second amputation the patient failed to keep the limb in the position in which it was placed and in which he was instructed to keep it, and thereby produced bleeding which to some extent impeded the healing; also that he refused to take the doctor's prescriptions about this time; and, further, that he left the hospital before he should have done so, which may also have aggravated the injury. This, the court held, was all proper evidence to be considered by the jury for the purpose of mitigating damages, but that it would not relieve the physician from the consequences of previous neglect or unskillful treatment.

---

* Lawson *vs.* Conaway, 37 W. Va., 159. Jones *vs.* Angell, 95 Ind., 376. Becker *vs.* Janinski, 27 Abb. N. C., 45. Scudder *vs.* Crossan, 43 Ind., 343. Geiselman *vs.* Scott, 25 Ohio St., 86.

† Du Bois *vs.* Decker, 130 N. Y., 325.

In the case of Sanderson *vs.* Holland,* the patient, a little girl of six years, had fractured her arm at a point about two inches above the elbow. The physician, in reducing the fracture, first extended the arm its full length in a straight line, and in that position bandaged it from fingers to shoulder. He then put on splints from the shoulder to the elbow, and then forced the arm into a right angle so as to swing it, thereby pressing the elbow ends of the splints into the forearm, causing the child to scream with pain, and stopping the circulation of the lower arm, which caused gangrene. Permanent injuries ensued for which suit was brought. Evidence was shown by the defendant of careless treatment of the patient by her parents and others which contributed to the injury. In regard to the effect of this evidence Justice Gill said: " If the defendant carelessly and unskillfully set, bandaged, and dressed the plaintiff's arm, and she was injured thereby, then the action will not be *defeated* by showing that subsequently her parents added to the extent of such injuries by their carelessness and negligence in nursing. This showing would not *defeat* plaintiff's case, but merely go to *mitigate* the damages as against the defendant."

On the other hand, the case of Young *vs.* Mason †illustrates the rule that where the negligence of the

---

* Sanderson *vs.* Holland, 39 Mo. App., 233.

† Young *vs.* Mason, 8 Ind. App., 264, 35 N. E. Rep., 521.

patient is either contemporaneous with that of the physician or contributes to the deleterious results of the original unskillful treatment of the physician in such a way that the result of the doctor's negligence and that of the patient can not be distinguished, then the contributory negligence is a complete defense to the action.

The patient had fractured the radius of her left forearm near the wrist, dislocated laterally both bones at the elbow, and fractured the inner condyle of the humerus.

The evidence showed that with one exception the physician dressed and treated the patient's injuries in a manner approved and followed by the most skilled surgeons in that vicinity, and which is approved by the standard authors and text writers upon the subject of surgery. The exception is that the evidence did not conclusively show that he used proper skill and care in reducing the fracture near the wrist joint. The evidence also showed that the patient, contrary to instructions, removed her arm from the sling numerous times, placing it in different positions while out of the sling, and that the effect of removing the arm from the sling was to aggravate the inflammation and swelling, which had a tendency to produce the stiff and useless condition of the arm for which suit was brought. The evidence also showed that the proper treatment of the arm for the stiffness of the elbow, wrist, and finger joints was passive motion; that the physician endeavored to apply this treatment at the proper time but was prevented from so doing by the patient.

The court was of the opinion that the negligence of the physician alone was not the cause of the injuries sustained, but that that of the patient entered into the general result in such a way as to make the result of each indistinguishable; therefore the negligence of the patient was a complete defense to the action against the physician. Justice Davis, in rendering the opinion of the court, said: " For instance, suppose a man fractures the bones in his leg below the knee, and calls a surgeon to treat the injuries, and the surgeon negligently fails to reduce one of the fractures, but in all other respects gives proper treatment, and the patient, in disobedience to the directions of the surgeon, negligently removes the bandages used as a part of the proper treatment by the surgeon, or is otherwise guilty of contributory negligence, and such combined negligence of the surgeon and patient unite in producing a shortness and stiffness of the leg, for which injuries an action is brought against the surgeon—can the patient recover? The patient is certainly not responsible in such a case for the original negligence of the surgeon in failing to properly reduce the fracture, but this negligence of the surgeon unites with the subsequent contributory negli-

gence of the patient in causing the shortness and stiffness of the leg." This being the case, a cause of action
does not exist against the physician.

An instructive case comes to us from a Massachusetts report of some years ago. The plaintiff complained that through the negligence of the physician
he became afflicted with a bedsore, from which by reason of negligent treatment he suffered damages. The
evidence tended to show that the injury complained of
was not a bedsore, but was caused by the patient's attendants carelessly dropping him on the bed rail. There
was evidence, however, which showed that the physician
did not give the injury proper treatment and that it
was thereby greatly aggravated. The instruction given
to the jury by the court learnedly and clearly presents
all of the law of contributory negligence relative to the
case, and is therefore quoted at length: " The burden
of proof is on the plaintiff to show that all the injury
for which he seeks damages proceeds solely from the
want of ordinary skill and care on the part of the defendant. If it be impossible to separate the injury occasioned by the neglect of the plaintiff himself from
that occasioned from the neglect of the defendant, the
plaintiff can not recover. If, however, they can be separated, for such injury as the plaintiff may show thus
proceeded from the want of ordinary skill or ordinary
care of the defendant he may recover. In the present

case the plaintiff claims damages of the defendant for want of ordinary care and ordinary skill in the treatment of him by the defendant, by which, as he says, first a bedsore was caused, and second, after the bedsore was caused, it was improperly treated and neglected. If the plaintiff should fail to satisfy you that the sore was caused by neglect of the defendant, for this damage he could not, of course, recover, but he might still recover for the injury occasioned to him solely by the subsequent neglect of the defendant in not taking proper care of it (should he prove such neglect), even if the sore was occasioned by the plaintiff's own carelessness. If, however, in the case last supposed, the injury has resulted to the plaintiff not solely from neglect in the subsequent treatment of it by the defendant, but also from his own subsequent neglect, and the jury are not satisfied but that both causes have combined to produce the subsequent injury, the plaintiff can not recover for it. While, on the one hand, the defendant would not be released from his duty to exercise ordinary care and ordinary skill in his subsequent treatment of a disease because at a previous stage of it the plaintiff had himself been negligent, and had thus contributed to the condition in which he was, on the other hand it would be for the plaintiff to show, if he seeks damages for want of ordinary care and ordinary skill on the part of the defendant in his subsequent treatment, that it proceeded solely from this, and not from any subsequent neglect of his own." *

The defense of contributory negligence is one which may be made in many cases; it is therefore thought that the importance of the subject will justify the particularity with which it has been treated.

Survival of Action.—At common law a cause of action arising from an injury to the person caused by want of skill or negligence of a physician and surgeon did not survive the death of either physician or patient.† The law in this respect has, however, been greatly altered in many of the States by statutes expressly providing for its survival, so that in case of death of either party suit may now be brought, or, if previously commenced, may be continued by or against the personal representative of the deceased.

To whom Liable.—To whom the physician becomes liable by reason of negligence or malpractice is often a question that would confuse one not understanding the fiction of the common law upon which these rights are often based.

At common law the family formed a legal unit, which was represented by the husband and father. An injury to his person was one which created a cause of

---

* Hibbard vs. Thompson, 109 Mass., 286.
† Wolf vs. Wall, 40 Ohio St., 111.

action in his favor alone and upon which he alone must sue; but should the injury be done to the wife, a double cause of action arose—one in favor of the husband for damages for the loss of her services and society during the time she was suffering from the injury, also for the cost of nursing and caring for her while ill. The other cause of action arose in favor of the wife for the injury inflicted upon her, in which the measure of damages was an amount adequate to compensate her for the inconvenience and suffering caused thereby. In this cause suit must be brought by the husband and wife jointly. In case of injury to the child, the rule is nearly the same. A cause of action arises in favor of the father for the loss of the child's services and for the cost of curing and caring for him. A separate cause of action arises in favor of the child for the personal injury which he has sustained and for the suffering to which he has been thereby subjected, and for any permanent injury reaching beyond his minority; upon this cause of action suit is brought for the infant by his guardian, or by a third person, who is styled the next friend or *prochein ami*. The father, if living, usually does, and by natural right may, appear for the infant as next friend.

In cases where the cause of action is made to survive the injured party by statute, the statute usually provides by whom the suit shall be brought and prosecuted, and in all such cases its provisions must be strictly followed.

Liability for Act of Partner.—As a general rule of law, each partner in a copartnership is bound by the acts of his copartners performed in the scope of the partnership business.

This law has been held to apply where a patient employed a firm of physicians to treat a broken leg. Both members of the firm attended him. The treatment of the one was skillful and proper, but the treatment of the other was negligent and unskillful. Suit was commenced against both, and the court held them to be equally amenable.*

Effect of Judgment against Patient for Fee upon Suit by him for Malpractice.—Although the effect of a judgment obtained by a physician against a patient for his fee in a given case upon a cause of action for malpractice in that particular case has already been treated,† it is thought advisable to refer to the subject again at this point.

Should a physician begin a suit, say before a justice of the peace, to recover the value of his services in a given case, and the defendant appears and defends upon the grounds that the services were valueless and that he sustained injury from the physician's negligence,

---

* Whittaker *vs.* Collins, 34 Minn., 299.

† See page 220.

etc., and a judgment is rendered in favor of the physician, this judgment, if unrepealed, stands as a complete adjudication of the patient's cause of action for damages, and will prevent him from subsequently bringing suit against the physician in another or higher court to recover damages. But supposing the patient does not appear, but suffers judgment to be entered against him by default, or supposing he appears and defends upon other grounds than those of the physician's negligence or incompetence; what, then, is the effect of a judgment for the physician? This is a question upon which the courts of different States differ. Those of Indiana, Iowa, Ohio, and Wisconsin* hold that such a judgment will not prevent the patient from afterward suing the physician to recover damages sustained by reason of his negligence or incompetency. Upon the other hand, the courts of New York, New Jersey,† and West Virginia ‡ hold that a judgment in behalf of the physician

---

* Goble *vs.* Dillon, 86 Ind., 327; Sykes *vs* Bonner, 1 Cin. Rep., 464; Ressequie *vs.* Byers, 52 Wis., 650; Whitesell *vs.* Hill, 101 Ia., 629, 66 N. W. Rep., 894.

† Gates *vs.* Preston, 41 N. Y., 113; Blair *vs.* Bartlett, 75 N. Y., 150; Dunham *vs.* Bower, 77 Id., 76; Ely *vs.* Wilbur, 49 N. J. L., 685.

‡ In West Virginia the court goes only so far as to hold that the judgment obtained by the physician for the amount of his fees is a bar to an action by the patient for malpractice in that case, where the patient appeared generally in the suit instituted by the physician. Had the judgment of the physician been obtained by default, or had the patient appeared specially to plead in abatement to the action, then he would

for his fees in a particular case is a complete bar to an action by the patient for damages sustained by him from improper treatment of the physician in that case, whether in the defense the character of the professional services rendered is subject to adjudication or not. Nor is the judgment in behalf of the physician for his fees the less efficacious because the suit in which it was obtained was begun before a justice of the peace after suit was commenced in a higher court by the patient to recover damages against the physician for negligent treatment in the particular case.*

In those States in which the courts have not passed upon this question it must be considered an open one.

Of Proving Malpractice.—In a former chapter of this work it has been stated that the implied contract of the physician is not that he will cure or even benefit his patients, but simply that he will use ordinary skill and diligence in that behalf; and the preceding pages of this chapter have shown that the physician's liability to a patient can not be predicated upon the mere failure of his skill to benefit the patient, or upon the mere fact that the patient has become worse under his treatment, but that such liability must be founded upon incompetency, unskillfulness, or negligence shown in the

---

not be precluded thereby from maintaining an action of malpractice against the physician. Lawson *vs.* Conway, 37 W. Va., 159.

* Bellinger *vs.* Craigue, 31 Barb., 534.

treatment of the particular case, from which unprofessional treatment injury has resulted.*　It therefore follows that, in an action brought to recover damages resulting from malpractice, proof of the mere fact that a fractured leg is shorter after healing does not amount to *prima facie* evidence of want of skill or care in the surgeon who attended the same.†

Justice Lyon, of the Wisconsin supreme court, in commenting upon the danger of receiving conditions as evidence of improper treatment, said: "The sad thought, 'it might have been,' forces itself upon all in hours of sorrow and gloom; but, unless the thought is verified by substantive and reasonably conclusive proof, it furnishes no safe basis of judicial judgment.

"It is a frequent occurrence that patients change their physicians; also, that the second physician called disapproves the treatment of his predecessor, and changes it, perhaps properly, and the patient dies. In such a case, if it should appear that the practice of the physician first called was incorrect, there is always room to conjecture that had the patient been properly treated in the first instance he would not have died. And yet, if a verdict based upon mere conjecture could be sustained, holding the physician first employed guilty of causing the death of the patient, the practice of med-

---

* Wurdemann *vs.* Barnes, 92 Wis., 206.
† Piles *vs.* Hughes, 10 Iowa, 579.

icine and surgery would be most perilous callings. The law does not subject the members of those or any other professions to any such peril." *

And so, where an oculist operated upon a girl of seven years, who had been cross-eyed for some years, for the purpose of straightening her eye, and the evidence showed that he performed the operation in the usual and approved manner, and bandaged the child's eyes and gave directions for her future treatment, other evidence will be required upon which to base a verdict against the oculist than that the child lost the sight of the eye after the operation. To justify such a verdict there must be evidence showing a want of the requisite skill, knowledge, or care on the part of the oculist. The court, on review of this case, said: "We feel certain that a verdict in favor of the plaintiff was not authorized by the evidence, and we believe that sympathy for the plaintiff unduly influenced the jury in rendering such a verdict." †

In the case of Sims vs. Parker,‡ the plaintiff, feeling certain pains, went to the defendant, who examined him and told him that he was ruptured, and thereupon applied a truss. After the truss was put on the plaintiff suffered great pain and went back several times, but

---

* Gores vs. Graff, 77 Wis., 174, 46 N. W. Rep., 48.
† Feeney vs. Spalding, 89 Me., 111, 35 Atl. Rep., 1027.
‡ Sims vs. Parker, 41 Ill. App., 284.

was told that the pressure of the truss was necessary. The evidence showed that the plaintiff was a fleshy man, that at the time he first applied to the defendant there was a slight swelling or protuberance at the point where he located the pain, and that the defendant adjusted the bulb of the truss over this. When the truss was taken off at the end of two weeks this swelling had increased and developed into an abscess. The physician who attended the plaintiff for the abscess was unable to say whether there was an incipient abscess at the time the truss was first adjusted or whether the abscess was produced by the truss.

The fair conclusion from the evidence given by the experts was that there was no rupture on the plaintiff. It was also shown that it is very difficult in certain cases to tell with certainty whether there is in fact a hernia or not, particularly in the case of fleshy persons.

There was also evidence that tended slightly to show that the abscess was caused by the pressure of the truss, but there was no evidence that the defendant was negligent or unskillful in his diagnosis or in fitting the truss.

This evidence was held to be insufficient to warrant a verdict for the plaintiff. The court said: " Proof that he was mistaken as to the existence of a rupture, or that the abscess was caused by the pressure of the truss, was not enough to entitle plaintiff to a verdict.

24

" Proof of a bad result or of a mishap is of itself no evidence of negligence or lack of skill. The defendant is qualified to practise medicine and surgery, and the evidence of the experts in his profession show him competent and skillful. Before a recovery could be had against him it must be shown that his treatment was improper or negligent, not merely that he was mistaken or that his treatment resulted injuriously to the plaintiff. A physician or surgeon, or one who holds himself out as such, is only bound to exercise ordinary skill and care in the treatment of a given case, and in order to hold him liable it must be shown that he failed to exercise such skill and care.

" The jury can not draw the conclusion of unskillfulness from proof of what the result of the treatment was, but that the treatment was improper must be shown by evidence."

From this and the preceding cases it may properly be inferred that the burden of proof is always upon the party attempting to show that the physician has been guilty of lack of skill or of want of care. This has been held to be the law in a number of cases,* whether the question arises in a suit against the doctor for malpractice, or whether the issue is raised in a suit begun by

---

* Chase *vs.* Nelson, 39 Ill. App., 53; Robinson *vs.* Campbell, 47 Ia., 625.

the doctor against his patient for the recovery of fees, and incompetence and negligence are pleaded by the defendant as a defense to the action.

The general rule regarding the burden of proof is very well stated by Justice Mayham as follows: " The burden of establishing affirmatively either want of ordinary skill, or a failure to use his best skill, or some negligence in the care or attention of the plaintiff's case, which resulted to her injury, must be met before she can recover." *

And so in a case where the patients had sustained a Pott's fracture and the physician, so the evidence seemed to indicate, diagnosticated and treated it as a fracture of both bones at a point about five inches above the ankle, the court held there was no evidence upon which to sustain a verdict of damages for permanent injury by stiffening of the ankle joint. In this case an expert witness introduced by the plaintiff stated, on cross-examination, that he recognized the fact as an expert witness that a Pott's fracture will probably leave the joint in a permanently inferior condition, even when the very best surgical skill is employed, and is employed at the most opportune time, and under the best circumstances. In answer to the question, " You are not prepared to say to the jury that the present condition that

---

* Winner *vs.* Lathrop, 67 Hun, 511.

the plaintiff presents is due to the fact of what he says in regard to the treatment he received at the hands of Dr. ——? " the expert replied, " I have not said it."

The court said : " It seems to us, therefore, that the case is absolutely barren of any evidence from which it may be inferred that the permanent injury which the plaintiff would suffer had come from any neglect or want of skill on the part of the defendant." *

But what is the character of proof required by the courts to fix liability upon the physician for the unfortunate results attending his treatment?

The case of Pettigrew *vs.* Lewis *et al.* † is instructive upon this point. The plaintiff had undergone an operation for strabismus. The evidence given by the plaintiff was that prior to the operation her eye was strong and in good condition, except as to the affection for which it had been treated; that the operation was successful in straightening the eye, but that afterward neither eye was as strong as before; that some time after the operation she had " a spell of sore eyes "; that the lids were afterward inflamed and her " eyes watered " when she went out in the wind or cold; that she found on attempting to use her eyes that they were weak, and that it was necessary to bring objects close

---

* Smith *vs.* Dumond, 6 N. Y. Supp., 242.

† Pettigrew *vs.* Lewis *et al.*, 46 Kan., 78, 26 Pac. Rep., 458.

to her in order to see clearly. This, it seems, is about the extent of the evidence offered on behalf of the plaintiff. The supreme court, in reviewing the case, discourses very comprehensively upon the character of evidence required in such a case to fix liability upon the physician. The following liberal extract is therefore taken from the opinion:

" To maintain her action, the plaintiff should have offered the evidence of skilled witnesses to show that the present condition of her eyes was the result of the operation, and that it was unskillfully and negligently performed. ' This evidence must from the very nature of the case come from experts, as other witnesses are not competent to give it, nor are juries supposed to be conversant with what is peculiar with the science and practice of the professions of medicine and surgery to that degree which will enable them to dispense with all explanations.' *

" ' The question whether a surgical operation has been unskillfully performed or not is one of science, and is to be determined by the testimony of skillful surgeons as to their opinion, founded either wholly upon an examination of the part operated on, or partly upon such examination, and partly on information derived from the patient; or partly on such examination, partly on

* Tefft *vs.* Wilcox, 6 Kan., 46.

such information, and partly on facts conceded or proved at the trial; or partly on such examination and partly on facts conceded or proved at the trial.' * It would have been easy for the plaintiff to have submitted to an examination by an experienced physician or oculist capable of determining whether the condition of her eyes was the result of the operation, and whether that operation was performed with reasonable skill and care. Cases may arise where there is such gross negligence and want of skill in performing an operation as to dispense with the testimony of professional witnesses; but not so in the present case. It is not conceded or proved that the weakness of her eyes had materially resulted from the operation; and even if it was the question would still arise, Was she in a fit physical condition to undergo the operation? Did the defendants, before beginning the operation, make due examination to determine her condition and the necessity for an operation? Was the operation performed in a careful and skillful manner? What was the standard of professional skill and scientific knowledge required of these men in that locality? Was the after-treatment and were the directions given for the subsequent care of the eye such as would meet the approval of the profession in its present advanced condition? If a mistake was

* McClel. Mal., 304.

made, was it a case of reasonable doubt or uncertainty or a mere error in judgment, for which there is no responsibility? It was the duty of the defendants to exercise ordinary care and skill; and, this being a duty imposed by law, it will be presumed that the operation was carefully and skillfully performed in the absence of proof to the contrary." *

Exceptions.—It will be observed that in the foregoing statement the court says: " Cases may arise where there is such gross negligence and want of skill in performing an operation as to dispense with the testimony of professional witnesses." This, in other words, means that cases may arise in which a presumption of unskillfulness or negligence on the part of the physician will arise from the condition in which such treatment has left the patient. Such a case, it will be clearly seen, forms an exception to all of the rules above laid down for proving negligence and incompetency. A recent Minnesota case appears to illustrate this exception. In this case, however, the evidence is so meagrely stated in the report that it can not be determined with certainty whether the opinion of the court was based upon the mere condition of the patient or whether there was evidence before it of particular acts of negligence or unskillfulness which the record fails to disclose. The case

---

* State *vs.* Housekeeper *et al.*, 70 Md., 162.

was as follows: The patient had suffered a miscarriage, having been delivered of a five-months-old fœtus.
The physician removed the placenta, but in so doing permitted a piece of it about two inches long and two thirds
of an inch thick to remain; blood poisoning and a septic
condition of the patient ensued from which her left leg
became gangrenous, necessitating amputation. Whether there was any evidence offered showing that the
defendant's treatment was improper may be reasonably
doubted from the report of the case, wherein the court,
upon this question, simply says: " Unexplained, the evidence was sufficient to justify the conclusion that the defendant, in the exercise of that degree of care and skill
which the law exacts of a physician, might and ought
to have reasonably discovered and removed the remnant
of the afterbirth." * A proper deduction from this
seems to be that the condition of the patient bespoke improper professional treatment, which it became incumbent upon the defendant to explain; thus forming an
exception to the general rule prescribed for proving the
physician's liability.

Another case which seems clearly to be an exception
to the rule is that of Lewis vs. Dwinell,† in which the
defendant, after repeated examinations, informed the
plaintiff that she was " all right," notwithstanding

---

* Moratzky vs. Wirth, 67 Minn., 46.
† Lewis vs. Dwinell, 84 Me., 497.

she had sustained a serious rupture of the perinæum. Upon the question of the defendant's liability as shown from the evidence and from the plaintiff's condition, Justice Haskell said: " If the defendant knew of the rupture and concealed it from the plaintiff, neither taking measures for its repair or relief himself nor giving an opportunity for other professional skill to be employed, little can be said in his excuse. But if the defendant neither discovered the lesion nor had any knowledge of it, a different question arises: Was he professionally negligent in his examinations? He was a physician of seven years' practice, a graduate of Boston University, and must have possessed the ordinary skill and learning required in such cases. His failure then to discover, after repeated examinations, the serious injury from which the plaintiff was suffering, must be held to be actionable negligence. Reasonable attention from a physician of ordinary intelligence would have discovered so palpable an injury."

Upon the trial of a suit for damages resulting from malpractice, the liability of the physician is a matter to be passed upon by the jury; aided by the evidence of expert witnesses, who are supposed to enlighten them upon all matters of professional knowledge involved in the case, and guided in their deliberations by instructions from the trial judge upon the law applicable to the questions before them.

Measure of Damages.—Damages is defined as "the injury or loss for which compensation is sought," * and the measure of damages refers to the amount or extent of such " injury," or " loss "; or, perhaps, more properly, to the amount of compensation to be awarded in adjustment of such " injury " or " loss."

In assessing the amount of damages which the injured party should receive to compensate him for the injury or loss he has sustained, three distinct classes are recognized and awarded to suit the merits of the case: First, nominal damages, or some trifling sum, which is awarded when a breach of duty or an infraction of the plaintiff's right is shown, but no serious loss is proved to have been sustained.

Second, substantial or compensatory damages. These are such as are designed and awarded to compensate for the actual loss or injury sustained.

Third, exemplary damages, also termed punitive and vindictive damages. This class of damages exceeds the loss actually sustained, and is given as a kind of punishment to the defendant.

Nominal Damages.—Nominal damages, it seems, are implied by law when there is shown to have been a violation of the plaintiff's right, but where no damages are shown by the evidence to have been sustained.

---

* Bouv. Law Dic. Title, Damages.

Nominal damages are also proper in those cases where lack of skill or care is shown, but where it is impossible to distinguish between the consequences of the physical ailment for which the patient was being treated and those of the lack of professional skill and care.*

Compensatory Damages.—Substantial or compensatory damages can be awarded only when there is evidence adduced at the trial of a loss or injury sustained from the defendant's wrongful act upon which suit is brought. In such a case it is the duty of the jury to weigh the evidence and fix such an amount as in their opinion properly compensates the injured party for the loss suffered, as determined from the evidence before them.

In estimating such damages it is proper for the jury, when there is evidence before them to justify their so doing, to take into consideration:

The expenses incurred by way of physician's or surgeon's fees, nursing, and drugs and medicines which have been rendered necessary by the unprofessional treatment complained of. They must, however, carefully exclude from this item all expenses of the sort necessitated by the original sickness or injury for which the defendant treated the patient. If the expenses for the original illness and those necessitated by

---

* Becker vs. Janinski, 27 Abb. N. C., 45.

the aggravated injuries or injuries caused by the act complained of can not be separated, then this item should not be considered.

The loss of time caused by such injury, together with the value of the same.

The physical and mental pain and suffering endured as a direct result of such improper treatment.

And in cases where the injury is shown to be permanent, the jury may consider its effect upon the plaintiff's capacity to earn money in the future, and also consider future pain and suffering, both physical and mental.

Exemplary Damages.—Whenever the unprofessional treatment upon which the suit is based is attended with fraud, malice, or gross negligence, and such fact is shown to the jury by the evidence, they may, in assessing the plaintiff's damages, consider not only the actual expense inflicted upon him, together with the amount proper to compensate him for physical and mental anguish, but may go still further and inflict damages upon the defendant for his intentionally vicious or grossly improper act. Such damages are exemplary or punitive, and are allowable upon the theory that they will act as a punishment to the wrongdoer, and thereby deter others from committing like flagrant acts.

While the foregoing general treatment of damages as involved in the scope of these articles is calculated to give the practitioner a comprehensive although rather superficial idea of the subject, it is thought that a more particular and less extended examination will be of greater value and more satisfactory to the reader. This effect is designed to be accomplished by examining particular cases, thus showing correctly the application of these governing rules.

Illustrations: Nominal Damages.—Nominal damages are proper and are the only damages that the jury will be permitted to assess either where no damages are shown by the evidence to have been sustained or where the injury sustained from the defendant's improper treatment can not be distinguished from the sickness or injury for which the plaintiff was treated.

In the case of Becker *vs.* Janinski,* the plaintiff had a miscarriage. The evidence showed some improper treatment by the defendant; it also showed that the patient's general health was impaired. There was evidence introduced on behalf of the defendant to show the injurious effect of a miscarriage upon the general health, from which it was argued that the injury complained of to the plaintiff's health was the result of the miscarriage, for which the defendant was not to blame; and, at least, that it was impossible to say the injury was due solely to the alleged improper treatment.

* Becker *vs.* Janinski, 27 Abb. N. C., 45.

Upon this point the jury was instructed that " The defendant not being responsible for the miscarriage, he is not to be made liable for any of its consequences. If liable at all, he is liable only for the effects of his maltreatment of the plaintiff. So that, should you find it impossible to distinguish between the consequences of the miscarriage and the consequences of the maltreatment—should you be unable to find upon the evidence that the plaintiff has suffered any injury distinctively due to maltreatment—you will award only nominal damages against the defendant."

Illustrations: Compensatory Damages.—In this class of damages the jury are supposed to determine as accurately as possible the extent of the injury suffered by the plaintiff and give him damages which shall fairly compensate him for the loss and injury sustained. There are, however, so many elements to be considered in determining damages in this kind of cases which can not be reduced to an accurate monetary basis that the verdicts of different juries will very materially differ in the same case.

This is very well illustrated in the case of Barnes *vs.* Means.* Here the plaintiff had sustained fractures of the tibia and fibula ; that of the tibia was oblique and near the upper part of the lower third of the limb, while that of the fibula was nearly transverse, and was

---

* Barnes *vs.* Means, 82 Ill., 379.

from three to four inches above the ankle joint. By reason of not applying extension and counter-extension at the proper time the bones were allowed to lap three quarters of an inch. This case was twice tried. The first jury assessed the damages at five hundred dollars. On motion of defendant the verdict was set aside, a new trial was had, and the damages were assessed by the new jury at one thousand dollars.

Probably the most satisfactory manner of arriving at an appropriate idea of what juries are disposed to consider a fair compensation in this class of cases is by observing the amount which they have given in a few of their verdicts.

In the case of Wood *vs.* Clapp.* a verdict of one thousand dollars was assessed where the evidence showed an improper and unsuccessful treatment of an arm which resulted in permanent disability.

In the case of Smothers *vs.* Hanks,† both bones of the plaintiff's arm were fractured near the wrist. The evidence showed unskillful treatment. The arm, hand, and fingers were crooked and stiff—perhaps permanently so. The jury gave a verdict for two thousand dollars. This, on motion for a new trial, was reduced to twelve hundred dollars, probably by mutual consent of the parties.

---

* Wood *vs.* Clapp, 4 Sneed (Tenn.), 65.
† Smothers *vs.* Hanks, 34 Ia., 286.

In the case of Teft vs. Wilcox,* the plaintiff, who had suffered from rheumatism and neuralgia in his shoulder, sustained a dislocation of the shoulder joint. From the improper treatment of this injury the shoulder became permanently disabled. His damages were assessed at two thousand nine hundred dollars.

It was held in the case of Kelsey vs. Hay † that a verdict of four thousand five hundred dollars was not excessive where the plaintiff was crippled in both legs for life by the ignorance and mismanagement of his physician. The deformity complained of resulted from improper treatment of fractures in both legs, at what points the report does not show.

In the case of Quinn vs. Higgins ‡ damages amounting to one thousand six hundred dollars were awarded for maltreatment of a fractured leg which resulted in a " false joint."

In the case of Williams vs. Poppleton # the plaintiff had received an injury at the ankle, probably a dislocation and slight fracture. There was some evidence of improper treatment; the bones became diseased and the leg was amputated above the knee. The jury found a verdict of nine hundred dollars. Whether this verdict

---

* Teft vs. Wilcox, 6 Kan., 57.

† Kelsey vs. Hay, 84 Ind., 189.

‡ Quinn vs. Higgins, 63 Wis , 664.

Williams vs. Poppleton, 3 Oregon, 139.

was intended as a compensation for the loss of the leg through improper treatment of the defendant, or whether it was for unnecessarily and improperly prolonging the plaintiff's sufferings in not performing the amputation for a considerable time after it should have been performed, does not appear. It was probably intended for the latter.

The jury awarded damages to the amount of two thousand and twenty-five dollars in the case of Howard *vs.* Grover,* where the defendant performed two amputations upon the plaintiff's thigh, both of which were unsuccessful. The first amputation was at the proper place, but the bone was left protruding too far; the second was not shown to have been improperly performed, but was not performed at the right place. The court, in commenting upon the amount of this verdict, said: " The practice of surgery is indispensable to the community, and while damages should be paid for negligence and carelessness, surgeons should not be deterred from the pursuit of their profession by intemperate and extravagant verdicts. The compensation to surgeons in the country is small in comparison with what is paid in cities for similar services, and an error of judgment is visited with severe penalty, which takes from one a large share of the surplus earnings of a long life."

---

* Howard *vs.* Grover, 28 Me., 97.

The court expressed the opinion that the jury must have been actuated " by some undue influence " in assessing the amount of damages; they expressed great reluctance, however, to interfering, and therefore stated that the verdict might stand if the plaintiff would remit five hundred dollars of the amount assessed.

It is perhaps proper to say that this case arose in Maine, and was tried in 1848.

For the improper treatment of an eye, from which loss of sight in that eye resulted, a Missouri jury gave a verdict of $362.75,* evidently a compromise verdict.

For the failure of a physician to discover and repair a serious rupture of the perinæum a Maine jury assessed damages at four hundred and fifty dollars.† And for improper uterine treatment, whereby the neck of the womb became closed, entailing much suffering and considerable expense, a Wisconsin jury assessed damages at three hundred and fifty dollars.‡

Illustrations: Exemplary Damages.—Upon the question of exemplary damages, the case of Brooke *vs.* Clark # is instructive. In this case the attending physician tied a ligature around the child's penis, instead of the umbilical cord, at his birth, whereby the glans of the penis came entirely off.

---

* McMurdock *vs.* Kimberlin, 23 Mo. App., 523.
† Lewis *vs.* Dwinell, 84 Me., 497.
‡ Gates *vs.* Fleischer, 67 Wis., 504.
# Brooke *vs.* Clark, 57 Tex., 105.

The facts may probably be best gathered from the evidence of the child's grandmother, which was as follows: " Dr. —— was the attending physician. He was standing at the foot of the bed and received the child from its mother. Before receiving the child from beneath the bedclothes he tied one cord or ligature, and then removed the cover, tied the second ligature, and cut the umbilical cord, when the child was by Dr. —— handed to the witness, who wrapped it in a blanket and sat by the stove trying to quiet it. When the first ligature was tied the child cried out like it was hurt, and continued to cry for about an hour. The doctor then took the child in his lap and examined it, and said the string had slipped off the navel cord. He asked for another string, which I gave him. I had given him one at his request before the child was born; both were common wrapping twine. Mrs. C. assisted Dr. ——, and he tied a string on the navel cord and returned the child to me, and I washed and dressed it and cared for it until morning. The child had spells of crying through the night; all the dressing that was done next day was changing its diaper, and that was done by me. When washing the child next morning I found a string hanging down, and, taking hold of it, I found it was tied to the child's penis; it was a part of the same cord witness gave to Dr. —— the night before. I had charge of the child at night. When Dr. —— came in I showed him what he had done, and he said it was probably owing to Mrs. C. being excited and holding up the wrong thing for him to tie. There was but one string around the navel cord when I dressed the child. There was no string tied after the child was dressed; no one had the child before it was dressed but Dr. —— and myself." Upon the trial of the case the jury fixed the damages at five thousand five hundred dollars.

In commenting upon the propriety of exemplary damages in this case Justice Gould said: " The criminal indifference of the defendant to results was a fact which the jury were at liberty to infer from the gross mistake which he either made or permitted to be made, and the grievous injury which was liable to result and did result therefrom. If there was other evidence tending to negative any wrong intent or actual indifference on his part, still the existence or non-existence of such criminal indifference was a question of fact for the jury, and was rightly submitted to them. If the conduct of the defendant in the discharge of his duty as accoucheur was so grossly negligent as to raise the presumption of his criminal indifference to results, we very greatly doubt whether it should avail to exempt him from exemplary damages for him to show that he had no bad motive, and that he acted otherwise in a manner tending to show that he was not, at heart, indifferent. Where the act is so grossly negligent as to raise the presumption of indifference, evidence that in other matters connected therewith he had shown due care, and that actual indifference would have been in fact indifference to his own interest, should, we think, not be allowed for any other purpose than to be considered by the jury in fixing the amount of exemplary damages."

It is believed that in this case the court expresses the true rule governing exemplary damages. The question is, however, one upon which there is conflict of authority. In an earlier Michigan case the court expresses the opinion that when the evidence shows no evil motive in the commission of an act, the jury can not give exemplary damages; and this opinion was expressed in the face of evidence sufficient, to use the language of the court, " to show such a total want of skill, and such a degree of carelessness, as would in law make the defendant below guilty of manslaughter." * The court in this case also expressed sentiments upon other phases of the question of damages which have not been approved by the wisdom of recent years, and it may reasonably be doubted that the law as expressed therein relative to exemplary damages will be recognized in future decisions as the correct doctrine.

Judgment for Plaintiff Bars Action for Subsequently Accruing Damages.—It has been shown that the jury, in

---

* Hyatt *vs.* Adams, 16 Mich., 180.

assessing damages, may properly consider the effect of the injury upon the plaintiff's capacity to earn money in the future; also the future pain and anguish, both physical and mental, that will necessarily or naturally result therefrom; in other words, the plaintiff's cause of action includes the right to recover for damages past, present, and future. The law will not tolerate a multiplicity of suits, but always compels a party litigating to enforce his whole right in a single suit, when the right is of such a nature as to render that possible; therefore if, in a suit against a physician for malpractice, the plaintiff fails, ignorantly or inadvertently, to prove future damages, and a judgment is entered in his favor against the physician for past and present damages only, such judgment will be a complete bar to another action brought for the recovery of such future damages.*

---

* Howell *vs.* Goodrich, 69 Ill., 556.

CHAPTER VIII.

Criminal Liability arises when Conduct becomes a Public Menace.—The liability of the physician resulting from the improper or wrongful exercise of the functions of his profession which has heretofore been the subject of examination is that of a civil nature, which is satisfied by the payment of an adequate compensation to the particular patient who was thereby injured. Usually in such cases of nonfeasance or malfeasance, the injury produced and the resulting right of prosecution is a matter affecting only the immediate parties to the transaction—viz., the physician and the patient—and is one in which third parties generally, or, in other words, the public or State, have no concern whatever. It is evident, however, that there may be cases in which the act complained of is so grossly unprofessional as not only to cause an injury to the patient for which he is entitled to compensatory damages but to amount as well to a serious menace to the peace and safety of the public. Such an act will, in addition to the civil liability heretofore considered, give rise to another and more

385

important liability in favor of the public or the State, known as a criminal liability.

Common Law and Statutes Regulate the Subject.— Our criminal law, like our law relative to civil matters, came from England as a part of the common law. To this many alterations and additions have been made in the several States by statutes, and in some few jurisdictions the common law relative to criminal matters is so abrogated by statutes that only those acts are considered as criminal which their legislatures have expressly declared so to be.*

The criminal law in its relation to the practice of medicine is in its nature very largely statutory, and differs in detail in the several jurisdictions; yet as a whole it is sufficiently uniform to render practicable a general treatment of the subject applicable to the several States.

Criminal Intent Presumed.—The civil liability of the physician, it has been observed, is based upon his failure to possess ordinary knowledge, or to exercise the usual or proper degree of care and diligence in applying the same. Such an act ordinarily lacks the essential element of a crime—viz., malice or a criminal intent—and can, therefore, be considered only in the light of a civil injury affecting the individual patient. That malice or crimi-

---

* This is the condition in the States of Iowa, Kansas, and Ohio.

nal intent need not always be shown to exist, but may be implied from the character of the acts complained of, is, however, a well-recognized principle of the law, it being held that one is presumed to contemplate the natural consequences of his acts, and, if these consequences are so disastrous or so fatal as to justify a presumption of malicious intent, the act will be deemed criminal even though it is in fact the result only of negligent or reckless conduct.

Gross Ignorance and Reckless Negligence; English Doctrine.—Whether or not the ignorance of a physician may be so gross, or his conduct so grossly and recklessly negligent, as to render him guilty of homicide where the patient dies from his maltreatment is a question that has been several times before the English and American courts. The doctrine established by the English courts seems to be that if the ignorance or the neglect is gross, then the criminal intent will be implied. Chief-Justice Parker says: " I call it acting wickedly when a man is grossly ignorant, and yet affects to cure people, or when he is grossly inattentive to their safety." * Some light is thrown upon the question of what degree of ignorance or what amount of negligence an English court considers gross by the words of Justice Miller, who says: " If a man knew that he was using medicine beyond his knowl-

---

* Rex *vs.* Long, 4 Car. and P., 410.

edge, and was meddling with things above his reach, that was culpable rashness. Negligence might consist in using medicines in the use of which care was required, and of the properties of which the person using them was ignorant. A person who so took a leap in the dark in the administration of medicine was guilty of gross negligence." [*]

Early American Policy.—The policy of the American courts, as manifested in the earlier cases, was that of much greater leniency, their policy being to hold the defendant guilty only when an evil or mischievous intent could be shown. In more recent cases, however, our courts have followed the English precedents, and, it is thought probable, will continue to do so, this doctrine being more in accord with the ever advancing spirit of medical and surgical science and better calculated to relieve the medical fraternity of those quacks and charlatans whose presence is a reproach upon the profession.

The earliest American case of any importance, and one which is doubly interesting because it not only illustrates the policy applied by our courts for over half a century, but also throws light upon the source of a system or school of medicine which enjoyed more or less patronage in this country for a number of years, is that

---

* Reg. *vs.* Markus, 4 F. and F., 356.

of Commonwealth *vs.* Thompson.* In this case, which was tried in 1809, Dr. Samuel Thompson, founder of the Thompsonian system of medicine, sometimes referred to as the botanical system or steam system, was tried for murder. The report of the case, it is thought, presents matter of sufficient interest to the medical profession to justify a liberal extract therefrom.

" On the trial it appeared in evidence that the prisoner, some time in the preceding December, came into Beverly, where the deceased then lived, announced himself as a physician, and professed ability to cure all fevers, whether black, gray, green, or yellow; declaring that the country was much imposed upon by physicians, who were all wrong, if he was right. He possessed several drugs, which he used as medicines, and to which he gave singular names. One he called *coffee;* another, *well-my-gristle;* and a third, *ramcats.* He had several patients in Beverly and in Salem previous to Monday, the 2d of January, when the deceased, having been for several days confined to his house by a cold, requested that the prisoner might be sent for as a physician.

" He accordingly came and ordered a large fire to be kindled to heat the room. He then placed the feet of the deceased, with his shoes off, on a stove of hot coals and wrapped him in a thick blanket, covering his head.

---

* Commonwealth *vs.* Thompson, 6 Mass., 134.

In this situation he gave him a powder in water which immediately puked him. Three minutes after he repeated the dose, which in about two minutes operated violently. He again repeated the dose, which in a short time operated with more violence. These doses were all given within the space of half an hour, the patient in the mean time drinking copiously of a warm decoction, called by the prisoner his *coffee*. The deceased, after puking, in which he brought up phlegm but no food, was ordered to a warm bed, where he lay in a profuse sweat all night. Tuesday morning the deceased left his bed and appeared to be comfortable, complaining only of debility; and in the afternoon he was visited by the prisoner, who administered two more of his emetic powders in succession, which puked the deceased, who, during the operation, drank of the prisoner's *coffee* and complained of much distress. On Wednesday morning the prisoner came and, after causing the face and hands of the deceased to be washed with rum, ordered him to walk in the air, which he did for about fifteen minutes. In the afternoon the prisoner gave him two more of his emetic powders, with draughts of his *coffee*. On Thursday the deceased appeared to be comfortable, but complained of great debility. In the afternoon the prisoner caused him to be again sweated, by placing him, with another patient, over an iron pan, with vinegar heated by hot stones put into the vinegar, covering them at the same time with blankets. On Friday and Saturday the prisoner did not visit the deceased, who appeared to be comfortable, although complaining of increased debility. On Sunday morning, the debility increasing, the prisoner was sent for, and came in the afternoon, when he administered another of his emetic powders with his *coffee*, which puked the deceased, causing him much distress. On Monday he appeared comfortable, but with increasing weakness, until the evening, when the prisoner visited him, and administered another of his emetic powders, and in about twenty minutes repeated the dose. This last dose did not operate. The prisoner then administered pearlash mixed with water, and afterward repeated his emetic potions. The deceased appeared to be in great distress and said he was dying. The prisoner then asked him how far the medicine had got down. The deceased, laying his hand on his breast, answered, Here; on which the prisoner observed that the medicine would soon get down and unscrew his navel; meaning, as was supposed by the hearers, that it would operate as a cathartic. Between nine and ten o'clock in the evening the deceased lost his reason and was seized with convulsion fits, two men being required to hold him in bed. After he was thus seized with convulsions the prisoner got down his throat one or two doses more of his emetic powders, and remarked to the father of the deceased that his son had got the *hyps* like the devil, but that his medicine would fetch him down; meaning, as the witness understood, would compose him. The next morning the regular physicians of the town were sent for, but the patient was so completely exhausted that no relief could be given. The convulsions and the loss of reason continued, with some intervals, until Tuesday evening, when the deceased expired."

The evidence showed that the "*coffee*" was a decoction of marsh rosemary mixed with the bark of the bayberry bush, which was not supposed to have injured deceased. The emetic powder, upon which the prisoner said he chiefly relied in his practice, and which was so frequently administered to deceased, was the pulverized plant commonly known as Indian tobacco, or the *Lobelia inflata* of Linnæus.

The prisoner in this case had been indicted for murder, but under the practice the jury could have found him guilty of manslaughter had they determined that the offense amounted to that crime only.

The court instructed the jury that to constitute the crime of murder the killing must have been with malice, either express or implied; that there was no express malice, and that they could not infer malice without being satisfied that the prisoner was willfully regardless of his duty and determined upon mischief.

Upon the question of the prisoner's guilt of the crime of manslaughter the court laid down the doctrine that the killing must have been a consequence of some unlawful act to constitute such a crime. This doctrine, it will be hereafter seen, has been distinctly repudiated by the supreme court of the same State in a recent decision. The court in this case continued: "Now, there is no law which prohibits any man from prescribing for a sick person with his consent, if he honestly intends to cure him by his prescription. And it is not felony if, through his ignorance of the quality of the medicine prescribed, or of the nature of the disease, or of both, the patient, contrary to his expectation, should die. The death of a man killed by voluntarily following a medical prescription can not be adjudged felony in the party prescribing, unless he, however ignorant of medical science in general, had so much knowledge or probable information of the fatal tendency of the prescription that it may be reasonably presumed by the jury to be the effect of obstinate, willful rashness, at the least, and not of an honest intention and expectation to cure." The court, after observing that if the evidence showed the administration of like remedies to have previously caused similar injurious or fatal effects, then the jury might have found the prisoner guilty of manslaughter, concluded its opinion as follows: "It is to be exceedingly lamented that the people are so easily persuaded to put confidence in these itinerant quacks, and to trust their lives to strangers without knowledge or experience. If this astonishing infatuation should continue, and men are found to yield to the impudent pretensions of ignorant empyricism, there seems to be no adequate remedy by a criminal prosecution, without the interference of the legislature, if the quack, however weak and presumptuous, should prescribe with honest intentions and expectations of relieving his patient."

Following this decision is one from the supreme court of Missouri, decided in 1844.* Here the prisoner was also a botanic physician. The patient, who was to be treated for " sciatica," was in the family way and lacked about six weeks of having completed the period of gestation. The patient's husband informed the accused of the patient's condition and told him that he had been cautioned against giving her vapor baths and emetics while in that condition. The accused declared his ability to treat the patient with perfect safety, and promptly began steaming and giving her lobelia. A few repetitions of this treatment brought on a miscarriage, from the effects of which the patient died.

The court applied the doctrine enunciated in the case of Commonwealth *vs.* Thompson, and said that as no improper motive or knowledge of the fatal tendency

---

* Rice *vs.* State, 8 Mo., 561.

of the treatment applied was shown the accused could not be held guilty.

The case of Honnard vs. People* presents a question rather of fact than of law. The patient, who was five months advanced in pregnancy, was suffering from bilious fever; the accused was attending her and, as the evidence shows, was extremely careful about giving her strong medicine, and was in no way responsible for her miscarriage. After the labor pains commenced the accused was sent for. The patient's labor being ineffectual, the doctor undertook to remove the fœtus by force. Of the first and, apparently, only presentation he succeeded in bringing away all but the head. Having no forceps, he undertook to improvise a substitute by the use of two spoons, but whether he used them to any extent is doubtful. Being himself ill, he gave up his endeavors to bring away the head and, going away, sent another doctor. The patient was then given ergot and, after a little time, the head and another fœtus besides came away. The patient from that time had no physician for about a week—why, the evidence does not show—when puerperal fever set in, from which she died in about two days. The court, in considering the criminal liability of the accused, said: "He may not have acted with either the best judgment or even ordinary skill. But

* Honnard vs. People, 77 Ill., 481.

no unprejudiced person can read the evidence without being convinced that he acted with good motives, and the evidence wholly fails to show that the puerperal fever, of which the patient died, was caused by anything done or omitted to be done by the accused.

"If physicians and surgeons can be convicted of manslaughter, and sent to the penitentiary, upon such evidence as this record contains, there would be witnessed a frightful devastation of their ranks. . . . There is wanting in this case every element of the crime of manslaughter, but that of the mere death of a human being."

In the case of State vs. Schulz,* in which the accused professed to be a Baunscheidtist, the evidence showed that the accused treated the deceased by using an instrument consisting of fine teeth or needles all over her body and applying oil; he also gave eight drops of the oil internally as a cathartic. In regard to the oil, the accused testified: "Do not know what the oleum Baunscheidtii is made of; it is a secret of the inventor."

Upon the trial the court instructed the jury that "a party, whether he be a physician or specialist, has no right to hold himself out to the public as competent to treat diseases, and induce the public to employ him, unless he knows what the medicine is he uses, and its rea-

---

* State vs. Schulz, 55 Ia., 628.

sonable effect upon the human system; and to do so, and administer internally poisonous medicines in sufficient quantities to ordinarily produce death, and death is produced thereby, he would be guilty of murder. And if the defendant in this case, through gross ignorance of the medicine used, or its reasonable effect upon the deceased as she was at the time, caused her death by an overdose of poisonous medicine, he would be guilty as charged."

The supreme court, in reviewing the case, held that this instruction was not the law, and that the physician could not be held guilty unless in prescribing and treating the patient he had so much knowledge of the fatal tendency of the prescription that it might be reasonably presumed that he administered the medicine from an obstinate, willful rashness, and not with an honest intention and expectation of effecting a cure. Thus following, it will be observed, the cases of Commonwealth *vs.* Thompson and Rice *vs.* State.

Present American Policy.—Upon the other hand, a disposition to follow the English doctrine and hold the profession to a more strict criminal accountability was first manifested by the supreme court of Arkansas in 1882.*

Here the question arose upon a point of law as to the sufficiency of the facts alleged in the indictment. These

---

* State *vs.* Hardister and Brown, 38 Ark., 605.

facts alleged in brief were that the accused unnecessarily administered to the patient, who was undergoing pains of childbirth, a large quantity of morphine, by reason of which the labor pains were retarded; that he then administered to her large and excessive quantities of fluid extract of ergot, by reason of which she had convulsions, and that he then bled the patient in the arm. That he then improperly and carelessly attempted to deliver the child with forceps. That he then improperly and carelessly administered excessive quantities of chloroform, and then, improperly, etc., punctured the head of the child with a pocket knife, unnecessarily killing it; that he inserted his finger in the mouth of the child and forced its head out of the mouth of the vagina, then tied a rope around its neck, and with force and violence, and without due caution, delivered the child; and that without delivering the afterbirth he abandoned the patient, from the effects of which she died in about six days.

The court, after reviewing all the principal authorities, English and American, said: " The court is of the opinion that the indictment in this case is sufficient. Whether the appellees are criminally responsible for the death of Mrs. S—— must depend upon the evidence. A felonious want of due care and circumspection in her treatment must be proved as alleged. For a mere mistake of judgment in the selection and

application of the remedies and appliances named in
the indictment, they would not be criminally liable.
Were they grossly ignorant of the art which they assumed to practise? Did they manifest gross ignorance
in the selection or application of the remedies? Were
the remedies unusual, inapplicable, or rashly applied?
Were appellees grossly negligent or inattentive? These
are all questions of evidence."

The next case in point of time seems to be that of
Commonwealth *vs.* Pierce,* passed upon by the same
court that decided the case of Commonwealth *vs.*
Thompson, but with quite a different result. Here
the physician caused the patient to be wrapped in
flannels saturated with kerosene for three days, from
which her flesh became so burned and blistered that
she died.

The counsel for the accused urged that if he made
the prescription with an honest purpose and intent to
cure the deceased, he was not guilty of the offense
charged, however gross his ignorance of the quality
and tendency of the remedy prescribed, or of the nature of the disease, and that to prove his guilt it must
be shown that he had so much knowledge or probable
information of the fatal tendency of the prescription
that the death may be reasonably presumed to be the

---

* Commonwealth *vs.* Pierce, 138 Mass., 165.

effect of obstinate, willful rashness, and not of an honest intent and expectation to cure. This, it will be remembered, is the doctrine enunciated by the supreme courts of Massachusetts and Missouri in the cases of Commonwealth *vs.* Thompson and Rice *vs.* State. The supreme court of Massachusetts, however, in the present case, denied the correctness of this doctrine and declared that recklessness, in the moral sense of indifference as to the result of one's actions, could not be applied as a test of criminal responsibility. That in criminal matters, as in civil, there must be an external standard of what would amount to moral recklessness in a man of reasonable prudence. That if the prescriptions used were dangerous, according to common experience, one who made use of them could not escape responsibility upon the ground that he had less than the common experience. The court said: " Common experience is necessary to the man of ordinary prudence, and a man who assumes to act as the defendant did must have it at his peril. When the jury are asked whether a stick of a certain size is a deadly weapon, they are not asked further whether the defendant knew it was so. It is enough that he used and saw it such as it was."

The principles laid down in this case have been followed in the late case of State *vs.* Gile,* and it is

---

* State *vs.* Gile, 8 Wash., 12; 35 Pac. Rep., 417.

believed will be recognized by other courts as the correct law.

Guilt to be Determined by Jury.—In determining whether or not, in a given case, a physician has been guilty of such gross professional conduct as to render him criminally liable, the question is one of fact which it is the defendant's constitutional right to have submitted to a jury for determination.* The jury, in arriving at their conclusion, are not to be governed by the usual test applicable in civil matters, and find the accused guilty because a preponderance of the evidence submitted shows guilt, but they must, before convicting, find the evidence showing guilt to be so strong as to exclude all reasonable doubt of innocence. Such a doubt must, however, be one founded upon the circumstances and evidence, and not a doubt resting upon mere conjecture or speculation.† This is the test applicable in all criminal matters.

Intoxication of Physician.—The fact that the fatal treatment may have been superinduced by drunkenness, or that the physician may have been in an intoxicated condition while rendering the services that resulted in the patient's death, would at common law be a circumstance for the jury to take into consideration in determining whether the defendant had been

---

* *Ex parte* Wong You Ting, 106 Cal., 296, 39 Pac. Rep., 627.

† U. S. *vs.* Knowles, 4 Saw., 521.

guilty of grossly improper conduct. The legislatures of several States have, however, expressly provided that a physician who administers while intoxicated a poisonous drug or medicine which results in death shall be held guilty of manslaughter, and many of the States have passed laws making it a misdemeanor for one to practise as a physician while intoxicated.*

No Right to Terminate Life.—The question of whether or not the physician ever has the right to terminate life, either that of a patient hopelessly ill and suffering intense agony, or that of a newly born monstrosity, has been very interestingly discussed, rather from an ethical than from a legal standpoint, before the Medico-Legal Society.† Legally speaking, no such right exists.

Obtaining Money under False Pretense.—Similar to the civil liability resulting from deceit is the criminal liability from obtaining money under false pretense. An interesting case of this sort was recently passed upon by the court of appeals of Maryland. Here the complaining witness called upon the defendant for medical treatment. The details of the inter-

---

* Such acts have been passed in the States of California, Idaho, Michigan, Minnesota, Montana, Nebraska, New Mexico, New York, North Dakota, Ohio, Oregon, South Dakota, Utah, Washington, Wisconsin, and Wyoming.

† An interesting paper on the subject, by Clark Bell, Esq., may be found in vol. lv, *Albany Law Journal*, p. 136.

view are perhaps best told in the words of the witness, which were as follows: " The professor offered me paper and told me to write my name and age upon it, and not let him see what I wrote. I wrote my name and age upon the paper, and he walked up and down the room and looked out of the window, and took the paper and folded it up, and placed it against his forehead, and then told me what I had written on the paper. He said, ' You suffer from stomach trouble, and I can and will cure you within six weeks; if not, I will return you your money.' I asked him when I should call again, and he said, ' Don't come; I will come and see you and work on you for hours, and after that you will be well.' He also gave me a charm to wear. I wore it around my neck for one hour. He said to wear it was essential to the treatment. I am not over the stomach trouble yet. He never came to my house and worked on me. I paid him twenty-six dollars and thirty cents." After this, and before the time fixed for curing the witness, the defendant left.

It will be remembered that no expression of opinion or promise of future events will ordinarily afford ground for an action based upon deceit. Upon similar grounds it is held that the criminal action for obtaining money under false pretense can not be based upon a promise of future profits or benefits. The counsel for the accused in the present case, therefore, contended that the accused's promise of future benefit would not sustain such a prosecution. The court was, however, of the opinion that the essential part of the transaction was the accused's representation that, in effect, he was then and there possessed of supernatural power whereby he could cure witness. This part of the transaction was no promise as to the future, but a positive assertion of a present condition, and the mere fact that a promise of future benefits operated with this representation as a part of the inducement under which the witness parted with his money would not operate to defeat the prosecution. The prisoner was held guilty.*

The purpose of this chapter being to examine only those questions of criminal liability resulting from the improper exercise of professional duties and the exercise of professional functions which are in themselves unlawful, notice will not be taken of those cases in which the physician has been guilty of criminal conduct of an ordinary character, even though committed in the course of his professional relations with his patients.

Criminal Abortions.—The most prolific source of criminal litigation growing out of the conduct of the physician in the exercise of the functions of his profession is the procurement of abortions.

---

* Jules vs. State, 85 Md., 305, 36 Atl. Rep., 1027.

Abortion as a criminal act seems to be of comparatively recent origin, as neither the ancient law writers nor the early English statutes refer to it as such.*

In many of the States the procurement of an abortion with the consent of the mother, before the child became quick, was not at common law considered a criminal act.† The theory upon which the courts arrived at this conclusion was that the procurement of an abortion, when the mother had given her consent to the operation, could be considered a wrong as against the child only. According to Blackstone, life begins, in contemplation of law, as soon as the infant is able to stir in the mother's womb; therefore, prior to this period the law did not, at least for the purposes of the present inquiry, recognize the child as *in esse* and capable of being the object of a criminal intent or act.‡ The early statutes in several of our States apparently recognized this distinction in providing that the killing of an unborn "quick" child should constitute the crime of manslaughter, etc.

This distinction is, however, forcibly repudiated by

---

* Archbold's Crim. Pr. and Pl., Pomeroy's ed., vol. i, 951.

† This was held to be the law in Iowa, Kentucky, Maine, Massachusetts, Michigan, Missouri, and New Jersey.

‡ State *vs.* Cooper, 22 N. J. Law, 52.

the Pennsylvania courts in the case of Mills *vs.* Commonwealth,* wherein the court, in reference to the contention that the absence of an allegation that the mother was quick, rendered the indictment defective, said: " Although it has been so held in Massachusetts and in some other States, it is not, I apprehend, the law in Pennsylvania, and never ought to have been the law anywhere. It is not the murder of a living child which constitutes the offense, but the destruction of gestation by wicked means and against Nature. The moment the womb is instinct with embryo life and gestation has begun, the crime may be perpetrated." This case was followed as a precedent by the supreme court of North Carolina.†

Notwithstanding the fact that it was at common law not generally considered criminal to commit an abortion upon a woman, with her consent, before the child quickened, yet if one performed such an act and the death of the mother ensued he was held guilty of murder. This was upon the ground that the act was without lawful purpose and dangerous to life, and that the consent of the mother could not take away the imputation of malice or criminal intent.‡

---

* Mills *vs.* Commonwealth, 13 Pa. St., 633.

† State *vs.* Slagle, 83 N. Car., 630.

‡ Commonwealth *vs.* Parker, 50 Mass., 263; Smith *vs.* State, 33 Me., 48.

It seems that at common law an abortion, when committed with the mother's consent, and after quickening, was not a crime, but only a misdemeanor, which could not be punished by imprisonment in the State prison.*

This question is now regulated by statutes in the several States which specify what acts shall be considered tantamount to the crime in consideration and provide penalties for their violation.† These statutes in most States now fail to draw any distinction between the commission of the offense or attempt at commission before and after the quickening of the child, making it a felony in either case. The statutes of some States, however, preserve the distinction by providing a more severe punishment when the act or attempt is committed after quickening.

A detailed examination of the statutes of the several States would require a greater space than can here be devoted to that purpose; we will therefore pass over the subject with a general statement of the most usual provisions contained in such statutes, which are that any person who shall administer to any pregnant woman any medicine, drug, or noxious thing, or who shall use or employ any instrument or other

---

* Evans *vs.* People, 49 N. Y., 86; Holliday *vs.* People, 9 Ill., 111.

† The matter in Kentucky seems to be without statutory regulation.

means with intent to produce a miscarriage, unless the same shall be necessary to preserve her life, shall be guilty of a felony.

Some States provide that the performing or attempting to perform an abortion shall be a misdemeanor, and that in case death results from the act the party performing the same shall be guilty of manslaughter. The effect of such statutes is, however, simply to reduce the crime of performing or attempting to perform an abortion from that of a felony to a misdemeanor, for the provision that the party performing the operation shall be guilty of manslaughter when death ensues does not in any material respect alter the common law. The common law upon this subject seems to be that where one attempts to cause an abortion in a way not to inflict serious injury upon the mother, and the mother dies from negligence in the operation, there being no intent to kill her, or to inflict serious injury, and no likelihood of such result, the offense is manslaughter; if, however, the act is one from which death or great injury would be likely to result, or if it were performed with intent to produce death or grievous injury, then the offense is murder.*

The liability of the mother for causing herself to

---

* Wharton's Crim. L., § 325.

miscarry, it seems at common law was regarded much the same as that of a third person. If she committed the abortion before the child had quickened she was not guilty of a crime, but if after quickening she was considered guilty. The statutes of the several States making it a crime for any person to administer to any pregnant woman any drug, etc., for the purpose of unlawfully producing an abortion, are construed as applying to third parties who commit such acts, but not as incriminating the mother who performs an abortion upon herself.* Nor was the submission of the mother at common law to the act of another in producing an abortion upon her held to render her an accomplice in the commission of the crime. She was looked upon rather as a victim of the act than as a *particeps criminis.*†

Statutes have, however, been enacted in some States making it a criminal offense for the mother to take any medicine or use or submit to the use of any instrument for the purpose of procuring her own miscarriage. Such a statute, it will be seen, entirely supersedes and alters the common law.‡

---

* Smith *vs.* Safford, 31 Ala., 45; Hatfield *vs.* Gano, 15 Iowa, 177.

† Dunn *vs.* People, 29 N. Y., 523; Com. *vs.* Wood, 11 Gray (Mass.), 85.

‡ Such laws exist in California, Connecticut, Idaho, Indiana, Minnesota, Montana, North Dakota, New York, South Carolina, South Dakota, Utah, and Wisconsin.

Advice to Produce an Abortion.—The mere solicitation or advice given to a pregnant woman that she
take medicine or adopt means to produce a miscarriage does not constitute a crime unless the solicitation or advice is acted upon. In the case of Lamb *vs.*
State,* the act upon which the prosecution was based
was the solicitation of a pregnant woman to take certain drugs for the purpose of causing an abortion, but
it was not shown that the woman did take the drugs.
In this case, after observing that the act complained
of was not included in the terms of the statute, the
court said: " It may be urged that a solicitation is
an attempt, and that an attempt to commit a misdemeanor is a misdemeanor. Pursuing the same train
of inference and reasoning, we may go a step farther,
and maintain that as the solicitation is a misdemeanor,
an attempt at solicitation would, by the same rule, be
also a misdemeanor. This process might be indefinitely
extended, so as to reach persons very remotely separated
from the act which the statute intended to punish. Certainly it would be a great calamity to invent crimes by
subtle, ingenious, and astute deduction. In all free
countries the criminal law ought to be plain, perspicu-
ous, and easily apprehended by the common intelligence
of the community. It is the essence of cruelty and

* Lamb *vs.* State, 67 Md., 524, 10 Atl. Rep., 208.

injustice to punish men for acts which can be construed to be crimes only by the application of artificial principles according to a mode of disquisition unknown in the ordinary business and pursuits of life."

A more recent and a stronger case than the above was decided by the New York court of appeals in 1892.* Here the crime was charged as having been committed by *advising* a pregnant woman to take a medicine, drug, or substance, and to use means to procure a miscarriage; but it was not shown that the advice was acted upon. The statute under which the defendant was prosecuted provided that " a person who, with intent thereby to procure the miscarriage of a woman, unless the same is necessary to preserve the life of the woman, . . . *advises* or causes a woman to take any medicine, drug, or substance, . . . is guilty of abortion, and is punishable, etc." The court said: " It would be a very strict and literal, if not extraordinary, construction of this section to hold that proof of mere suggestion or advice, without evidence of its being acted upon, could convict a man." The court, in discussing the question further, after observing that it would be competent for the legislature to impose a penalty for mere giving advice to a woman to take a medicine to produce an abortion, irrespective of its being acted

---

* People *vs.* Phelps, 133 N. Y., 267; 30 N. E. Rep., 1012.
27

upon, said: " For the man to be 'guilty of abortion' within the provisions of this chapter, who has advised the woman to take a drug, it is necessarily and logically to be implied that his advice should have been followed by the act. Otherwise we should have to draw the apparently absurd conclusion that the legislature intended that abortion could be committed or caused by the act of offering advice."

Intent, Rather than Efficacy of Means Employed, Governs.—In one of the first English statutes * enacted for the purpose of preventing the procurement of abortions, the expression " any poison or other noxious thing " was made use of in describing an unlawful means of performing the forbidden act. This expression has been reenacted in the statutes of many of our States, and is judicially defined as being any drug, medicine, or other thing which is hurtful or harmful.

Under the New Jersey statute which makes it a crime to administer any drug, poison, medicine, or noxious thing with intent to produce an abortion, the court held that it was not necessary that the drug or medicine used should accomplish the effect designed, or should even be capable of producing a miscarriage; but if it is hurtful and is administered, prescribed, or

* 9 Geo. IV, c. 31, § 13.

advised with the intent to cause a miscarriage, the crime is complete the moment the medicine is taken. The reasoning of the court in this case is based upon sound policy, and should commend itself as correct law whenever the question may in the future arise. Justice Scudder, in assigning the reason for this conclusion, said: " The design of the statute was not so much to prevent the procuring of abortions, however offensive these may be to morals and decency, as to guard the health and life of the female against the consequences of such attempts. . . . It is dangerous to the life and health of the mother and to the existence of the child to experiment with any drug, medicine, or noxious thing to produce a miscarriage. The ignorance of the operator may lead him to select something that will not have the effect he designs; but if it be noxious in any degree, though in the judgment of others who have greater knowledge it can not produce the effect intended, it is within the statute." *

In a case † similar to the one above, and in which the law was held substantially as there stated, the supreme court of Colorado held that the character and capabilities of any drug alleged to have been used in the procurement or attempted procurement of an abortion are questions of fact to be determined by the jury

---

* State *vs.* Gedicke, 43 N. J. Law, 86.
† Dougherty *vs.* the People, 1 Colo., 514.

upon the evidence before them. In referring to the essential element of the crime the court said: " The acts sought to be prohibited and the crime sought to be punished are the using of noxious substances and instruments with intent to produce miscarriage. It is not necessary that the miscarriage should take place—that is, that the administering of the drugs or the use of the instrument should be followed by the expulsion of the fœtus. That is not necessary to constitute the crime. It is the administering the noxious substance or the use of the instruments with intent to produce miscarriage that makes up the crime."

A recent case in apparent conflict with the doctrine upon which the preceding cases are based comes from the Texas court of appeals.* A more careful examination of the case, however, shows that the conflict is only apparent, for the decision is based upon the wording of the Texas statute which requires that the means employed to produce the abortion shall be calculated to be efficacious. Here the accused administered cotton-root tea. Experts for the State testified that while medical books said an abortion was liable to follow the administration of cotton-root tea, they knew nothing of it by personal observation, and thought that as administered to the prosecuting wit-

---

* Williams *vs.* State, Tex. App., 19 S. W. Rep., 897.

ness by the defendant it was not calculated to produce an abortion.

Upon the question in consideration the case of Commonwealth *vs.* W.* is instructive. The statute under which the defendant was prosecuted was as follows: "If any person, with intent to procure the miscarriage of any woman, shall unlawfully administer to her any poison, drug, or substance whatsoever, or shall unlawfully use any instrument, or other means whatsoever, with like intent, such person shall be guilty of felony." The evidence in this case tended to show that the defendant had been guilty of improper liberties with the complaining witness; that shortly thereafter her fears were excited by an irregularity in her monthly courses, and that she made this known to the defendant. He expressed the belief that she had taken cold, and advised the use of a tea, and afterward brought her a phial of iron tincture, instructing her to take ten or fifteen drops before meals for the purpose of strengthening her. Professional evidence was given that the iron could do her no harm, but on the contrary was a benefit to her.

The court instructed the jury, in effect, that the motive or intent of the defendant in furnishing the prosecutrix with the iron should govern in determin-

* Com. *vs.* W., 3 Pittsb. R., 463.

ing his liability; that at the time the iron was given there was no certainty of pregnancy, and that his motive as expressed did not indicate a criminal intent; yet if they concluded from all the circumstances that the drug was administered with intent to procure a miscarriage, they should find the defendant guilty. The evidence further showed that the prosecutrix, after undergoing violent and excessive exercise, jumped from a ladder, the effect of which was to cause a miscarriage. Whether or not this means, if induced by the defendant, rendered him liable under the statute was a question strongly opposed by the defense, who urged that the words of the statute defining the crime, " or shall use any instrument or other means whatsoever," imply some act to be done by the defendant and not by the woman herself under his advice. Upon this question of law the court said to the jury: "We have given this question some reflection, and our conclusion is, to submit the case to you upon the evidence, with the instruction that the third count (alleging the excessive exercise and jump as an act induced by the defendant) sets forth the offense within the intent and meaning of the act of assembly.

"We are not prepared to adopt the view of the law presented by the defendant's counsel, for the reason that such an interpretation would greatly abridge what we conceive to be the remedial design of the act, and to a great extent frustrate the expressed intention of its framers. If a person intent on inducing an abortion must not only prescribe the drug, but with his own hand put it to the victim's lips, or, after contriving the mechanical means, must to moral constraint superadd physical force, we can readily perceive how the abortionist may practise his nefarious schemes with impunity in the very face of the statute. Upon the commonwealth's evidence, the case is one of criminal abortion—that is, unlawful means were made use of to procure a miscarriage. The defendant, according to the evidence, contrived these means, and used the prosecutrix in rendering them efficacious; what she did was as much his act as if she had been moved to it by outward constraint. The means used to produce the abortion, therefore, were used by the defendant just as much as if he had employed physical instead of moral force."

Upon the question of fact to be determined by the jury the court instructed them that they were to consider carefully all the evidence, and from that determine whether the defendant conceived the violent and excessive exercise as a means of producing a miscarriage, and whether he induced her to employ it with intent on his part of producing a miscarriage.

The jury failed to agree and were discharged. The prosecutrix soon removed to another State, and it seems was prevented from returning and appearing in court by declining health. A *nolle prosequi* was therefore entered and the defendant dismissed.

Pregnancy not Necessary for Commission of the Crime; Statutory Exceptions.—In harmony with the above decision, and probably based upon the same reason—viz., that the chief aim of the law is to protect the woman from injurious attempts to cause her to miscarry—is the rule that it is not essential that the woman shall, in fact, be pregnant when operated upon, in order to render the person attempting to produce her miscarriage criminally liable.* This rule can not, of course, exist where the statute under which the attempted abortion is sought to be punished expressly provides that the woman shall be pregnant; such statutes sometimes provide that it shall be a crime to produce or attempt to produce an abortion upon a woman "pregnant with child." In such a case it is an essential part of the crime that the person upon whom the attempt has been made was in fact so pregnant, and if the prosecution fails in showing this condition to have existed the accused can not be convicted even though it is clearly shown that he has attempted to produce an abortion. Nor will it make any difference in the necessity of prov-

---

* Regina *vs.* Goodchild, 2 Car. and K., 292; Com. *vs.* Taylor, 132 Mass., 261.

ing the pregnancy that a new law may have been enacted obviating this necessity by eliminating the words "pregnant with child," after the time of the alleged attempt to perform an abortion and before trial,* it being a constitutional guarantee that no person shall be convicted of a criminal act upon less evidence or evidence inferior to that which would have been requisite to a conviction at the time the alleged criminal act was committed.

Vitality of Fœtus not Essential to Commission of the Crime.—It has been contended that if the fœtus had lost vitality at the time the act intended to cause a miscarriage was committed, this will relieve the defendant of criminal liability. Upon this question we have two cases nearly contemporaneous—one from the supreme court of Massachusetts, decided in 1858, and one from the supreme court of Vermont, decided in 1859, which at first blush appear to be in conflict. The Vermont case lays down the rule squarely that where a physician attempts, with unlawful intent, to produce an abortion, it is no defense that it may be subsequently discovered that the fœtus had lost vitality previous to the operation or that the case was one in which it would have been necessary to destroy the fœtus to save the mother. If the physician did not know this fact at the time of treat-

---

* Com. vs. Grover, 82 Mass., 602.

ing the patient and attempted to produce the miscarriage for other than a lawful purpose, he is criminally liable.* In the Massachusetts case † there appears at first glance to be a more lenient application of the law. There the court says that if there had been evidence that the fœtus had lost its vitality, it might have been the duty of the judge to say directly to the jury that, if they so found, the case was not within the statute. Upon examining the case more carefully, however, it is apparent that the court had in contemplation the effect that would have been produced by the introduction of evidence on behalf of the defendant to show the existence of a condition justifying and requiring the operation performed. In such a case, it is apprehended, the question of intent upon the part of the defendant at the time he administered the drug or performed the operation would properly be submitted to the jury for determination, and that they should properly find him guilty or innocent accordingly as they determine his motive and purpose to have been to unlawfully relieve the mother of the burden of bearing the child, or to save her from the impending danger. With this interpretation it will be observed that the Massachusetts case is in complete harmony with the Vermont case.

---

* State *vs.* Howard, 32 Vt., 380.

† Com. *vs.* Wood, 77 Mass., 85.

Justification for Performing.—These cases bring us to an examination of the question of when a physician is justified in performing an abortion. The statutes of many States, in making it a crime to procure an abortion, expressly except those cases in which the abortion may be necessary to preserve the life of the mother, or shall have been advised by one (sometimes two) physicians to be necessary for such purpose. The proper construction of such an act seems to be that if the physician operating believes the performance of an abortion necessary to save the mother's life, and acts upon this belief without availing himself of counsel and obtaining the advice of the number of physicians named in the statute of his State that such operation is necessary, he is not exonerated unless he is correct in such belief. But if he calls in counsel, and, after proper examination, they advise him that the operation is necessary, he is then justified in performing it, and will be held harmless whether his advice was correct or not. It is apprehended that the law is substantially the same in those States having no provisions in their statutes for securing the advice of other physicians as to the necessity of performing such an operation. The fact that the preservation of the mother's life requires that a miscarriage be performed upon her is always a justification for producing an abortion, whether the statute expressly so provides or not; if, however, the physician performing the abortion assumes the responsibility of determining that the operation is necessary, and acts upon his own judgment, he will be bound at his peril to judge correctly; but if he acts in good faith in securing a consultation he will then be protected in acting upon the advice of the consultants, whether their opinion of the patient's condition is, in fact, correct or not. Should the physician's good faith in obtaining the consultation be questioned, it would then be for the jury to determine, from all the attendant circumstances, whether the consultation was a mere sham and collusive pretense made to give color of legality to an unlawful act, or was, in fact, an honest effort made to determine the patient's actual condition with a view to rendering to her such medical services as her real needs required. Probably the physician's best safeguard against an attack of this sort is the exercise of a wise discrimination in the choice of consultants, for if a consultation is secured with consultants whose professional integrity is irreproachable, no imputation of bad faith can be safely made, much less maintained.

The supreme court of Massachusetts, in a case before them some years ago,* expressed their approval of an instruction given to the jury in the trial court, wherein the legal duty of the physician in an emer-

---

* Commonwealth *vs*. Brown, 121 Mass., 69.

gency of the sort in contemplation was said to be at a much lower standard than that above fixed. Therein the trial judge said: " A physician may lawfully procure the miscarriage of a woman pregnant with child by any means applicable and reasonable for that purpose, directly or indirectly, if in so doing he acts in good faith for the preservation of the life or health of such pregnant woman. The justification of a physician thus acting must depend upon his exercising his best skill and judgment, and in the honest belief that the acts directly applied to produce a miscarriage, or applied to the treatment of a disease so as to involve a miscarriage as a not unusual incident of such treatment, are necessary to save such pregnant woman from great peril to her life or health."

While the standard upon which this instruction is based is the one underlying nearly the whole law of civil and criminal liability, yet it can not be safely advised that the courts will in similar cases follow the opinion therein expressed. Moreover, should this opinion be followed, the question of fact to be determined by the jury of whether or not the physician did exercise " his best skill and judgment " and act " in the honest belief " that such operation was necessary, will be a perilous one which will be eliminated from all cases in which the physician observes the legal duties herein first laid down.

The necessity of destroying the child to save the mother's life, as contemplated by the statute, applies to those cases only where the death of the mother can reasonably be anticipated to result from natural causes unless the child is destroyed. For example, it is evidently not within the meaning of the statute that the physician's conduct in destroying the child is justified as necessary to save the mother's life when the only reason to anticipate the mother's death from a continuation of her condition of pregnancy is that she has threatened to commit suicide if she is not operated upon.* Nor is the consent of the mother to the operation, nor a desire to screen her from exposure and disgrace, any justification for the act.†

Burden of Proving Existence or Non-existence of Necessity for Operating.—Whether it is necessary for the State to prove as an essential feature of the case of the prosecution that an abortion was not necessary to save the life of the mother, or whether, on the other hand, this fact will be presumed and the burden of proving that such operation was necessary to the mother's safety devolve upon the defendant, should he desire to make such a defense, is a question upon which the courts are divided.

The general rule of evidence regulating the burden

---

* Hatchard *vs.* State, 79 Wis., 357.

† Com. *vs.* Wood, 77 Mass., 85 ; Com. *vs.* Snow, 116 Mass., 47.

of proof is that the burden or requirement of proving any fact lies upon the party who substantially asserts the affirmative of the issue. This rule is, however, subject to a number of well-recognized exceptions, among which is the rule that when a statute, in creating or defining an offense, makes negative matter or a negative condition a material element of the offense described, then this negative condition must be proved by the party enforcing the operation of the statute. That the statutes of the several States prohibiting the production of abortion, as usually worded, come within this exception, seems evident; yet in apparent conflict with this rule, at least in the present case, is the rule that where facts are peculiarly within the knowledge of either party to a suit the burden is upon that party to prove them.

The supreme court of Oregon, in a well-considered opinion, denies the application of the last rule mentioned to this class of cases. The court, speaking through Justice Thayer, says: " The relative convenience of the parties to make the proof ought not, it seems to me, to be taken into consideration; but, in any event, no such rule should be applied to a criminal case, where the accused is presumed to be innocent, and the prosecution is required to prove him guilty beyond a reasonable doubt. . . . Proof that a physician, in his professional treatment of a woman pregnant with a child, had used means, with the intent thereby to destroy the child, and the death of the child was thereby produced, is not evidence that the treatment was not necessary to preserve the life of the mother; nor, if it produced the death of the mother, that it was not an honest effort on the part of the physician to preserve her life. The experience of mankind shows that cases have often arisen in which such treatment has necessarily been resorted to, and, in the absence of other proof, the law, in its benignity, would presume that it was performed in good faith, and for a legitimate purpose. The extent of proof to establish the negative averment in such a case would necessarily be limited by the circumstances. It could not, in the nature of things, be made positive, except as aided by the fact that the accused was able to refute it absolutely, if untrue, and had failed to attempt to do so." * The supreme court of Minnesota, in examining a question very nearly related to this one, indicated its disposition to hold the law as above laid down,† while the supreme court of Ohio very clearly expressed its opinion that it was incumbent upon the State to prove that the producing of the abortion was not " necessary to preserve the life of such mother." The ground, however, upon which this court arrived at this conclusion was that the facts showing whether or not it

---

* State *vs*. Clements, 15 Ore , 237, 14 Pac. Rep., 410.
† State *vs*. McIntyre, 19 Minn., 93.

was necessary to perform the abortion to save the mother's life were not peculiarly within the knowledge of the defendant. Upon this point the court, speaking through Chief-Justice Day, said: "The circumstances attending the procurement of an abortion, tending to prove that it was unnecessary for the purpose of preserving the life of the mother, ordinarily can be shown quite as easily upon the part of the prosecution as it can be proved by the defendant that it was necessary for that purpose." The negative of the fact that the abortion was advised by two physicians, the court holds, for a like reason, is not necessary to be proved by the State. Here the fact that the physician obtained the advice of two physicians of the necessity of the operation, if indeed he did, is one which is peculiarly within his knowledge and one of which it might be impossible for the State to prove the negative.*

Upon the other hand, it is held in several well-considered cases that it is not incumbent upon the State to show that the operation is not necessary, but that this is a matter of defense peculiarly within the knowledge of the defendant, which he must prove if available.

The supreme court of New York lays down the rule unqualifiedly that it is not for the State to prove the absence of a necessity for performing the operation,

---

* Moody *vs*. State, 17 Ohio St., 110.

but that this is a matter of defense which must be affirmatively proved by the defendant.* The same rule is adhered to in the State of Wisconsin.†

Constitutional and Legal Safeguards in Criminal Cases.—When one accused of a criminal offense enters a court of justice sitting for the purpose of determining his innocence or guilt of the crime charged, he is protected by constitutional guarantees and presumptions of law, wisely designed to guard the innocent from the untoward and sometimes perilous chain of circumstances which often falsely bespeak guilt. In all criminal cases the place of trial must, by virtue of the United States Constitution, be in the State and district where the crime has been committed. This provision prevents the possibility of taking the prisoner to a distant State, where it would probably be impossible for him to secure evidence to disprove or combat that produced by the prosecution. The manner of trial, according to the guarantee of the United States Constitution, shall be, in federal cases, by jury, and by a similar guarantee contained in the constitutions of the several States the trial of prisoners for crimes against the respective States shall also be by jury. These guarantees, together with the wise laws which generally pre-

---

* People *vs.* McGonegal, 17 N. Y. Supp., 147, 136 N. Y., 62; Bradford *vs.* People, 20 Hun, 309.

† Hatchard *vs.* State, 79 Wis., 357, 48 N. W. Rep , 380.

vail for the purpose of securing unprejudiced juries, insure the prisoner a reasonably fair trial.

The first, and probably one of the most important, intendments of the law in the prisoner's favor is the presumption of his innocence. This presumption can only be overcome by the production of evidence on the trial so strong as to remove from the mind of the jury every reasonable doubt as to his guilt. In civil matters it has been shown that the jury, after weighing the evidence, are to give their verdict in accordance with the preponderance of evidence; but in criminal matters, it must be observed, the rule is different. Here the jury can not find the accused guilty unless the evidence indicating guilt preponderates so greatly over that calculated to show innocence as to remove from the mind of the jury every reasonable doubt of the defendant's guilt.

In the manner of producing the evidence against the prisoner the solicitude of our Constitution and laws for justice to the accused is again shown. In civil matters, if a witness is far distant from the place of trial, or if he is sick and unable to appear in court, his deposition may be taken and produced upon the trial with a like effect as his personal statement made before the jury, or perhaps even greater; but not so in criminal matters. Here the Constitution says the accused shall be confronted by the witnesses against him—that is, he shall meet them face to face—and they shall testify in open court and in his presence. The prisoner is insured the right of compulsory process to obtain witnesses in his favor, and is spared the necessity of being himself required to testify. Moreover, he is guaranteed the right of being informed of the nature and cause of the accusation against him, and is assured the assistance of counsel for his defense. And, above all, when once acquitted of the crime charged, his innocence can never again be judicially questioned. But, notwithstanding all these legal barriers thrown about the accused, it is apprehended that many innocent men have suffered because of inadvertent circumstances, or perhaps through indiscretions. The evidence of circumstances is, as all know, often most convincing, and yet sometimes leads to absolutely false conclusions.

Rules Governing Admission of Evidence in Abortion Cases.—In order to understand more particularly what character of evidence is admissible to prove the commission of the crime in consideration and the amount and weight of such evidence necessary to fix the guilt, an examination will be made of a few cases in which the evidence has been passed upon and the prisoner's guilt or innocence determined by the jury. But first a brief reference will be had to the general rules of law regulating the admission of evidence.

In the trial of a case before a jury, whenever either party offers evidence, the admissibility of that evi-

dence is a question of law to be decided by the judge.
If the judge decides that the evidence is proper and
admissible, it then becomes the province of the jury to
weigh and determine the effect of that evidence. The
judge, in passing upon the admissibility of the evidence,
must determine whether it is relevant to the question
at issue. In determining this, recourse is had, if in a
civil matter, to the pleadings, or preliminary written
statements of the facts or conditions claimed by the
respective parties; if in a criminal matter, to the indictment or information, and herein will be found many
technical discussions, which can be neither interestingly
nor profitably examined.

The general rule, that the best evidence of which
the case in its nature is susceptible is required, has been
heretofore referred to. This rule simply means that
when a certain fact can be shown by authentic evidence
a secondary or inferior grade of evidence will not be
admitted to prove the same; if, for instance, the contents of a certain letter or writing are desired to be
proved, then the letter or original writing itself is the
only admissible evidence; if, however, it can be shown
that the letter is lost or destroyed, then secondary evidence of its contents may be admitted.

Similar in principle to this rule is the one rejecting
as incompetent all hearsay evidence. The rule regarding hearsay evidence is that the witness may testify as

to facts lying within his own knowledge, but that he can not testify from information given by others. There are, however, a number of exceptions to this rule which figure very importantly in the trials of the class of cases we are about to examine. One of these exceptions, or apparent exceptions, is that the expressions of another showing his bodily or mental feelings at the time they were made may be given in evidence by a witness who was present, where the physical or mental condition of such party at that time is relevant to the question in issue. Another and important exception, and one which it is difficult to adequately and clearly express in few words, is the rule that the circumstances and statements forming part of the *res gestæ* are admissible in evidence; by the term *res gestæ* is meant all of those circumstances and things which are related to or throw light upon the real question in issue. Mr. Greenleaf, in his philosophical work upon *Evidence*, in describing this rule, said: "The affairs of men consist of a complication of circumstances so intimately interwoven as to be hardly separable from each other. Each owes its birth to some preceding circumstance, and in its turn becomes the prolific parent of others; and each, during its existence, has its inseparable attributes and its kindred facts, materially affecting its character, and essential to be known, in order to a right understanding of its nature. These surrounding circumstances,

constituting parts of the *res gestæ*, may always be shown
to the jury, along with the principal fact; and their admissibility is determined by the judge, according to the
degree of their relation to that fact, and in the exercise
of his sound discretion; it being extremely difficult, if
not impossible, to bring this class of cases within the
limits of a more particular description." * To illustrate this rule, if one running from a room in which a
murder had just been committed were heard to use certain expressions or make certain statements, those expressions or statements would be competent as part of
the *res gestæ*, they tending to throw light upon the
main question in issue. As a general rule, the circumstances or declarations offered in proof as part of the
res gestæ must be contemporaneous with the main fact
under consideration and so connected with it as to illustrate its character. It has been held, however, that
where the witness reached the murdered person twenty
seconds after the injury and heard him say, " I'm
stabbed; I'm gone; Dan Hackett stabbed me," this evidence could be admitted as part of the *res gestæ*. The
admissibility of evidence under this rule must depend
largely upon the circumstances of the particular case,
as will be more particularly and practically seen in observing its application in the cases hereafter examined.

---

* 1 Greenleaf on Evidence, § 108.

More properly the foregoing rules admitting evidence of statements expressive of bodily and mental feelings, and statements which are part of the *res gestæ*, are not, in fact, exceptions, but are apparently exceptions to the rule debarring hearsay evidence, for the witness in neither of these cases attempts to testify as to the truth of the subject matter of the declaration, but simply as to statement or expression which he heard.

There are, however, several real exceptions to the rule. One of these exceptions, which is of material importance in this class of cases, is that dying declarations will be received as evidence of the fact which they recite. This rule is not applicable in civil matters, but only in cases of homicide, and such declarations are then admissible only for the purpose of showing the circumstances of the death. Such declarations must, however, be made while *in extremis*, the party realizing his condition and entertaining no hope of recovery. The theory upon which this class of statements is received as evidence of the fact recited is that a situation so solemn and so awful is considered by the law as creating an obligation equal to that which is imposed by a positive oath in a court of justice.*

Another exception which sometimes has an important bearing in this class of cases is the rule that con-

---

* 1 Greenleaf on Evidence, § 156.

fessions of the prisoner, or, in civil matters, admissions against interest, may be admitted in evidence to prove the subject matter of their contents. In view of this exception and of the great zeal shown by certain ministerial officers whose duty it is to apprehend and retain custody of the accused, to procure condemning evidence, often irrespective of the merits of the case, one who is so unfortunate as to have fallen under suspicion, perhaps by force of untoward circumstances, for which he is not accountable, should have this rule in mind, and carefully guard his utterances lest some intentionally innocent remark, made under the excitement of the occasion, be repeated in court, possibly with a slight alteration of wording or a change of expression, to convey an impression of guilt not intended and not justified by the facts.

These are the principal rules of evidence adverted to in determining the admissibility of evidence in this class of cases. An examination will now be made of the cases themselves for the purpose of ascertaining the weight and effect of the evidence when admitted before the jury.

Proving Unlawful Performance of Abortion; Illustrations.—In cases where the mother dies from the operation it may happen that the fact that an abortion has been performed can not be shown by any living witness. In such cases the only manner of proving the *corpus delicti,* or body of the wrong, is by having a competent medical man perform a post-mortem and then testify before the jury as to the condition which he found present. In addition to the evidence which such a physician gives as to the condition of the deceased, it is competent for him to also express his opinion or belief as to whether she was pregnant, and, if so, whether or not an abortion had been performed upon her, and give his reasons for such belief.* And so, where the defendant alleges that the deceased operated upon herself, and that he was called in after such operation and superintended her delivery of a dead fœtus and afterbirth, and acted only as an honest medical practitioner should act when called to attend a woman suffering from such injuries, it is competent for a skillful physician and surgeon who has examined the uterus of the deceased to testify whether or not in his opinion the injuries he found thereon were self-inflicted.†

The case of State *vs.* Howard ‡ is a revolting one, in which the fact that an abortion had been performed seems to have first become known through a post-mortem examination. Here the evidence showed that two girls, the deceased and her sister, left their homes for

---

* State *vs.* Smith, 32 Me., 369.
† State *vs.* Lee, 65 Conn., 265, 30 Atl. Rep., 1110.
‡ State *vs.* Howard, 32 Vt., 380.

the purpose of visiting relatives in a neighboring town. Soon afterward they left the house where they were visiting for the ostensible purpose of taking an excursion into an adjoining State, but instead they went to the house of the defendant, a practising physician; about two weeks after arriving there the deceased expired. Her body was placed in a coffin and she was sent to her home and buried, but a few days afterward was disinterred and a post-mortem examination made. The examination extended through the body and internal organs, but no examination was made of the brain. The external opening of the vagina was greatly extended, so that the hand, without much difficulty, might be passed in; the uterus was enlarged in size, its walls were thickened, and its blood-vessels were increased in size and number, as is usual in case of pregnancy, and internally there were marks of the attachment of a *placenta*, that had been removed, leaving open sinuses; the breasts were distended, and contained milk, and there was a dark areola about each nipple; the mouth of the womb was then about half an inch in diameter; the neck of the womb was greatly inflamed, and the lining membrane had all been taken off; there were sloughs and holes in the substance of the neck; the body of the womb was healthy, and all the internal organs of the body were in a natural and healthy condition. The physician who performed the post-mortem examination testified, upon the trial of the case, that in his opinion the direct cause of the death was the inflammation of the neck of the womb, and perhaps hæmorrhage; that that was a sufficient cause of death; that there had been a fœtus in the womb from four to seven months old that had been expelled before the examination. He also testified that he had removed the uterus and preserved it in alcohol, and upon request of the counsel for the State he produced it. It was exhibited to the jury and the various parts and marks were pointed out and described.

The State then produced a witness who testified to the finding of a fœtus upon the premises of the defendant. The admissibility of this evidence was contested by the defendant, but it was admitted as tending strongly to show the *corpus delicti.*

Deceased's sister then testified that when she and deceased left home it was understood between them that an abortion was to be performed upon deceased; that just before going to the defendant, who lived in a village some miles distant from the one in which they were visiting, deceased met the father of her child, who, it seems, had arranged with defendant to take the case; that arriving at the house of the defendant they told him deceased's condition, that she was six months advanced, and that they desired him to procure an abortion; that he did not consent at first, but, after corre-

sponding with the child's father, agreed to go through
with the operation for one hundred dollars; that defendant first gave deceased medicine in the form of
bitters, about a gobletful at a dose, which operated as an
emetic and cathartic. That about a week after their
arrival defendant performed an operation upon deceased with instruments, she lying on the bed in their
room, the witness being present; that he used two or
three instruments; that he used the instruments internally upon the private parts of deceased, who complained of pain and its hurting while the operation was
going on; that discharges of water came from her,
which continued to flow for two or three hours more;
that on the next day defendant made another operation
in a similar manner and attended by pain, which was
indicated by complaints and gripping of the hands;
that the result of this operation was flowing, and that
the witness saw considerable blood; that near night of
the same day defendant performed a third operation,
making the same use of instruments as in the former
operation, and in connection therewith introduced his
hand; that the result was a child about two thirds
grown; that defendant took the child from the room
and witness saw it no more. From the further evidence it seems that deceased lived a week after the
first operation; that she was delirious several days before death and became violent.

The theory upon which the defense was conducted was that deceased, before going to defendant's house, had taken strong medicines, which were accountable for the miscarriage and her subsequent death, and that the professional services rendered to her by defendant were only such as her condition required from a physician in the honest and conscientious practice of his profession. To show this, an inmate of the defendant's household was introduced as a witness, who gave in evidence as a *dying declaration* the following statement of the deceased. The witness said that on Thursday, the day before the patient's death, about noon she had a conversation with her while her sister was at dinner; that deceased told witness she thought she could not live, and did not expect to; that she had been taking powerful, poisonous medicines before she came to defendant's, and she thought she had destroyed her life, and that that was what had caused her mouth to be sore; that she hoped they would not blame the doctor; and that she thought he had done everything he could to restore her health, and that she had been out of health a long while. The witness testified that she did not see any indication that deceased was not perfectly sane, and that witness had never discovered any insanity about her, and had no suspicion of it; that she seemed sane through that day, but that on the next morning she seemed to have lost her reason.

The State introduced witnesses who testified that about four o'clock Thursday morning, the day upon which the above conversation was said to have taken place, the deceased became violent and kicked off the footboard, and that she was not in a condition to be able to converse during the day.

Other evidence of a cumulative or corroborative character was given by both sides. The jury found the defendant guilty of the procurement of an abortion. The case was appealed to the supreme court and there affirmed, after which the defendant was sentenced to the State prison.

In the case of State *vs.* Glass * is an illustration of the application of the rule admitting evidence of statements which form part of the *res gestæ*. Here the deceased applied to two physicians, informing them of her condition and asking them to perform an abortion upon her; they both refusing, she then went to the defendant. The State, in order to prove the condition of the deceased, called these two physicians as witnesses and had them testify regarding the statements made to them by deceased. The introduction of this evidence was objected to by the defendant, but it was admitted as part of the *res gestæ*. The supreme court, in reviewing the case, held that the trial court ruled cor-

---

* State *vs.* Glass, 5 Or., 73.

rectly in admitting this evidence. Here the statements admitted related so intimately to the condition which was the principal inducement to the crime for which the defendant was being tried, and were made under circumstances where every possible inducement to suppress, conceal, or distort the truth was overcome, that they could not well be considered.otherwise than as admissible upon the grounds named.

Nor, generally speaking, can the evidence of a physician who is called upon professionally to perform an unlawful abortion be objected to upon the ground that the knowledge thereby gained by him is privileged.*

This rule is illustrated in the case of State *vs.* Smith.† In this case the evidence showed that the prosecuting witness, an unmarried woman of twenty-three, who was advanced between five and six months in pregnancy, came to the house of the defendant, a practising physician, on the 25th of September, where she remained for some time, and that on the morning of October 5th she had a miscarriage.

The prosecuting witness testified that previous to the time of her going to defendant's house she was in sound physical health and that no attempt had been made to produce a miscarriage. She testified that on the morning of her arrival defendant began treating her

---

* See pp. 483, 514 *et seq.*
† State *vs.* Smith, 99 Ia., 26, 68 N. W., 428.

for the purpose of producing a miscarriage, and that certain medicines and instruments were used upon her, and that a miscarriage followed their use.

The testimony of the defendant was that the complaining witness came to her for treatment and that she was in a deranged condition; " that the uterus was sore, swollen, and very much inflamed, and it looked like it had been punctured in the mouth of it, and all around the sides "; and that it was " tipped," the parts swollen, and a discharge coming therefrom. Defendant admitted that she used the kind of instruments named by prosecuting witness, but testified that they were used in a different way and for a different purpose from that stated. She described the treatment given, and said it was proper treatment under the conditions to prevent a miscarriage. Several experienced physicians confirmed her in this statement as to the propriety of the treatment, under conditions such as she stated existed, while one or two others condemned the treatment. Defendant further testified that on the fourth day of October she found the head of the fœtus in the vagina, and that it had commenced to leave the uterus; believing that a miscarriage could not be prevented, and that the obstruction must be removed, and having no instruments, defendant sent for another physician who, upon arriving, refused to have anything to do with the case, but, according to defendant's testimony,

29

advised that Nature be allowed to take her course. Whether anything further was done to prevent or produce the miscarriage the evidence does not show.

The physician who was called to remove the fœtus was produced as a witness by the State at the trial and asked to state what he saw and did in the presence of the defendant. The defendant objected to the witness answering the question on the ground " that the things he saw, and the conversation he had with this defendant upon the occasion of the visit mentioned by him, were confidential, and that the knowledge he obtained upon that occasion was obtained in his capacity as a physician." The trial court admitted the testimony of the witness. The defendant's counsel excepted to the ruling and the question was reviewed by the supreme court, who held, in accordance with the rule above laid down relative to privileged communications, that as the facts and the testimony of this witness showed " that the communication of defendant to him was for an unlawful purpose and had for its object the commission of a crime," it therefore was not privileged.

The witness testified as follows: " I went into the room and took off my overcoat, and laid down my instruments. (Defendant) told me that she had a friend from the southern part of the State; that she came there to be treated; that she was in the family way, and was to be married to a man in Pennsylvania, and must get out of this fix before she was to be married. She wanted that I should go into the room and examine the patient, and I refused to go. She told me that the girl was sick. I told her that I would have nothing to do with the case. I went into the other room and put on my coat."

There was considerable other evidence given on behalf of both the defendant and of the State, yet the foregoing seems to have been the principal evidence upon which the case was decided. The jury found the defendant guilty of producing a miscarriage and she was sentenced to imprisonment in the penitentiary.

The question of what length of time will be considered sufficient to afford an opportunity to operate is answered to a certain extent in the cases of Commonwealth *vs.* Drake * and People *vs.* McGonegal.† In the former case the evidence showed that the woman upon whom the abortion was performed and the defendant were together fifteen minutes; this was thought to be sufficient time to afford opportunity for the operation. Here the woman upon whom the abortion was performed, and who for convenience will be designated S., and a friend came from a distant town to the city where defendant lived for the purpose of having the abortion performed. The friend testified that they

---

* Com. *vs.* Drake, 124 Mass., 21.

† People *vs.* McGonegal, 17 N. Y. Supp., 147, 136 N. Y., 62.

went to defendant's house, where S. told defendant of her condition; defendant and S. were then alone together for some fifteen minutes. In answer to a question by defendant's counsel, the witness testified that S. told her that defendant had operated on her with something which she concealed with her handkerchief. Witness further testified that S. suffered great pain that night; that two days later, having been ordered from their lodging house by their keeper, they went to the house of defendant and remained there three days.

The defendant denied that either S. or her friend had ever been in the house.

A hack driver testified that he drove the two girls from their lodging house to the corner near where defendant lived, but that he did not know where they went.

There was nothing further to connect the defendant with the procuring of the miscarriage except that the friend, who had always lived in a distant town, described accurately the interior arrangement of the house of the defendant. The jury found the defendant guilty of the crime of procuring an abortion.

In the case of People *vs.* McGonegal the deceased and defendant were alone together in defendant's office for a length of time not exceeding five minutes in duration. The State showed by expert testimony that this length of time might have been sufficient for the purpose; this, in addition to the fact that the evidence showed that defendant had met deceased some days previously, and that there had then been an opportunity to arrange for the operation, was held sufficient to justify the jury in finding that there was an opportunity to commit the crime. In this case the defendant was convicted upon circumstantial evidence. The evidence showed that a friend and intimate companion of the deceased, who knew of her pregnancy and her desire to obtain relief by prohibited means, accompanied her to the office of defendant on July 2d; that the friend remained in the reception room while the defendant and deceased were in the private office together, but that they remained there not longer than five minutes. On the 4th of July deceased was taken sick and defendant went to see her at her lodging house, and, it seems, was informed by the landlady that if there was anything wrong with the patient she must be removed. That night at about eleven o'clock defendant took the patient to another house where she remained until her death, which occurred eight days later. Upon the death of the patient the defendant removed the body himself at about twelve o'clock at night to the undertaker's, and gave a certificate of death, ascribing it to inflammatory rheumatism of the heart. It also appeared that several days subsequent to the patient's death defendant went to deceased's friend for the purpose of getting her to write or sign a letter purporting to come from the deceased which should say that she was doing nicely with an old friend of hers, working every day and Sunday, and would be home in a month or two; not to worry. About ten days after patient's death the body was exhumed and an autopsy held which showed that the death was caused by peritonitis, resulting from an abortion which had been performed upon deceased.

The defendant's evidence was that when deceased called upon him on July 2d she informed him of her condition, from which he apparently inferred that she desired him to operate upon her. She said that she had been making efforts in that direction herself, and that she was then complaining of the pains that are usually regarded as a premonition of a miscarriage; that he would not do anything to aid her in the way of procuring a miscarriage, but told her to go home and take care of herself, and that he would treat her, if she wanted him, to the best of his ability. Defendant stated when he called upon deceased on 4th of July he did not recognize her as having called upon him before, and that he did not make any particular examination of her, apparently because of the demand of the landlady for her immediate removal. The defendant's evidence does not show when he recognized deceased as the person who visited him at his office on July 2d. It seems

that defendant testified that during all the time he was
treating deceased for rheumatism, he made no examination whatever to ascertain whether the efforts made by
deceased to produce an abortion, as previously testified
to by him, had had any results or not.

The jury found the defendant guilty of manslaughter. An appeal was taken to the general term of
the supreme court where the judgment of conviction
was affirmed, and from there the case was taken to the
court of appeals, with like result. The court of appeals,
after reviewing the evidence, said: " If innocent, it was
his misfortune to voluntarily environ himself in a net-
work of circumstances which, to the minds of intelligent men required to reach results by rational pro-
cesses, would admit of no other conclusion than that
of guilt."

Evidence of Willingness and Capability Admissible.
—While it is essential for the State, in proving the commission of this sort of a crime, to show an opportunity,
it is also competent, although not essential, for it to
show a state of preparedness or of willingness on the
part of the defendant to render such services. It was
accordingly held proper to admit the evidence of a witness who testified that, several months before the alleged crime was committed, she saw a metallic instrument in the defendant's hands, in two parts, about a
foot long, round and hollow, and that the defendant

said it was the best kind of an instrument for procuring an abortion, because safer than any other kind.*

Upon the trial of a physician in New York State it was held proper to admit in evidence a circular which the defendant had issued several years previously.

In commenting upon the admissibility of this circular,† which, it seems, was a most flagrant production,

---

* Com. *vs.* Blair, 126 Mass., 40.

† The following is the principal part of the circular:

"Dr. ——'s female regulator; married ladies should not take it. For reference apply at his office. Office hours from 8 to 11 A. M., and from 1 to 5 P. M.

"*A Card.*—Dr. —— would respectfully announce to the ladies of S—— and vicinity that he is at all times ready and happy to have a social consultation upon all matters relating to pregnancy or confinement, or in regard to lawful production of a premature birth, which, in all proper cases, he will produce in a skillful manner, guarantee an easy time, and speedy recovery. For the information of all I insert the statute in reference to the unlawful production of premature birth, which is as follows, to wit:

"Every woman who shall solicit of any person any medicine, drug, or substance, or anything whatsoever, and shall take the same, or shall submit to any operation or other means whatsoever, with intent thereby to procure a miscarriage, shall be deemed guilty of a misdemeanor, and shall, upon conviction, be punished by imprisonment in the county jail not less than three months nor more than one year, or by a fine not exceeding one thousand dollars, or by both such fine and imprisonment. 2 R. S., 694, § 21.

"It is a well-settled rule of law that a person can not be compelled, under any circumstances, to answer a question where the answer would convict or tend to convict the person of a crime. Ladies, your secrets are with yourselves, and yourselves alone, whether in the street, at your homes, or as a witness, and you need answer no question when the answer would in any way tend to harm you, as stated above, or to make

and might well be calculated to strongly influence the minds of the jury, Justice Miller, of the supreme court, said: " The circular was, I think, competent as a declaration of the prisoner that he made a specialty of this business, and was versed and skilled in regard to it. It corroborated the proof introduced upon the trial, and was a statement of himself to the effect that he made it a part of his business to attend to cases of this kind. With evidence that an abortion had been procured while deceased was under prisoner's charge, his own advertisement that he was ready to perform operations of such a character certainly tended to strengthen the testimony already introduced, and was clearly admissible." *

In the case of Commonwealth *vs.* Brown † two women appeared upon the trial and testified positively to the details of the procurement of abortions upon them. A police officer appeared and testified as to the arrest of the defendant and produced the instruments in court which he had found at the defendant's office,

---

you liable under this statute to a criminal action. And, ladies, should you ever require legal assistance in any of these matters, of course employ such counsel as you think proper; but, if you are not pecuniarily able, or too delicate to act in the matter, notify me, and I will protect you at my own expense.

       (Signed.)   " Dr. ——

                                  " S——, N. Y."

* Weed *vs.* People, 3 Thomp. & C., 50.

† Com. *vs.* Brown, 121 Mass., 69.

also a speculum chair. Experts testified that most of the instruments exhibited were adapted to procuring the abortion of pregnant women, although none of them could be said to be so exactly designed for that purpose as not to also be appropriate for use in necessary and lawful acts of surgery.

The defendant in his own behalf testified that none of the instruments exhibited were adapted to use in producing abortion, but were all in common use in lawful and necessary surgical operations; he then explained to the jury the use and purpose of each instrument and of the speculum chair. He then offered to read to the jury from books of medical authority to substantiate his testimony, but was not permitted to do so. In answer to the evidence of the two women above referred to, he testified that the first one came to him to be treated for a tumor on the neck of her womb, and that she did not think she was pregnant; that he examined and treated her medicinally and surgically for a tumor which he discovered on the neck of her womb; and that he gave her no medicine capable of producing an abortive effect, nor did he use any instruments for the purpose of producing an abortion. In answer to the evidence of the second woman, he testified that she came to his office, in company with a man, who stated to him that the woman had been operated upon by a midwife to procure an abortion, and that at the request of the man he undertook to treat the woman, medicinally and surgically, to relieve her of a dead fœtus.

The police officer, above referred to, testified that on the day after arresting the defendant, he took him before the two women and asked them if they knew the prisoner, and if they had been operated upon by him, to both of which questions they answered in the affirmative, and that the prisoner then asked them if they had previously been operated upon by another person. The prisoner's counsel objected to the admission of this evidence, but it was admitted on the ground heretofore referred to—viz., that it was an admission against interest. The court very clearly stated the rule applicable in the following words: "The rule is that a statement made in the presence and hearing of a defendant, to which no reply is made, is not admissible against him, unless it appears that he was at liberty to make a reply, and that the statement was made by such person and under such circumstances as naturally to call for a reply unless he intends to admit it. But if he makes a reply wholly or partially admitting the truth of the facts stated, both the statement and the reply are competent evidence." The court in applying the rule expressed the opinion that the reply was such as to justify an inference that the defendant admitted the truth of the statements, and therefore that the statements both of the women and of the defendant were admissible.

In regard to the effect and importance which the jury should give the evidence relative to the surgical instruments, the trial judge properly instructed them as follows: " The possession by a physician of surgical instruments adapted to use in procuring the miscarriage of pregnant women would be explained consistently with that physician's innocence of any intention to use them for unlawfully procuring miscarriages, if they were instruments also adapted equally to other and legitimate uses in surgery or midwifery, unless their extraordinary number and variety was in more than ordinary proportion to the whole number and variety of surgical instruments possessed by him, or the exigencies of his practice furnished him occasion for using; but the significance, as evidence, of the possession of any number or variety of surgical instruments adapted especially to procuring miscarriage of pregnant women, would more or less depend upon circumstances, usual or unusual, ordinary or extraordinary, attending the mode of their possession and keeping, and the exigencies of such physician's practice."

The jury in this case rendered a verdict of guilty, which the supreme court, upon appeal, refused to interfere with.

Similar to the rule of evidence admitting the circular and the instruments in evidence in the cases above examined is that under which a mother-in-law was permitted to testify that defendant had a conversation with her in which the defendant, after being informed that deceased was pregnant and desired to be relieved of her child, said, "Send her to me," and stated in effect that she had operated successfully five times on one person. Upon further questioning the witness testified that she informed her daughter-in-law of this conversation before leaving home to undergo the treatment which proved fatal.*   And so, in another case,† the State was permitted to show by four different witnesses conversations had with the defendant extending through a period of four years preceding the act of which defendant was accused, showing a willingness and a preparedness to commit the crime for which she was then on trial. The evidence showed that to one witness defendant stated that she had the instruments with which to produce abortion, and had got rid of a number of children; that she showed witness the instruments, at the same time saying that if she wanted any help she could help her. To another she stated that she had committed abortion, and could do it again; that she had the instruments to use in doing it. And to another she stated her terms for perform-

---

* Com. vs. Holmes, 103 Mass., 440.

† People vs. Sessions, 58 Mich., 594, 26 N. W. Rep., 291.

ing such services, which she then proffered to the witness, who was in the family way, and told her she had the instruments for the purpose. The admissibility of this evidence was vigorously contested, but the court held it admissible and proper.

Dying Declarations.—From the very nature of this class of cases, dying declarations, and facts and statements forming parts of the *res gestæ,* are often essential features in the chain of evidence upon which the jury is asked to base a verdict of guilt. It is therefore desirable to examine more particularly the character of evidence of this sort which is admissible and proper to prove the case.

It has been heretofore shown that dying declarations must be made while *in extremis,* with a realization of the approaching end and after hope of recovery is abandoned. Also that they are admissible only in cases of homicide. Whether this condition does not entirely bar out dying declarations in abortion cases is a question upon which the courts of different States differ, some of them holding that they are not admissible in this class of cases at all. Among the latter are the courts of Pennsylvania,* Ohio,† and New York.‡ In New York, however, the legislature has, since the deci-

---

* Railing *vs.* Com., 110 Pa. St., 100.
† State *vs.* Harper, 35 Ohio St., 78.
‡ People *vs.* Davis, 56 N. Y., 95.

sion referred to, made dying declarations admissible in this class of cases. In these States the reasoning of the court is that the crime for which the defendant is being tried is not the killing of the patient, but the procurement of the abortion, and that the incidental death of the patient does not change the nature of the prosecution, but merely aggravates the penalty. The better opinion probably is that the death of the patient from the unlawful act of the accused gives to the offense the character of a felonious homicide, and that the reason for applying the rule is quite as plain as in cases of any other sort of homicide.*

A dying declaration, in order to be competent, must, however, be a statement of material facts concerning the cause and circumstances of the homicide. Thus, when deceased said, " O Aleck, what have we done? I shall die ! " the statement was held inadmissible, as it contained no reference to the cause of death, and was not made for the purpose of explaining any act connected with the death.† Nor is it sufficient that the statement should relate to a distinct fact or transaction which is the remote cause of the act producing the death. Thus, in the case where the theory of the prosecution was that the defendant had seduced the deceased, the following dying statement was held inadmissible:

---

* Montgomery vs. State, 80 Ind., 338, 41 Am. Rep., 815.

† People vs. Olmstead, 30 Mich., 431.

"He is the cause of my death. Oh, those horrible instruments! Laws is the cause of my death, he is my murderer. They abused me terribly." In regard to the nature of this statement, the court said: "These declarations did not necessarily refer to any attempt to produce an abortion. They are as plainly referable to the former relations of the parties. If it be true that the defendant had gotten the deceased with child, then her declarations were such as she might naturally make in her extremity, about her seducer, without intending to charge him with any more than her seduction. The expression, 'Oh, those horrible instruments!' might indicate that instruments were used, but in no wise charges the defendant with having used them or aided in their use." * In another case † the court, in commenting generally upon the admissibility of this class of evidence, said: "The rule that dying declarations should point distinctly to the cause of death, and to the circumstances producing and attending it, is one that should not be relaxed. Declarations at the best are uncertain evidence, liable to be misunderstood, imperfectly remembered, and incorrectly stated. As to dying declarations, there can be no cross-examination. The condition of the declarant in his extremity is often unfavorable to clear recollection, and to the giving of

---

* State *vs.* Baldwin, 79 Iowa, 714, 45 N. W. Rep., 297.

† State *vs.* Center, 35 Vt., 378.

a full and complete account of all the particulars which it might be important to know. Hence, all vague and indefinite expressions, all language that does not distinctly point to the cause of death and its attending circumstances, but requires to be aided by inference or supposition in order to establish facts tending to criminate the (defendant), should be held inadmissible."

Res Gestæ.—In regard to the admissibility of statements as part of the *res gestæ*, the general rule has been observed that the statements must be contemporaneous with the main fact under consideration. The meaning of the term contemporaneous, as here used, is not necessarily that the conversation must have taken place at the same moment that the operation was performed. Thus, when deceased left defendant's office, where the operation had presumably just been performed, walked across the street, and met a friend who accompanied her to that spot, and said, " Oh, dear, I feel weak! " the exclamation was held admissible.* This exclamation, however, might have been admitted also upon the ground that it was an expression of bodily feelings. Also, conversations had relative to the purpose of an intended visit to the physician's office before departure are held admissible to show that the patient had formed the purpose of going to the defendant to have an abor-

---

* Com. *vs.* Fenno, 134 Mass., 217.

tion performed. Thus it was held proper to allow the
roommate of deceased to testify that on the day the
abortion was alleged to have been committed, she loaned
deceased ten dollars, and to state what deceased said
she was going to do with it, and where she was going
that afternoon, and for what purpose. It was also held
proper to permit the witness to testify as to conversations had with deceased on the Wednesday and Friday
before the Saturday on which the operation was supposed to have been performed. In these conversations
witness testified that deceased said that she understood or had found out that she was in the family way;
that she had been to see the defendant about it; had
been or was going to defendant to get some medicine
or a syringe; that she had made an arrangement with
the defendant to have an operation performed upon her;
was to give twenty-five dollars, and was to return to
the defendant's on Saturday afternoon for the purpose
of having instruments used to get rid of the child.
Upon the admissibility of these conversations the supreme court said: " It was certainly competent to prove
that the deceased went to the house of the defendant
at the time it was charged in the information the abortion was produced. Upon the authorities, her intent
or purpose in going there might be shown by her declarations then made or previously made; because such
declarations become part of the *res gestæ.* For it is evi-

dent the declarations were connected with the act of
her going to the defendant; were expressive of the character, motive, or object of her conduct; and they are to
be regarded as verbal acts indicating a present purpose
or intention, and therefore are admitted in proof like
any other material facts." *

In the case of Hays *vs.* State † the evidence showed
that deceased left her home and came to the house of
the defendant, where she was operated upon to produce
an abortion.   After the operation was performed a
physician was called to attend her.   This physician
was subsequently placed on the witness stand by the
defense and testified that deceased complained of a
pressing and burning in the stomach; he also testified
that she said that she had " been taking some stuff,"
and that on the way from her home to the defendant's
house, a distance of six or seven miles, something like
a lump dropped from her, and that she did not know
what was the matter with her.   In regard to the admissibility of this evidence the court held that such
part of her statements as related to her then condition,
the seat of her pain, its character and extent, and any
expression of mental or bodily feelings was admissible
and proper; but that which she stated regarding her
having " been taking some stuff " and what happened

---

* State *vs.* Dickinson, 41 Wis., 299.

† Hays *vs.* State, 40 Md., 633.

to her on her journey was a mere narrative of what
had taken place before the physician visited her, and was
not legally admissible, either as a dying declaration (the
deceased not having been shown to be *in extremis* when
the statement was made) or as part of the *res gestæ*.

**Conditions Existing Subsequent to Alleged Opera-
tion Admissible.**—Facts and conditions existing subsequent to the alleged operation, but which tend to explain the patient's condition, are also relevant and may
be shown upon trial. It was accordingly held proper
to permit a witness to state that she had been sent
for the day before deceased's death to wash her and
change her clothes, and that she found blood stains
upon the bed and clothing, and that there was a peculiar
offensive odor which she had never noticed before at
any time or place, although she had noticed something
like it.* And so, a witness was permitted to testify
that about the middle of February (the operation being
alleged to have been committed about the middle of
January) she slept one night in the same bed with the
complaining witness, who looked unusually pale and
feeble, and sighed and groaned a good deal; that the
witness made the bed next morning and saw red stains
upon it, through the feather bed and upon the straw
bed, which she thought were quite recent, and some of

---

* People *vs.* Olmstead, 30 Mich., 431.

them more recent than others. And another witness in the same case was permitted to testify that she lived in the same house with complaining witness; that about January 20th complaining witness was confined to her bed and that witness was called to aid her and found that she had fainted; that after she began to get well, witness found her washing stains from the tick of her feather bed, and noticed stains upon her straw bed. Regarding the admissibility of this evidence the court said: " The objection that the facts occurred or appearances were observed a month after the alleged abortion does not render the evidence incompetent, though it may affect its weight. That they were not connected with the abortion we can not presume. We can not know that the result of the injury did not continue thus long."

Effect of Proving an Alibi.—An element of defense sometimes available is that of an *alibi*, or the proving by the defendant that he was at another place than that at which the crime was committed at the time of the performance of the criminal act. The effect of such evidence is admirably shown in the case of Commonwealth *vs.* Snow.* Here the woman upon whom the abortion was alleged to have been performed testified positively that the operation was performed on

---

* Com. *vs.* Snow, 116 Mass., 47.

May 20th; "that she knew it was upon that day; that she set it down in her diary upon the evening of that day or the next morning; that she had seen the memorandum upon her diary a number of times since then, the last time within a week prior to her testimony."

The woman's sister, also the father of her child, each testified that May 20th was the day upon which the operation was performed. The former testified that her sister left home that day to have the operation performed, and the latter testified that he took the complaining witness to defendant upon that day, and that defendant performed an operation upon her with an instrument.

The defendant introduced evidence tending to show that upon May 19th, 20th, and 21st he was more than one hundred miles distant from the place where the operation was alleged to have been performed. The court, in instructing the jury upon the weight and effect they should give this conflict of evidence, instructed them that the exact day was not material; that "if the jury were satisfied that the witnesses for the government were in error as to the date stated by them, this was a proper matter to be considered upon the question of the degree of credit they were entitled to as to other matters; and if this, either alone or in connection with other evidence, caused the jury so far to doubt as to their truth and the reliability of their testimony in other matters that they were not satisfied beyond doubt that the defendant did perform the operation as alleged, then they should acquit the defendant." The supreme court, in reviewing this case, said: " These rulings and instructions were right. If the *alibi* was satisfactorily proved, it was for the jury to say what effect it ought to have upon the testimony of the witnesses for the prosecution. It might discredit them altogether. If it did not have that effect, then it required an inference of some mistake on their part, either as to the person who performed the operation, or the true date of its performance. Their testimony was no more positive as to the date than it was as to the person; and they were at least quite as liable to have made a mistake as to the true date as they were in regard to the identity of the person. But in any respect it was entirely a question of fact for the jury, and was rightly left to them to decide."

Illustrations.—Having generally reviewed the law relative to this class of cases, the chapter will be brought to a close with a brief examination of the evidence as shown in the reported cases upon which juries have based their verdicts in several instances.

The statute under which the case of State *vs.* Van Zile * was prosecuted provides that any person who

---

* People *vs.* Van Zile, 73 Hun, 534, 26 N. Y. Supp., 390.

with intent, etc., "either, first, prescribes, supplies, or administers to a woman, whether pregnant or not, or advises or causes a woman to take any medicine, drug, or substance; or, second, uses, or causes to be used, any instrument or other means, is guilty of abortion, and is punishable, etc." The evidence in this case shows that deceased, in company with a young man, went to defendant's office for the purpose of having deceased examined to determine whether or not she was pregnant. Defendant made an examination, announced that the girl was pregnant, and advised the young man, who for the sake of convenience will be hereafter designated A., to marry her. For the examination defendant charged and received twenty-five dollars. Three days afterward, and on the eleventh day of November, defendant and A. met at a drug store, and, after a conversation in the corner, which was not heard by the clerk, defendant asked for pen and ink and paper, and wrote a prescription, which he gave to the drug clerk and said: "Put it up and give it to this young man." The prescription specified several drugs, which were required to be compounded and made into twenty capsules, one of which was to be taken after each meal. This compound was pronounced by a professor of materia medica to be an abortive mixture. On December 19th deceased had a miscarriage and sent for defendant. Upon his arrival the following conversation took place, so he testified:

"The girl said, 'You don't remember me?' And I said, 'No; who are you?' And she said, 'I am the girl that A. had at your office.' And I says, 'What is your trouble?' and she said, 'I am all through my trouble.' 'When did it occur?' and she says, 'Last night.'" The girl became worse, and on the 24th of December the family physician was called in, who testified that the following conversation took place between himself and defendant. "He (defendant) told me that he had been called into the case, I think the Thursday previous, and that she had been getting rapidly worse, and was now in a very bad condition. He did not seem to understand what was the matter—what the trouble was." To the question, "Did he say so?" the family physician replied, "He said so." On the following day the girl died. Defendant went to the druggist and told him that the girl had died, and he thought if the druggist would lend him two hundred and fifty dollars he could pay the funeral expenses and in that way settle with and satisfy the mother. That night defendant fled from the city and remained absent for about three months.

The jury rendered a verdict of guilty. The general term of the supreme court, in reviewing the case, said: "A careful examination of the testimony leaves no doubt of the guilt of the defendant. While it is true that the evidence is circumstantial, and leaves the question of guilt to be determined by inferences drawn from established facts, yet the facts proved are not only entirely inconsistent with the innocence of the defendant, but they can be reconciled upon no theory except that of guilt."

The case of Solander *vs.* People * is also one in which there was no direct evidence of the commission of the crime, and yet it is one in which the circumstances point so strongly to the guilt of the accused as to exclude all reasonable doubt as to her guilt. The principal witness was a man, who, for convenience, will be designated K. This witness testified that about three weeks before deceased's death he procured some medicine from Denver at her request for the purpose of producing an abortion, and that she took the medicine. That a little more than two weeks afterward, on Thursday, deceased went to see defendant, and that on the way home she told him that she had visited defendant for the purpose of employing her to procure an abortion, and that defendant had stated that it would be necessary to use an instrument and to procure medicine from St. Louis, and that she would charge thirty dollars for the services. K. further testified that on the following Saturday he returned with deceased, a distance of some eight miles, to defendant's office, and

* Solander *vs.* People, 2 Colo., 48.

that defendant and deceased were alone about an hour; that defendant and K. then returned with deceased to her home, and that defendant remained there until Monday morning. Witness said that defendant left some powders with deceased Monday morning, and that he gave deceased some of them, and that after taking each powder she fainted. Next day deceased died. Shortly before her death, however, the witness K. went for defendant and told her that deceased desired to see her. Witness testified to a conversation which then took place between him and defendant in which defendant disclosed knowledge of deceased's condition, and of the nature of her illness. That defendant stated that deceased had been taking medicine from Denver, and that if she should die that medicine would be the cause of her death; that, defendant said, would clear her. Witness testified that defendant inquired for the fœtus which had come from deceased, and requested him to take it away, as inquiry might be made for it. Witness testified that on the following day he returned with defendant to her home and that she then told him that she wanted to get a certain man, naming him, for her lawyer, and that she wanted to get two certain doctors, who were good friends of hers to go over for the examination, and that she would be all right; and that if any one should ask witness what was the matter he should say that he did not know.

There was expert evidence offered to show that death was caused by an attempt to produce an abortion, and that an instrument was used for that purpose. Evidence was also adduced by the State that a bougie, broken into three pieces, was found upon the premises of the deceased, and that the injuries observed in the womb of deceased might have been produced by that instrument; also that the powders left with deceased bore a striking resemblance to gossypium, and that the effect of the drug was abortionary. A witness testified that when the bougie was found defendant disclaimed any knowledge of it, and said she did not know what instrument was used for procuring abortions; that she had never seen one. The coroner testified that at the inquest defendant told him that she supposed deceased was laboring under *prolapsus uteri*, and that she was treating deceased for that, but that he saw no indications in the body of deceased of *prolapsus uteri*. Defendant took the witness stand in her own behalf and denied having used any instrument, and also that she had advised it. She admitted having given powders, but denied that they were gossypium, and averred that they were not intended to produce abortion.

Among other instructions, the court gave the jury the following: " Neither is it necessary that it should appear by the evidence that the prisoner, with her own hands, used any instrument upon the person of deceased, or that with her own hands prisoner administered to the deceased any drug or substance. If prisoner furnished any instrument to deceased or to any other person with intent that deceased or any other person should use such instrument for the purpose of procuring the miscarriage of deceased, she being then pregnant, or if prisoner provided any noxious drug or substance with intent that deceased, being then pregnant, should administer the drug or substance herself, or that any other person should administer it to her in order to produce the miscarriage of the deceased, prisoner thereby constituted the deceased, or the person to whom such instrument or drug was delivered or provided, her agent, and is accountable for all the acts of such person done in pursuance of the agency. And if such person, whether the deceased herself or any other, used such instrument upon the person of deceased, or administered such drug to deceased with the intent to produce the miscarriage of deceased, and by reason of such treatment the deceased came to her death, the prisoner is guilty as charged in the indictment, even though she was not present at the time of the use of the instrument or administration of the drug."

The jury returned a verdict of guilty, and the prisoner was sentenced to confinement in the penitentiary for a term of three years.

The supreme court, in reviewing the case, approved of the instruction above quoted, and also gave their opinion that the trial court had made no error in permitting the witness K. to testify to the conversation had between himself and deceased while returning from their first visit to defendant. The court, in discussing the question of admissibility of this conversation, affirms the correctness of the rule that a mere narrative of past events, not made in furtherance of the criminal design, is not evidence against one who was not present when it was uttered, and consequently can not be repeated on the witness stand. But the court continued: " Although the statement of deceased was made after the interview with prisoner, and was, in one sense, a history of a past event, it was during the pendency of the criminal enterprise, and closely attendant upon an act done to promote the illegal purpose. If the evidence was admissible upon the principle of *res gestæ*, as I think it was, it would not have been proper to exclude it upon the ground that it was merely a narrative of past events."

The case of State *vs.* Clements * impresses one very forcibly as illustrating the danger attending the professional life of the medical man. Here the unfortunate combination of circumstances which entangled the

---

* State *vs.* Clements, 15 Or., 237, 14 Pac. Rep., 410.

defendant and brought disgrace and conviction upon him is one that is liable at any time to ruin an honest practitioner who has not the opportunity of protecting himself by the counsel and assistance of his reputable professional brothers, and it is one against which the honest physician can not take too great precaution.

The evidence in this case showed that the deceased was a young unmarried woman who had been stopping for some time at the hotel where she died; that on the morning of her death defendant locked her door and passed out of the hotel, and remarked to some one that she was sleeping quietly, and that he did not want her disturbed. A few hours afterward, at about nine o'clock A. M., defendant came back, and, upon going to deceased's room, called some one and stated that "Lena was dying." The defendant was immediately arrested and placed in charge of the constable. Upon leaving the hotel defendant told the constable that he had something to show him at his office. Upon arriving at the office he exhibited to the constable a fœtus of which he said deceased had been delivered. Shortly before this, and at about the time deceased was first taken sick, the defendant exhibited in the drug store to the druggist a stout sharpened quill about six inches long, being bloody, and having the appearance of having been recently imbedded in living animal tissues, which he claimed to have taken from her room. He stated to the druggist: " I want you to examine this. I may need it for my protection. I am afraid this case will get me into a scrape yet. Some woman has been using this for a criminal purpose."

The post-mortem examination showed that there was some abrasion or scratching of the interior walls of the uterus, apparently caused by some rough instrument, but that the injuries were slight. There was no indication that deceased met her death by abortion produced by drugs.

The principal witness for the State was the colored cook of the hotel, who testified to finding deceased lying upon the floor of her room about the time she was taken ill, and, contrary to the objections of defendant's counsel and contrary to the law of evidence, was permitted to testify to the following conversation: " I asked her if the doctor had used instruments upon her. She said, ' Yes.' " This statement, it will be seen, was not admissible as a dying declaration, nor was it a part of the *res gestæ*, but was mere hearsay and inadmissible. It appeared also that defendant while attending deceased misrepresented the nature of her illness.

The evidence given by defendant upon his own behalf was that deceased applied to him on August 12th, nineteen days before her death, to perform an abortion upon her; that he refused absolutely to do it; that some ten or twelve days prior to her death deceased called

upon him to treat her professionally for some derange-
ment of the uterus; that he made an examination and
found a sponge imbedded in the tissues in the mouth of
the womb; that he used a metallic speculum and forceps,
and removed the sponge; that he found the place occupied by the sponge lacerated, the sponge covered with
pus, and very offensive; that he treated her for about
six days, and dismissed the case. Defendant testified
that he did not see deceased again until August 25th,
when he was called by her; that she complained of
nausea of the stomach, and pains in the abdomen, and
upon being questioned denied having made any attempt
at abortion; that symptoms rapidly disclosed themselves indicating labor pains; that he prescribed anti-
abortive treatment; that there were no other physicians
in reach with whom to consult, and deceased had no
means to employ medical assistance; that he continued
such treatment; that deceased then informed him she
had made an attempt to accomplish a miscarriage by
inserting a quill into the uterus, and told him where
the quill could be found, and which was shown to be
the same quill before referred to; that thereafter, on
the night of August 30th, deceased gave birth to a dead
fœtus; that for a considerable time prior to this deceased was in such a condition that to have exposed the
cause of her illness would have resulted in a nervous
shock extremely dangerous to her life; that defendant
31

removed the fœtus and its appendages, and afterward surrendered them to the officer; that he administered opiates to deceased, placed her in bed for the purpose of securing repose, gave directions that she should not be disturbed, left the hotel, and went to his breakfast. That upon returning in about an hour afterward, he found her dying, uterine hæmorrhage having set in during his absence, and caused her death.

The jury returned a verdict of guilty, and judgment was entered thereupon. The supreme court, however, upon reviewing the case, reversed the judgment and sent the case back for a new trial, because of errors committed by the court below. One of these errors was permitting the cook to testify to the conversation between himself and deceased which was above referred to. The result of the second trial of the case is not known to the author.

Another case which shows to what extreme verdicts juries will sometimes allow themselves to be persuaded by the great zeal that often actuates prosecuting attorneys to secure a conviction, irrespective of the merits of the case, is that of Clarke *vs.* People.* Here the defendant was convicted of procuring an abortion upon the deceased, a young unmarried woman. There was much evidence taken, but very little of it reflects

---

* Clarke *vs.* People, 16 Colo., 511.

unfavorably upon the defendant. The substance of the evidence of the prosecution was that a miscarriage had taken place from the effects of which death ensued; that defendant was the sole attending physician at the time of the abortion and for some time prior and subsequent thereto; that defendant burned the fœtus instead of burying it; and that in reply to a question propounded by the landlady of the house where deceased was stopping, defendant stated that the patient was suffering from inflammation of the bowels.

Defendant testified that deceased first sought his services on the twenty-fourth day of February, and that she was at that time suffering from " bearing-down pains "; that upon his next visit, which occurred next day, he cautioned her in reference to the danger she was incurring, and warned her against the effects of the course she had entered upon, advising her that she should reconcile herself to her condition and let the full time elapse before birth. At the end of this visit he was paid for his services and considered himself discharged from the case. Defendant testified that a few days later he was called again, and that deceased was threatened with a miscarriage; that it was too late to prescribe medicine to counteract the effect of the drugs she had previously taken, but that he did prescribe quiet and rest; that, finding this would not prevent the abortion, he did what he could to relieve the patient and save her life. It was shown that on the day before the patient's death defendant informed her she was not progressing so favorably as he had hoped, and that he desired a physician in consultation, and advised that her parents be notified. To both of these propositions deceased objected. Finding deceased worse next morning instead of better, defendant telegraphed her father and sent out for another physician, but, owing to delay, the latter arrived only shortly before her death. In explanation of the burning of the fœtus, defendant testified that decomposition had set in, rendering an immediate disposition of it necessary; that the patient required his immediate attention, and that there was no other man about the premises to bury it, and that burning was the most effective as well as the most convenient way to dispose of it.

It also appears that deceased, shortly before her death, fully exonerated defendant, and said that he was not the cause of her sickness. It further appears that immediately after the death of deceased, defendant took her effects to the coroner, and notified that official of the cause and circumstances of her death.

How a jury of intelligent men could have rendered a verdict of guilty upon this evidence it is difficult to understand. The forces of eloquence and personal magnetism moved by a mistaken zeal are often potent factors in working injustice and may have been largely accountable for the termination of the present suit. It is extremely gratifying, however, to observe the wholesome check which our higher courts place upon the trial courts which are sometimes betrayed into a display of feeling prejudicial to justice. In the present case it is believed that every reader will heartily approve of the sentiment expressed by the supreme court, which, in reversing the judgment, says: " The crime charged is one that strikes at the foundation of our social fabric, and is well calculated to arouse the indignation of all right-thinking people; but to allow this conviction to stand would be to violate the fundamental rule of the criminal law fixing the quantum of proof necessary to sustain a conviction. We fully agree with the attorney-general that prudence would have dictated the calling of counsel at an earlier period in the case; but the neglect in this particular can not be taken as a justification to the verdict and judgment rendered in the court below."

At an early period in the examination of the subject of criminal abortions in this chapter it was stated that the matter was regulated by statutes in the several States. The cases and general rules of evidence which have been examined will be found applicable in nearly every instance in proving that the statute has been violated, but the exact act or series of acts which shall in any given State amount to the crime of procuring an abortion can be determined with certainty only by carefully examining the local statute regulating the matter.

CHAPTER IX.

Privileged Matter Generally.—Upon the broad and urgent ground of *public policy* certain matters are held so sacred in the eyes of the law that one can not be compelled to disclose his knowledge relative thereto, even as a witness in a court of justice. Matters of this sort may be generally classified as follows:

I. POLITICAL MATTERS.—Under this head are included state secrets, official transactions and communications between the heads of departments of state and their subordinate officers, and all like communications.

II. JUDICIAL MATTERS.—Herein are included proceedings in the jury room, consultations of judges, and the like.

III. PROFESSIONAL COMMUNICATIONS.—Under this head are included all communications between client and counsel or attorney necessarily made for the purpose of securing professional services or assistance; communications between patient and physician or surgeon necessary to secure proper professional treatment; and all confessions or communications of like character made to one's spiritual adviser.

480

IV. Social Matters.—Under this head are in-cluded all communications of a confidential nature made between husband and wife.

Professional Communications at Common Law.—At common law the protection accorded to professional communications was in its scope very limited, applying only to the legal profession, nor does the protection which that profession enjoyed seem to have been as full and adequate as that now accorded to it by the courts and legislatures.* The medical † and clerical ‡ professions were both outside the protection of the common law, both of England and the United States, and whatever privileges of protected professional confi-dence they now enjoy are expressly conferred by statute.

Statutory Protection to Communications between Physician and Patient.—In recognition of the impor-tance of a full and absolute confidence existing between physician and patient in all matters of professional intercourse, the legislatures of about half the States #

---

* Duchess of Kingston's case, 20 Howell's St. Tr., 573, 613.

† Rex *vs.* Gibbons, 1 C. and P., 97; Broad *vs.* Pitt, 3 C. and P., 518.

‡ Baker *vs.* Arnold, 1 Caine's Rep., 257.

The following States have passed laws extending the privilege to professional communications between physician and patient: Arizona, Arkansas, California, Colorado, Idaho, Indiana, Iowa, Kansas, Michigan, Minnesota, Missouri, Montana, Nebraska, Nevada, New York, North Carolina, North Dakota, Ohio, Oklahoma, Oregon, Pennsylvania, Utah, Washington, Wisconsin, Wyoming.

have passed wholesome laws which in effect assure the patient that the information necessarily imparted to secure proper and legitimate medical treatment shall not be wrested from the physician to whom he confided it, even in behalf of justice. The wording of the statutes upon the subject, as enacted by the several States, varies considerably; in New York, which was probably one of the first States to recognize the need of this sort of protection to the physician and patient by legislative enactment, the law in force provides that:

"A person duly authorized to practise physic or surgery shall not be allowed to disclose any information which he acquired in attending a patient in a professional capacity, and which was necessary to enable him to act in that capacity." *

The restraining clause that the "physician or surgeon shall not be allowed to disclose any information, etc.," is reenacted almost *verbatim* in the States of Iowa, Michigan, Pennsylvania, and Nebraska; the majority of the States having statutes upon the subject impose practically the same restriction by using the expression that the physician "shall not (or can not) be examined," † or "shall not be a witness," ‡ or "shall not testify." # The statutes of four States, to wit, Indi-

---

* Code of Civil Procedure, § 834.

† California, Colorado, Idaho, Minnesota, Nevada, North Dakota, Oregon, Utah, and Washington.

‡ Montana.   # Ohio and Wyoming.

ana, Kansas, Missouri, and Oklahoma, provide that a physician shall not be competent to testify as to information professionally obtained, while the statutes of three States, to wit, Arkansas,* North Carolina, and Wisconsin, provide that the physician " shall not be required (or compelled) to " testify.

The statutes in several States expressly restrict the application of the protection to civil cases.† Whether the protection of the statute in the absence of this restriction extends to criminal cases is a question which has been the subject of judicial decisions, which will be examined in their proper order.

The statute of North Carolina is subject to the provision that " the presiding judge of a superior court may compel such disclosure (of knowledge professionally obtained), if in his opinion the same is necessary to a proper administration of justice." While the statute of Arizona provides that the physician " can not without the consent of his patient be examined in civil or criminal cases as to any information acquired in attending the patient which was necessary to enable him to prescribe or act for the patient." ‡

The privilege conferred by these statutes is pri-

---

* In Arkansas the privilege is extended by statute to include the " trained nurse."   Laws of 1899, Act XXXI, p. 38.

† The statutory restriction to civil cases exists in California, Idaho, Minnesota, Montana, Oregon, Pennsylvania, Utah, and Washington.

‡ Laws of Arizona, 1899, p. 75.

marily for the benefit of the patient, and he, therefore, either by his acts or by express consent, may waive the privilege and allow the physician to testify. By the statutes of several States * it is expressly provided that the privilege is waived whenever the patient voluntarily testifies regarding the subject matter of the same. The question of what acts shall in the absence of express statutory provision be considered a waiver of the privilege has been passed upon in a number of cases.

Communications with Unlicensed Physicians not Protected.—The statute usually provides that communications shall be protected when made to persons "duly authorized to practise," or to "licensed physicians or surgeons," or to "qualified physicians and surgeons." These statutes will therefore not protect communications of a confidential nature made to one not legally qualified to practise medicine, but who is exercising the functions of a physician; such a person, upon being called as a witness, may be required to disclose all information that he has gained from a patient, and the patient's protest will avail nothing.†

Relation of Physician and Patient must Exist to Create Privilege.—Having learned that the physician to whom the confidential communications were made was duly licensed and authorized to practise medicine

---

* Kansas, Nevada, Ohio, Oklahoma, and Wyoming.
† Wiel *vs.* Cowles, 45 Hun, 307.

and surgery, it next becomes pertinent to determine whether or not the relations existing between the patient and the physician to whom the communications were made were of such a character as to bring such communications within the protection of the law.

The general proposition that because one is a licensed physician and surgeon he is incompetent to testify regarding the condition in which he found a certain person without that person's consent is too absurd to require refutation; this privilege must be based upon a relation of confidence similar to that of physician and patient, and unless such relation, in fact, exists at the time the information is obtained there is no privilege; * nor will the court presume the existence of such confidential relations. The party invoking the aid of the law must show that the relations which existed between the physician and himself were of the confidential nature contemplated by the statute.†

In order to constitute the confidential relation of physician and patient it is not essential that the physician should have been called or employed by the patient himself; the legal effect is quite the same whether the physician is summoned by the patient himself, by the

---

* Jacobs *vs.* Cross, 19 Minn., 523.

† People *vs.* Schuyler, 106 N. Y., 298, 12 N. E. Rep., 783; Edington *vs.* Insurance Co., 77 N. Y., 564; Stowell *vs.* Am., etc., Assn., 5 N. Y., Supp., 233.

patient's attending physician, by friends of the patient, or even by strangers.* It therefore logically follows that where the defendant in a suit for personal injuries sends his physician to the plaintiff to make an examination for the purpose of testifying as to the plaintiff's condition, and the physician, instead of simply making the examination for the purpose intended, undertakes the treatment of the plaintiff, the relation of physician and patient immediately arises, and the physician becomes incapable of disclosing the information obtained.† In the case of Freel *vs.* Market Street Cable Railway Company,‡ the plaintiff testified that defendant's physician called upon her several times and prescribed for her. The doctor, when questioned upon the subject, failed to remember whether he did or did not prescribe for her. Thereupon the plaintiff's counsel asked him the following question: " It was during this time that you were making these visits *and prescribing for her* that you obtained any knowledge that you have of her case? " to which the physician answered, " Yes, sir; that is all, except conversations with Dr. ——." The court was of the opinion that even though the physician was sent for the sole and exclusive purpose of examining the plaintiff to enable him to disclose her

---

* Renihan *vs.* Dennin, 103 N. Y., 573.

† Weitz *vs.* Mound City Ry Co., 53 Mo. App., 39.

‡ Freel *vs.* Market St. Ry. Co., 97 Cal., 40.

condition, yet by "visiting and prescribing for her" the confidential relation of physician and patient was created, which would preclude the disclosure of any information gained while making such visits. And so in the case of People *vs.* Murphy,* where the public prosecutor selected a physician and sent him to examine a woman upon whom an abortion had been performed, for the apparent purpose of obtaining evidence, and the physician treated the patient professionally, he was not permitted to give any information obtained while so treating her.

Where, however, a physician calls upon a person and examines him only for the purpose of information, and it is understood that the purpose of the call and examination is not for professional treatment, no question of privilege can be successfully urged.† Therefore, where a physician, at the request of the prosecuting attorney, entered the cell of a prisoner and had a talk with him for the purpose of determining his mental condition, but rendered to him no medical assistance or advice, the physician's observations were properly admitted in evidence.‡ And so, when a physician, at the request of the prosecuting attorney, examined a pris-

---

* People *vs.* Murphy, 101 N. Y., 126.

† Nesbit *vs.* People, 19 Colo., 441, 36 Pac. Rep., 221.

‡ People *vs.* Kemmler, 119 N. Y., 580; People *vs.* Sliney, 137 N. Y., 570, 50 S. R., 391.

488 THE LAW IN ITS RELATIONS TO PHYSICIANS.

oner while in jail for the purpose only of determining
whether or not he was afflicted with a venereal disease,
the court held that no confidential relation existed, and
that the information gained might properly be disclosed.* And for a like reason it is held, where two
physicians, not attending upon the testatrix professionally, are taken to her bedside for the purpose of
determining her mental condition, and while there witness the execution of her will, that no professional relation is thereby created between the testatrix and witnesses, and that they are competent to disclose what they
learned at the examination. One of the physicians, in
answer to questions propounded to him at the trial, said
that he was not testatrix's physician or surgeon at the
time, and didn't prescribe for her; was not called, as
he understood it, to prescribe for her; that he was not
her family physician; that he made a charge for making
the examination upon his books to the attorney who
prepared the will and was present at the examination;
that he made the examination the same as he always
did when called upon to examine a person with regard
to sanity, and after the examination the will was at
once executed. The other physician's statement of the
purpose of his visit was in legal effect much the same.
In considering the admissibility of the evidence of

---

* People vs. Glover, 71 Mich., 303.

these physicians the court said: " In the present case the physicians were not called to prescribe for the deceased or to advise as to professional treatment; nor did they so prescribe or advise. If the deceased at the time of their visit had been in great need of good medical advice, and they had given no advice, they would not have been chargeable with malice or neglect of duty; because they were not under any obligation to advise or to prescribe. Any advice or prescription would have been an improper act, because they were not the attending or consulting physicians, and they were under no obligation to her. If they had conversed with her as to her health, then, possibly, she might have conceived the idea that they were consulting physicians. And if, in such mistaken belief, she had stated anything as to her health, very possibly that might have come within the prohibition of this section. But . . . there is no reason to believe that she thought them to be consulting physicians, or recognized them to be anything more than proper witnesses to her will." *

The proper test, it seems, to apply in determining the competency of the physician to testify, is whether he met the party professionally or non-professionally at the time the information in question was obtained.†
Thus, when a physician offered to give evidence as to

---

* *In re* Freeman, 46 Hun, 458.
† Fisher *et al. vs.* Fisher *et al.*, 129 N. Y., 654.

the mental capacity of the deceased, and this evidence was objected to upon the ground that he had been the attending physician of the deceased, the court, upon being shown that the knowledge regarding which the physician proposed to testify was not obtained while acting in that capacity, properly permitted the physician to testify.* And upon the same principle a physician who had attended the deceased was permitted to state what he had observed relative to deceased when he called upon him for the purpose of collecting some money which was due for professional services. The physician was also permitted to testify that he met deceased in the road near his home, and that the old gentleman did not know him, and asked who he was.† The physician must, however, be able to separate the knowledge which he acquired from the patient while attending him in a professional capacity from that which he obtained upon meeting him in a non-professional way, otherwise he will not be permitted to testify as to the latter.‡

In the case of the Colorado Fuel and Iron Company vs. Cummings,# the defendant, the Colorado Fuel and Iron Company, together with a certain railroad com-

* In re Will of Peck, 42 N. Y. S. R., 898, 17 N. Y. Supp., 248.
† Bower vs. Bower, 142 Ind , 194, 41 N. E. Rep., 523.
‡ In re Darragh, 52 Hun, 591.
# Colorado Fuel and Iron Co. vs. Cummings, 8 Colo. App., 541, 46 Pac. Rep , 875.

pany, had established a hospital for the use of the two companies, which was supported by contributions from the employees, certain amounts being deducted from their monthly wages for that purpose, the general contribution being termed the "hospital fund." The plaintiff, who had been injured while in the course of his employment with the defendant, was taken to this hospital and attended by a physician who was employed by the company and received his salary from it, probably from the "hospital fund." This physician offered to testify regarding the plaintiff's condition, but his evidence was refused. The court, in considering the question of whether or not the relation of physician and patient existed between the plaintiff and witness, said: "We are, however, entirely satisfied that the circumstances under which the doctor was employed and the relation existing between the company and its employees and the doctor were such as to put the physician and the plaintiff directly in the relation of doctor and patient. The plaintiff's contributions may have been slight, but the circumstances of the situation were such as to lead him to put himself implicitly under the care of the surgeon and to trust himself in his hands for care to the same extent and under the same circumstances as though he had sent out for another physician and put himself directly in his charge."

From this case an inference seems deducible that the

32

confidential relation of physician and patient can not exist when the physician is wholly paid by a third party. However justly such an inference may be drawn from the opinion of the learned court in this case, it is apprehended that such a statement would not be correct law. The law is probably better illustrated in the case of Grossman *vs.* Supreme Lodge of Knights and Ladies of Honor.* In this case the patient was at a hospital and her regular attending physician was a Dr. W. A Dr. N. was called as a witness to testify to the patient's condition, but his evidence was objected to upon the ground that the knowledge he possessed was privileged. In order to determine the relation existing between the patient and Dr. N., he was permitted to state his connection with the hospital and the circumstances under which he met the plaintiff. He stated that he and Dr. W. had charge of different wards in the hospital and that he and Dr. W. made the rounds of the hospital together, and generally examined the cases together; that he was not the physician attending the patient, although he partly attended her. Referring to the patient, he said: " I went with Dr. W., who was the attending physician. We generally tried to confirm diagnosis. I went there to find out the condition of the patient, and the ailments." And again he said: " I

---

* Grossman *vs.* Supreme Lodge of Knights and Ladies of Honor, 6 N. Y. Supp., 821.

went there just out of curiosity to acquire information in interesting cases." And later in his examination he said that when Dr. W. went to examine the patient he went with him " and assisted him in making the examination." Regarding the admissibility of Dr. N.'s evidence of the condition of the patient, the learned court said: " We think the court properly held that the witness was disqualified. ' To bring the case within the statute it is sufficient that the person attended as a physician upon the patient, and obtained his information in that capacity.' * Whether the witness was actuated by curiosity or a higher motive makes no difference. His own admission that he attended the patient, although he qualifies the statement by the use of the adverb ' partly,' suffices to establish the existence of the professional relation which debars him from disclosing what he learned of her condition under the circumstances."

A jail physician, it seems, is also incompetent to testify as to the condition of a prisoner whom he has attended in a professional capacity; but unless it can be shown that the information he offers to disclose was obtained while attending such prisoner professionally he will not be prevented from testifying.†

Whether or not the professional relation of physi-

---

* From Renihan vs. Dennin, 103 N. Y., 573.

† People vs. Schuyler, 106 N. Y., 298, 12 N. E. Rep., 783.

cian and patient exists to such a degree as to protect
the communications made to the physician where a
third party comes to him and makes disclosures for the
purpose of getting medicine or a prescription for the
patient is a question that is largely dependent upon the
circumstances of the particular case. In an early New
York case * the defendant repeatedly applied to a
physician for drugs to produce an abortion, and upon
one occasion told him the name of the female for whose
use the drugs were desired. The physician was permitted
to disclose the subject of these interviews, the court
expressing its opinion as follows: "The witness (the
physician) I think was not privileged. It is very doubtful whether the communications made to him by the
defendant can be considered as consulting him professionally within the meaning of the statute." And so,
in the case of Babcock *vs.* People,† a physician was permitted to testify that defendant came to him and told
him that he wanted some medicine for a certain young
lady who had taken a cold and was suffering from suppressed menses, and that subsequently, in about a
month, the defendant returned the medicine and said
it was for his wife and was not given because she was
pregnant. The court said: "The defendant was not
consulting him (the physician) for himself, nor does it

* Hewitt *vs.* Prime, 21 Wend., 79.
† Babcock *vs.* People, 15 Hun, 347.

appear that he was representing any one else who needed or desired medical assistance." If, however, a third party appears before a physician and confidentially discloses to him the condition of a patient and procures the physician to undertake the treatment of such patient, the relation of physician and patient exists in its full sense, and the information conveyed through the third party is as adequately protected as though communicated by the patient direct.*

It has been observed that the confidential relation of physician and patient is not dependent upon the employment by the patient, but that such a physician may be called by another. Similar to this is the rule that a physician who is called by the attending physician as consultant is within the law and not permitted to disclose knowledge gained in the course of such consultation.† The partner of the attending physician also comes within the rule and is not permitted to disclose knowledge imparted to him by the attending physician.

Justice Berkshire, in considering a question of the sort, said: " Dr. L. (the partner) comes clearly within the spirit, if not the letter, of the statute. He was the partner of Dr. W. (the attending physician). They were in active practice, occupying the same office. The

* People vs. Brower, 53 Hun, 217.
† Renihan vs. Dennin, 103 N. Y., 573.

business of the one was the business of the other; when necessary, it was the duty of one to consult with the other, and in the absence of the one who was giving special attention to a patient, it was proper for the other, if not obligatory on him, to take his place." In this case the court, after stating that the information possessed by Dr. L. was obtained while the patient was at the firm's office to consult Dr. W., expressed itself positively that to have permitted Dr. L. to disclose this information " would have been a perversion " of the statute.* It seems, however, that a physician merely having office privileges with the attending physician, but not interested in his business, does not come within the law and will be permitted to disclose information imparted to him by the other's patients.†

Nor does the relation of physician and patient exist as contemplated by the law when the physician performs an autopsy, as a dead man can not be considered a " patient," " but is a mere piece of senseless clay which has passed beyond the reach of human prescription, medical or otherwise." Therefore information disclosed at such autopsy is not privileged.‡

---

* The Ætna Life Insurance Co. vs. Deming, 123 Ind., 384, 24 N. E. Rep., 86.

† Kendall vs. Grey, 2 Hilt., 300.

‡ Harrison vs. Sutter Street Ry. Co., 116 Cal., 156, 47 Pac. Rep., 1019.

The statutes, in designating to what relations the privilege shall extend, more frequently use the expression that no person authorized to practise " physic or surgery " shall be permitted to testify, etc. Such a designation as this is restricted to a physician or surgeon and is not construed to include a dentist; for while the duties of a dentist include to a very limited extent those of a surgeon, yet it has been held that a dentist is not, in law, to be considered a surgeon; * therefore communications made to him will not be privileged.†

Knowledge Coming within the Law.—The question of what knowledge is within the meaning of these statutes is often a very nice one, and it is a question upon which the courts have many times been unable to agree.

There is no doubt, however, that the statute does not preclude one from stating that he is the family physician of another, nor from giving the number and dates of his professional visits,‡ and the date upon which he discharged the patient.# The disclosures which the law aims to preclude the physician from making are those facts which he learns in the course of his pro-

---

* State *vs.* Fisher, 24 S. W. Rep., 167, 22 L R. A., 799.

† People *vs.* De France, 104 Mich., 563, 62 N. W. Rep., 709.

‡ Briesenmeister *vs.* Knights of Pythias, 81 Mich., 525; Patten *vs.* U. L. and A. Ins. Assn., 133 N. Y., 450, 31 N. E. Rep., 342.

Dittrich *vs.* City of Detroit, 98 Mich., 245, 57 N. W. Rep., 125.

fessional employment,* and to construe the statutes so as to give them this effect is the apparent design of the courts.

The statute of New York provides that one practising medicine and surgery shall not be permitted to disclose " any information which he acquired in attending a patient in a professional capacity." With the exception of five States † to be hereafter referred to, each of the States having statutes upon this subject has almost literally reenacted that part of the New York statute included within the quotation, which describes the knowledge that is protected.

It seems well settled that this clause in the statutes includes all knowledge gained in the professional intercourse of a physician with his patient, whether obtained from statements made to him by the patient or gained from observing and examining the patient. A leading case upon this subject is that of Edington vs. Mutual Life Insurance Company.‡ In this case Justice Miller says : " When it (the statute) speaks of information, it means not only communications received from the lips of the patient, but such knowledge as may be acquired from the patient himself, from the statement of others who may surround him at the time, or

* Kelley vs. Highfield, 15 Or., 277.

† The five States not following the wording of the New York statute in the above particular are Indiana, Iowa, Nebraska, Ohio, and Wyoming.

‡ Edington vs. Mutual Life Insurance Co., 67 N. Y., 185.

from observation of his appearance and symptoms. Even if the patient could not speak, or his mental powers were so affected that he could not accurately state the nature of his disease, the astute medical observer would readily comprehend his condition. Information thus acquired is clearly within the scope and meaning of the statute." The law, as stated by the learned judge in this case, has been cited with approval and followed in a number of succeeding cases in New York and elsewhere.* The examination of the patient referred to in these cases covers not only the thorough and careful examination made for the purpose of prescribing, but includes as well impressions or opinions regarding the patient's condition formed from his general appearance as disclosed at first sight, before the physician has had an opportunity to examine or converse with him.† Nor will the seal of silence be removed from the doctor's lips because the examination may have been conducted in the presence of others.‡

In the States of Indiana, Iowa, Nebraska, Ohio, and Wyoming the statute provides that physicians shall

---

* Grattan *vs.* National Life Insurance Co., 15 Hun, 74 ; Briggs *vs.* Briggs, 20 Mich., 34 ; Gartside *vs.* Conn. Mutual Life Insurance Co., 76 Mo., 446 ; Corbett *vs.* St. L. I. M. and S. Ry. Co., 26 Mo. App., 621.

† Grattan *vs.* Metropolitan Life Insurance Co., 28 Hun, 430, 92 N. Y., 274.

‡ Grattan *vs.* Metropolitan Life Insurance Co., 80 N. Y., 281.

not be allowed to disclose matter " communicated " to them by their patients, or to disclose any " communication," etc. The wording of these statutes would seem at first sight to restrict the protection of privilege to such information as the physician received by communications from the lips of his patients; such, however, does not seem to be the understanding of the courts which have passed upon the question. The supreme court of Indiana, after quoting the statute of that State, says: " It sets the seal of secrecy and con-fidence upon what a physician observes in respect to the condition of his patient's person in the course of his professional examinations, as well as upon communications made to him by his patient. Accident or disease may compel the submission of one's person to examination by a physician, who thus acquires information which would be confided to no one else. The fear of disclosure often induces persons to suffer from bodily ailments rather than submit to examination by persons of skill. The policy of the statute is to protect and render inviolable the confidence which should exist between physician and patient. A physician is not permitted to disclose the result of observations or examinations made by him upon the person of his patient, unless with the consent of the latter, or unless the patient in some way waives his privilege." * And in

* Williams *vs.* Johnson, 112 Ind., 273.

a late case * the supreme court of Iowa says: " Although the statute of this State uses the word ' communication ' it means much the same as the word ' information ' in the statutes of other States to which we have referred.   The prohibition of our statute refers not merely to verbal communications, but to those of any kind by which information of the character of that specified in the statute is imparted."   The courts of last resort in the other three States having statutes similarly worded have not yet passed upon this particular question.   It is hoped, however, that when a case involving this point shall be placed before them, they will be able to reach the same conclusion as that arrived at by the courts of the two sister States, for such a construction of the statute is more in accord with the true professional spirit of reserve regarding matters necessarily and confidentially disclosed to enable the physician to properly perform the functions of his profession.

By the statute of nearly every State the protection of the law is restricted to the knowledge gained by the physician which was " necessary and proper to enable him to discharge the functions of his office."   The wording of the statutes of several of the States is different, yet the meaning conveyed is quite the same.   In constru-

---

* Prader *vs.* Accident Association, 95 Ia., 149.

ing this clause of the statute there has been a lack of harmony, the courts at one time having shown a disposition to place a strict construction upon the statute and exclude all matter from the protection of the privilege which was not essential or necessary for diagnosticating or prescribing for the ailment; while the courts at a subsequent and previous period as well have shown a disposition to give the statute a more liberal construction, and include within its protection all communications which might reasonably or even remotely relate to the subject of the professional services.

There are certain communications that are manifestly outside of the protection of the law. Thus, where an unmarried woman told the physician who attended her at her confinement that the father of her child had never promised to marry her, the communication could not be withheld as privileged, for the statement was neither designed nor calculated to throw any light upon the patient's condition nor aid the physician in the remotest degree in his professional treatment of her.* The courts have, however, in many cases shown a disposition to admit every doubt in behalf of a liberal construction of the statute. Thus, the evidence of a physician that he had treated a certain patient for venereal disease and that the patient told him he had contracted the disease

---

* Collins *vs.* Mack, 31 Ark., 684.

from the cook on his canal boat, was excluded as coming within the statute.* In this case the nature of the patient's affliction and the length of time he had been suffering from it are clearly within the protection of the statute, but there is room for doubt that the statement by the patient that he had had intercourse with his cook could have been intended or in any way designed to assist the doctor in the professional treatment of the case.

Probably the case most cited in favor of a strict construction of the statute is that of Edington *vs.* Ætna Life Insurance Company.† Herein Justice Earl says: " It will not do to extend the rule of exclusion so far as to embarrass the administration of justice. It is not even all information which comes within the letter of the statute which is to be excluded. . . . Suppose a patient has a fever or a fractured leg or skull, or is a raving maniac. All these ailments are obvious to all about him. May not the physician who is called to attend him testify to these matters? In doing so there would be no breach of confidence, and the policy of the statute would not be invaded. These and other cases which might be supposed, while perhaps within the letter of the statute, would not be within the reason thereof." Justice Earl gives it as his opinion in this

---

* Hunn *vs.* Hunn, 1 T. and C., 499.
† Edington *vs.* Ætna Life Insurance Co., 77 N. Y., 564.

case that the party attempting to avail himself of the privilege of the statute must show that the information acquired by the physician was such as was necessary to enable him to prescribe or to do some act as a surgeon. In harmony with the spirit of this decision is the case of Campau vs. North,* wherein a physician was permitted to testify to the date upon which a patient had told him she received a breach, for which he was treating her professionally. The court thought that the time the patient received the rupture, or rather the existence of the rupture, prior to a certain date, was not information " necessary to enable the doctor to prescribe for her as a physician or to do any act for her as a surgeon." The case of Linz vs. Massachusetts Mutual Life Insurance Company † presents the views of a court favoring a strict construction of the statute. Justice Hayden, in this case, after quoting with approval from the opinion of Justice Earl in the Edington case, says: " Objective signs that are obvious, or such an observation as implies no disclosure—symptoms which are apparent before the patient submits himself to any examination—the statute gives no authority for excluding. That a patient had an inflamed face, a bloodshot eye; that fumes of alcohol proceeded from his person; that he talked deliriously, could be excluded

---

* Campau vs. North, 39 Mich., 606.

† Linz vs. Mass. Mut. Life Ins. Co., 8 Mo. App., 363.

only on the basis that the statute forbids a physician to be a witness. These objective signs, and others which imply no knowledge obtained as the result of submission or exposure by the patient, and which would be apparent before the initial act of service on the physician's part, the latter should testify to under our statute."

These three cases present the extreme view favoring a strict construction of the statute. This view has not been approved or followed by later cases, and it is very much doubted whether it may be considered the law. The case of Kling *vs.* The City of Kansas * probably presents the true doctrine. In this case the question was presented to the court whether or not a physician should be permitted to disclose the condition of a patient with regard to sobriety at the time of calling upon him to render professional services. The court, in an elaborate and learned opinion, explains clearly and satisfactorily the meaning of the statute with reference to the question of what information is "necessary information." The court is of the opinion that all information, although unimportant in itself, which is necessarily communicated to the physician in order to give him the knowledge needed to act in a proper professional capacity is "necessary information." It is evi-

* Kling *vs.* City of Kansas, 27 Mo. App., 231.

dent that the information necessarily imparted to a physician to give him a clear understanding of all the conditions and circumstances of the case to enable proper professional treatment may, and oftentimes does, include much irrelevant matter, and matter which has no relation to the case as viewed from a medical standpoint, but which in its relation to matter more intimately related to the main question was necessarily communicated to give a correct and comprehensive view of the whole case. To illustrate, the court says: " If the patient, suffering from a gunshot wound, necessarily communicates the information to the physician that the wound was received in a personal encounter, in order to explain the probable course of the ball, information of which latter fact is needed or desired by the physician, information of the fact that the patient was wounded in a personal encounter, although that fact is unimportant, would be privileged. If the patient, suffering from a broken leg, in explaining to his physician the manner in which he received the injury, in order to give needed information concerning the injury, communicate to the physician information that he was under the influence of intoxicating liquor at the time of the accident, such information would be excluded." It will be remembered that the protection of the statute applies as well to information gained by seeing and observing the patient as to that acquired from oral communications of the patient; therefore, if a patient, to enable a physician to treat an injury, necessarily exposes his person, and thereby discloses a hidden defect or a mark indicating the presence or former existence of a loathsome disease, such an exposure, though having no relation to the cause of the present professional services, was necessarily made, and should therefore be considered within the protection of the law.

The court then refers to the distinction made by the strict construction case, above illustrated, between the obvious signs and conditions, such as the "bloodshot eye" and "fumes of alcohol," and the secret and hidden signs and defects. After showing that the Edington case is practically overruled, at least so far as the subject of the present inquiry is concerned, the court asserted that such a distinction had no support either from the words or spirit of the statute. The court said: "The physician called upon the plaintiff as his physician; any information as to the plaintiff's condition as to sobriety, acquired by the physician by seeing him, was necessarily acquired in order to treat him, and is excluded by statute."

It logically follows that a physician attending a patient that has been injured in an accident, railroad or otherwise, will not be permitted to disclose statements made to him by the patient as to how the accident occurred, especially if the communication was
33

imparted to the physician for the purpose of aiding him in determining the character or extent of the injury. The decisions upon the subject are nearly all in harmony with this proposition.* Thus, in the case of Raymond *vs.* The Burlington, Cedar Rapids, and Northern Railway Company,† where the physician questioned the patient regarding the accident and said it was absolutely necessary to enable him to obtain a diagnosis, and that the injury would be more severe if the cars were in motion, the court held that the description of the accident given in response to these questions was privileged. In the case of The Pennsylvania Company *vs.* Marion,‡ the court very justly went much further. Here the questions were asked by the physician, as contended by the defendant's counsel, for the purpose of learning whether the railroad company was to blame for the injury. But the court said: " The physician has no business to interrogate his patient for any purpose or object other than to ascertain the nature and extent of the injury, and to gain such other information as was necessary to enable him to properly treat the injury and accomplish the object for which he was called professionally; and such communications are privileged, and he can not disclose them. If the physician took ad-

---

* Heuston *vs.* Simpson, 115 Ind., 62, N. Y. C. and St. L. Ry. Co. *vs.* Mushrush, 11 Ind. App., 192.

† Raymond *vs.* B. C. R. and N. Ry. Co., 65 Ia , 152.

‡ The Penn. Co. *vs.* Marion, 123 Ind., 415.

vantage of the fact of being called professionally, and while there in that capacity made inquiries of the injured party concerning matters in which he had no interest or concern professionally, or for the purpose of qualifying himself as a witness, he can not be permitted to disclose the information received. The patient puts himself in the hands of his physician. He is not supposed to know what questions it is necessary to answer to put the physician in possession of such information as will enable the physician to properly treat his disease or injury, and it will be conclusively presumed that the physician will only interrogate his patient on such occasions as to such matters and facts as will enable him to properly and intelligently discharge his professional duty, and the patient may answer all the questions propounded which in any way relate to the subject or to his former condition, with the assurance that such answers and communications are confidential, and can not be disclosed without his consent." Nor, as shown in an earlier part of this chapter, will it make any difference with regard to the seal of secrecy placed upon the lips of the physician that he was employed and paid by the railroad company, or party accountable for the accident, provided the relation of physician and patient actually exists.*

* Louisville, etc., R. R. Co. *vs.* Berry, 9 Ind. App., 63; Citizens' Street R. R. Co. *vs.* Stoddard, 10 Ind. App., 278.

In conflict with the above cases is that of Kansas City, Fort Scott, and Memphis Railroad Company vs. Murray,* wherein the court held that it was allowable for a physician to state that his patient told him he was leaning over the edge of a car and negligently fell off, causing the injury. The court based this decision squarely upon the ground that the statement in question did not relate to the injury or ailment for which he was being treated, but referred to circumstances preceding the injury. This case, it will be observed, is in direct conflict with those preceding, which are thought to present the better view of the law.

In harmony with those decisions, representing a liberal construction of the statute, a physician was precluded in New York from disclosing statements made to him by his patient regarding the condition of her health previous to the time she came under his professional care.†

The law, in order to adequately protect all matter confided to the physician, not only seals his lips, but guards every avenue whereby such information might be improperly disclosed. Thus, in a New York case, the court refused to direct that a physician's original books of account, which contained information regarding the

---

* K. C., Ft. S., and M. Ry. Co. vs. Murray, 55 Kan., 336, 40 Pac. Rep., 646.

† Barker vs. Cunard Steamship Company, 91 Hun, 495.

nature of the maladies of his patients, be turned over
to a receiver, who under ordinary circumstances would
have been entitled to their possession. The court, in
assigning the reason for its refusal to grant the order,
said: " In the complicated affairs and relations of life,
the counsel and assistance of clergymen, physicians,
surgeons, and those learned in the law often become necessary; and to obtain it, men and women are frequently forced to make disclosures which their welfare, and
sometimes their lives, make it necessary to keep secret.
Hence, for the benefit and protection of the confessor,
patient, or client, the law places the seal of secrecy upon
all communications made by those holding confidential
relations, and the courts are prohibited from compelling
a disclosure of such secrets. The safety of society
demands the enforcement of this rule." *   A like conclusion would undoubtedly have been reached by the
court of every State having a statute protecting this
class of information.

**Rule Applies to Knowledge Regarding Testamen-
tary Capacity.**—There are certain classes of cases to
which the applicability of the statutes sealing the lips
of the physician regarding information gained in his
professional capacity have been or are seriously questioned.

---

* Kelly *vs.* Levy, 8 N. Y. Supp., 849.

At an early date it was thought that the statutes enjoining secrecy upon physicians could not have been intended to apply to testamentary cases. Justice Bradford, in 1850, after a somewhat extended examination of the question, expressed it as his opinion that he did not think they were within the reason or the intention of the statute.* As late as 1883 this opinion was cited with approval and followed in the surrogate court,† but in 1886 the court of appeals of New York repudiated the distinction between testamentary cases and those of the ordinary sort. Justice Earl, in delivering the opinion of the court, logically said: " But it is claimed that the statute should be held not to apply to testamentary cases. There is just as much reason for applying it to such cases as to any other, and the broad and sweeping language of the two sections can not be so limited as to exclude such cases from their operation. There is no more reason for allowing the secret ailments of a patient to be brought to light in a contest over his will than there is for exposing them in any other case where they become the legitimate subject of inquiry." ‡ This decision has been followed by an almost unbroken line of decisions in several of the States having such statutes, so that it may now be stated with reasonable

---

* Allen *vs.* Public Administrator, 1 Bradf., 221.
† Whelpley *vs.* Loder, 1 Demarest, 368.
‡ Renihan *vs.* Dennin, 103 N. Y., 573.

certainty that the knowledge of a physician gained from a professional relation with his patients is protected as fully in testamentary cases as in those of any other sort.* There has, however, in New York been a disposition shown to relax from the liberal and broad interpretation of the law by permitting the physician to be asked whether or not the information acquired by him, which is desired to be shown in the case, was necessary to enable him to act in his professional capacity, and, upon his answering this question in the negative, to permit him to disclose such information.†

The privilege which prevents the physician from disclosing all information gained in the course of his professional intercourse is one which may be waived by the patient, and it has been very properly held that, where the patient requests the physician to place his name upon the patient's will as subscribing witness, he thereby waives the privilege and invites a full and proper examination of the matters and facts as to which the physician's lips would otherwise have been sealed.‡

* *In re* Flint, 100 Cal., 391, 34 Pac. Rep., 863; *In re* Redfield, 116 Cal., 637; Heuston *vs.* Simpson, 115 Ind., 62, 17 N. E. Rep., 261; Gurley *vs.* Park (Ind.), 35 N. E. Rep., 279; Denning *vs.* Butcher, 91 Ia., 425, 59 N. W. Rep., 69; Fraser *vs* Jennison, 42 Mich , 206; Thompson *vs.* Ish, 99 Mo , 160.

† *In re* Halsey Estate, 9 N. Y. Supp., 441; Herrington *vs.* Winn, 14 N. Y. Supp., 612.

‡ *In re* Mullin's Estate, 110 Cal., 252, 42 Pac. Rep., 645; McMaster *vs.* Scriven, 85 Wis., 162.

Regarding Inquisition of Lunacy.—The question whether or not a regular attending physician is competent in an inquisition of lunacy to testify regarding his patient's condition is one upon which there does not seem to be a decision by a court of last resort. Justice Werner was of the opinion that the statute did not disqualify the physician; he said: " I do not think the section applies to a proceeding of this character. No physician can be better qualified to testify to the sanity or insanity of a person than he who has for some time attended such person in a professional capacity." * The latter part of this proposition is undoubtedly correct, yet the same statement may be made with equal force in case of the contest of a will upon the ground of a want of testamentary capacity on the part of the testator; and, yet we have just seen that the law applies in such cases. Until this question is settled by a more authoritative decision it may well be considered in doubt.

Application in Criminal Cases.—It has been observed that by the express limitation contained in the statutes of several States the privilege extended to knowledge professionally obtained by the physician applies only to civil cases. This limitation precludes both the physician and patient from the right of with-

---

* *In re* Benson (Co. Ct.), 16 N. Y Supp., 111.

holding, or having such information withheld, where it is relevant to the subject of inquiry in a criminal proceeding.* In those States where the privilege is not expressly limited by statute to civil proceedings there is some difficulty in determining with certainty the extent to which the courts allow the privilege. A careful examination of the cases relative to the subject discloses precedents extending to such knowledge the protection of the law and others denying it such protection. The facts and circumstances upon which these conflicting decisions have been rendered seem to suggest a classification of the precedents under three heads, by which arrangement the apparent conflict of authority is overcome, and, it seems, a uniform rule may be laid down, as follows:

I. Communications had for the purpose of doing an unlawful act or committing a crime are not within the meaning of the law, and will not be protected.† Thus, a consultation had with a physician relative to the unlawful producing of an abortion is not within the protection of the law, and the witness may be compelled to disclose the same.‡ The procuring of an abortion is not, however, necessarily a criminal act;

---

* People *vs.* Lane, 101 Cal., 513, 36 Pac. Rep., 16; People *vs.* West, 106 Cal., 89, 39 Pac. Rep., 207.

† 19 Am. and Eng. Enc. of Law, 140; State *vs.* Kidd, 89 Ia., 54.

‡ State *vs.* Smith, 99 Ia., 26, 68 N. W. Rep., 428.

therefore in some jurisdictions it is held that before the protection of the privilege will be denied it must be shown that the mother's life or health did not necessitate the operation.*

II. When the object of the criminal action is the prosecution of the patient's murderer, then the privilege can not be insisted upon by the accused murderer so as to preclude the deceased's physician from disclosing the condition in which he found deceased. Thus, where a physician was called to attend a patient who had been feloniously poisoned, the poisoner, upon trial, objected to a disclosure by the physician of the condition in which he found the patient, claiming that such information was privileged; but the court denied that the privilege applied in such a case.† The reason for denying the privilege in such a case is that the evident intention of the legislature in passing these laws was to protect the patient from an improper disclosure of his infirmities, whereas the application of the rule in such a case would act as a shield to the patient's murderer, a purpose which the legislature neither contemplated nor designed the act to accomplish.‡

III. In ordinary criminal actions the privilege

---

* Guptill *vs.* Verback, 58 Ia , 98.
† People *vs.* Harris, 136 N. Y., 423.
‡ Pierson *vs.* People, 79 N. Y., 424.

applies equally as in civil matters.* Thus, where an abortion had been performed and, after the discovery of the commission of the crime, the district attorney sent a physician to attend the girl, such physician was not permitted to testify regarding knowledge which he gained in attending her. The court, in discriminating between this case and those coming under the second class, said: "But in that decision (one coming under the second class) the statute was construed, and we held it did not cover a case where it was invoked solely for the protection of the criminal, and not at all for the benefit of the patient, and where the latter was dead, so that an express waiver of the privilege had become impossible. The present is a different case." †
In this connection it might be pertinent to inquire whether the death of the patient after the witness assumed professional care over her would have left him free to disclose those facts which he learned in his treatment of her, or whether the dishonorable and criminal acts causing her death would, if disclosed, cast such a cloud of dishonor and shame upon her memory as to still preserve a distinction between this case and the one referred to under classification II, where deceased came to his death by poisoning. There seems to be no

---

* Post vs. State, 14 Ind. App., 452, 42 N. E. Rep., 1120; State vs. Depoister, 21 Nev., 107, 25 Pac. Rep., 1000.

† People vs. Murphy, 101 N. Y., 126.

case marking the exact line of distinction. It is believed, however, that so long as the physician's silence is necessary for the welfare of the patient, whether living or dead, the privilege will be enforced.*

To whom Privilege Belongs.—The privilege of secrecy insured by legislative enactment respecting all professional communications is a right extended to the patient and not to the physician,† and it is a right which the patient may assert or waive as he chooses; and in the event of the patient's waiver the physician may be compelled to testify. Nor does the right cease with the death of the patient, as the physician is as strongly bound to preserve silence after that event as while his patient was in life.‡ Nor does it seem that the rule is otherwise regarding the extent of the right vested in the patient in those States in which the statute reads that the physician " shall not be *compelled* to disclose," etc. The supreme court of Wisconsin, in an opinion both cogent and logical, shows that the protection of the patient, who alone would have been injured

---

* In the case of State *vs.* Harris, *supra*, a disposition was shown to sacrifice the honor of the deceased patient, where knowledge professionally obtained was material in the prosecution of deceased's murderer, rather than impede justice. The evidence there offered was admissible upon other grounds, however, and therefore the opinion can not be considered authoritative upon this particular point.

† Johnson *vs.* Johnson, 14 Wend, 641.

‡ Grattan *vs.* Met. Life Ins. Co., 80 N. Y., 281.

by the disclosure of his infirmities, was the object and aim of the legislature, and that in order to accomplish this end that right to make a disclosure can not be left discretionary with the physician, but that " the physician can neither be *compelled* nor *allowed* to disclose it, as a witness, against the will or without the consent of the patient." *

The protection which the statute conveys to the patient relates, it seems, only to the physician's giving evidence in court relative to information professionally acquired, but does not prohibit such disclosures in his general intercourse.† The legislature, in framing this law, evidently assumed that in all cases where the physician is not subject to coercion, as is an ordinary witness upon the witness stand, the patient's secrets would be as sacred and inviolable in the breast of the physician, unprotected save by his own sense of professional propriety, as though secrecy were enjoined by the strictest legislative enactment. In this connection it may be proper to add that no professional man having a proper regard for the important relation which he bears to society, and a just appreciation of the absolute confidence which the proper performance of his duties necessitates being reposed in him, will under any cir-

---

* Boyle *vs.* N. W. Mut. Relief Assn., 95 Wis., 312, 70 N. W. Rep., 351.

† See dictum in Boyle *vs.* N. W. Mut. Benefit Assn., *supra.*

cumstances be betrayed into violating such confidence, or outraging the honor of his profession by improperly disclosing facts necessarily learned in the course of his professional duties. The temptation is undoubtedly strong at times to publish the details of an opera- tion or treatment which reflects favorably upon one's professional skill, yet such a publication, unauthorized by the patient, can not be regarded otherwise than rep- rehensible in the extreme. In a Michigan case, which arose nearly twenty years ago, Justice Campbell, in delivering the opinion of the court, went beyond the question at issue to rebuke one of the parties, a physi- cian, who had published the details of an operation recently performed by him. The justice said: " We can not forbear, in the interest of public morality, to call attention to the fact that the plaintiff, if a physi- cian, has no right to publish matter of professional con- fidence, and that the article, if published as he wrote it, without the approbation of the person operated on, would have been a very plain breach of professional duty. Such publications, for no purpose of public in- struction and only for private gratification or laudation, deserve severe censure." *

Waiver.—We have just seen that the privilege is a right belonging to the patient; therefore the patient is

---

* Sullings *vs.* Shakespeare, 46 Mich., 412.

capable of waiving this privilege, and permitting or, if necessary, compelling his physician to testify regarding matters of professional confidence between them; and this is the law even in States where, by the wording of the statute, the physician is *incompetent* to disclose information obtained in the course of his professional employment.*

The waiver need not always be express, but may be implied from the acts or, under some circumstances, from the silence of the patient; but to determine whether or not the conduct of the patient in a particular case amounts to a waiver is often a very difficult matter. The patient, by calling his physician to testify, waives the privilege.† Also, the patient's attorney waives for him when he calls the physician as a witness and states that as the patient's attorney he waives the privilege of the statute.‡ It is also held that a patient, by permitting a physician to testify regarding privileged matters, either as his own or his opponent's witness, waives the privilege.# It is advisable to state, however, in this regard that a physician, whenever placed upon the wit-

---

* Davenport *vs.* Hannibal, 108 Mo., 471, 18 S. W. Rep., 1122.

† Carrington *vs.* St. Louis, 89 Mo., 208; Squires *vs.* City of Chillicothe, 89 Mo., 226.

‡ Alberti *vs.* N. Y., L. E., and W. R. Co., 118 N. Y., 77, 23 N. E. Rep., 35.

Hoyt *vs.* Hoyt, 112 N. Y., 493; Lincoln *vs.* City of Detroit, 101 Mich., 245, 59 N. W. Rep., 617; Wheelock *vs.* Godfrey, 100 Cal., 578.

ness stand by another than his patient, for the purpose of disclosing privileged matter between himself and that patient, should, in justice to that patient, inform the court that the matter he is asked to divulge was learned by him in the course of his professional attendance, and that he desires to submit the question to the court whether he may, consistently with the confidence reposed in him by the patient and with his own professional integrity, disclose such confidential matter. A case similar to the one supposed, in which the physician disclosed matter that should have been carefully guarded, went to the supreme court of Michigan several years ago, and Justice Conley, in delivering the opinion of the court, took the opportunity to censure both the physician and the commissioner who permitted the evidence to be received, in the following words: "Every reputable physician must know of the existence of this statute (protecting confidential communications); and he must know from its very terms, as well as from the obvious reasons underlying it, that it is not at his option to disclose professional secrets. A rule is prescribed which he is not to be 'allowed' to violate; a privilege is guarded which does not belong to him, but to his patient, and which continues indefinitely, and can be waived by no one but the patient himself. What was done in this case may have been thoughtlessly done; but if a physician is found disposed to violate both the law of the land and the precepts of professional ethics by making such a disclosure, and if counsel invite him to do so by their questions, the commissioner, in the case of so plain a disregard of the law to the prejudice of a third party, may well decline to be an instrument of the wrong." *

In case of a criminal prosecution instituted by the patient, who is prosecuting witness, he will be deemed to have waived his privilege, and the physician who attended the patient for the injuries inflicted by the accused will be properly permitted to testify. Thus, in a rape case where the criminal act was committed upon a child, and the prosecution was inaugurated by the child's parents, and the child and her mother testified at the trial regarding the criminal act and the injuries thereby inflicted, the supreme court of Nevada was of the opinion that the parents by their conduct showed a desire to waive the protection of the statute, and that the physician's evidence was therefore properly admitted.†

But whether or not the patient, by taking the witness stand in a civil suit and testifying regarding his health, waives his privilege of objecting to the evidence of his physician as to the condition of his health at the time referred to in his testimony is a question upon

---

* Storrs vs. Scougale, 48 Mich., 388.

† State vs. Depoister, 21 Nev., 107, 25 Pac. Rep., 1000.

34

which the decisions are not in harmony. It has been observed that in several States the statute extending the privilege to the patient expressly provides that when the patient voluntarily testifies he will be deemed to consent to the examination of his physician.* In States having such a statute there can be no doubt that the patient, by testifying concerning matter within the knowledge of his physicians, in law authorizes them to make a full disclosure relative thereto, but whether his testifying will have such effect in other States is seriously doubted. In the court of common pleas of New York, however, Justice Pryor held that the plaintiff, who testified minutely and circumstantially to the effect of a blow upon her physical condition, and disclosed to the jury without reservation all the ill consequences of the injury to her health and comfort, thereby waived the privilege of objecting to the evidence of the physician who had attended her for the particular injuries.† Almost contemporaneous with this case is one from the supreme court of Iowa, in which the plaintiff testified minutely regarding the health she enjoyed previous to the accident upon which the suit was based, in such a way as to justify the belief that she was an unusually vigorous and healthy woman. The defendant

---

* The statutes contain such a clause in Kansas, Ohio, Oklahoma, and Wyoming.

† Treanor vs. Manhattan Ry. Co., 28 Abb. N. C., 47.

then offered the evidence of the physician who had attended the patient occasionally during the time referred to in her testimony, but the court denied that the plaintiff by her evidence had waived her privilege of objecting to the disclosure proposed,* and therefore refused to permit the physician to testify. The authorities seem to be uniform upon the proposition that where a patient at the trial testifies regarding his condition at a certain time physicians who attended him at another time than that covered in his testimony can not be permitted to testify regarding the patient's condition at such other time contrary to his objection. In the case of Butler *vs.* Manhattan Railway Company, the plaintiff, who was pregnant, upon attempting to board a car upon the elevated railroad, was struck a severe blow in the side by the iron gate as it was forcibly closed by the brakeman, producing a miscarriage. At the trial the plaintiff testified regarding her physical condition subsequent to the accident, whereupon the defendant attempted to prove by the physicians who had attended the patient previous to the accident what her condition was during that period, but the court refused to permit the disclosure offered.†

It also seems well settled that when a patient is attended by several different physicians at different

---

* McConnell *vs.* City of Osage, 80 Ia., 293, 45 N. W. Rep., 550.

† Butler *vs.* Manhattan Ry. Co., 23 N. Y. Supp., 163.

periods, and he calls one physician to testify to his condition during the period in which that physician treated him, he does not thereby waive his privilege as to the other physicians.* Thus, where the patient, who had been injured in a railway accident, first employed Dr. A., but before recovering discharged him and employed Dr. B., it was held that by calling Dr. B. to testify regarding his condition he did not waive his privilege as to Dr. A., and that Dr. A. could not be placed upon the witness stand by the defendant to testify, contrary to the patient's objection, to facts learned while attending him professionally.† And so, when a patient called physicians to testify to his condition previous and subsequent to a certain period, he did not thereby waive his privilege to object to the evidence of another physician, who had attended him during the intervening period, regarding his physical condition during such intervening period.‡ But when two or more physicians attend a patient at the same time the question of whether, by calling one of them to disclose his condition, he waives his privilege as to the others is one upon which the decisions are conflicting. The court of appeals of New York holds that by such an act he does

---

* Hope *vs.* Troy and Lansingburg Ry. Co., 40 Hun, 438.

† Mellor *vs.* The Mo. Pac. Ry. Co., 105 Mo., 455.

‡ Barker *vs.* Cunard Steamship Co., 91 Hun, 495, 36 N. Y. Supp., 256.

waive his privilege of objecting to the evidence of the others. The court says: " We think that a construction of the statute which permits a patient who has been attended by two physicians at the same examination or consultation to call one of them as a witness to prove what took place or what he learned, thus making public the whole interview, and still retain the right to object to the other, is unreasonable and unjust, and should not be followed. The waiver is complete as to that consultation when one of them is used as a witness." * Upon the other hand, the supreme court of Iowa in a recent case held that a patient, by placing on the stand one of several physicians who had attended her, presumably at the same time, did not waive her right of objecting to the evidence of the others as privileged.†

The question of whether the privilege, having once been waived in a given case, may ever again be asserted, is also one in which there is conflict of authority. In the case of Grattan vs. Insurance Company,‡ the New York court of appeals held that a party having waived the privilege at one trial could claim it upon a new trial of the same case; but the same court, in the case of

---

* Morris vs. N. Y., O., and W. Ry. Co., 148 N. Y., 88, 42 N. E. Rep., 410.

† Baxter vs. City of Cedar Rapids, 103 Ia., 599, 72 N. W. Rep., 790.

‡ Grattan vs. Insurance Co., 92 N. Y., 274.

McKinney *vs.* Grand Street, etc., Railroad Company,* decided four years later that the patient having once consented to the disclosure of privileged information could never again assert his privilege regarding the subject of his former waiver. The supreme court of Michigan, in a late case,† in passing upon practically the same case, reviewed the decisions of the New York court and, after expressing its preference of the rule laid down in the Grattan case, held that a privilege having been waived at one trial might be asserted at a new trial of the same case.

That a patient fully and completely waives all privilege as to matters connected with the physician's treatment of him when he sues the physician for alleged malpractice in such treatment can not be justly doubted. "To establish a contrary rule," said Justice Gavin, "would be most manifestly unfair." ‡ But a rule of similar justice does not prevail where a physician sues a patient to recover for the value of his professional services, and the patient interposes an answer containing a general denial. In such a case the patient does not waive his privilege, and the physician may not testify as to any information protected by the statute.# He may, how-

---

* McKinney *vs.* Grand St., etc., R. R. Co., 104 N. Y., 352, 10 N. E. Rep., 544.

† Briesenmeister *vs.* K. of P., 81 Mich., 525.

‡ Becknell *vs.* Hosier, 10 Ind. App., 5, 37 N. E. Rep., 580.

Van Allen *vs.* Gordon, 83 Hun, 379.

ever, testify that he is the family physician, and that he attended the patient, giving the dates and number of such visits made, and mentioning the examinations, prescriptions, and operations, but he may not describe them if the patient objects.*

The question of privilege has repeatedly arisen in cases where insurance companies have sought to avoid liability upon an insurance policy by showing by the assured's physician that at or previous to the time of entering into the contract of insurance he was afflicted with a disease, the existence of which he had denied in his application for insurance.

In an application for insurance it is usually required of one to give the name of his physician for the purpose of verifying the applicant's statements regarding the condition of his health. This reference does not, however, amount to a waiver of the privilege, and will not enable the insurance company to place such physician upon the witness stand and elicit from him the assured's physical condition at the time or times mentioned in the application.†

When, however, the application contains a clause waiving all provisions of the law preventing a physi-

---

* Van Allen *vs.* Gordon, *supra;* Briesenmeister *vs.* K. of P., 81 Mich., 525.

† Edington *vs.* Mutual Life Assn., 67 N. Y., 185 ; Masonic Mut. Ben. Assn. *vs.* Beck, 77 Ind., 203.

cian from disclosing any information acquired in attending the applicant in a professional capacity, the effect will be to completely waive the privilege, not only as to the assured, but also to any one claiming a benefit under the contract of insurance.*

The legislature of New York in 1891 amended the law providing for the protection of professional communications so that a physician could not be examined regarding information obtained in the course of his professional intercourse " unless the provisions thereof are expressly waived *upon the trial or examination* by . . . the patient." This act was held by the court of appeals not to apply to a waiver executed prior to the amendment of the law.† And the supreme court has, in two well-considered decisions,‡ held that a waiver executed subsequent to the enactment of the law may be used upon the trial after the patient's death to authorize a disclosure. In the case of Dougherty *vs.* Metropolitan Life Insurance Company, the court said: " If the patient be alive, an entry upon the record at his trial by his counsel would be sufficient. In case of his inability to attend the trial, a written stipulation signed by

---

* Adreveno *vs.* Mut. Res. Fund Life Assn., 34 Fed. Rep., 870.

† Foley *vs.* Royal Arcanum, 151 N. Y., 196, 45 N. E. Rep., 456.

‡ Dougherty *vs.* Metropolitan Life Ins. Co., 87 Hun, 15, 33 N. Y. Supp., 873 ; Holden *vs.* Metropolitan Life Ins. Co., 11 App. Div., 426, 42 N. Y. Supp., 310.

him and entered upon the record would remove the prohibition.

"That being so, it must certainly be immaterial when the stipulation is signed. In this case it was signed long before the trial in anticipation of that event, and with design of having it used thereat. . . . The reasonable construction of the statute, therefore, is that the provisions are expressly waived upon the trial if a proper stipulation to that effect be produced thereat and entered upon the record, regardless of the time when the waiver was executed."

With the evident intent of overcoming the effect of this decision and nullifying the waiver contained in the application for an insurance, the legislature of New York, in 1899, amended the statute by adding to it the following words: " The waivers herein provided for must be made in open court, on the trial of the action or proceeding, and a paper executed by a party prior to the trial, providing for such waiver, shall be insufficient as such a waiver. But the attorneys for the respective parties may, prior to the trial, stipulate for such waiver, and the same shall be sufficient therefor." * What the effect of this amendment may be can not be stated until the parties interested in its avoidance have devised means to accomplish that end, and those means have been passed upon by the courts.

---

* Code of Civil Procedure, § 836.

It has been observed that the privilege does not expire with the life of the patient. The question therefore naturally arises whether or not the privilege may be waived after the patient's death, and, if so, to whom does this right descend?

The New York statute previous to its amendment in 1892 provided that privileged communications should not be disclosed unless the "provisions of the statute were expressly waived by the patient." It was therefore held under this statute that a patient by dying without first waiving his privilege rendered it impossible to remove the seal of secrecy from the lips of his physician.* Thus, where one who was insured committed suicide, and his insurance policy contained a clause providing that it should be void if the insured committed suicide, it became vital to the validity of the policy to show that the deceased was insane and either unconscious of the act which he performed, causing his death, or was unable to understand what the physical consequences of it would be. In order to show this the physician who had attended him was called, but upon the evidence being objected to by the insurance company, the court held that under the statute the patient alone could waive the privilege, and, as the patient was dead, the right of granting permission to disclose privi-

---

* Loder vs. Whelpley, 111 N. Y., 239.

leged matter between him and his physician had also ceased, and that the physician could not properly be permitted to make the disclosure asked.* That the injustice worked by this law was realized is evident, for the legislature in 1892 amended the statute so as to permit the physician to testify when the privilege was waived by the personal representative of the deceased, or in case of a will contest by the executors, surviving husband or wife, or an heir-at-law, or next of kin, or any other party in interest, except that the physician should not be permitted to disclose confidential communications and such facts as would tend to disgrace the memory of the patient.†

The rule enforced by the New York courts previous to the amendment of the statute is followed by the courts of California, where it is held that if the patient dies without having waived the privilege, the matter forever is closed, and the physician will under no circumstances be permitted to disclose the knowledge obtained in rendering professional services to the deceased.‡ The reason assigned for this strict rule is the similarity of the California statute to that of New York as it formerly existed.

---

* Westover *vs.* Ætna Life Ins. Co., 99 N. Y., 56.

† L., 1892, p. 1042, ch. 514.

‡ *In re* Flint, 100 Cal., 391, 34 Pac. Rep., 863; Harrison *vs.* Sutter St. Ry. Co., 116 Cal., 156, 47 Pac. Ref., 1019.

The supreme courts of Michigan, Missouri, and Indiana hold to a contrary doctrine and permit the personal representative of the deceased to waive the privilege, thus qualifying the physician to testify regarding matters otherwise prohibited.*

In Indiana it is held that in the contest of a will the waiver can be made only by a personal representative of the deceased—viz., an executor or administrator —and if there is no such personal representative the physician can not be permitted to testify; † but in case of a suit upon an insurance policy the wife of deceased, who is named as beneficiary, is competent to waive the privilege.‡

The rule which seems best calculated to do justice to all parties is that laid down by the supreme court of Missouri in the case of Thompson *vs.* Ish,# which is that in a will contest any party claiming under the deceased, whether a devisee or heir-at-law, may waive the privilege and call the attending physician to testify regarding deceased's mental capacity.

---

* Fraser *vs.* Jennison, 42 Mich., 206; Morris *vs.* Morris, 119 Ind., 341; Denning *vs.* Butcher, 91 Ia., 425, 59 N. W. Rep., 69.

† Gurley *vs.* Park, 135 Ind., 440, 35 N. E. Rep., 279.

‡ Penn. Mut. Life Ins. Co. *vs.* Wiler, 100 Ind., 92.

Thompson *vs.* Ish, 99 Mo., 160, 12 S. W. Rep., 510.

INDEX.

Abortion, at common law, how regarded, 404.

at common law, not criminal before quickening, 405.

at common law, murder when death of mother ensued, 406.

at common law, misdemeanor after quickening, 407.

as regarded by statutes, 407.

advice to procure, when becomes criminal, 410.

conditions existing subsequent to operation, competent to show, 462.

corpus delicti, how shown, 435.

efficacious means, not necessary to show adoption of, to establish crime, 412.

instruments for performing, possession of, admissible, 449–456.

justifiable, when legally, 421–424.

mother, when regarded guilty, 408.

necessity for performing, burden of proving, 424.

necessity for performing, how to be shown, 421.

pregnancy, not necessary to establish, 418.

proof of, illustrations, 436–449, 465–479.

time sufficient for performing, 445.

vitality of fœtus not essential to commission of crime of, 419.

willingness to perform, evidence of, admissible, 449.

Adjudication, effect of former, 56, 158, 220, 358.

Advanced state of medical science, skill to be judged by, 61, 269–274.

Advertising, when unprofessional conduct, 51.

Agent, when act of, binds corporation for physician's fees, 105.

Alabama, qualifications to practise in, 10.

Alibi, effect of proving, 463.

Appeal from decision of examining board, 24.

Arizona, qualifications to practise in, 10.

communications between physician and patient privileged in, 481, n.

Arkansas, qualifications to practise in, 10.

communications between physician and patient privileged in, 481, n.

Assistance, refusal of, by physician does not increase obligations, 284.
Assistant, physician entitled to fees for services of, 141.
Attendance, physician not to discontinue, without notice, 72, 297.
Attendant, non-professional, at confinement case, 325.
Autopsy, consent to perform, necessary, 315.
    consent to perform, from whom to be obtained, 136, 317.
    consent to perform, when not necessary, 319.
    physician performing by coroner's orders protected, 136, 319.

Bandaging, case of improper, 241.
    liability of physician operating but not attending for too tight, 258.
Best judgment, what is, 276–284.
    what it implies, 68.
    knowledge and skill necessary for its exercise, 274.
    physician required to use, 68.
    physician not liable for error of, 277.
    physician should not operate contrary to, except, 69, 281.
Board of Medical Examiners. See Examining Board.
Books of account, how to be kept, 200–209.
    what should show, 200.
    admissibility of, in evidence, 197.
    inadmissible because disclosing privileged communications, when, 203, 510.

California, qualifications to practise in, 11.
    communications between physician and patient privileged in, 481, n.
Care and diligence, contract to use, implied, 63.
Care, degree required, 240, 254–262.
    degree of required, not proportionate to injury treated, 65.
Certificate of admission, how issued and filed, 13.
    registration or filing of, 32.
    registration or filing of, failure of, when excusable, 37.
    registration or filing of, rights of physician in other counties, 32.
Character of physician, not competent to be shown in defense of action for compensation, 216.
Cherokee nation. See Indian Territory.
Child, adult, liability of parent to pay physician's fee for attending, 84.
Child, liability of parent to pay physician's fee for attending, 80.
Choctaw nation. See Indian Territory.
" Christian Scientist," entitled to compensation, 142.
Claims. See Estates of Decedents.
Clairvoyant, absent husband not liable for fees of, in attending wife, 88.

Colles's fracture. See Fracture.

Colorado, qualifications to practise in, 11.

    communications between physician and patient privileged in, 481, n.

Common law, described and defined, 2.

    in the United States, 4.

    stability of, how secured, 4.

Compensation. See Fees.

Compensation. See Recovery of Compensation.

    right to, usually based on implied contract, 140.

    physician entitled to, without rendering services, when, 140.

    recovery of, 171–238.

    proof of license when necessary to recovery of, 187.

    right of unqualified practitioner to recover, 172–177.

    right of unqualified practitioner to recover for medicines furnished, 177–181.

    right of unqualified practitioner to recover compensation after legal disability removed, 181.

    proof of employment, 194.

    statute of limitations, right to, when barred by, 184–187.

    assistant, physician entitled to, for services of, 141.

    carelessness in regard to contagious diseases, effect upon, 168.

    " Christian Scientist," entitled to, 142.

    failure to benefit patient, right to, not affected, 153–158.

    gratuitous, intent that services shall be, 164–167.

    incompetency and neglect, effect of, upon right to, 158.

    intoxication of physician, effect of, upon right to, 167.

    mistake as to disease does not affect right to, 157.

    " no cure, no pay," right to, under contract of, 159–164.

    services to physicians, right to, for, 167.

    " spiritualist " entitled to, 142.

    student, physician entitled to, for services of, 141.

    subsequent visits, physician entitled to, for, 141, 215.

    Sunday, physician entitled to, for services on, 143.

Conductor, no authority in, to bind railroad for physician's fees, 111.

Confessions. See Evidence.

Confidential communications. See Privileged Communications.

Connecticut, qualifications to practise in, 10.

    non-resident physician, right of, to consult in, 16.

    non-resident physician, right of, to practise in, 15.

Consent, examining without, 336.

    necessity for, before operating, 313.

    necessity for, before performing autopsy, 315.

    to performance of operation presumed, 134.

Consideration, contract must be based upon, 92.

Consultant's fee, patient liable for, 151.

Consultation, meeting of physicians does not necessarily constitute, 152.
    right to meet in, in foreign States, 16–20.
Contagious disease, duty of physician to protect patients from, 72.
    effect of carelessness in regard to, upon right to compensation, 168.
    liability of physician for conveying, to patient, 338.
    physician destroying property in case of, protected, 137.
Contract, defined and classified, 59.
    express, defined, 59.
    implied, defined, 59.
    for medical treatment includes surgical cases, 73.
    Sunday, for medical services valid, 79.
Contract of patient, implied by law, 75.
    payment of physician's fees, 75.
    to obey instructions of physician, 78.
Contract of physician, implied by law, 60.
    implied, not altered by refusal of proffered assistance, 65.
    not implied to effect a cure, 71.
    payment of consultant's fees, 77.
    to continue attendance while needed, 72.
    to follow established modes of treatment, 69.
    to give proper instructions, 71.
    to protect patients from contagious disease, 72.
    to use best judgment, 68.
    to use care and diligence, 63.
    to use skill and knowledge, 60.
    where services are gratuitous, 66.
Contributory negligence, what is, 347.
    in mitigation of damages, 351.
    when a defense to suit by patient, 348.
    when not defense to suit by patient, 350.
Coroners, right of, to choose physician to perform post-mortem, 128, 129.
Coroners' inquests, fees for performing post-mortems at, liability of towns for, 122.
Corporation, liability of, for fees when summoning physician to attend employee, 102, 104–121.
    who has authority to bind, for payment of fees, 105–111.
    who has not authority to bind, for payment of fees, 111–113.
    except when, 113, 114.
    ratification of unauthorized employment for, 114.
    ratification of unauthorized employment, method of securing, 119.
Counties and towns, services to paupers, liability of, for, 121.
Counties, negligence of physician in treating patients at county hospitals, not liable for, 132.

Counties, partial allowance of bill by, extinguishes claim against patient, 169.
Criminal abortion. See Abortion.
Criminal intent, when presumed, 386.
Criminal law, subject to statutory regulation, 386.
Criminal liability, distinguished from civil, 385.
    jury to determine when negligence amounts to, 401.
    when ignorance or negligence becomes, 387-401.
Criminal trials, legal safeguards to accused in, 428.
Cure, no implied contract to, by physician, 71.

Damages, measure of, defined, 372.
    nominal, defined, 372.
    nominal, illustrated, 375.
    substantial or compensatory, defined, 372.
    compensatory, includes what, 373.
    compensatory, illustrated, 376.
    exemplary, defined, 372, 374.
    exemplary, illustrated, 380.
    assessment of, to include future loss, 374, 383.
Dead body, legal status of, 315.
    right to, in whom, 136, 317.
    of child, right to, in father, 136, 317.
    of husband, right to, in wife, 136, 317.
    of parent, right to, in child, 317.
    of wife, right to, in husband, 136, 317.
Deceit and misrepresentation, what amounts to, 344.
Delaware, qualifications to practise in, 10.
    non-resident practitioners, right of, to consult in, 16.
Dentist, implied by contracts to use skill and care, 67.
Diagnosis, incorrect, legal effect of, 246.
Diligence. See Care.
Diploma, as requirement to practise, 10.
    must be shown to belong to applicant, 11.
    how proved, 192.
Dishonorable. See Revocation of License.
Dislocation, failure to reduce, legal effect, 247-252.
District of Columbia, qualifications to practise in, 10.
    non-resident practitioners, right of, to consult in, 16.
    non-resident practitioners, right of, to practise in, 15.
Division superintendent, authority in, to bind railroad for physician's fees, 108.
Doctor, physician and surgeon defined, 21.
Drunkenness of physician defense to action for compensation, 219.
Dying declaration. See Evidence.

Emergency case, what is, 49.

540 THE LAW IN ITS RELATIONS TO PHYSICIANS.

Employer, not liable for negligence of physician in treating employee, 131.

Employer. See Corporation. Servant. Seaman.

Engineer. See Corporation.

Established mode of treatment, what is, 69, 288.
  physician's contract to follow, implied, 69.
  physician must follow, 69, 286.

Estates of decedents, collection of claims against, 221.
  amount of claim affected by value of, 146.
  claims against, by whom to be presented, 222.
  claim against, to whom to be presented, 223.
  claims against, manner of presentation, 223.
  claims against, how to be prepared, 223.
  order of payment of debts against, 225.
  validity of claims against, 231.
  claim for services to deceased wife not valid against estate of, except when, 231.
  contested claims against, how proved, 233 et seq.
  communications with deceased when not admissible to prove claim against, 233.
  competency of evidence of physician's wife to prove claims against, 235.
  books of physician, when admissible to prove claim against, 234. See 197.

Evidence, admissibility of, to be decided by judge, 430.
  admissions against interest, admissible, 434, 453.
  best evidence only is admissible, 431.
  conditions existing subsequent to operation, competent to show abortion, 462.
  confessions admissible, 434.
  dying declarations, admissibility of, 434.
  dying declarations, must state material facts, 457.
  dying declarations, when admissible, 456.
  expressions showing feelings as competent, 432.
  hearsay not competent, 431.
  hearsay not competent, exceptions, 432–435.
  possession of suitable instruments for performing abortion admissible as, 449–456.
  res gestæ, admissible, 432.
  res gestæ, what admissible as, 459–462.
  res gestæ, what constitute, 432.
  willingness to perform abortion admissible as, 449–456.

Examination, consent necessary before making, 336.
  liability for erroneous conclusion at, 335.
  medical college can not arbitrarily refuse, 28.

Examining board, power to issue license, 13.
  power to revoke license, 51.

Examining board, action not final, 27.
  appeal from decision of, 24.
  decision of, reviewed by mandamus, when, 25.
  irregularly appointed, certificate from, valid, 50.
Extension. See Fracture.

False pretense, what amounts to obtaining money under, 402.
Fees. See Compensation. Counties and Towns. Coroners' Inquest. Estates of Decedents. Recovery of Compensation.
  amount of, affected by value of patient's estate, 146.
  amount of, not affected by patient's financial circumstances, 149.
  collection of, from estates of decedents, 221.
  consultant's, patient liable for, when, 77, 151.
  consultant's, physician liable for, when, 77, 151.
  contract reserving right by employer to determine amount of, when valid, 110.
  corporation, liability of, for summoning physician to attend employee, 102, 104–121.
  father, liability of, for payment of, 80.
  husband, liability of, for payment of, 86.
  judgment for, effect upon action for malpractice, 220.
  implied contract of patient to pay physician's, 75.
  implied contract of patient to pay consultant's, 77.
  malpractice as defense to action for recovery of, 217.
  master, liability of, for attendance upon servant, 89.
  mother, liability of, for attendance upon child, 83.
  prolonged visit, increase of, for, 143.
  rate of, determined by local customs, 143.
  rate of, not determined by local customs, when, 144, 151.
  rate for performing operation less affected by customs, 144, 149.
  third parties, liability of, for summoning physician, 94.
  third party, liability of, must be based on consideration, 92.
  third party, when contract of, for payment of, must be in writing, 91.
  unqualified physicians, right of, to, prohibited by statute, 14.
  vessels, liability of, for attendance on seamen, 89.
  who may bind corporation for payment of, 105–111.
  who may not bind corporation for payment of, 111–113; except when, 113, 114.
Felony, definition of, 12, note.
  disqualification to practise in certain States, 12.
Filing certificate. See Certificate of Admission.
Florida, qualifications to practise in, 10.
Former adjudication, effect of, 56, 158, 220, 358.
Fracture, Colles's, illustrating case of, improper treatment of, 242.
  effect of failure to discover, 246.

542 THE LAW IN ITS RELATIONS TO PHYSICIANS.

Fracture, failure to apply extension to, legal effect of, 252–254.
Future damages, can not be recovered in separate action, 374, 383.

General manager, authority in, to bind railroad for physician's fees, 108.
Georgia, qualifications to practise in, 10.
  non-resident practitioners, right of, to consult in, 16.
Gratuitous services, contract of physician with patient not altered, 66, 308.
Gross negligence, when criminal, 387–401.

Husband, consent of, to operation on wife, 133.
  liability of, for fees in attending wife, 86.
  absent, not liable for fees of clairvoyant for attending wife, 88.
  rights of, 133–137.
  supposititious, liability of, for physician's fees in attending supposed wife, 87.

Idaho, qualifications to practise in, 10.
  non-resident practitioners, right of, to consult in, 16.
  communications between physician and patient privileged in, 481, n.
Illinois, qualifications to practise in, 10.
Immoral conduct. See Revocation of License.
Incompetency, effect of, upon right to compensation, 158.
Indiana, qualifications to practise in, 11.
  non-resident practitioners, right of, to consult in, 16.
  non-resident practitioners, right of, to practise in, 15, 16.
  communications between physician and patient privileged in, 481, n.
Indian Territory, qualifications to practise in, 11.
Inquisition of lunacy, privileged communications, application of, 514.
Insanity, liability for wrongful certificate of, 327.
Instructions, physician required to give proper, for care of patient, 70, 293.
Instructions of physician, patient bound to obey reasonable, 78, 348.
Intoxication of physician, legal effect of, 401.
  effect of, upon right to compensation, 167.
Iowa, qualifications to practise in, 10.
  communications between physician and patient privileged in, 481, n.
Irregularly appointed board, certificates or licenses from, valid, 50.
Issuing and filing certificate or license, 13.
Itinerant and traveling doctors, who are, 38.

Judgment. See Best Judgment. Qualifications of Physicians.
Jury trial, guaranteed in criminal cases, 428.

Kansas, qualifications to practise in, 11.
    communications between physician and patient privileged in, 481, n.
Kentucky, qualifications to practise in, 11.
    non-resident practitioners, right of, to practise in, 15.
Knowledge, degree of, required, 60, 254–262.
    admission of inadequacy of, effect, 284.

Last illness, expenses of, when preferred, 227.
    what is construed to be, 227.
Law, origin and development of, 1.
    divisions of, 2.
    statute, construction of, 6.
Laws, how enforced, 14.
Legislature has authority to prescribe qualifications of physicians, 9.
Liability, to whom right of action accrues, 356.
Liability of physicians. See Qualifications of Physicians.
    how affected by dismissal from case, 244.
    to father for injury to child, 356.
    to husband for injury to wife, 356.
License. See Certificate.
    registration of, 32.
    registration of, failure of, when excusable, 37.
    when necessary prerequisite to recovery of compensation, 172, 187.
License to practise, to be issued by examining board, 13.
    how issued and filed, 13.
    previous practice as qualification for, 19.
    proof of, 192.
    revocation of, 51.
Life, right of physician to terminate, 402.
Limitations, statute of, when bar to recovery of compensation, 184–187.
Location of physician, considered in determining amount of skill and knowledge required, 62, 255.
Louisiana, qualifications to practise in, 10.
    non-resident practitioners, right of, to consult in, 16.

Maine, qualifications to practise in, 10.
    non-resident practitioners, right of, to practise in, 15.
Malpractice, as defense to action for recovery of fees, 217.
    burden of proving, 364.
    burden of proving on party alleging, 217.
    character of proof required to show, 218.
    effect of judgment for fees upon action for, 220, 358.
    how must, be proved, 360.
    may be assumed, when, 369.

Mandamus, writ of, definition, 25.
  proper to review decision of examining board, when, 25.
Maryland, qualifications to practise in, 10.
  non-resident practitioners, right of, to consult in, 16.
Massachusetts, qualifications to practise in, 10.
  non-resident practitioners, right of, to practise in, 15.
Master, liability of, for physician's fees in attending servant, 89, 105.
Master and servant. See Corporation.
Messenger summoning physician, liability of, for physician's fees, 94.
Michigan, qualifications to practise in, 11.
  communications between physician and patient privileged in, 481, n.
Minnesota, qualifications to practise in, 10.
  non-resident practitioners, right of, to consult in, 16.
  communications between physician and patient privileged in, 481, n.
Mississippi, qualifications to practise in, 10.
  non-resident practitioners, right of, to practise in, 15, 16.
Missouri, qualifications to practise in, 11.
  communications between physician and patient privileged in, 481, n.
Montana, qualifications to practise in, 10.
  non-resident practitioners, right of, to consult in, 16.
  communications between physician and patient privileged in, 481, n.

Nebraska, qualifications to practise in, 11.
  non-resident practitioners, right of, to consult in, 16.
  communications between physician and patient privileged in, 481, n.
Neglect, effect of, upon right to compensation, 158.
Negligence, counties not liable for that of physicians in treating patients in county hospitals, 132.
  employer not liable for that of physician in treating employee, 131.
  liability for, in making examination, 139.
  liability of physician for that of physician recommended, 304.
  physician liable for that of partner, 358.
  physician liable for that of student, 286.
Nevada, qualifications to practise in, 11.
  communications between physician and patient privileged in, 481, n.
New Hampshire, qualifications to practise in, 10.
  non-resident practitioners, right of, to consult in, 16.
  non-resident practitioners, right of, to practise in, 15, 16.
New Jersey, qualifications to practise in, 10.
  non-resident practitioners, right of, to consult in, 16.
  non-resident practitioners, right of, to practise in, 15, 16.

New Mexico, qualifications to practise in, 11.

New York, qualifications to practise in, 10.

non-resident practitioners, right of, to consult in, 16.

non-resident practitioners, right of, to practise in, 15, 16.

communications between physician and patient privileged in, 481, n.

"No cure, no pay," rights to compensation under contract of, 159–164.

Non-professional attendant, physician liable for having, at confinement case, 325.

Non-resident physician, privileges accorded to, by certain States, 15–20.

North Carolina, qualifications to practise in, 10.

non-resident practitioners, right of, to consult in, 16.

non-resident practitioners, right of, to practise in, 15.

communications between physician and patient privileged in, 481, n.

North Dakota, qualifications to practise in, 10.

non-resident practitioners, right of, to consult in, 17.

communications between physician and patient privileged in, 481, n.

Ohio, qualifications to practise in, 11.

non-resident practitioners, right of, to consult in, 17.

non-resident practitioners, right of, to practise in, 15, 16.

communications between physician and patient privileged in, 481, n.

Oklahoma Territory, qualifications to practise in, 11.

communications between physician and patient privileged in, 481, n.

Operation, consent to, when necessary, 133, 313.

consent to, when presumed, 134, 313.

duty to advise against, when contrary to best judgment, 69.

Oral contracts, defined, 60.

Oregon, qualifications to practise in, 10.

communications between physician and patient privileged in, 481, n.

Parent, liability of, for physician's fees, 80.

liability of, for physician's fees when divorced, 83.

liability of, for fees for attendance on adult child, 84.

Partner, liability of physician for negligence of, 358.

Passengers, railroad liable for services rendered to, upon request of certain officers, 105.

railroad not liable for services rendered to, upon request of certain agents, 111.

Patent medicines, when venders of, held to be practising medicine, 47.

Paupers. See Counties and Towns.
Pennsylvania, qualifications to practise in, 10.
    non-resident practitioners, right of, to consult in, 17.
    non-resident practitioners, right of, to practise in, 15, 16.
    communications between physician and patient privileged in, 481, n.
Physician, surgeon, doctor, defined, 21.
Physicians, right to compensation for medical services rendered to, 167.
Place of trial in criminal cases, 428.
Police power of the State defined, 18.
Post-mortem. See Autopsy.
    fees for performing, at coroner's inquest, 122.
Practice, right of a physician to leave temporarily, considered, 299.
Practice of medicine, early English statutes regulating, 8.
    no restrictions upon, at common law, 8.
    right to practise, generally, 8.
    general classification of requirements for, 9.
    former practice in other State as qualification for, 30.
    statutory restrictions on, in United States, 9.
    statutory regulations constitutional, 17.
    statutory regulations, certain, unconstitutional, 21.
    laws regulating, how enforced, 14.
    without license, improper refusal of certificate no defense, 50.
Practising medicine, what constitutes, 39.
    without license, effect of repeal of statute, 58, 181.
Prescriptions, liability for negligence in writing, 343.
President of railroad, authority in, to bind railroad for physician's fees, 106.
Presumption of innocence, how overcome, 420.
Previous practice as qualification of candidate to practise, 30.
Privileged communications, classification of, 480.
    professional communications as regarded at common law, 481.
    autopsy, knowledge gained at, is not, 496.
    based upon public policy, 480.
    books of account when inadmissible because disclosing, 510.
    consultant, knowledge obtained by, at consultation is, 495.
    criminal cases, application to, 483, 514.
    dentist, information imparted to, is not, 497.
    criminal case, not extended to, by several States, 483.
    inquisition of lunacy, application in, 514.
    jail physician, information imparted to, in professional way is, 493.
    mental condition may be shown by physician when, 488.
    partner of attending physician, information imparted to, is, 495.
    regulations of, by laws of several States, 481.
    relation of physician and patient must exist, 484.

Privileged communications, relation of physician and patient, patient must show exists, 485.
  testamentary capacity, applies to knowledge regarding, 511.
  third party, when information imparted by, is, 494.
  to whom privilege belongs, 518.
  unlicensed physicians, communications with, not, 484.
  waiver of, 520.
  waiver, effect of, in application for insurance, 529.
  waiver, effect of, made at former trial, 527.
  waiver, general denial of patient in suit by physician for fees does not amount to, 195, 528.
  waiver, how made, 521.
  waiver, in whom is right of, after patient's death, 532.
  waiver, suit for malpractice against physician constitutes, 528.
  waiver, what amounts to, 521.
  what information is, 497–511.
  what information not included, 497–511.
Professional communications. See Privileged Communications.
Promissory note, for future services conditional, 168.
Proprietary medicines, when seller of, is practising medicine, 47.
Proving diploma, 12.

Qualifications of physicians, general, required by law, 240.
  general rule of, illustrations of application of, 240.
  required of all professing to act as physicians, 63.

Railroad. See Corporation.
Railroad physician, no power in, to bind railroad for care and board of employee, 112.
  not bound to attend trespasser injured by railroad, when, 111.
Ratification, by corporation of unauthorized employment, 114.
  by corporation of unauthorized employment, method of securing, 119.
  chief surgeon, not authorized to bind corporation by, 120.
  must be by whom, to bind corporation, 115.
Reason, foundation of law, 6.
Recovery of compensation. See Estates of Decedents.
  action for, did not lie in England, 182.
  books of account, when admissible to prove case, 197.
  defenses to actions for, 215.
  drunkenness of physician as defense to, 219.
  license, when necessary to prove, 14, 187.
  negligence of nurses in hospital no defense to action for, 219.
  professional services, how may be shown, 194.
  proof of, value of services, 209.
Refusal to accept patient, physician's right of, 239.
Registration of certificate, 32.

548 THE LAW IN ITS RELATIONS TO PHYSICIANS.

Registration of certificate, rights of physician in others than county of, 32.
  when failure to, excusable, 37.
Removal to another county, 13.
Removal to another State, 12.
Repeal of statutes restricting practice, effect of, 58, 181.
Requirements of physician, general classification of, 9.
  admission of inadequacy of skill, effect upon, 284.
  not affected because services gratuitous, 66, 308.
  not increased by refusal of proffered assistance, 284.
  same attach to all exercising functions of physician, 310.
Res gestæ. See Evidence.
Res judicata, effect of judgment for fees upon action for malpractice, 158, 220, 358.
Revocation of license, grounds for, 51.
  misrepresenting character of disease, ground for, 52.
  power usually in examining board, 51.
  practise in, 57.
  unprofessional, dishonorable, and immoral conduct ground for, 51.
  act of board not final, 57.
  rights of physician pending appeal from order revoking license, 57.
Rhode Island, qualifications to practise in, 11.
  non-resident practitioners, right of, to practise in, 15.
Roadmaster, no authority in, to bind railroad for physician's fees, 111.

School of medicine, skill to be judged by one's, 262-269.
  clairvoyants belong to none, 267.
Seaman, liability of vessel's owners and masters for attendance upon, 89.
Servant, liability of master for payment of physician's fees in attending, 89, 105.
Skill. See Qualifications of Physician.
  degree required, 60, 254-262.
  liability for absence of, in making examination, 139.
  rules for determining, 61-63, 262-274.
  admission of inadequacy of, effect, 284.
Skill and knowledge, location of physician considered in fixing amount required, 62, 255.
South Carolina, qualifications to practise in, 10.
  non-resident practitioners, right of, to consult in, 17.
South Dakota, qualifications to practise in, 11.
" Spiritualist," entitled to compensation, 142.
Splints, improper application of, 245.
Station agent, no authority in, to bind railroad for physician's fees, 111.

Statute law, what is, 6.
Statute of frauds, what contracts fall within, 91.
Student, physician entitled to fees for services of, 141.
　　physician liable for negligence of, 286.
Summoning physician, liability of party, for payment of fees, 94.
Summoning physician for employee, liability of corporation for part
　　of fees, 102, 104–121.
Sunday contracts for medical services valid, 79.
Sunday, physician entitled to compensation for services on, 142.
Superintendent, authority of, to bind railroad for physician's fees,
　　106.
Surgeon, physician, doctor, defined, 21.
Survival of action, common-law doctrine changed by statute, 356.

Tennessee, qualifications to practise in, 10.
　　non-resident practitioners, right of, to consult in, 17.
Texas, qualifications to practise in, 10.
Third parties, who are, 80.
　　liability of, for physician's fees, 80–131.
　　liability of, for fees when summoning a physician, 94.
　　liability of, for physician's fees must be based upon considera-
　　　tion, 92.
　　must be privity of contract with physician to be bound for fees,
　　　110.
　　rights of, 133.
　　when promise of, to pay must be in writing, 91.
Towns, liability of, for services to paupers, 121.
　　partial allowance of bill by, extinguishes claim against patient,
　　　169.
Traveling doctor. See Itinerant.

Unlicensed physicians, communications with, not privileged, 484.
Unprofessional conduct. See Revocation of License.
Unqualified practitioner, right to compensation for services ren-
　　dered before repeal of disqualifying act, 181.
　　right of, to recover compensation, 172–177.
　　right of, to recover for medicines furnished, 177–181.
Utah, qualifications to practise in, 10.
　　non-resident practitioners, right of, to consult in, 17.
　　communications between physician and patient privileged in,
　　　481, n.

Value of services, how proved in suit to recover compensation, 209.
Vermont, qualifications to practise in, 11.
Vessel, liability of, for attendance upon seamen, 89.
Virginia, qualifications to practise in, 10.
　　non-resident practitioners, right of, to consult in, 17.

Washington, qualifications to practise in, 10.
 communications between physician and patient privileged in, 481, n.
West Virginia, qualifications to practise in, 10.
 non-resident practitioners, right of, to consult in, 17.
Wisconsin, qualifications to practise in, 11.
 non-resident practitioners, right of, to consult in, 17.
 communications between physician and patient privileged in, 481, n.
Witnesses, accused may compel attendance of, 430.
 accused to be confronted by, 429.
Written contracts defined, 59.
Wyoming, qualifications to practise in, 11.
 non-resident practitioners, right of, to practise in, 15, 16.
 non-resident practitioners, right of, to consult in, 17.
 communications between physician and patient privileged in, 481, n.

THE END.

www.ingramcontent.com/pod-product-compliance
Lightning Source LLC
Chambersburg PA
CBHW021938220326
41599CB00010BA/290